SWIFT IN PRINT

Published Texts in Dublin and London, 1691–1765

Presenting a fresh perspective on one of the most celebrated print canons in literary history, Valerie Rumbold explores the expressive force of print context, format, typography, ornament and paratext encountered by early readers of Jonathan Swift. By focusing on the books, pamphlets and single sheets in which the Dublin and London book trades published his work, this revealing whole-career analysis, based on a chronology of publication that often lagged years behind dates of composition, examines first editions and significant reprints throughout Swift's lifetime, and posthumous first editions and collections in the twenty years after his death. Drawing on this material evidence, Rumbold reframes Swift's publishing career as a late expression of an early modern formation in which publishing was primarily an adjunct to public service. In an age of digital reading, this timely study invites a new engagement with the printed texts of Swift.

VALERIE RUMBOLD is Professor of English Literature at the University of Birmingham. She is author of *Women's Place in Pope's World* (1989) and has edited Pope's *Dunciads* (1999, 2007) and Swift's *Parodies, Hoaxes, Mock Treatises* (2013). She is a General Editor of the *Cambridge Edition of the Works of Jonathan Swift* and of the *Oxford Edition of the Writings of Alexander Pope*.

SWIFT IN PRINT

Published Texts in Dublin and London, 1691–1765

VALERIE RUMBOLD

University of Birmingham

CAMBRIDGE
UNIVERSITY PRESS

University Printing House, Cambridge CB2 8BS, United Kingdom

One Liberty Plaza, 20th Floor, New York, NY 10006, USA

477 Williamstown Road, Port Melbourne, VIC 3207, Australia

314–321, 3rd Floor, Plot 3, Splendor Forum, Jasola District Centre, New Delhi – 110025, India

79 Anson Road, #06–04/06, Singapore 079906

Cambridge University Press is part of the University of Cambridge.

It furthers the University's mission by disseminating knowledge in the pursuit of education, learning, and research at the highest international levels of excellence.

www.cambridge.org
Information on this title: www.cambridge.org/9781108839440
DOI: 10.1017/9781108878036

© Valerie Rumbold 2020

This publication is in copyright. Subject to statutory exception and to the provisions of relevant collective licensing agreements, no reproduction of any part may take place without the written permission of Cambridge University Press.

First published 2020

Printed in the United Kingdom by TJ International Ltd, Padstow Cornwall

A catalogue record for this publication is available from the British Library.

Library of Congress Cataloging-in-Publication Data
NAMES: Rumbold, Valerie, author.
TITLE: Swift in print : published texts in Dublin and London, 1691–1765 / Valerie Rumbold, University of Birmingham.
DESCRIPTION: Cambridge, United Kingdom ; New York, NY : Cambridge University Press, 2020. | Includes bibliographical references and index.
IDENTIFIERS: LCCN 2019059900 (print) | LCCN 2019059901 (ebook) | ISBN 9781108839440 (hardback) | ISBN 9781108878036 (ebook)
SUBJECTS: LCSH: Swift, Jonathan, 1667–1745 – Criticism, textual. | Swift, Jonathan, 1667–1745 – First editions. | Literature publishing – England – London – History – 18th century. | Literature publishing – Ireland – Dublin – History – 18th century. | Printing – England –London – History – 18th century. | Printing – Ireland – Dublin – History – 18th century.
CLASSIFICATION: LCC PR3727 .R87 2020 (print) | LCC PR3727 (ebook) | DDC 823/.5–dc23
LC record available at https://lccn.loc.gov/2019059900
LC ebook record available at https://lccn.loc.gov/2019059901

ISBN 978-1-108-83944-0 Hardback

Cambridge University Press has no responsibility for the persistence or accuracy of URLs for external or third-party internet websites referred to in this publication and does not guarantee that any content on such websites is, or will remain, accurate or appropriate.

To Jim McLaverty
'DETUR DIGNISSIMO'

Contents

List of Illustrations	*page* ix
Preface	xi
Acknowledgements	xx
Note on Conventions	xxiii
List of Abbreviations	xxv

PART I BEGINNINGS

1   First Impressions: Dublin and London to 1699 — 3

PART II LONDON

2   The Shock of the Normal: From Temple to the *Tale* (1693–1705) — 33

3   Material Voices: The Bickerstaff Effect (1705–1710) — 66

4   Politics and Permanence: *Miscellanies*, Politics and a *Proposal* Declined (1710–1714) — 102

PART III DUBLIN

5   The Irish Patriot in Print (1720–1725) — 143

6   Delegating in London, Recouping in Dublin: *Travels*, *Miscellanies*, the *Intelligencer* and *A Modest Proposal* (1726–1729) — 177

viii *Contents*

7 *The Works of J. S, D. D, D. S. P. D.* (1730–1735)   211

PART IV INTO THE FUTURE

8 Ending and Going On (1736–1765)   251

Works Cited   292
Index   303

Illustrations

1. Jonathan Swift, dedicatory letter to *Ode to the Athenian Society*, in John Dunton's *Fifth Supplement to the Athenian Gazette* (London, 1692). Reproduced by kind permission of the Master and Fellows of Trinity College, Cambridge, Wren Library, RW.70.1.   *page* 22

2. Jonathan Swift, *A Tale of a Tub ... To which is added, An Account of a Battel between the Antient and Modern Books in St. James's Library* (London, 1704), title and facing page. Reproduced by kind permission of the Master and Fellows of Trinity College, Cambridge, Wren Library, RW.1.12.   59

3. Jonathan Swift, *A Tale of a Tub ... To which is added, An Account of a Battel between the Antient and Modern Books in St. James's Library* (London, 1704), pp. 44–5. Reproduced by kind permission of the Master and Fellows of Trinity College, Cambridge, Wren Library, RW.1.12.   64

4. Jonathan Swift, *An Elegy on Mr. Patrige, the Almanack-maker, who Died on the 29th of this Instant March, 1708* (London, 1708). © The British Library Board, C.40.m.11.(74).   77

5. Jonathan Swift, *A Letter from a Member of the House of Commons in Ireland to a Member of the House of Commons in England, concerning the Sacramental Test* (London, 1709), p. 14. Reproduced by kind permission of the Master and Fellows of Trinity College, Cambridge, Wren Library, RW.62.20.   88

6. Jonathan Swift, *T—l—nd's Invitation to Dismal, to dine with the Calves-Head Club. Imitated from Horace, Epist. 5, Lib I* (London, 1712). Reproduced by kind permission of the Master and Fellows of Trinity College, Cambridge, Wren Library, RW.70.9.   113

ix

x   *List of Illustrations*

7. Jonathan Swift, *Some Arguments against Enlarging the Power of Bishops, in Letting of Leases* (Dublin, 1723), p. 18. Reproduced by kind permission of the Master and Fellows of Trinity College, Cambridge, Wren Library, RW.53.13.   156

8. Jonathan Swift, *A Letter to the Shop-keepers, Tradesmen, Farmers, and Common-People of Ireland, concerning the Brass Half-Pence coined by Mr. Woods . . . By M. B. Drapier* (Dublin, 1724), p. 5. Reproduced by kind permission of the Master and Fellows of Trinity College, Cambridge, Wren Library, RW.53.15.   163

9. Jonathan Swift, *Travels into Several Remote Nations of the World . . . By Lemuel Gulliver* (London, 1726), p. 1. Reproduced by kind permission of the Master and Fellows of Trinity College, Cambridge, Wren Library, RW.53.31.   181

10. *The Penny London Post*, 25 November 1726, p. 2. Reproduced by kind permission of the Master and Fellows of Trinity College, Cambridge, Wren Library, RW.53.31.   190

11. *The Works of J. S, D. D, D. S. P. D.* (Dublin, 1735), vol. I, series title. Reproduced by kind permission of the Master and Fellows of Trinity College, Cambridge, Wren Library, RW.53.1.   224

12. *The Works of J. S, D. D, D. S. P. D.* (Dublin, 1735), vol. IV, p. 23. Reproduced by kind permission of the Master and Fellows of Trinity College, Cambridge, Wren Library, RW.53.4.   229

13. *Proposals for Printing by Subscription a Beautiful and Correct Edition of the Works of Dr. Jonathan Swift* ([London], 1752), title. Chetham's Library, H.P.746.   270

14. *The Works of Jonathan Swift, D. D. Dean of St. Patrick's, Dublin*, ed. John Hawkesworth (London, 1755), vol. I, series title. © The British Library Board, 90.d.1.   276

Preface

This is a study of the printed books, pamphlets and single sheets in which, over the span of Swift's lifetime and the two following decades, the Dublin and London book trades offered his writings for sale. Suppose, for example, that in the early 1730s you had subscribed for the first four volumes of the Dublin *Works* published by George Faulkner, what would you have found when you unwrapped your purchase? What did the volumes look and feel like? Which works were included, and how were they organised and presented? How did these texts of the works compare with previous ones? How did paratexts such as prefaces and notes frame the reading experience, and how did frontispieces and ornaments interact with the verbal texts?[1] By considering, in chronological order, a generous selection of first editions and significant reprints and collections, this study attempts to trace patterns less easily discerned from the viewpoint of a single work or group of works. By analysing change over time and tracing interactions between the print trades of Ireland and England, it seeks a better understanding of the early printed forms in which the published writings reached their readers. In a vast and diverse canon now dominated by a mere handful of works, these original printings also remind us that the writings offered for sale in Swift's lifetime were much more numerous and varied than the selection commonly read now, and that they appeared in a sometimes surprising range of material texts.

Early publications were extraordinarily diverse in print quality and genre (to which their relation was often parodic), but they were remarkably consistent in their dominant formats, which clustered towards the middle and lower reaches of the market. Many pieces were issued as half sheets, or as quarto or octavo pamphlets, and the most aspirational medium for

---

[1] For a comparison of Faulkner's expanded *Works* as it stood in 1758 with a rival Dublin edition of that year, see Andrew Carpenter, 'Reading Swift's *Works* in Dublin in the 1750s', in Kirsten Juhas, Patrick Müller and Mascha Hansen (eds.), *'The First Wit of the Age': Essays on Swift and his Contemporaries in Honour of Hermann J. Real* (Frankfurt am Main: Peter Lang, 2013), pp. 117–31.

xii *Preface*

a lifetime collection or substantial single work was a well-printed octavo, with a few copies on large paper. (Only later in Swift's life, notably in the 1735 Dublin *Works*, would the option of a duodecimo format become crucial; and an octodecimo option emerged only twenty years after his death.[2]) Volumes in folio, the large old-fashioned prestige format, hardly featured at all; and it was only ten years after his death, in 1755, that his works first appeared in the large quarto that had begun to displace the folio earlier in the century.[3] Both the modesty of format and the range of print quality and genre were deeply characteristic of Swift in print, structuring in significant ways the interplay between the folded sheet and what was printed on it.

Swift in print, however, is not Swift; and what was good for the one was not necessarily good for the other. Indeed, Swift in print profited from experiences that were deeply unwelcome to Swift; it developed on many occasions in ways that he would not have chosen; and it carried on, without his further input, during his years of cognitive decline and into the years after his death. So this is not a book about Swift, or his writings, or even about his attitude to authorship and his publishing strategies and relations with the print trade, although all of these are vital contexts. (Nor does it focus on the intentions and decisions of print professionals, which are for the most part even more sparsely documented than Swift's.) In order to focus on the books, pamphlets and papers themselves, I have largely forgone the familiar pleasures of tracing Swift's emotions and intentions, quoting his works and private letters, and debating the various views of critics. In Swift's lifetime, direct knowledge of what he was thinking, feeling, composing and contriving was restricted to a relatively small circle (as, indeed, was knowledge of the motives, intentions and decisions of his booksellers and printers): readers without privileged access to inside knowledge might glean advance information from printed proposals and advertisements, but for most readers Swift's work effectively came into existence when it was printed and offered for sale. In the case of verse, composition was particularly likely to be separated from publication by intervals of varying duration, during which new pieces might be known through relatively restricted manuscript circulation or not at all.[4] (Significant numbers of manuscript works did not come to press until after Swift's death.) By adopting a chronology of first publication rather than the usual chronology of composition, this study therefore prioritises

---

[2] See Chapter 7.   [3] See Chapter 8.
[4] Stephen Karian, 'Swift as a Manuscript Poet', in *JS Book*, pp. 31–50 (pp. 33–6).

Preface xiii

the works' successive emergence into print – which was often significantly out of sequence with their writing. By focusing on the books themselves rather than on the intentions and processes of their making (and adopting a cautious approach to the attribution of individual responsibility), it brings into the foreground evidence that is plentiful, accessible – and often relatively neglected.

In general, the discussions that follow focus primarily on first publications, as distinct from the later revised and supplemented editions from which our modern texts of major works typically derive (notably in the cases of *A Tale of a Tub* and *Gulliver's Travels*).[5] First publications and their early reprints might come from Dublin or from London; they might be cheap half sheets or pamphlets or substantial volumes; and they might or might not have been authorised by Swift. But whatever their status and credentials, they were still the first printed texts available. Swift, however, took for granted his right as author to revise for subsequent editions. This was a principle that he had learned young, while assisting his elderly patron Sir William Temple in applying his final lifetime intentions to the text of his letters and memoirs; but as time went on it tended to dignify Swift's works for posterity by distancing them both from their contexts of composition and from the printed texts in which they had first been instantiated.[6] Changing fashions in book design also played their part, particularly after Swift's death. By emphasising the first publication of a given work, the present study prioritises the books that the first purchasers handled in print-shops or on book-stalls, the pamphlets and single sheets that they passed around in coffee houses or brought into their homes. Revised editions might later adjust, but hardly efface, the impact of these early publications.

One perhaps surprising feature of the Swift canon is the number and persistence of dubious attributions. This is in one sense a problem: some works unlikely to be Swift's continue to influence his reception because attributions remain embedded in library catalogues, older editions, secondary scholarship and popular accounts; and others are the subject of continued disagreement among scholars.[7] Yet such disputed attributions reflect something important about Swift in print, which was nearly always issued anonymously, and often purported to be the work of a fictitious named person, or of some unnamed person from a social category to which

---

[5] *CWJS Tale*, pp. 275–80; *CWJS Travels*, pp. 652–3.   [6] See Chapters 2 and 3.
[7] For recent progress in this regard, see the deattributed poems section of *CWJS Poems* IV (forthcoming).

xiv *Preface*

Swift himself did not belong. When he became famous, particularly during the Drapier affair of the 1720s, it was tempting for contemporaries to surmise (or actively suggest) that printed work by others might be his, and it helped that some of those who published views similar to Swift's were also accomplished writers. In other cases Swift gave his friends 'hints' that they incorporated into their own publications. Unless otherwise stated, the present study focuses on works of whose attribution to Swift I am reasonably confident: the fuzzy edges of the canon figure less as puzzles to be solved than as reminders of the media phenomenon that was Swift in print.

In offering a whole-career overview of a major writer's published works, the present study also confronts a realisation that is familiar to published authors, if not always reflected in everyday talk about literature, namely that books are as they are not primarily because their authors desire them to be so, but because they are the outcomes of a collaborative process with established norms and practices. In Swift's time these norms and practices were shaped not only by hierarchical structures of apprenticeship in the print trade, but also by the different regulatory frameworks of Dublin and London print: Moxon's account in *Mechanick Exercises on the Whole Art of Printing* (1683) is particularly valuable for the way in which it relates print processes to a specific print community. Bertrand Bronson speaks of the book as 'the collaborative product of many minds and many hands: hands trained to habitual skills and set in traditional ways, and minds predisposed by knowledge, judgment and taste'; and attention to material texts underlines the fact that the individual book is not designed from scratch, but as a variant of what might be called 'printers' normal', a set of working templates in which some elements are easily varied and others less so.[8] What counted as normal in the hand-press period varied with time, place, price and genre; but many basic conventions remain so deeply acculturated, even today, as to pass largely below the threshold of authorial intention. While authors may well desire a particular size or quality of book, or a particular typographical design, they are less likely to put in a specific request for the title to appear on a recto. Indeed, in *Edmund Spenser and the Eighteenth-Century Book*, Hazel Wilkinson draws on recent reassessments of authorial involvement in the lifetime printings of works by Spenser, Milton and Jonson to argue that 'In the early modern period, the author was often the recipient, not the sole originator, of the authority

---

[8] Bertrand H. Bronson, *Printing as an Index of Taste in Eighteenth-Century England* (New York Public Library, 1963), pp. 5–6.

Preface   xv

constructed by print.'[9] This is also suggestive in relation to Swift. Instead of framing Swift in print in terms of an eighteenth century often associated with modernity and enlightenment, it is worth at least considering the published works as a late expression of an early modern formation – one that significantly predated the professional authorship modelled by Swift's younger friend Alexander Pope.[10]

Swift in print began as a Dublin presentation of the writing of an Anglo-Irish child of the 1660s, and developed in the context of an asymmetrical relationship between the print trades of Ireland and England. Swift's publications, usually anonymous, relatively unpretentious in format and hugely varied in material quality, did not constitute a livelihood in themselves, but were part of the professional career of a university-educated Church of Ireland clergyman. In contrast, Pope in print was an English phenomenon through and through, the long-term livelihood of a Londoner born in the 1680s who found himself debarred by Catholicism and disability from standard routes through education into the professions. As James McLaverty emphasises in his 2001 study *Pope, Print and Meaning*, Pope's poems, taken up from the beginning by leading booksellers, were consolidated into a self-edited *Works* by the time he was thirty and were routinely marketed in prestige formats, while his exploitation of the London copyright law introduced in 1710 made him a pioneer in the authorial management of intellectual property. Later publications were in effect self-published, as he cut out the bookseller and commissioned printing as required. If such a view of Pope in print foreshadows the literary livelihoods enterprised in print and digital media by writers today, it also suggests that Swift in print, though overlapping in time, was importantly different. The present study considers some of the material evidence of that difference.

Stephen Karian begins his 2010 study *Jonathan Swift in Print and Manuscript* with an important recognition:

> Swift's dealings with the book trade are known and documented; nonetheless, no one has yet examined these relationships in a way that covers his entire career. As a result, we do not yet understand the changes and continuities that characterize Swift as a print author.[11]

---

[9] Hazel Wilkinson, *Edmund Spenser and the Eighteenth-Century Book* (Cambridge University Press, 2017), p. 12.

[10] James McLaverty, *Pope, Print and Meaning* (Oxford University Press, 2001); Dustin Griffin, *Swift and Pope: Satirists in Dialogue* (Cambridge University Press, 2010).

[11] Karian, *Print and Manuscript*, p. 11.

xvi   *Preface*

The present book, however, though still concerned with changes and continuities across the whole career, focuses less on print-trade relationships and transmissions between manuscript and print than on the print products that resulted. This is because, while I love the work of scholarly editing that has occupied me for most of my career, it also frustrates me by revealing, in the lifetime printed texts, expressive traces of human skill, effort and difficulty that are not easy to share. The end users of an edition can certainly consult textual accounts and historical collations, and they can also now look online at images of various printed texts; but the editor's reading text still tends to dominate – in some ways functioning less as an additional text of the work than as a stand-in for the work itself. Yet the irony is that while talk of book formats and print processes often seems abstruse or irrelevant to those not directly involved, the opportunity to work directly with a press, or to handle rare books, is typically greeted with delight and a sense of illumination. All this encourages me to attempt, in deliberately straightforward terms, a career-long view of Swift in print. While it is a privilege to be able to draw on the extraordinarily detailed and subtle textual and bibliographical scholarship being produced within the Swift community, this is not a technical study. It offers instead a long-term perspective on effects which may in themselves be relatively superficial, but are nonetheless significant.

* * *

Swift in print, as introduced in Part I, 'Beginnings', was predicated on an awkward straddling of the Irish Sea: on the one side lay the world of London print, where delegated regulation by the Stationers' Company allowed the trade to expand and diversify; on the other lay the heavily restricted Dublin trade, where, nominally at least, only the King's Printer in Ireland was allowed to print at all. Implications for the formation of Swift in print are addressed in Chapter 1, 'First Impressions: Dublin and London to 1699', which focuses on the revealing oddities of Swift's first two printed works: *An Ode. To the King*, published by John Brent in Dublin, and *Ode to the Athenian Society*, published by John Dunton in London. By contextualising these early poems in the distinct but connected Irish and English print worlds of the late seventeenth century (aided by Dunton's *The Dublin Scuffle*, his account of a working visit undertaken in 1698), the chapter shows how some of the print-trade structures and individuals of

Preface xvii

Swift's early formation would continue to exert an influence on the future development of Swift in print.

Part II, 'London', moves on to the years up to 1714, when publication was centred in England. Chapter 2, 'The Shock of the Normal: From Temple to the *Tale* (1693–1705)', begins by analysing Swift's paratexts to the posthumous editions of the works of his patron, Sir William Temple, which first presented Swift's words in high-quality print. Having chosen Benjamin Tooke the younger as his bookseller, Swift published *A Tale of a Tub* in 1704 – a notorious and expensive production, which, considered *as* a book, turns out, despite its modern reputation, to be surprisingly normal. Chapter 3, 'Material Voices: The Bickerstaff Effect (1705–1710)', focuses on the intensely productive years up to 1710, tracing the process by which Swift in print consolidated its techniques of anonymity, reaching a climax in the Bickerstaff hoax of 1708–9, and presenting in 1710 the elaborated but still technically anonymous fifth edition of the *Tale*. Finally, Chapter 4, 'Politics and Permanence: *Miscellanies*, Politics and a *Proposal* Declined (1710–1714)', shows how, during the hectic period of Swift's service to the Tory ministry from 1710 to 1714, print not only disseminated the day-to-day political interventions published by the ministry's official printer, John Barber, but also supported claims for longer-term significance. In 1711 Tooke published the *Miscellanies in Prose and Verse* that first brought together the beginnings of a canon; and in the following year he produced, to particularly expressive effect, Swift's doomed *Proposal* to found an academy, fix the language and celebrate Queen Anne and her ministers to posterity.

With the fall of the ministry and the death of the Queen in 1714, Part III, 'Dublin', returns, with Swift, to the politics and print trade of Ireland. Chapter 5, 'The Irish Patriot in Print (1720–1725)', demonstrates how, after a long silence, Swift in print achieved a new degree of public engagement, ultimately exploding with unprecedented force in the Drapier's letters against Wood's halfpence. These shabby but effective pamphlets staged print and its processes in notably self-referential terms, representing print as a means of bringing people together for the common good; and by the triumphant end of the campaign Swift in print was a dynamic brand in a growing Dublin print trade. Yet London publication still offered the apparent advantages of legally secured copyrights, high-quality printwork, effective distribution and assistance from established contacts, and Chapter 6, 'Delegating in London, Recouping in Dublin: *Travels*, *Miscellanies*, the *Intelligencer* and *A Modest Proposal* (1726–1729)', examines a brief period when

xviii   *Preface*

publication once more centred in London, arguably to the benefit of Swift in print, though not to the satisfaction of Swift himself. Now that Tooke was dead, Swift sold the copy of his *Travels* to his successor, Benjamin Motte the younger, and provided Pope with material for a joint set of London *Miscellanies*. Later, enraged by the selection and censorship they had exercised, Swift responded by conniving at the appearance of authorial revisions in Dublin reprints – even while entrusting Irish friends with more poems to carry to press in London. Yet the established momentum of Swift in print continued to favour the Dublin trade, and it reached its climax in George Faulkner's 1735 Dublin edition of the *Works*, whose expressive force is the focus of Chapter 7, '*The Works of J. S, D. D, D. S. P. D.* (1730–1735)'. This Dublin *Works* was the nearest thing to an authorised collected edition to appear in Swift's lifetime. While rightly regarded as a monument, and a significant step in the consolidation of Swift in print, it is clear from the proposal and the 1735 tranche of volumes that it was a radically – and expressively – compromised one.

Part IV, 'Into the Future', shows Swift and Swift in print in the process of final separation. Chapter 8, 'Ending and Going On (1736–1765)', begins with Swift's last lifetime publications, considers the new publications that followed his death in 1745, and addresses the changes brought about by the major collections of the next twenty years. First, in the short time remaining before cognitive decline prevented Swift from acting on his own behalf, important poems appeared in significantly odd forms in London, while *Polite Conversation* was published in strategically different editions there and in Dublin. *Directions to Servants*, finally sent to press unfinished, was brought out by Faulkner a few days after Swift's death in 1745. But Faulkner soon lost ground to the London copy-holders, whose new 1755 edition boasted the novelty of a fashionable large quarto. The copy-holders still began by proposing a subscription; but now the editor himself became a selling point, with his personal connection to Swift advertised as a crucial qualification. Yet when the copy-holders' reliance on 'an intimate Friend of the Author' was disappointed they turned to John Hawkesworth, a representative of a new breed of professional men of letters – and the first publication of *The History of the Four Last Years of the Queen* in 1758 showed that even an editor who had known Swift personally could still denounce his politics. In 1765 Swift's cousin Deane Swift, having dropped previous plans for Oxford publication, brought to press in London new material from

Preface xix

family manuscripts which attracted subscribers from constituencies old and new. Exemplifying the clean, modern elegance of the Hawkesworth edition into which it was incorporated, Deane Swift's handsome quarto confirmed just how much Swift in print had changed from the modest formats and expressive typography of its author's lifetime.

Acknowledgements

As this study emphasises, it takes much more than an author to make a book, and it is a pleasure to put on record the generosity, expertise and enthusiasm that so many people have brought to the making of this particular book. For indispensable guidance through the 'printers' normal' of a digital age, I would like to thank Bethany Thomas and Bethany Johnson at Cambridge University Press and Gayathri Tamilselvan at Integra. Two anonymous readers also provided much-valued advice and encouragement, and Rose Bell was the ideal copy editor, bringing an enviable combination of rigour and finesse to the final preparation of the text. I also want to thank past and present colleagues at the University of Birmingham for their help and encouragement during planning and writing. Particular gratitude is due to Hugh Adlington, Sally Baggott, Maureen Bell, Louise Curran, Rob Doolan, Andrzej Gasiorek, Oliver Herford, John Holmes, Susan Hunston, Jo Keogh, Martin Killeen, Helen Laville, Tom Lockwood, Deborah Longworth, Rebecca Mitchell, Sebastian Mitchell, Kate Rumbold, Marcus Walsh, Emily Wingfield, Hazel Wilkinson and Gillian Wright. The conversations generated over recent years by the Centre for Literary Editing and the Materiality of the Text have made me realise afresh what a privilege it is to work with so many outstanding colleagues in the study of book and text. Further afield, many other individuals have shared their knowledge and pointed me towards crucial materials, notably John Barnard, Nicolas Bell, Giles Bergel, Carol Conlin, Sophie Evans, Moyra Haslett, Máire Kennedy, Tom Keymer, Gregory Lynall, Jason McElligot, John McTague, Anne Markey, Sandy Paul, Hermann Real, Michael Suarez and Fergus Wilde. Conferences of the British Society for Eighteenth-Century Studies, the Eighteenth-Century Ireland Society, the Bangor Conference on the Restoration and the Swift350 Conference at Trinity College Dublin have all provided congenial and stimulating contexts for sharing ideas.

Acknowledgements xxi

My attention was first turned to Swift by an invitation from the General Editors of the *Cambridge Edition of the Works of Jonathan Swift* to edit his prose parodies. After decades of working on the poetry of Pope, this was a life-changing experience, which introduced me for the first time to the Dublin book trade and led in turn to the conception of the present book. It also introduced me to the *CWJS* editorial team, and I'd like to thank Linda Bree, Paddy Bullard, Andrew Carpenter, Daniel Cook, David Hayton, Ian McBride, James May, Claude Rawson, Adam Rounce, Marcus Walsh, Abigail Williams and David Womersley for their support and collegiality over the years. James Woolley and Stephen Karian have given me the benefit of their textual expertise right from the planning stage; and it is now a pleasure to direct readers, for up-to-date accounts of Swift's printed verse, to their forthcoming four-volume *CWJS Poems*. (Consulting this transformatory edition is going to be a priority for everyone interested in Swift's poetry; any mistakes in the meantime are entirely my own.) I also owe Ian Gadd and Ian Higgins particular thanks not only for their help along the way, but also for sharing their recent work towards *CWJS English Political Writings, 1701–1711*. Finally, my long-standing debt to Jim McLaverty for his tact, wisdom and insight into Scriblerian printing is acknowledged, but in no sense repaid, by the Dedication.

Research based on examining books rather than reading them is arguably as much work for their custodians as it is for the researcher, and my requests to see so many of the different material forms in which Swift was published in his lifetime have entailed laborious and repeated rounds of book-fetching both in UK libraries and in Dublin. Heartfelt thanks are due to the staff of the Rare Books Room of Cambridge University Library, the Wren Library of Trinity College, Cambridge, the Armagh Robinson Library, the Bodleian Library, the British Library, the London Metropolitan Archives and the Cadbury Research Library at the University of Birmingham. In Dublin, I am enormously grateful to the staff of the Trinity College Early Printed Books department, Pearse Street Library, the National Library of Ireland, the Royal Irish Academy and Marsh's Library. Without permission to exceed daily allowances for book-ordering and to inspect copies not normally available to readers, writing this book would have been much less practicable. Chetham's Library, the Huntington Library, the Kroch Library of Cornell University and the National Library of Scotland also responded quickly and conclusively to enquiries at a distance. For generous assistance with illustrations I should like to record my thanks to the Wren Library of Trinity College, Cambridge, the British Library and Chetham's Library.

xxii *Acknowledgements*

This is also the place to acknowledge the particular contributions of three pioneering scholars of print and book history whom I did not have the privilege of meeting in person: it will be obvious from what follows how fundamental the insights of Donald McKenzie, Mary ('Paul') Pollard and Michael Treadwell have been. With the completion by Hermann Real and Dirk Passmann of David Woolley's *Correspondence of Jonathan Swift*, and the steady advance of the *Cambridge Edition of the Works of Jonathan Swift*, it has also been time to say a respectful farewell to routine citation of such long-familiar scholarly editions as the *Correspondence*, *Poems* and *Journal to Stella* edited by Harold Williams, and the volumes of Herbert Davis's *Prose Works* now superseded by *CWJS* volumes. Yet we are all standing, as long as we can stand at all, on the shoulders of giants (the labours of Herman Teerink and Arthur Scouten on *A Bibliography of the Writings of Jonathan Swift* are an enduring example); and only from such a vantage point can we hope to see, in and through the intricate challenges posed by the material texts and their contexts, the larger patterns of Swift in print. To take on such a subject is necessarily to pay tribute to the many other kinds of book that have constituted Swift studies over the generations, and to recognise the excitement of a digital moment in which books themselves, now relieved of many of their everyday duties, are once more reminding us of their strangeness and allure.

But there is, as always, the most important person still to thank. Without Ian's support and resilience over the last forty years, not to mention the stimulus of his own very different work in editing and textual transmission, I would probably never have begun this or indeed any of my books – let alone finished them.

Note on Conventions

The scholarship and modern editions that provide the secondary material for this study are listed in the Works Cited at the end of the book; but a different method has been adopted for the early printed books, pamphlets and papers that constitute the primary material. These are instead introduced in the body of the book (and can be traced from the Index). This allows a fuller and more contextualised account of items whose titles, places of publication and relative dates are not necessarily straightforward. These first references are primarily designed to distinguish the edition under discussion from others with which it might be confused, making it as easy as possible for readers to identify available library copies and digital simulacra (for which the listings of holding libraries and digital resources in *ESTC* are particularly helpful). TS numbers, Foxon numbers and *ESTC* numbers are therefore provided as relevant, although it should be borne in mind that TS was last revised in 1963, Foxon's *English Verse, 1701–1750* dates from 1975, and *ESTC* does not include all the publications discussed in the present work. (*ECCO* images can be accessed quickly and accurately by using the *ESTC* number search facility; but some Swift publications included in *ESTC* are not included in *ECCO*.)

Titles of works by Swift are normally given in italics. (The modern convention of distinguishing between italics for works first published separately and roman in inverted commas for those first published as part of a collection sits awkwardly with the diversity of early Swift printings.) Where discussion focuses on typographical variation, titles and quotations are transcribed in roman or italic or black letter, upper case or lower case, large or small capitals as required.

All classical quotations and translations are taken from Loeb Classical Library (www.loebclassics.com).

In choosing illustrations for this book I have focused primarily on less familiar publications and on less familiar pages from better-known publications, and it has been a joy to be able to draw on the resources of the

British Library, Chetham's Library and the Wren Library of Trinity College, Cambridge. Some of the images have been reproduced from items of relatively poor quality (an important aspect of early Swift in print); some, though perhaps harder to read in detail at reduced size, provide a necessary overview of the designs of page and opening that framed Swift's writings for early readers. Many other images of Swift in print are already accessible in editions of his works, in books about him, and in online resources, so the present selection aims to widen the range by prioritising images not so easily found elsewhere – even if they are not always the clearest or most elegant.

Abbreviations

Ault, *Pope's Own Miscellany*	Alexander Pope, *Pope's Own Miscellany*, ed. Norman Ault (London: Nonesuch Press, 1935)
Baines and Rogers, *Curll*	Paul Baines and Pat Rogers, *Edmund Curll, Bookseller* (Oxford: Clarendon Press, 2007)
BBTI	*British Book Trade Index* (bbti.bodleian.ox.ac.uk)
BL	British Library
Bond, *Tatler*	*The Tatler*, ed. Donald F. Bond, 3 vols. (Oxford: Clarendon Press, 1987)
Bowyer Ledgers	Keith Maslen and John Lancaster (eds.), *The Bowyer Ledgers* (London: Bibliographical Society, revised online edition, 2017: www.bibsoc.org.uk; book and microform first published London: Bibliographical Society, and New York, Bibliographical Society of America, 1991)
Carpenter, *Scuffle*	John Dunton, *The Dublin Scuffle*, ed. Andrew Carpenter (Dublin: Four Courts Press, 2000)
Corr.	*The Correspondence of Jonathan Swift, D.D.*, ed. David Woolley, with index by Hermann J. Real and Dirk F. Passmann, 5 vols. (Frankfurt am Main: Peter Lang, 1999–2014)
CWJS	*The Cambridge Edition of the Works of Jonathan Swift* (Cambridge University Press, 2008–): vol. I, *A Tale of a Tub and Other Works*, ed. Marcus Walsh (2010); vol. II, *Parodies, Hoaxes, Mock Treatises: Polite Conversation, Directions to Servants and Other Works*, ed. Valerie Rumbold (2013); vols. III–VI, *Poems* I–IV, ed. James Woolley and Stephen Karian (forthcoming); vol. VII, *English Political Writings, 1701–1711: The Examiner and Other Works*, ed. Ian Gadd and Ian Higgins

	(forthcoming); vol. VIII, *English Political Writings, 1711–1714: The Conduct of the Allies and Other Works*, ed. Bertrand A. Goldgar and Ian Gadd (2008); vol. IX, *Journal to Stella: Letters to Esther Johnson and Rebecca Dingley, 1710–1713*, ed. Abigail Williams (2013); vol. XII, *Writings on Religion and the Church after 1714*, ed. Ian Higgins (forthcoming); vol. XIV, *Irish Political Writings after 1725: A Modest Proposal and Other Works*, ed. David Hayton and Adam Rounce (2018); vol. XV, *Gulliver's Travels*, ed. David Womersley (2012)
Davis, *Drapier's Letters*	Jonathan Swift, *The Drapier's Letters to the People of Ireland against Receiving Wood's Halfpence*, ed. Herbert Davis (Oxford: Clarendon Press, 1935)
ECCO	*Eighteenth Century Collections Online* (www .gale.com/intl/primary-sources/eighteenth-century-collections-online)
Ehrenpreis, *Swift*	Irvin Ehrenpreis, *Swift: The Man, His Works, and the Age*, 3 vols. (London: Methuen, 1962–83)
Ellis, *Discourse*	Jonathan Swift, *A Discourse of the Contests and Dissentions between the Nobles and the Commons in Athens and Rome*, ed. Frank H. Ellis (Oxford: Clarendon Press, 1967)
Ellis, *Examiner*	Jonathan Swift, *Swift vs. Mainwaring: The Examiner and The Medley*, ed. Frank H. Ellis (Oxford: Clarendon Press, 1985)
ESTC	*English Short Title Catalogue* (estc.bl.uk)
Foxon	David Foxon, *English Verse, 1701–1750: A Catalogue of Separately Printed Poems with Notes on Contemporary Collected Editions*, 2 vols. (Cambridge University Press, 1975)
HLQ	*Huntington Library Quarterly*
JSA	*Jonathan Swift Archive* (ota-qa.bodleian.ox.ac.uk)
JS Book	Paddy Bullard and James McLaverty (eds.), *Jonathan Swift and the Eighteenth-Century Book* (Cambridge University Press, 2013)
J. Woolley, *Intelligencer*	Jonathan Swift and Thomas Sheridan, *The Intelligencer*, ed. James Woolley (Oxford: Clarendon Press, 1992)

List of Abbreviations

Karian, *Print and Manuscript*	Stephen Karian, *Jonathan Swift in Print and Manuscript* (Cambridge University Press, 2010)
Lonsdale, *Lives*	Samuel Johnson, *The Lives of the Most Eminent English Poets*, ed. Roger Lonsdale, 4 vols. (Oxford: Clarendon Press, 2006)
Münster (date)	*Proceedings of the First Münster Symposium on Jonathan Swift*, ed. Hermann J. Real and Heinz J. Vienken (Munich: Wilhelm Fink, 1985); *Reading Swift: Papers from the Second Münster Symposium on Jonathan Swift*, ed. Richard H. Rodino and Hermann J. Real (Munich: Wilhelm Fink, 1993); *Reading Swift: Papers from the Third Münster Symposium on Jonathan Swift*, ed. Hermann J. Real and Helgard Stöver-Leidig (Munich: Wilhelm Fink, 1998); *Reading Swift: Papers from the Fourth Münster Symposium on Jonathan Swift*, ed. Hermann J. Real and Helgard Stöver-Leidig (Munich: Wilhelm Fink, 2003); *Reading Swift: Papers from the Fifth Münster Symposium on Jonathan Swift*, ed. Hermann J. Real (Munich: Wilhelm Fink, 2008); *Reading Swift: Papers from the Sixth Münster Symposium on Jonathan Swift*, ed. K. Juhas, H. J. Real and S. Simon (Munich: Wilhelm Fink, 2013); *Reading Swift: Papers from the Seventh Münster Symposium on Jonathan Swift*, ed. Janika Bischof, Kirsten Juhas and Hermann J. Real (Munich: Wilhelm Fink, 2019)
ODEP	*The Oxford Dictionary of English Proverbs*, 3rd edition, ed. F. P. Wilson (Oxford: Clarendon Press, 1970)
ODNB	*Oxford Dictionary of National Biography* (www.oxforddnb.com)
Pollard, *Dictionary*	Mary Pollard, *A Dictionary of the Members of the Dublin Book Trade, 1550–1800* (London: Bibliographical Society, 2000)
PW	Jonathan Swift, *The Prose Writings of Jonathan Swift*, ed. Herbert Davis and others, 16 vols. (Oxford: Basil Blackwell, 1939–74)

xxviii	*List of Abbreviations*

SCEBC (date)	*Stationers' Company Entry Book of Copies* (images in *Literary Print Culture: The Stationers' Company Archive, 1554–2007*, Adam Matthew Digital, www.literaryprintculture.amdigital.co.uk)
Scott, *Works*	Jonathan Swift, *The Works of Jonathan Swift*, ed. Walter Scott, 2nd edition, 19 vols. (Edinburgh, 1824)
SStud	*Swift Studies*
SwJ	Alexander Lindsay, 'Jonathan Swift, 1667–1745', in *Index of English Literary Manuscripts*, Vol. III: *1700–1800*, Part 4 (London: Mansell, 1997)
TCD	Trinity College, Dublin
TS	H. Teerink, *A Bibliography of the Writings of Jonathan Swift*, 2nd edition revised and corrected by the author, ed. Arthur H. Scouten (Philadelphia, PA: University of Pennsylvania Press, 1963)
Ward, *Prince of Dublin Printers*	George Faulkner, *Prince of Dublin Printers: The Letters of George Faulkner*, ed. Robert E. Ward (Lexington, KY: University Press of Kentucky, 1972)

PART I

Beginnings

CHAPTER I

First Impressions
Dublin and London to 1699

Swift in print began in the early 1690s with two oddly printed poems. Published in two different kingdoms, one in Dublin and one in London, they anticipate an uneasily asymmetrical relation between Ireland and England that would shape Swift's publications as decisively as it did his life and writing. Slender (even nugatory) as these two first publications are, their material oddities present a striking contrast with the higher standards later available to Swift. Yet their publishers were also linked with networks that would continue to shape Swift in print well into the future – a future in which cheap popular print would also display its own particular force. These scanty and erratic first publications offer revealing insights into the print cultures that Swift in print inherited and would to a degree transform.

That Swift in print should be so deeply marked by the asymmetrical power relations that connected and differentiated the Irish and English print trades is hardly surprising. Born in 1667 into the Anglo-Irish professional community around Dublin Castle, Swift would later claim that as a child he had been taken away to England by his nurse.[1] By about 1673 he had been placed at Kilkenny School, 70 miles south of Dublin, and in 1682 he entered Trinity College, staying until 1688, when the War of the two Kings prompted an exodus of Protestants to England. There Swift became secretary to the retired diplomat and family patron Sir William Temple (1628–1699), returning to Ireland in 1690, the year of William III's victory at the Battle of the Boyne: Swift's first printed work, *An Ode. To the King*, celebrates this event and is dated Dublin 1691. In the same year Swift rejoined Temple in England, and 1692 saw the London publication of his second printed work, *Ode to the Athenian Society*. He began a career in the Church of Ireland: having been ordained deacon in 1694 and priest in

---

[1] For Swift's early life, see *Family of Swift, PW*, vol. V, pp. 192–5, and chronology in each volume of *CWJS*.

3

4   Part I: Beginnings

1695, he took on a thankless ministry in Presbyterian-dominated Ulster, which he left to return to Temple again in 1696. By now he was almost thirty, and for the next three years he stayed in England as Temple's secretary, also working during this time on *A Tale of a Tub*. On Temple's death in 1699 he took on the role of literary executor, overseeing the London printing of Temple's as yet unpublished works.

Swift had grown up in a print world where Dublin and London exemplified opposite approaches to the threats and advantages posed by print to the early modern state.[2] In Restoration Dublin the advantages were secured by appointing a King's Printer in Ireland, and the threats were suppressed by giving him a monopoly: apart from the King's Printer, no one in Ireland had any business to be printing or selling books at all. London print, in contrast, had long operated under the more expansive regime run by the Stationers' Company, which effectively managed the trade on the Crown's behalf. As John Feather puts it: 'The interests of the Company and the Crown coalesced in a desire to control the trade, the Crown to control content and the Company to protect the commercial interests of its members.'[3] Crucially, the Stationers' Company enjoyed monopoly rights in the works of the so-called English Stock – notably almanacs, the Bible, the Book of Common Prayer and Lily's Latin grammar (all of which would be important to Swift). The English Stock was powerfully constitutive of authority, whether in presenting a Protestant understanding of the Bible, promulgating Anglican liturgy, systematising the language fundamental to elite education, or tabulating times of sunrise and sunset. Both London and Dublin had systems to ensure that print and authority went hand in hand, but, as Swift in print would amply demonstrate, the instantiation of that union in traditional print genres also invited co-option and challenge.

Swift's well-known preference for London publication might at first sight seem to align Swift in print with a London-orientated Anglo-Irish outlook: Pollard notes that London, 'the centre of all social, political, and literary excellence in the eyes of most of the Anglo-Irish', gained further traction for Irish authors, after the British Copyright Act of 1709, from what was for many (if not for Swift) 'the compelling attraction of payment

---

[2] Mary Pollard, *Dublin's Trade in Books, 1550–1800*, Lyell Lectures, 1986–7 (Oxford: Clarendon Press, 1989), p. 1, and, for overview, Charles Benson, 'The Irish Trade', in Michael F. Suarez and Michael L. Turner (eds.), *The Cambridge History of the Book in Britain*, vol. V: *1695–1830* (Cambridge University Press, 2009), pp. 366–82.

[3] John Feather, 'The Stationers' Company and Copyright: Evidence in the Company Archives', in *Literary Print Culture* (www.literaryprintculture.amdigital.co.uk).

First Impressions: Dublin and London to 1699 5

for copy'.[4] The material texts of Swift's writings tell more complicated stories: London publications could prove problematic, Dublin publications might achieve what London publications could not, and additional advantages, as well as difficulties, arose from the interplay between them. The printed canon of a major author was also likely to exert a different cultural and commercial force in the two kingdoms: in the 1730s Swift's first collected *Works*, published in Dublin by George Faulkner (*c.* 1703–1775), constituted an unprecedented achievement for an indigenous author and a proportionately valuable investment for his bookseller; but in the much larger London trade, which had long boasted impressive folios of Chaucer, Jonson, Spenser and Shakespeare, a single author could hardly have loomed so large (though Swift's friend Alexander Pope arguably came close).[5]

The changes in scale and range that facilitated Swift's later Dublin profile were already well under way in his youth. Gillespie's table of the output of Irish presses in the seventeenth century (based on *ESTC* data from 2003) confirms the overwhelming dominance of Dublin within a relatively small national output.[6] The table provided by Bullard and McLaverty (based on *ESTC* data from 2012) further suggests that over the first half of the eighteenth century Dublin's production almost doubled – although the preponderance of London production remained massive.[7] Gillespie also suggests the restricted range of seventeenth-century Dublin printing: in the final decade he identifies around 250 official items, around 100 reprints (typically from London originals) and around 200 other items.[8] (As for poetry, the core of imaginative writing in the period,

---

[4] Pollard, *Dublin's Trade in Books*, p. 67.

[5] See David Foxon, *Pope and the Early Eighteenth-Century Book Trade*, revised and edited by James McLaverty (Oxford: Clarendon Press, 1991); McLaverty, *Pope, Print and Meaning*.

[6] Raymond Gillespie, *Reading Ireland: Print, Reading and Social Change in Early Modern Ireland* (Manchester University Press, 2005), table 1, p. 186. For booksellers in Dublin in the late seventeenth and early eighteenth century, see James W. Phillips, *Printing and Bookselling in Dublin, 1670–1800* (Dublin: Irish Academic Press, 1998), pp. 26–30, and, for printers and journeymen, pp. 34–6.

[7] Bullard and McLaverty, 'Introduction', in *JS Book*, pp. 1–28 (p. 8, and, for necessary cautions, p. 26 n. 29, citing Stephen Karian, 'The Limitations and Possibilities of the *ESTC*', *The Age of Johnson: A Scholarly Annual*, 21 (2011), 283–97 (pp. 291–3)). Suarez breaks English imprints down by region but treats Ireland (like Scotland and Wales) as a single unit, using *ESTC* data from 2002–4 (Michael F. Suarez, 'Toward a Bibliometric Analysis of the Surviving Record, 1701–1800', in Michael F. Suarez and Michael L. Turner (eds.), *The Cambridge History of the Book in Britain*, vol. V: *1695–1830* (Cambridge University Press, 2009), pp. 39–65 (pp. 39, 50–1), noting, *passim*, the cautions necessary in estimating from *ESTC* data). For poor survival rates of Dublin publications for 1710–35, see James May, 'False and Incomplete Imprints in Swift's Dublin, 1710–35', in *Münster* (2019), pp. 59–99 (pp. 66–7).

[8] Gillespie, *Reading Ireland*, table 2, p. 188.

6   Part I: Beginnings

Carpenter notes its relative rarity in Dublin print right through into the 1680s; and James Woolley, noting the small size of 'the poem-buying public in Dublin' in the time of Swift, suggests 'the likelihood that when Dublin poems were published, they were published with a subvention from the author or a patron or both'.[9]) Pollard's account of the seventeenth-century printer William Bladen (*d.* 1695), who printed successively for Charles I and the Commonwealth from the 1640s until 1660, gives a stark perspective: 'Bladen was the only printer in Dublin and for most of this thirty-odd years the only bookseller . . . From 1640 to 1660 he issued a mere 20 or so works that were not official pub[licatio]ns, news, or propaganda.'[10] Both scale and range would change markedly under his successors, as the King's Printer's monopoly was largely ignored by rival tradesmen, and official strategy for the control of offensive books relied increasingly on prosecutions for seditious libel (which would also bear on Swift in print).[11] Nonetheless, the King's Printer remained a pervasive presence in the Dublin print of Swift's youth.

The King's Printer in Ireland

Early modern books customarily included, usually at the foot of the title page, a formal statement ('imprint') that declared their city of publication, the name of the person responsible, and the year of publication.[12] In Swift's youth the Dublin imprint of the King's Printer generally featured the name of the London bookseller Benjamin Tooke the elder (*c.* 1642–1716), often accompanied by one or more of the Crooke family.[13] John Crooke (*d.* 1669), who received the patent in 1660, had been Tooke's apprentice in London, and had married Tooke's sister, Mary. While John Crooke

---

[9] Andrew Carpenter, 'Circulating Ideas: Coteries, Groups and the Circulation of Verse in English in Early Modern Ireland', in Martin Fanning and Raymond Gillespie (eds.), *Print Culture and Intellectual Life in Ireland, 1660–1941: Essays in Honour of Michael Adams* (Dublin: Woodfield Press, 2006), pp. 1–23; James Woolley, 'The Circulation of Verse in Jonathan Swift's Dublin', *Eighteenth-Century Ireland: Iris an dá chultúr*, 32 (2017), 136–50 (p. 138). Such payments were not unknown in the London trade: see *The Correspondence of Alexander Pope*, ed. George Sherburn, 5 vols. (Oxford: Clarendon Press, 1956), vol. III, p. 489.

[10] Pollard, *Dictionary*, p. 39; Pollard, *Dublin's Trade in Books*, pp. 4–5.

[11] Pollard, *Dublin's Trade in Books*, pp. 1–11.

[12] For imprint conventions (and ways of evading them), see May, 'False and Incomplete Imprints', pp. 70–2 and *passim.*

[13] E. R. McClintock Dix, 'The Crooke Family', *Bibliographical Society of Ireland* [papers], 2 (1921), 16–17; Pollard, *Dictionary*, pp. 128–36 (family tree, p. 128). For the Crookes as 'a highly successful printing dynasty' and an example to later entrants to the trade, see Colm Lennon, 'The Print Trade, 1550–1700', in Raymond Gillespie and Andrew Hadfield (eds.), *The Oxford History of the Irish Book*, vol. III: *The Irish Book in English, 1550–1800* (Oxford University Press, 2006), pp. 61–73 (p. 73).

First Impressions: Dublin and London to 1699   7

looked after his London interests, Mary Crooke ran the King's Printer's business in Dublin. When John Crooke died in 1669 (the year of Swift's second birthday), Tooke acquired the patent in trust for his sister and her sons, and his name appeared in the imprint, alongside a shifting combination of Crooke names and roles, until John and Mary's son Andrew Crooke (*d.* 1732) acquired the patent in 1693. The King's Printer's Printing House (initially on Skinner Row, bounding Christ Church Cathedral yard to the south, and later on Ormonde Quay, on the north bank of the Liffey) was a central fixture in the Dublin print world: in 1673, the Franciscan Peter Walsh commented on the utility of Mrs Crooke's house as a 'randevue', 'by reason of a publick shopp', a sociable space where surreptitious contacts could pass unremarked.[14]

Mary Crooke's output featured an extensive official repertory of proclamations, acts of parliament, loyal sermons and editions of the Book of Common Prayer and psalter, along with liturgical supplements for special occasions. At the heart of her operation was the new type that her husband had commissioned when he took up the patent: featuring royal arms, elaborate initials, the traditional authority of archaic black letter type and an Irish harp motif, it affirmed the restoration of Church and King in Ireland.[15] (In 1673 the Crookes also acquired the type used by Bladen, and by the 1690s they were deploying a range of type that descended from even earlier King's Printers.[16]) The expressive force of the Crookes' loyal typography is well illustrated by a warning issued in 1662 by the Lords Justices and Council, complaining that 'Recusants, Non-conformists, and Sectaries have grown worse by Clemencie.'[17] As a brief notice for public display it was printed on one side only, in the typical format of a half sheet (also useful for news-sheets, poems and other short pieces – as many later Swift publications would testify). Authority was emphasised by a headpiece of the royal arms, surmounted by a border of crowned roses and acorns (the latter recalling the oak in which Charles II had escaped capture after the Battle of Worcester). The main text, in black letter, had a heading in large lower-case roman type, beginning with a large upper-case roman initial wreathed in foliage; and at the foot were the names of the signatories, surmounting the imprint of '*John Crook*, Printer to the Kings most

---

[14] Pollard, *Dictionary*, p. 135, quoting Bodleian, Carte MS 45, f. 400v.

[15] Pollard, *Dictionary*, p. 134.

[16] Lennon, 'The Print Trade, 1550–1700', p. 71; Pollard, *Dictionary*, p. 131.

[17] Ireland, Lords Justices and Council, *Whereas in expectation of Conformity to the Laws of the Land, concerning uniformity of Common-Prayer and Service in the Church and the Administration of the Sacraments* (Dublin, 1662; *ESTC* R39307).

8   Part I: Beginnings

Excellent Majesty'. Royal imagery, traditional black letter and names of authority underlined the coercive force of the verbal text, exemplifying the King's Printer's power to give material expression to the restored order of Church and King.[18]

Yet this order would be challenged in the following reign; and when in June 1688 the order went out for a supplement to the Book of Common Prayer to celebrate the birth of a son to James II and Mary of Modena, it was the Crookes who printed it: *A Form of Prayer with Thanksgiving for the Safe Delivery of the Queen, and Happy Birth of the Young Prince. To be used on Sunday the first of July, in the City of Dublin, and the Liberties thereof; and upon the 8th day of the same month in all other places throughout this Kingdom of Ireland. By His Excellency's Command.*[19] The pamphlet adopted the typographical scheme of large black letter with roman headings and rubric that was usual for such supplementary prayers. But the familiarity of the format can only have underlined, for Anglican congregations, the unprecedented threat of the content (also expressed in a procession to High Mass in Dublin Castle accompanied by public feasting and fireworks).[20] The prayers, part of daily worship for Swift and his fellow students at Trinity College, envisioned a Catholic succession extending to the crack of doom: 'That when the Kings days shall be fulfilled, and he shall sleep with his Fathers in Peace and Glory, his Seed may be set up after him, and his House and Kingdom may be established for ever before Thee.'[21] The Crookes' role was to print for the king, whoever he was and whatever he stood for: when in 1689, after the Revolution, James arrived in Ireland to reassert his right to the throne, it was the Crookes who set Tooke's name to James's 'Act of Supply for his Majesty for the Support of his Army', which once more flourished the royal arms on its title.[22] Even when James's ordinances began to appear under the imprint of a new King's Printer,

---

[18] Nearly a century later, John Smith's *Printer's Grammar* would declare that 'Black Letter is so far abolish'd *here*, that it is seldom used in any other matter than what belongs to Law, and more particularly to Statute Law', while conceding its occasional use 'to serve for matter which the Author would particularly enforce to the reader', or 'instead of printing in Red, what is designed to be made more conspicuous than common' (*The Printer's Grammar, 1755*, English Bibliographical Sources, Series 3, No. 2 (London: Gregg Press, 1965), pp. 18–19).

[19] *ESTC* R173987.

[20] John Gerald Simms, *Jacobite Ireland, 1685–91* (London: Routledge & Kegan Paul, 1969), pp. 44–5.

[21] Andrew Carpenter, 'A School for a Satirist: Swift's Exposure to the Wars of Words in Dublin in the 1680s', in *Münster* (2003), pp. 161–75 (pp. 163, 165–6); S. J. Connolly, *Divided Kingdom: Ireland, 1630–1800* (Oxford University Press, 2008), p. 178.

[22] *Anno Regni Jacobi II. Regis. Angliæ, Scotiæ, Franciæ & Hiberniæ Quinto. At the Parliament begun at Dublin the seventh day of May, Anno Domini 1689. In the fifth year of the reign of our most Gracious Soveraign Lord James the Second, by the grace of God, of England, Scotland, France and Ireland King, Defender of the Faith, &c.* (Dublin, 1689; *ESTC* R215420).

First Impressions: Dublin and London to 1699

the Catholic bookseller and book importer James Malone (*d.* 1721), who held James's patent with his relation Richard Malone for a few months in 1690, it seems that most of the printing was actually done by Andrew Crooke, continuing a stable coding of royal authority through a period of radical uncertainty.[23] But by this time Swift had left for England.

The output of the King's Printer, even when supplemented by the publications of rival presses, was insufficient to satisfy national demand, and readers of English books in Ireland were substantially reliant on imports.[24] Another possibility was Dublin reprinting of London titles, for by convention this was regarded as entirely legitimate, provided that no other Dublin printer had already laid a claim.[25] Such reprints were cheaper to supply than imports, especially if corners were cut on materials and printwork; and since the Copyright Act of 1709 would not extend to Ireland, these older, more permissive conventions, which persisted in Dublin throughout Swift's lifetime, encouraged the circulation of different printed texts (often of the same work) on the two sides of the Irish Sea. In the case of school books, for example, the Crookes were by the 1690s advertising their own range:

> Whereas such *Chapmen* as deal in *Books* have been forced to send to *England* for all their Histories and School-Books. These are to give them an account that the Books under-named may be had at the Kings Printing-House on *Ormonde-Key*, or at *Eliphel Dobsons*. Bookseller at the Stationers-Arms, *Dublin*: And all other School Books and Histories useful in this Kingdom will be done so fast as possible, and afforded as cheap as can be had in *London*.[26]

Their list includes reprints of standard Latin textbooks, but also 'The Church Catechism, with the Bishop of *Cork*'s Notes upon it', such favourite chapbooks as 'Valentine and Orson' and 'Seven Champions', and two items on military topics: 'Military Discipline' and 'Arlicles [*sic*] of War'. It is an eloquent reminder of the unsettled times, as well as the schoolboy culture, in which Swift had his formation.

The Crookes, however, did not always work to a quality commensurate with their royal authority, particularly since they supplemented their

---

[23] Pollard, *Dictionary*, pp. 395–6, 480–1.   [24] Pollard, *Dublin's Trade in Books*, pp. 32–65.
[25] *Ibid.*, pp. 66, 169–73.
[26] Advertisement on the final leaf of the Crookes' erratically printed *Mercurius Hibernicus, or, an Almanack for the Year of Christ, 1693 ... Fraught with Variety of Matter Befitting such a Work ... By John Whalley, Esq; Student in Pphysick [sic] and Mathematicks* (Dublin, 1693; *ESTC* R170269); Pollard cites a similar advertisement from 1690 (*Dictionary*, p. 130). For cheap Dublin reprints of English school books commissioned by the Catholic bookseller James Malone, see also Pollard, *Dictionary*, p. 395, and J. W. Phillips, *Printing and Bookselling*, p. 75.

Part I: Beginnings

official business with cheap popular print such as almanacs. Gillespie points out that 'at least part of the success of the almanac lay in its low cost', which was often no more than a penny; but the traditional design was fussy and labour-intensive, requiring tables, astrological symbols and rubrication.[27] Combined with low prices, small type and cheap paper, the results were predictably tawdry. The Crookes' *Bourks Almanack Hiberniae Merlinus for the Year of our Lord 1685*, for example, loyally affirmed the legitimacy of English rule by offering a chronology 'of all the Kings of Ireland, with the Remarkable things done by them from the time of *St. Patrick*, till *Henry* the 2d. the first English *Monark* of this *Kingdom*', but it also littered the text with mis-spaced words and transposed letters, and resorted to a last-minute reduction in type size (in November) to fit in the remaining text.[28] It is not surprising that the Crookes, though tried out by the Whig almanac-maker John Whalley (1653–1724), failed to give satisfaction: in the end Whalley set up a printshop of his own.[29] Complaints of the Crookes' textual errors, illegible type and poor paper intensified during the 1670s, and recurred in the 1700s.[30] The new type commissioned at the Restoration began to wear; and the type inherited from previous King's Printers was even older. Even new type would have required good paper for best effect, but paper was a major target for economy, particularly as Irish printers relied mainly on imports from France and Holland.[31] In the absence of constant reinvestment, some of the texts issued over Benjamin Tooke's imprint teetered on the verge of unsustainable pretension.

Meanwhile the patent monopoly was ceasing to be an effective reality. In 1670 the Dublin Guild of St Luke the Evangelist had been incorporated to admit 'Cutlers, Painter-stainers and Stationers', and within this body members of the Dublin book trade were admitted to the faculty of stationers.[32] Since one of the two patentees in this faculty was none other than Tooke, Pollard surmises that 'it may be taken as legitimizing the

---

[27] Gillespie, *Reading Ireland*, pp. 168–9; Pollard, *Dublin's Trade in Books*, p. 3; Valerie Rumbold, 'Ignoring Swift in Dublin? Swift's Bickerstaff Hoax in the Dublin Print Trade', *Publishing History*, 57 (2017), 9–42 (pp. 16–18).

[28] *ESTC* R170116. For Bourke's attempts to shape his material to attract Irish readers, see Gillespie, *Reading Ireland*, pp. 168–9.

[29] Pollard, *Dictionary*, p. 603. See Whalley, *Mercurius Hibernicus . . . 1693*, printed by Andrew Crooke under the Tooke imprint, and for discussion, Rumbold, 'Ignoring Swift', pp. 16–19.

[30] Pollard, *Dictionary*, pp. 131, 136. For an overview of Irish papermaking and of imported papers used in Dublin, see J. W. Phillips, *Printing and Bookselling*, pp. 151–96.

[31] Pollard, *Dublin's Trade in Books*, pp. 145–6.

[32] Pollard, *Dictionary*, pp. ix–xxxiv; Pollard, *Dublin's Trade in Books*, pp. 5–6.

First Impressions: Dublin and London to 1699

bookselling trade in Dublin' – if not the printing trade, to which the Crookes long continued to assert their monopoly rights. No King's Printer sought admission to the Guild until Andrew Crooke was admitted in 1696, and Pollard judges this likely to have been a compromise on his part.[33] In her view, despite repeated official confirmations of the King's Printer's monopoly, 'from the 1690s for most practical purposes it ceased to exist': the real benefits conferred by the patent were status and a steady supply of official work.[34]

Print-shops like Mrs Crooke's remained a focus of fascination for Swift, both in Dublin and in London: his early familiarity with such premises is suggested not only by his being disciplined in 1687 for 'neglect of duties' and 'frequenting the town', and his later recollection that he had spent most of his student days reading history and poetry (subjects not well represented in the library of Trinity College), but also by his lifelong taste for book-trade company. Formed in a Dublin market structurally reliant on London imports, Swift's lifelong aspiration to London publication may itself reflect a young man's sense that life was elsewhere; but when in 1701 he sought a London bookseller of his own, his choice fell on Benjamin Tooke the younger (1671–1723), son of the former King's Printer in Ireland, whose imprint was highly reminiscent of Dublin imprints of Swift's youth.[35] Swift remained deeply engaged with official publications, whether attacking or supporting the authorities that they served to instantiate, and his Dublin-printed texts would also invoke the national rhetoric of ornaments such as harps, roses and thistles (the first of these by far the rarest in eighteenth-century Dublin print-shops). In the late Stuart crises of Swift's youth in Ireland print authority had been undermined by dramatic transfers of power: the Restoration dispensation of his early life, in Connolly's words, 'strongly coloured by the values and principles of the Laudian era', had been challenged in print by the Catholicism of James II, and was further challenged by Whig support for Presbyterianism after 1688, helping to set the tone for Swift's pugnacious defence of Anglican privilege.[36] Yet the standing of the King's Printer had also been damaged by failures in print quality, and poor printwork would irritate Swift throughout his life: even when his works imitated cheap popular print

---

[33] Pollard, *Dublin's Trade in Books*, pp. 8–9. [34] Pollard, *Dictionary*, pp. 128, 133, 480.
[35] It was long believed that Swift's bookseller was Benjamin Tooke the elder: for correction, see Michael Treadwell, 'Swift's Relations with the London Book Trade to 1714', in Robin Myers and Michael Harris (eds.), *Author/Publisher Relations during the Eighteenth and Nineteenth Centuries*, Publishing Pathways (Oxford Polytechnic Press, 1983), pp. 1–36 (pp. 9–10).
[36] Connolly, *Divided Kingdom*, p. 139; Gillespie, *Reading Ireland*, p. 117.

Part I: Beginnings

they would tend to be implausibly well printed, although the Drapier's letters were to demonstrate the potential of genuinely shabby print to reach a wide audience. Swift himself never published under the imprint of the King's Printer in Ireland: his first publication issued instead from one of the members of the Guild whose very existence posed an implicit challenge to the monopoly.

An Ode. To the King (1691)

Swift in print begins with *An Ode. To the King on His Irish Expedition, and the Success of his Arms in general. Presented to His Majesty upon His departure from Ireland* (Dublin, 1691).[37] It survives in only one known copy, identified by James Woolley in the library of the Diocese of Derry and Raphoe as recently as 1993.[38] Its colophon, under a rule at the foot of the last printed page, is '*Dublin*, Printed by *Jo. Brent*; and are to be Sold at the Printinghouse over against the Sign of the *Cock* in *Capel-street*, near *Essex-Bridge*. 1691'. The north end of Essex Bridge (on the site of the later Grattan Bridge) was at the junction of Capel Street, which runs north from the river, and Ormonde Quay, where the Crookes had their King's Printing House: at the heart of a print neighbourhood, John Brent (1639–1714) was only a few minutes' walk from Trinity College. But despite the explicitness of *An Ode. To the King* about its material origins, it is silent as to who wrote it, inaugurating at the outset the lifetime habit of anonymity typical of Swift in print. In this case, as J. Woolley points out, the acknowledgement came in 1692, when 'in his "Ode to the Athenian Society," published that year, he refers to "an *Humble Chaplet for the King*", glossed as "The Ode I writ to the King in *Ireland*."'[39] To judge by the survival of just one known copy, *An Ode. To the King* was a very small beginning for a very major author.

Brent created an attractive quarto pamphlet, which would turn out to be a staple format for Swift in print.[40] Quartos, already well established as a format for printed plays, were about to take on two new major roles; and only one of them would be relevant to Swift in print. This was the use of the quarto for pamphlets, which from the late seventeenth century made

---

[37] James Woolley, 'Swift's First Published Poem: *Ode. To the King*', in *Münster* (2003), pp. 265–83; *CWJS Poems* I (forthcoming). *Ode to the Athenian Society* (see below) was previously believed to be Swift's first published work.

[38] J. Woolley, 'Swift's First Published Poem', pp. 266–7.   [39] *Ibid.*, p. 265.

[40] For this and other book formats (with diagrams), see Philip Gaskell, *A New Introduction to Bibliography* (Oxford: Clarendon Press, 1972), pp. 80–109.

First Impressions: Dublin and London to 1699

possible a new kind of extra-parliamentary controversy, to which Swift would make a crucial contribution. The less relevant quarto trend would be promoted in the new century by his younger friend-to-be, Alexander Pope (whose birth in 1688 barely preceded the publication of *An Ode. To the King*). Pope would from 1717 offer subscribers to his *Works* and Homer translations a choice between two prestige formats: a traditional folio and the newer option of a large quarto.[41] By mid-century the stylish large quarto would have largely displaced the older folio, but Swift in print eschewed both. (Only in 1755 would John Hawkesworth's posthumous London collected edition of Swift feature the first large quarto option.[42])

Brent, however, launched Swift in print with a much humbler kind of quarto, made from just one sheet of paper: seven of the eight pages were printed, and the last left blank, forming a back cover. The poem begins on the first page, immediately below the title: to have provided a separate title page with a blank verso would have entailed either the expense of extra paper, or a relatively cramped presentation of the verse – even if the poem had been allowed to run onto the final verso. In a poem blazoned as '*Presented to His Majesty*', it probably seemed best to prioritise the spacious effect of the verse itself.[43] Verse, as mentioned above, was rarely printed in Dublin at this time, and Brent was probably more a bookseller than a printer; but he made a careful and effective use of limited resources. (In contrast, two contemporary London quarto poems in praise of William, which also begin directly under the title, lack even the refinement of a blank back cover.[44]) Although there are indications that Brent made a few literal errors, his printing is clear and sharp throughout.[45] The title contrasts large full capitals for principal words with smaller full capitals; lower-case roman and italic are also used for contrast; and the composition is set off by straight, well-executed composite rules.[46] (Brent may have lacked the long rules of a better-equipped print-shop, but his skill with short ones puts him well ahead of less accomplished Dublin printers.[47]) The type is large and legible; varying indentation emphasises the different line lengths characteristic of a Pindaric ode; italic contrast is used for emphasis; and care is taken to keep adjacent rhyming lines together

---

[41] McLaverty, *Pope, Print and Meaning*, p. 47.   [42] See Chapter 8.

[43] I am grateful to Andrew Carpenter and James McLaverty for discussion on these points.

[44] E. W., *A Poem to his Most Sacred Majesty King William upon his Return from Flanders* (London, 1691; *ESTC* R5717); *A Pindarick Ode on His Majesties Return from the Campaign, 1691* (London, 1691; *ESTC* R181804).

[45] J. Woolley, 'Swift's First Published Poem', pp. 280–3.   [46] For images, see *ibid.*, pp. 267–73.

[47] For Dublin printers' use of composite rules, see May, 'False and Incomplete Imprints', p. 61.

Part I: Beginnings

between pages. Yet there is some shaky alignment in the title where full capitals and lower case occur in the same line, and an inappropriate comma marks the title's end. There are also signs that Brent lacked type to carry out his design in full: from page 4 capital VV appears instead of W, and numerous lines begin with an italic capital *A* or *H* mismatched with a word in roman.[48] These oddities suggest that he had run out of upper-case roman type in this large size, which in turn highlights the young poet's particular fondness for beginning lines with the word 'And' (approximately 20 per cent of the lines in the poem) – and, to a lesser extent, with 'How', 'His' and 'Her'. When we consider the traditional story that Swift's cousin Dryden, the exponent of the Pindaric ode *par excellence* in this period, discouraged his efforts by telling him that 'Nature has never formed you for a Pindaric poet', we might also reflect on the material evidence of those mismatched capitals.[49]

Swift would soon abandon the Pindaric vein in favour of what Philmus calls 'poems whose matter and manner we can now pronounce to be decidedly Swiftian', but his steps to that decision are obscure.[50] His choice of topic was not in itself unpromising, for, by celebrating the triumph of William of Orange (whom he may already have met through Temple) at the Battle of the Boyne in 1690, he not only published a tribute that might have advanced his own preferment, but also embraced what Abigail Williams identifies as one of the master themes of Whig poetic culture.[51] He would always maintain, despite his reservations about the later consequences of William's triumph, that 'we ought to remember him with gratitude'; and this publication catches that gratitude in its first and relatively uncritical flush.[52] The title also claims that the poem was presented to the King before his departure from Ireland (5 September 1690). But the 1691 imprint of the printed text suggests publication either late in 1690 (postdating being a routine ploy for prolonging the currency of end-

[48] For a view from 1755 on the advantages and disadvantages of retaining 'large Founts of Letter', and on the uses of large capitals, see Smith, *The Printer's Grammar*, pp. 47–8, 50–2. Smith also details ingenious 'shifts and contrivances to which Printers are drove who live at a great distance from Founders; and who have no neighbours to assist them' (p. 84).

[49] Theophilus Cibber, *The Lives of the Poets of Great Britain and Ireland*, 4 vols. (London, 1753), vol. V, p. 98; Robert M. Philmus, 'Dryden's "Cousin Swift" Re-Examined', *SStud*, 18 (2003), 99–103, suggesting possible transmission via Colley Cibber's conversations with Laetitia Pilkington (pp. 101–2).

[50] Philmus, 'Dryden's "Cousin Swift" Re-Examined', p. 103.

[51] Abigail Williams, *Poetry and the Creation of a Whig Literary Culture, 1681–1714* (Oxford University Press, 2005), pp. 1–2, 112–16. For page images, dating and contexts, see J. Woolley, 'Swift's First Published Poem', and *CWJS Poems* I (forthcoming).

[52] *A Sermon upon the Martyrdom of K. Charles I.*, *PW*, vol. IX, p. 224.

First Impressions: Dublin and London to 1699

of-year publications) or early in 1691, too late for the King to have been given a printed copy – which would in any case have been a *faux pas*, since, as J. Woolley points out, it lacks the requisite 'epistle dedicatory' to a monarch. Whether or not the poem had actually been presented to the King, the pamphlet was an ambitious production in a market where verse was well out of the ordinary. With its clearly advertised availability at Brent's shop, it was a creditable publication of record. Bearing in mind Carpenter's view that pre-1680 printed verse connected with Ireland was largely 'custom-printed in very small print-runs and so intended, not for general circulation to miscellaneous purchasers, but rather to be passed around closed groups or sent to specific recipients', and that post-1680 'original Irish-printed verse . . . is still meagre in comparison with the riches available in English-printed material of the period', it seems not unlikely that Swift's poem was printed less to reach a general readership than to testify his loyalty and accomplishment to a small group of crucial gatekeepers.[53] In that case the omission of his name might have seemed not so much mystificatory as tactful, combining the formality of print with a modest abstention from self-advertisement. A small print-run of this economically designed single-sheet pamphlet may indeed have been paid for by Swift himself, or by a well-wisher, in the hope of gaining a Fellowship at Trinity College (a possibility that Temple had suggested to William's Secretary of State for Ireland, Sir Robert Southwell, at the end of May 1690).[54] The surviving copy of *An Ode. To the King* certainly seems to have passed through the collection of Trinity's vice-provost and librarian, John Hall; but in the event the 1691 election was cancelled owing to the College's losses during the war, and no other preferment materialised.[55] For such purposes, given the Crookes' known problems with print quality, Brent's clear, careful work may well have made him a better option than the King's Printer.

Stephen Karian computes that only twenty-nine of '366 poems that can be confidently attributed to Swift alone and in collaboration' were published in authorised editions within a year of composition.[56] This makes *An Ode. To the King* highly unusual, a verse debut that gives no hint of the dominant pattern to come: whereas Swift's prose would often be sent quickly to press, verse would typically circulate in manuscript, or not at

---

[53] Carpenter, 'Circulating Ideas', pp. 1, 18.
[54] *Corr.*, vol. I, pp. 101–3, 106 n. 4; J. Woolley, 'Swift's First Published Poem', pp. 266, 278; *CWJS Poems* I (forthcoming); *PW*, vol. V, p. 195.
[55] J. Woolley, 'Swift's First Published Poem', pp. 274–5, 280.
[56] Karian, 'Swift as a Manuscript Poet', pp. 32–3.

16   Part I: Beginnings

all, and reach print publication much later – if at all. Both verse and prose might engage issues of public urgency and importance, but poems in Swift's mature style were particularly likely to do so in libellous or otherwise inadvisable terms; and they were also a preferred medium for sociable exchange arguably too trivial and intimate for publication. But in material if not generic terms this first publication is deeply characteristic of lifetime Swift in print. The careful work of a somewhat meagrely equipped printshop, it occupies just a single sheet of paper: Swift in print will often require only a half, and will aspire at most to the modest pomp of a decently printed octavo volume.

As May points out, 'With Dublin books more than London books, to discover the printer is to discover the publisher or at least approach him, for the two functions were more often shared by the same individual and, when they were not, ideological and familial relations bound printers and publishers more than in London.'[57] This politically and religiously charged face-to-face world was so constitutive of Swift's outlook that it may well have conditioned his approach to the larger London print trade, but it is overwhelmingly relevant to this first Dublin relationship with Brent: as J. Woolley notes, Swift's 'friendship with the Brents was apparently the first and most long-lasting in a series of friendships Swift had with printers and booksellers, including the Tookes, Barber, Waters, Hyde, the Hardings, Motte, and Faulkner'.[58] But in some ways it was also the most surprising, because Brent's wife, Jane, was a Presbyterian; and despite Swift's notorious hostility to dissenters he chose for the rest of his life to entrust his housekeeping first to her, and subsequently to her daughter. Swift's mother apparently got on well with Mrs Brent when she stayed with her on an early visit to Dublin; and David Woolley infers, on the basis of Swift's 1728 statement that Mrs Brent had worked for him 'above thirty years', that she may have been keeping house for him as early as 1694–6.[59] By the time of her death John Brent had been dead for twenty years, but Swift still turned to their daughter, Ann Ridgeway, to be his housekeeper.[60]

Swift consistently made a joke of the ideological mismatch that his choice of Mrs Brent set at the heart of his domestic world: in 1722, for

---

[57] May, 'False and Incomplete Imprints', p. 72.
[58] Ehrenpreis, *Swift*, vol. I, p. 66; J. Woolley, 'Swift's First Published Poem', p. 274; Bullard and McLaverty, 'Introduction', p. 3.
[59] J. Woolley, 'Swift's First Published Poem', p. 274; Bullard and McLaverty, 'Introduction', p. 8; Ehrenpreis, *Swift*, vol. I, p. 29; *Corr.*, vol. I, p. 613 n. 7.
[60] Ehrenpreis, *Swift*, vol. III, p. 806.

First Impressions: Dublin and London to 1699 17

example, he teased his friend Thomas Sheridan (1687–1738) that his foolishness had made Mrs Brent so 'angry' with him that she 'swears as much as a Fanatick can do'; in 1728 he told Pope that she was 'my Walpole'; and in 1731 he elaborated to his correspondent Lord Bathurst a mock-complaint of his 'hard circumstances', founded on the misfortune that 'I have an old Presbyterian Tory house keeper whom the Neighborhood call Sr Robt W—', whom he depicts as conspiring against him at every turn.[61] Swift would also tease her in domestic verses such as *Dingley, and Brent. A Song* – a piece evidently not intended for publication.[62] He also wrote from London to his friends Esther Johnson and Rebecca Dingley in 1712 with a report (presumably for Mrs Brent) that he was trying, at her request, to establish in the London trade a young man whom he had formerly placed as an apprentice with her late husband: her good opinion evidently mattered to him.[63] Yet there is in Swift's writing about her a persistent coupling of ideological exasperation with abiding attachment, which takes on a new dimension in the light of the revelation that her husband was Swift's first printer. John Brent may have worked for William III in 1690 in the Dublin print-shop set up (probably from London) by the King's Printer in England, Edward Jones (*d.* 1706); and although he seems to have been happy enough to collaborate with printers of various outlooks (even Tories), the relationship between Swift and the Brents may well have been grounded in their shared relief at William's victory at the Boyne.[64] If in the longer view it seems ironic that Swift's first published work should have had its origins so close to the Presbyterian dissent that he would spend his life denouncing, it is even more ironic that in 1758 *The History of the Four Last Years of the Queen*, the last of his major works to come to press after his death, should have been published for the first time by Andrew Millar, a London bookseller from a distinguished family of Presbyterian divines.[65] But that publication, unlike Brent's helpfully painstaking *An Ode. To the King*, would be framed in terms overtly hostile to Swift's established record as Tory apologist.

Ode to the Athenian Society (1692)

Swift left Ireland in 1691 and once more joined Temple in England, where his second publication, *Ode to the Athenian Society*, appeared in 1692,

---

[61] *Corr.*, vol. II, p. 439; vol. III, pp. 180–1, 405.
[62] For its posthumous publication, see *CWJS Poems* II (forthcoming).   [63] *CWJS Journal*, p. 447.
[64] Pollard, *Dictionary*, pp. 52, 321–2.   [65] See Chapter 8.

Part I: Beginnings

probably with Temple's encouragement.[66] This time things were much more complicated: as well as the poem, there was a covering letter; the context was not a separate publication but a collection supplementary to a larger periodical project; and they were handled by a bookseller whose commercial and domestic disasters could hardly have been more removed from the probity and comfort that Swift seems to have associated with the Brents. That bookseller was John Dunton (1659–1732), a visionary print entrepreneur friendly to religious dissent, whose career was visibly dwindling into marital strife, bankruptcy and eccentricity.[67] His Athenian project, the stimulus for Swift's new publication, had been inaugurated in 1691, although there never was an Athenian Society as such, only a commercial collaboration between Dunton and his brothers-in-law Samuel Wesley the elder, a clergyman married to his wife's sister, and Richard Sault, a mathematician married to his half-sister.[68] After the first number, entitled the *Athenian Gazette*, the title of the sheets was changed to *Athenian Mercury*; the original title would be reserved for bound volumes.[69]

The journal's unique selling point was its promise to answer readers' questions: focusing on what Berry identifies as 'the concerns of the middling sort' of both sexes, it was ideally pitched for popular consumption.[70] Among other printers, Richard Baldwin (*c.* 1653–1698), a voluminous trade publisher and printer of popular Whig polemic, was heavily involved.[71] The flimsy half sheet was printed on both sides, with advertisements at the end; the questions and answers were crammed into double columns of patchily impressed small type; literal errors and mis-sorted and reversed letters were frequent; and the advertisements rarely strayed far beyond Dunton's own projects. One hallmark, typical of the lower end of the market, was last-minute switching to smaller type as space ran out,

---

[66] *CWJS Poems* I (forthcoming).

[67] Stephen Parks, *John Dunton and the London Book Trade: A Study of his Career with a Checklist of his Publications* (New York: Garland, 1976), pp. 20–1, 42; *ODNB* ('John Dunton').

[68] For the Athenian project in the context of Dunton's career, see Parks, *John Dunton*, pp. 74–108. See also Gilbert D. McEwen, *The Oracle of the Coffee House: John Dunton's Athenian Mercury* (San Marino, CA: Huntington Library, 1972); Helen Berry, *Gender, Society and Print Culture in Late-Stuart England: The Cultural World of the Athenian Mercury* (Aldershot: Ashgate, 2003).

[69] For possible pressure from the authorities to avoid confusion with the official *London Gazette*, see John Dunton, *The Life and Errors of John Dunton, late citizen of London* (London, 1705; *ESTC* T75140), p. 256.

[70] Berry, *Gender*, pp. 63–103 (p. 63).

[71] Parks, *John Dunton*, pp. 41, 86; D. F. McKenzie, 'The English Book Trade in the Later Seventeenth Century' (Sandars Lectures, 1976; typescript held in Cambridge University Library), p. 28; *ODNB* ('Richard Baldwin'). For the role of trade publisher, see Chapter 2.

First Impressions: Dublin and London to 1699 19

revealing a failure of the process by which, in Gaskell's words, 'the compositor – or sometimes the master or overseer – "cast off" the copy by counting words and by computation according to the sizes of type and page that had been decided on'.[72] Although Swift's Athenian poem escaped unscathed in this respect, some of his later work would not be so lucky (notably Dublin reprints of London-published pamphlets). Yet in 1692, in what was only Swift's second publication, his writing was already passing through the hands of printers for whom botching was all in a day's work.

The *Ode to the Athenian Society* was published, with a covering letter dated 14 February 1691 (i.e. 1692), as a commendatory poem at the front of Dunton's 1692 *Fifth Supplement to the Athenian Gazette*.[73] At the foot of the volume's title page it was billed as the second of two new attractions: 'The New Project concerning the / 𝕹atural & 𝕬rtificial 𝕽arities / OF / ENGLAND. / AS ALSO / AN ODE / TO THE / Athenian Society'.[74] The '𝕹atural & 𝕬rtificial 𝕽arities' were dignified with so-called 'ENGLISH' black letter and the largest type on the title was reserved for 'ENGLAND': Swift's poem was worth having, but could hardly compete with such patriotic fanfare. The imprint at the foot of the title vividly communicates Dunton's irrepressible preoccupation with marketing:

> *LONDON*, Printed for *John Dunton* at the Raven in the *Poultrey*, where is to be had the *First, Second, Third Fourth*, and *Fifth Volumes* of the *Athenian Gazette*, (and the *Supplements* to 'em) compleating the Entire Set for the Year 1691. (or single ones to this time.)

Yet, as the lack of a comma to separate '*Third Fourth*' shows, the struggle between ambition and print quality was endemic. The verso of the title was, as usual, left blank, and the second leaf provided two pages for Dunton's 'Preface', which was set, on his usual plan, in large italics with reverse roman for emphasis (although a mismatched upper-case roman U sits awkwardly upright throughout – *PARTICULAR DRAUGHT* being particularly striking). Dunton, dedicating yet another new initiative to 'the Honour and Profit of the English Nation', proposed a range of topics both vast and miscellaneous:

---

[72] E.g. *Athenian Gazette*, vol. I, no. 7; Gaskell, *A New Introduction*, p. 41. Moxon, writing in the 1680s, gives detailed instructions for casting off (Joseph Moxon, *Mechanick Exercises on the Whole Art of Printing (1683–4)*, ed. Herbert Davis and Harry Carter, 2nd edition (London: Oxford University Press, 1962), pp. 239–44); Smith, in the 1750s, provides tables (*The Printer's Grammar*, pp. 147–69). Smith describes it as 'unpleasant and troublesome work, which requires great attention; and therefore ought not to be hurried, but to be done with deliberation' (p. 155).

[73] *ESTC* R223319.   [74] In transcription, '/' indicates line divisions.

Within the compass of our Design will not only be comprehended the Natural History, *but as exact an Account as we can receive of all* Artificial and Civil Things Remarkable in *England* and Wales, Scotland, Ireland, *and all the Forreign Plantations depending on them,* &c. All Appearances *in the Heavens, Air, as strange Lights, Noises,* &c. The Natural *Growth and Improvements, their Productions, Qualities of the Soil,* Earth's, Minerals, *and Things Dug*; the Local History, *or an Account of the Civil Transactions of each Place, as* Battels, Sieges, *&c. which have happen'd there. The various sorts of* Fowls, *the several species of* Fishes *common to our Seas, the* Murders *that have been formerly or lately committed in every County, and by whom, and when discovered.* Princes, *Famous and Great Men who have been Natives of each Province, County, Shire, Hundred, Town,* &c. Immemorial Customs. In short, we shall endeavour to present the World *with whatever is* Curious & Entertaining *on every Subject, which if it be of too great Extent, will in some measure Excuse the Faults of our Performance.*

After a few more explanations and excuses, Dunton was finally ready for Swift; but the material text immediately highlighted the difficulty of finding space for such a long commendatory poem. As the volume is in folio (not so much the solid grandeur of a prestige edition as a deft commandeering facilitated by the project's association with a half-sheet periodical), each signature produced only four large pages.[75] The title, its blank verso, and the two pages of Preface had already filled the first signature ([A]), and, as it seems to have been decided that Swift's contribution would require more space than was available on the four pages of B, a half sheet (signed lower-case a) was inserted between [A] and B.[76] The recto of this half sheet (p. [1]) bore Swift's covering letter, and the poem began awkwardly on its verso (rather than on the next recto) and went on to fill all four pages of B (making five pages in all, numbered 2–6).

Although David Woolley correctly notes that 'the deferential tone of Swift's letter was given exaggerated emphasis typographically', Dunton's 'Preface' had already set the tone with the hyper-expressive roman/italic contrast normal for Athenian preliminaries. (Though less extreme than the typographical effects analysed by Harold Love as the distinctive journalistic voice of Sir Roger L'Estrange, it certainly suggests Dunton's preference for what Love calls 'noisy' print.[77]) In Swift's letter, however, the swaggering

[75] For the signing and assembly of sheets to form signatures, see Moxon, *Mechanick Exercises*, pp. 210–11, 317–18.

[76] The square brackets for [A] indicate that the first signature letter is inferred, in contrast with B, which is actually so signed.

[77] Harold Love, 'L'Estrange, Joyce and the Dictates of Typography', in Anne Dunan-Page and Beth Lynch (eds.), *Roger L'Estrange and the Making of Restoration Culture* (Abingdon: Routledge, 2016), pp. 167–79.

First Impressions: Dublin and London to 1699

typography came in particularly useful for asserting the sophistication and social connections of the project's supporters. The letter, set out on the recto of the half sheet signed a, displayed a prominent centred heading in which 'Athenian Society' was selected for size and emphasis, with Temple's Moor Park address, from which Swift dated his letter, tucked in beneath. The letter itself, in much smaller type, occupied little more than the upper half of the page, so that the large space below floated Swift's highly complimentary subscription gracefully across the page (Figure 1). Such a studiedly deferential layout (whether or not derived from Swift's hand-written copy) conferred an entirely undeserved honour on Dunton's fictitious society. This (and not, as Swift would later claim, his 1712 subscription of his name to *A Proposal for Correcting, Improving and Ascertaining the English Tongue*) was the first instance of his putting his name to a printed work, and the 'Jonathan Swift' here conjured is, as Ann Cline Kelly emphasises, an exercise in 'self-mythologizing'.[78] This was not a young Irish-born secretary and well-nigh invisible published author, but a world-weary lamenter of prevailing 'Follies', 'an English-man' who dated his letter from the address of a distinguished author and diplomat, where he was by implication a long-term guest rather than an employee. Indeed, his poem had been endorsed not only by '*a Person of very great* Learning and Honour' (presumably Temple himself), but also, in traditional coterie style, by '*the best of my Acquaintance*', staging a suggestive negotiation between the elite culture of manuscript circulation and the increasingly important role of print in reaching a broader readership, effectively offering his work for the latter while preserving the refinement of the former. The whole presentation gave a strong sense of the social disadvantages to be negotiated if Swift's name was to appear in print as author, as it now did for the first time.

Swift's coterie-style positioning is a reminder that, as a child of the 1660s, he was not born into a literary world based solely or even principally on print. His long withholding from the press of compositions (particularly poems) which were already circulating in manuscript was indeed to be one of the major factors that would give Swift in print its characteristically dislocated late early modern chronology. In Swift's early years print figured principally as an opportunity for a clergyman and writer to position himself for preferment; later it served to provide maximum dissemination for confrontational polemic. Where neither motive was pressing, or there were countervailing risks, it was easy enough to allow friends to make copies. Swift's deep personal

---

[78] *CWJS Parodies*, p. 156; Ann Cline Kelly, *Jonathan Swift and Popular Culture: Myth, Media, and the Man* (Basingstoke: Palgrave, 2002), pp. 14–20 (p. 16).

(1)

TO THE

Athenian Society.

Moor-park, Feb. 14. 1691.

GENTLEMEN,

SINCE every Body *pretends to trouble you with their* Follies, *I thought I might claim the Priviledge of an* English-man, *and put in my share among the rest. Being last year in* Ireland, *(from whence I returned about half a year ago) I heard only a* loose talk of your Society, *and believed the design to be only some new* Folly *just suitable to the Age, which God knows, I little expected ever to produce any thing* extraordinary. *Since my being in* England, *having still continued in the Countrey, and much out of Company ; I had but little advantage of knowing any more, till about two Months ago passing through* Oxford, *a very learned* Gentleman *there, first shew'd me two or three of your* Volumes, *and gave me his Account and Opinion of you ; a while after, I came to this place, upon a Visit to ——— where I have been ever since, and have seen all the* four *Volumes with their Supplements, which answering my Expectation. The perusal has produced, what you find inclosed.*

As I have been somewhat inclined to this Folly, *so I have seldom wanted some-body to flatter me in it. And for the* Ode *inclosed, I have sent it to a* Person *of very great* Learning *and* Honour, *and since to some others, the best of my Acquaintance, (to which I thought very proper to inure it for a greater light) and they have all been pleased to tell me, that they are sure it will not be unwelcome, and that I should beg the Honour of* You *to let it be* Printed *before* Your *next* Volume *(which I think, is soon to be published,) it being so usual before most* Books *of any great value among* Poets, *and before it's seeing the World, I submit it wholly to the* Correction *of your* Pens.

I intreat therefore one of You *would descend so far, as to write two or three lines to me of your* Pleasure *upon it. Which as I cannot but expect from* Gentlemen, *who have so well shewn upon so many occasions, that greatest* Character *of* Scholars, *in being favourable to the* Ignorant, *So I am sure nothing at present, can more highly oblige me, or make me happier.*

I am,

(Gentlemen)

Your ever most Humble,
and most
admiring Servant.

Jonathan Swift.

a

O D E.

Figure 1 Jonathan Swift, dedicatory letter to *Ode to the Athenian Society*, in John Dunton's *Fifth Supplement to the Athenian Gazette* (London, 1692).

First Impressions: Dublin and London to 1699   23

attachment to manuscript circulation, partly practical and partly generational, indicates one of the ways in which Swift in print pulls away, decisively if erratically, from the practices of Swift as an individual.

Manuscript circulation would not presumably have answered the purposes of *Ode to the Athenian Society* or *An Ode. To the King*, whose flourishes of compliment suggest the public performance of a place-seeking author. Like *An Ode. To the King, Ode to the Athenian Society* also belongs to the select minority of Swift's poems published in authorised printings within a year of composition.[79] Unfortunately, in comparison to the spacious printing accorded to the aspirationally misleading covering letter, the *Ode to the Athenian Society* itself received short shrift. It begins directly on the verso of the letter, and the lack of spacing between the numbered stanzas of the ode further demonstrates that the extra half sheet was not nearly enough. If Swift's offering had been allocated a full two sheets, instead of one-and-a-half, the letter could have been backed with a gracefully blank verso, the poem could have begun in proper dignity on a new recto, and there would have been room for suitable spacing between stanzas and generous margins at head and foot. As if in compensation, the questionable benefits of Dunton's busy typography were lavished with unsparing hand: roman type is varied with frequent italic contrast, and there is occasional emphasis in black letter. But such elaborations did not require extra paper. Refinements that did were not a priority in the Athenian struggle between pomp and economy.

It may be significant that Swift had not, apparently, seen many issues of the *Athenian Mercury* in the original half sheets, but had instead formed his opinion from the superficially more impressive folio-sized bound volumes of the *Athenian Gazette*. According to his covering letter to the *Ode*, he had encountered in Oxford (presumably in 1691) '*two or three of your* Volumes', and, at Moor Park, '*all the* four Volumes with their Supplements' – which is consistent with his explanation to his cousin Thomas Swift that 'S^r W^m T speaking to me so much in their Praise made me zealous for their cause'.[80] Each volume contained thirty numbers, with a newly printed title, preface and contents list, and came ready bound in marbled paper.[81] But if the ambition of this repackaging was obvious, so were its shallow

---

[79] Karian, 'Swift as a Manuscript Poet', p. 33.
[80] The first number is dated 17 March 1690 (i.e. 1691). For Swift's covering letter, see *Corr.*, vol. I, pp. 107–10, and, for his letter to Thomas Swift, pp. 109–13.
[81] For a single volume (vol. I) in its original marbled paper, see Bodleian Library J.C. 43.1/25. In contrast, Bodleian Library (Vet.) Per. 3986 c.1 has been made up by removing the covers of several volumes and binding them together.

24 Part I: Beginnings

foundations. The first volume began well enough, with a title framed in respectably aligned double rules: 'THE / 𝔄𝔱𝔥𝔢𝔫𝔦𝔞𝔫 𝔊𝔞𝔷𝔢𝔱𝔱𝔢: / OR CASUISTICAL MERCURY, / Resolving all the most / *Nice and Curious Questions* / PROPOSED BY THE / INGENIOUS: / From *Tuesday* March 17*th*, to *Saturday* May 30*th*, 1691. / The First Volume, / TREATING / On the several Subjects mentioned in the CONTENTS / at the Beginning of the Book.'[82] The effect, with its lively mixture of type and sizes, fell somewhere between elegant simplicity and the unrestrained miscellaneity of popular print. The verso of the title was left blank, and the following leaf presented a closely printed Preface of two pages, set in italics across the full width of the page with exuberant use of contrasting roman. The remaining four pages of the preliminaries were then devoted to listing the contents in double columns in small roman, forming a transition to the poorly printed single sheets that followed. By a typically ingenious piece of re-marketing, Dunton had transformed ephemera into collectable items – which throws into relief Swift's imagining in the *Tale* of a luxury multi-volume edition of gallows speeches 'worthy of such a Hand'; for malefactors' last dying words were also, in the first instance, produced as cheap single half sheets.[83]

It is possible that Swift, encouraged by Temple (whose gentry status made him a somewhat atypical outlier of the Athenians' core readership), was to some extent deceived by these volumes in their marbled covers.[84] The tone of his letter to Thomas Swift is archly ambivalent:

> ... the Poem I writ to the Athen: Society was all ruff drawn in a week, and finishd in 2 days after, and yet it consists of 12 stanza and som of them above thirty lines, all above 20. and yet it is so well thought of that the unknown Gentlemen have printed it before one of their Books, and the Bookseller writes me word that another Gentleman has in a book calld the History of the Athen Society, quoted my Poem very Honorably (as the fellow call'd it) so that perhaps I was in a good humor all the week ...[85]

Quite apart from the injudicious boast of speedy composition, this is the voice of someone who hardly knows whether to be proud of being mentioned 'Honorably' or to dismiss such a 'fellow' as a mere bookseller. (And

---

[82] Cf. Berry, *Gender*, pp. 50–2.
[83] For Dunton's offers to assist collectors in making up sets, see Berry, *Gender*, pp. 51–2. For Dunton in the *Tale*, see *CWJS Tale*, p. 38.
[84] Berry, *Gender*, pp. 22–3, 64, 82–4. For Dunton's claims about the favour shown to his project by Temple and other elite readers, see Parks, *John Dunton*, pp. 89–90.
[85] *Corr.*, vol. I, pp. 109–10.

First Impressions: Dublin and London to 1699

the 'History' in which Charles Gildon quoted Swift's poem proved to be a piece of transparent hack-work, rehashing material already in print.) Although the 14 February date on Swift's covering letter has prompted speculation about a possible publication date on or around All Fools' Day, once he had sent it to press the publication date would have been under Dunton's control, not his, making it even harder to discern which of the two might have been attempting to brand the other a fool.[86] Moreover, although anti-Athenian gibes were beginning to emerge in print, the most pretentious articulations of the myth would come too late for Swift.[87] Yet despite the poem's references to favourite topics such as the Society's supposedly learned secrecy, its gallantry to female readers, and its interest in such matters as the source of the Nile and the aftermath of the Flood, it is unlikely that Swift was universally impressed.[88] The Athenians' regular professions of religious moderation presumably jarred with his recent experience as Anglican priest of a largely nonconformist Ulster parish; and his reading of the bound volumes could hardly have failed to reveal the basic alignment of *Athenian Gazette* with cheap commercial print.

It therefore seems unlikely that he was much surprised by the mingled grandiosity and penny-pinching with which his letter and poem were finally published, or by the preposterous conceptual and material improvisations in which they were embedded. The enlarged circulation constituted by this London publication had been achieved at the cost of shifting considerably downmarket. In the process, Swift had set his name to a performance of deference whose object was a fiction, and whose political, religious and cultural agenda was at odds with his own. It was the first of many published epistolary performances by Swift, typically voiced by spokesmen who stand, as here, in ambiguous relation to their author. Temple, the encourager of this second publication, had not long to live, and his views would soon cease, like the Pindaric ode itself, to be a dominant concern. Dunton, meanwhile, was easily relegated to a niche

---

[86] *CWJS Parodies*, pp. 527–8 (but *An Ode. To the King*, not the *Ode to the Athenian Society*, was Swift's first published work).

[87] A. C. Kelly, *Jonathan Swift and Popular Culture*, p. 16. Gildon's *History* and the *Young-Students-Library* (with its 'Emblem' of the Society seated in state amid assorted enquirers, framed by vignettes of Athens, Rome, Oxford and Cambridge) in fact postdated Swift's poem (Parks, *John Dunton*, pp. 269, 274), as did Elkanah Settle's *The New Athenian Comedy*, not staged (if at all) until the 1692–3 season, and published only in 1693. For Tom Brown's rival paper the *London Mercury*, whose detailed allegations began to appear on 1 February, just a fortnight before the date on Swift's covering letter, see McEwen, *Oracle*, pp. 34–8. See also *CWJS Poems* I (forthcoming).

[88] For the Athenian project as a long-term resource for Swift, see Parks, *John Dunton*, pp. 92–3, citing Mabel Phillips (Mrs. William C. DeVane), 'Jonathan Swift's Relation to Science' (unpublished thesis, Yale University, 1925).

26   Part I: Beginnings

in Swift's modern rogues' gallery. Swift in print would still, from time to time, take periodical form; but future periodicals would not bear their author's name – and Swift would see to it that he was either the principal writer or his close associate.

Dunton's Dublin

After publishing the *Ode to the Athenian Society* Dunton had little more to contribute to Swift in print. He would plagiarise, in desultory fashion, parts of *An Ode. To the King* – extending its reach, but leaving readers to assume that he had written it himself.[89] (It is not even clear whether Dunton knew that Swift had written it, or whether Swift knew that Dunton had plagiarised it.[90]) He would also advertise the *Ode to the Athenian Society* for sale as a separate item (although no copy is now known).[91] In 1698, however, while Swift was away in England, Dunton made a visit to Dublin to conduct book auctions (which went badly, because the premises he had planned to use were claimed instead by a rival bookseller); but his rambles around the print-shops and personnel of the Dublin book-trade did at least provide him with material for his next book, *The Dublin Scuffle*. Strategically evasive about the deep professional and ideological fissures that divided the Dublin trade, its interest for students of Swift lies rather in Dunton's conjuring of the Dublin book world as a walkable space in which nearly every encounter is a pleasure.

Dunton had planned to conduct his auctions in the coffee house run by Richard Pue (active from 1698, *d.* 1722), popularly known as Dick's (which had strong Tory, even Jacobite associations, though this did not seem to worry Dunton).[92] To print his catalogues he engaged 'my three printers, Mr Brent, Mr Powel, and Mr Brocas', who operated 'at the back of Dick's coffee house in Skinner Row'.[93] Thus, in a busy street by Christ Church Cathedral, came together Brent and Dunton, the two men who had

---

[89] Mackie Langham Jarrell, '"Ode to the King": Some Contests, Dissensions, and Exchanges among Jonathan Swift, John Dunton, and Henry Jones', *Texas Studies in Literature and Language*, 7.2 (1965), 145–59 (pp. 146–50); J. Woolley, 'Swift's First Published Poem', p. 266; *CWJS Poems* I (forthcoming).

[90] For discussion, see Jarrell, '"Ode to the King"', pp. 157–8.

[91] Parks, *John Dunton*, p. 91; TS 467; and for a Dublin reprint of 1724 under the title of *The Sphinx*, TS 468.

[92] Pollard, *Dictionary*, pp. 473–4. For the Tory associations of Pue and his coffee house, see Robert Munter, *The History of the Irish Newspaper, 1685–1760* (Cambridge University Press, 1967), pp. 50–52; Gillespie, *Reading Ireland*, p. 14.

[93] Carpenter, *Scuffle*, pp. 101–3. For Powell and Brocas, see Pollard, *Dictionary*, pp. 469–70, 54–5.

First Impressions: Dublin and London to 1699   27

between them inaugurated one of the major print canons of the coming century. It may even have been Brent who drew Dunton's attention to *An Ode. To the King*, perhaps hoping he would do Swift a service by reprinting it in London (but not, presumably, by plagiarising it). Dunton, for his part, singled out Brent as the oldest of his three printers, and praised him as 'a scrupulous honest, conscientious man', 'so that he's what we may truly call a religious printer' who 'hates vice, almost as much by nature as by grace'. Such approval suggests Brent's congeniality to Dunton's much-vaunted religious moderation; but even Swift seems to have agreed with him on the solid merits of the Brents.

Dunton also put on record a somewhat bland appraisal of two key figures whose conflicting interests were crucial to the print contexts within which Swift in print would develop. By 1698 Andrew Crooke had held for five years the King's Printer's patent once exercised on his family's behalf by his uncle, Benjamin Tooke the elder; and Dunton tellingly characterises him in terms of princely virtues – if not commensurate wealth – while asserting his respect for the printing community as a whole:

> Nor must I (Madam) forget the extraordinary civility of the King's Printer, Mr Andrew Crook, 'Who is a worthy and generous gentleman, whose word and meaning never shake hands and part, but always go together: he is one that is as far from doing other men an injury, as he is from desiring to be injured; and though his circumstances are not so great, yet his soul is as large, as if he were a prince, and scorns as much to do an unworthy action. He is a great lover of printing, and has a great respect for all that are related to that noble mystery.'[94]

Yet the patent monopoly rested precisely on there being no Dublin printers but himself; and Dunton remains entirely silent about the campaign waged against the King's Printer's privileges by 'the ingenious Mr Ray' (Joseph Ray, *d.* 1709), 'who is both printer and bookseller, and the best situated of any man in Dublin'.[95] Ray, who printed both for the City of Dublin and for the Dublin Philosophical Society, had protested formally against the monopoly in the early 1680s. Although his case failed, his argument effectively bolstered the practical defiance of Dublin printers.[96] Pollard concludes that Ray's 'determined opposition to the King's pr[inter]'s monopoly was of immense importance to the Dublin book trade, resulting as it did in freedom to expand to match the growth in population of the

---

[94] Carpenter, *Scuffle*, p. 186.   [95] *Ibid.*, p. 182.
[96] J. W. Phillips, *Printing and Bookselling*, pp. 18–19; Pollard, *Dublin's Trade in Books*, pp. 6–11.

28 Part I: Beginnings

18th century'.[97] Ray thus played a vital role in making possible Swift's unprecedented emergence as a major Dublin-published author in the 1720s and beyond.

In saying his final farewells, Dunton also called on two near neighbours whose opposing political and religious views would mark the ideological extremes of the print world within which Swift in print took shape in Dublin. First Dunton called at the premises of John Whalley, who in Dunton's view 'justly merits the esteem he has with ingenious men', and whose 'Almanack bears the bell from all the rest in Ireland'.[98] Whalley was a committed no-popery Whig and a friend of John Partridge (the London Whig astrologer to be satirised in Swift's 1708 Bickerstaff hoax), although his idealisation of William III, his dark hints at *'Popish or Jacobite Rogery'* and his constant zeal in denouncing Tory and Catholic printers were arguably even more virulent, suggesting that Swift's contempt for Whig almanac-making may well have been primed by Whalley in Dublin long before it was unleashed on Partridge in London.[99] Finding that Whalley was not at home, Dunton moved on to visit his neighbour, Cornelius Carter (active from 1696, *d.* 1734), who, like Brent and his colleagues, also had links with Dick's coffee house, but had recently moved to the Post Office coffee house in Fishamble Street.[100] Carter, an extremist of the opposite kind, was notorious for Tory, High Church, and even Jacobite printing (as well as for some of the worst printwork in Dublin); but what Dunton chooses to emphasise is the social allure of 'a genteel honest printer', 'a witty man' who 'charms a thousand ways'. Ironically, Carter was printing Whalley's almanac at about this time, but it predictably failed to charm Whalley, who was no more satisfied with Carter's work than he had earlier been with Crooke's. He later set up his own print-shop for almanacs and newspapers, and, since newspapers were Carter's established staple, they were by 1714 embroiled in a paper war. Its ramifications would generate, shortly before Swift took up the persona of the Drapier in the 1720s, Dublin allusions to Isaac Bickerstaff, the fictional mask for Swift's attack on Whalley's friend Partridge in the London Bickerstaff hoax.[101]

---

[97] E. R. McClintock Dix, 'The Ray Family', *Bibliographical Society of Ireland* [papers], 2 (1921), 84–5 (p. 84); Pollard, *Dictionary*, p. 182.
[98] Carpenter, *Scuffle*, p. 257; Pollard, *Dictionary*, pp. 603–4.
[99] John Whalley, *Advice from the Stars, or an Almanack for the Year of Christ 1699* (Dublin, 1699; *ESTC* R223598), 'Monthly Observations' for May; Pollard, *Dictionary*, pp. 92–3; J. W. Phillips, *Printing and Bookselling*, p. 37; Rumbold, 'Ignoring Swift', pp. 14–16.
[100] Carpenter, *Scuffle*, p. 257; E. R. McClintock Dix, 'Cornelius Carter, Printer', *Irish Book Lover*, 17 (1929), 84–5; Pollard, *Dictionary*, pp. 92–3.
[101] Rumbold, 'Ignoring Swift', pp. 29–35.

First Impressions: Dublin and London to 1699

Well before that, the 1705 Dublin reprint of *A Tale of a Tub* had been sold from Carter's address, and he may also have been the reprinter in 1709 of a strangely altered edition of one of Swift's Bickerstaff papers; in the 1710s he was one of the most active reprinters of Swift's London-produced political propaganda; and in the 1720s he printed a poem in praise of the Drapier.[102] He had also been involved with Powell and Brocas, whom Dunton presents in threefold partnership with Brent at the back of Dick's coffee house. Powell collaborated with Carter from 1700 to 1704; and in the late 1720s he impinged on Swift in print from a different direction by publishing tracts by Swift's antagonist, John Browne.[103] Brocas too had collaborated with Carter, confirming the multiple connections between this in some ways extreme figure, with his messy printwork and run-ins with authority, and the network that made Swift in print.[104]

With hindsight, *The Dublin Scuffle* also serves to introduce individuals whose younger relations or apprentices would go on to play significant roles in Swift in print. Benjamin Tooke the younger, son of his cousin Andrew Crooke's patent-holder in trust, Benjamin Tooke the elder, would later become Swift's London bookseller. Sarah Ray (*d.* 1750), daughter of Joseph Ray, would marry John Hyde (active from 1707, *d.* 1728), who printed Dublin editions of *Gulliver's Travels*; and after her husband's death she acted as Swift's agent in receiving correspondence from his London bookseller, Benjamin Motte the younger (1693–1738), as well as producing, in 1734, a Dublin edition of Swift's inflammatory *On Poetry: A Rapsody.*[105] Samuel Fairbrother (*c.* 1684–1758?), Ray's apprentice, would also establish himself as a major bookseller, printer and bookbinder, and would in the 1730s publish, in surreptitious collusion with Swift, textually significant but technically unauthorised Dublin editions of the joint *Miscellanies* produced by Pope in London.[106]

In addition, the printed text of *The Dublin Scuffle* has its own suggestive associations with the transmission of Swift's work in Irish manuscript and

---

[102] For Carter and the *Tale*, see Chapter 2; for the version of *The Accomplishment of the First of Mr. Bickerstaff's Predictions* (1709) represented by a unique copy in the Armagh Robinson Library, see *CWJS Parodies*, pp. 650–1, and Chapter 3. For Carter's reprints of the *Examiner*, see Ian Gadd, '"At Four Shillings per Year, Paying One Quarter in Hand": Reprinting Swift's *Examiner* in Dublin, 1710–11', in *Münster* (2013), pp. 75–94 (pp. 75–94), and for his reprinting of this and other political writing by Swift, Chapter 4. For Carter's printing in praise of the Drapier, see *A Poem on the Drapiers Birth-day* (Dublin 1725; *ESTC* T202787, Foxon P610).

[103] Pollard, *Dictionary*, p. 469. For Browne, see *CWJS Irish Political Writings after 1725*, pp. xlii–xliii; for Powell's publications of his tracts, see *ESTC*.

[104] Pollard, *Dictionary*, p. 54.   [105] *Ibid.*, pp. 304–7; *CWJS Poems* IV (forthcoming).

[106] Pollard, *Dictionary*, pp. 195–7; *CWJS Parodies*, pp. 624–5.

Part I: Beginnings

English print. In Ireland, the Colonel Butler to whom Dunton dedicated *The Dublin Scuffle* may have been father to Theophilus Butler, Lord Newtown Butler, a friend of Swift's at Trinity College whose manuscript collection 'The Whimsical Medley' would later emerge as a source for Swift's verse.[107] Although Newtown Butler and Swift seem later to have been estranged by politics, there was also an enduring print-related connection between them in the person of Brent's daughter, Ann, who worked for Newtown Butler until his death in 1724 and received in his will an annuity in recognition of her 'Fidelity and Care' – qualities from which Swift in turn benefitted when, under her married name of Ridgeway, she replaced her mother as his housekeeper.[108] In England, meanwhile, Dunton's *Dublin Scuffle* was 'Sold by *A. Baldwin*', widow of his associate Richard Baldwin: Abigail Baldwin (*bap.* 1658, *d.* 1713) would also in 1709 issue Swift's hoax *A Famous Prediction of Merlin*. Swift also had a cousin, Dryden Leach the elder (1684–1731), who printed a newspaper for the Baldwins; and it was to Leach that Swift turned in 1711 to print a continuation of the *Tatler* by his protégé William Harrison.[109] All in all, though Swift would understandably cast Dunton on the side of the spider and himself on the side of the bee, the *Dublin Scuffle* maps intriguingly onto the book worlds within which Swift in print was about to take shape.[110] Dunton's notoriously rambling career not only demonstrated some of the potentials for cultural modernity that Swift would come to oppose, but also exemplified – not least in *The Dublin Scuffle*, stuffed as it is with flattering correspondence of dubious authorship – something of the shapeshifting potential that Swift in print would make its own. Dunton ironically unites, in relation to the beginnings of Swift in print, the roles of Dublin guide, London publisher, and revealingly repudiated *alter ego*.

---

[107] Carpenter, *Scuffle*, p. 307. For 'The Whimsical Medley', see James Woolley, 'John Barrett, "The Whimsical Medley", and Swift's Poems', in Howard D. Weinbrot, Peter J. Schakel and Stephen E. Karian (eds.), *Eighteenth-Century Contexts: Historical Inquiries in Honor of Philip Harth* (Madison, WI: University of Wisconsin Press, 2001), pp. 147–70 (and for the inferred relationship between Newtown Butler and Dunton's dedicatee, p. 166 n. 29), and 'The Circulation of Verse', pp. 143–4; for nineteenth-century misattributions to Swift from this source, see Introduction and individual discussions in the deattributed poems section of *CWJS Poems* IV (forthcoming).

[108] J. Woolley, 'John Barrett', p. 153 and p. 167 n. 41.

[109] Treadwell, 'Swift's Relations', pp. 4, 30; *CWJS Parodies*, pp. 78–87, 106–20, 657–9, 663–4; Valerie Rumbold, 'Merlinus Verax, T. N. Philomath, and the Merlin Tradition: Print Contexts for Swift's *A Famous Prediction of Merlin* (1709)', *The Library*, 12.4 (2011), 392–412.

[110] *CWJS Tale*, pp. 149–51.

PART II

London

CHAPTER 2

The Shock of the Normal
From Temple to the Tale *(1693–1705)*

So far Swift in print had been haphazard in its material forms and sparse to the point of invisibility, but in the following decade Swift's engagement with well-placed London booksellers raised both its quantity and its quality. The new normal that resulted – what we might think of as the characteristic look of early Swift – reflects the resources of a print trade much larger and better resourced than Swift had known in Dublin. The Stationers' Company, entrusted by the Crown with the regulation of the trade and endowed in return with the English Stock, oversaw a milieu in which it was worth developing sophisticated skills. Its leading businesses were not simply investing in type, paper, craftsmanship and purchase of copy, but also working adeptly to calculate costs against sales, estimate format and paper quantity, design and execute an effective printed page, correct proofs accurately and facilitate distribution. Swift in print was now about to be reshaped by the processes that printers at this level assumed to be normal.

Underlying the next steps for Swift in print was a clear set of professional assumptions about what a book ought to look like, namely a group of alphabetised signatures forming an orderly sequence of clearly and accurately printed pages.[1] The main body of the book would begin on the first recto of a signature, and would typically be signed in capitals and paginated with arabic numerals. Preliminaries such as prefaces and titles (usually printed last) would be placed in one or more additional signatures (or, if brief, a part-signature), often signed in lower case and paginated in roman numerals or not at all.[2] Much depended on the chosen format, and the format that now emerged as crucial for Swift in print was the octavo, a format that could equally well produce a substantial volume or

---

[1] For the signing and assembly of signatures, see Moxon, *Mechanick Exercises*, pp. 210–11, 317–18.

[2] Smith would reflect ruefully, in 1755, that these final elements, left 'still to do' after completing the body of the book, 'are such Parts as try not only a Compositor's judgment, but also patience' by their complex requirements (*The Printer's Grammar*, pp. 216–23).

34 Part II: London

a diminutive pamphlet. At the upper end of its quality range, elaborated with ornaments and illustrations, it would provide, in the large-paper octavo series of Faulkner's 1735 *Works*, the nearest approach of lifetime Swift in print to a prestige edition.[3] At the lower end it would provide the cheap bulk-purchase pamphlets that in the 1720s enabled the Drapier to mobilise public opposition to Wood's halfpence.[4] Now, at the turn of the seventeenth century into the eighteenth, octavos provided for the routine production of well-produced volumes, first in Swift's curation of the unpublished works of his late patron, Sir William Temple, and later in the publication of *A Tale of a Tub*.

In contrast with the first two published poems, these publications were produced to a robust standard, both by the team that Swift inherited from Temple and by his own subsequent choice of bookseller.[5] It did not mean that Swift's works would never again appear in cheap or inept forms, nor even that Swift himself would invariably eschew printers at the lower end of the market. What it did mean was that there was now a default level of competence against which the significance of inferior work (whether deliberate and authorised, or mischievous and unauthorised) could be effectively measured. Swift laid the foundations by working in this decade with professionals very different from the under-resourced but careful Brent or the carelessly flashy Dunton; and although he introduced oddities of his own, printing-house routines were resilient enough to cope. In effect, like all authors who entrust the making of their books to professional publishers, he submitted his works to a set of templates and expectations that we might think of as 'printers' normal' – but this time it was the 'normal' of printers who were much more able to raise the long-term status of Swift in print. Given that the decade would reach its climax with the early editions of the *Tale*, such emphasis on normality may seem perverse; but, even for the *Tale*, the underlying normality is the making of the performance.

The ambiguities of Swift's attachments to England and to Ireland consequent on his family's client relation to the Temples continued to exert their influence. Despite the Temples' long-established connections with Ireland, Swift's employer had long lived and published in England, a choice whose consequences Swift effectively inherited. Ireland, however, remained the nation of Swift's birth, education and earliest print networks, and when Temple died in 1699, Swift, disappointed in his hope of gaining

---

[3] See Chapter 7.   [4] See Chapter 5.
[5] For printing-house practice, see Gaskell, *A New Introduction*, pp. 5–185.

The Shock of the Normal (1693–1705)

'a Prebend of Canterbury or Westminster' that he believed the King had promised him, returned to Ireland as chaplain to another Whig dignitary, Charles Berkeley, second Earl of Berkeley (1649–1710). From 1699 to 1700 Berkeley was one of the Lords Justices at Dublin Castle, but he did not promote Swift to the Deanery of Derry as he had hoped.[6] In 1701, however, soon after becoming vicar of Laracor and prebendary of St Patrick's Cathedral, Swift went so far as to encourage two favourite inmates of the Temple household, the young Esther Johnson (1681–1728) and her companion Rebecca Dingley (c. 1666–1743), to move to Dublin. Yet London continued to exert a compelling force, focused at first on the publication of Temple's remaining letters, memoirs and essays. Although Swift began by using Temple's established publishing arrangements, he soon chose a new London bookseller of his own, whom Michael Treadwell identified in the early 1980s as Benjamin Tooke the younger, son of Benjamin Tooke the elder, former King's Printer in Ireland.[7] By this discovery Treadwell opened up new understandings of Swift's choices at the point when he first began to publish his own original work in London. Around his visits in 1701, 1702 and 1703–4 he consolidated the distinctive rhythms of writing and printing that would form the context for his first two major original publications, *Contests and Dissensions* (1701) and *A Tale of a Tub* (1704).

Inheriting Temple (1699, 1700)

The literary inheritance that Swift received from Temple on his death in 1699, though no doubt welcome, also contributed a potential complication. Swift's role as Temple's editor provided him with readily saleable copy and a means of displaying his credentials, and it led to the making of impressive volumes that brought Swift's name before the public – as editor, if not as author. Yet it also prolonged his involvement with a patron whose elaborately staged exasperation with commercial print might have been an awkward model for a thirty-year-old who still aspired to greater preferment

---

[6] *Family of Swift*, *PW*, vol. V, p. 195. See also James Woolley, 'Swift and Lord Berkeley, 1699–1701: Berkeley Castle Swiftiana', in Kirsten Juhas, Patrick Müller and Mascha Hansen (eds.), *'The First Wit of the Age': Essays on Swift and his Contemporaries in Honour of Hermann J. Real* (Frankfurt am Main: Peter Lang, 2013), pp. 31–68 (pp. 32–7); for a new Swift letter written in this role, pp. 37–41; for chronology of Swift's movements in connection with Berkeley, pp. 42–7; for the appointment of the Dean of Derry, pp. 47–54.

[7] Michael Treadwell, 'London Trade Publishers, 1675–1750', *The Library*, 4.2 (1982), 91–134; Treadwell, 'Swift's Relations', pp. 9–11. Swift's bookseller had previously been misidentified as the elder Tooke.

36   Part II: London

than anyone was disposed to give him.[8] In the event, however, Temple's authorial self-projection turned out to be an apt introduction to print as a theatre of authorial strutting, cajolery and bluster.

The role of published author went back three generations in Temple's family. His grandfather (also Sir William) had founded his reputation on an edition of *Dialecticae Libri Duo* by Peter Ramus (1584), 'one of the first books to be printed at the Cambridge university press', and went on to become provost of Trinity College, Dublin.[9] His son, Sir John Temple, established his reputation with a classic of anti-Catholic Irish historiography: *The Irish Rebellion: Or, An History of the Beginnings and first Progresse of the Generall Rebellion Raised within the Kingdom of Ireland, upon the three and twentieth day of October, in the Year, 1641. Together with the Barbarous Cruelties and Bloody Massacres which ensued thereupon.*[10] The title page of this solidly assertive London-published quarto, 'Printed by R. White for Samuel Gellibrand, at the Brasen Serpent in Paul's Church-yard', emphasised his status as Master of the Rolls and Privy Counsellor for Ireland. When Swift's Sir William Temple came in his turn to publish with Gellibrand, the title page of his spaciously printed 1673 octavo *Observations upon the United Provinces of the Netherlands* continued the emphasis on public distinction, presenting Sir William as landowner, baronet and diplomat, '*of* Shene, *in the County of* Surrey, *Baronet, Ambassador at the* Hague, *and at* Aix la Chappellè, *in the year* 1668'; but Temple's Preface (set in the dignity of comfortably sized italic, lightly contrasted with reverse roman) positioned him as loftily self-deprecating in his approach to authorship, contemptuous of commercial print and instrumental reading, and only barely willing to concede that publication of his writings might be of benefit to fellow statesmen. After his prefatory brush-off, it was left to the bookseller, in a note printed at the foot of the contents list, to represent the difficulty in which he found himself: '*The Author having not concerned himself in the publication of these Papers; It has happen'd that for want of his Care in revising the Impression, several faults are slipt in, and some such as alter the sense; For which I am to ask the* Reader's *Pardon, and desire his trouble in correcting such as occur to me, according to the following* / ERRATA'. Nine instances are listed.

---

[8]   For a summary of Swift's disappointments to date, see Ehrenpreis, *Swift*, vol. II, pp. 12–13.

[9]   William Temple, *P. Rami Dialecticae libri duo, scholiis G. Tempelli Cantabrigiensis illustrati. Quibus accessit, eodem authore, de Porphyrianis prædicabilibus disputatio. Item: epistolæ de P. Rami Dialectica contra Iohannis Piscatoris responsionem defensio, in capita viginti novem redacta* (Cambridge, 1584; *ESTC* S108367); K. H. D. Haley, *An English Diplomat in the Low Countries: Sir William Temple and John De Witt, 1665–1672* (Oxford: Clarendon Press, 1986), pp. 2–3.

[10]   London, 1646; *ESTC* R201974, R14603; Haley, *An English Diplomat*, pp. 3–6.

The Shock of the Normal (1693–1705)

Even more striking was the elaborate 'AUTHOR's Letter to the *Stationer*, upon occasion of the following Papers' that prefaced Temple's *Miscellanea* in 1680 (by which time Samuel Gellibrand had been succeeded by his son, Edward).[11] The title page did not this time name Temple, although the black-letter attribution to '𝔞 𝔓𝔢𝔯𝔰𝔬𝔫 𝔬𝔣 𝔥𝔬𝔫𝔬𝔲𝔯' gestured towards his status. 'The AUTHOR's Letter', however, which was set in italics significantly larger than the body of the book, showed him writhing in contortions of authorial exasperation. He claimed that he had left his papers with the stationer's father (Samuel Gellibrand) while he was in Holland (in itself a clue to his identity), on the basis that they were to be published, for the benefit of the stationer, only in the event of his death. He declares that he has now received the '*Excuses and Desires*' of the son and accuses him of allowing the works to circulate both in print and in manuscript (dismissing his excuse that the type had been broken up after only two copies had been printed). Now, apparently, the bookseller says he wants to print the works in order to prevent others from doing so, to which the author gives his irritated consent, complaining at the same time that because of such proceedings two other books have already been wrongly attributed to him. He therefore refuses to have anything to do with organising the papers, devising a title, reading proofs or writing a preface, but leaves it all to the bookseller who stands to profit by it. For his own part, his professed aim is solely to destroy the curiosity value of the contents by making them common: '*If this happens, I shall be at quiet, which is all I ask of them or of you.*' By glossing publication as making common, Temple emphatically distanced himself from the vulgar aims of fame or profit. When, in the next year, Gellibrand brought out a second edition, this time under Temple's name, Gellibrand prefaced the 'Letter' with an 'Advertisement of the *Stationer* to the *Reader*' in which he claimed that he had been given permission to use Temple's name in order to prevent the misattribution of anonymous publications, and that 'apart from these and the Observations nothing has been published, or will be, without his name'.[12] The contest between Temple's disdain for commercial

---

[11] *Miscellanea. I. A Survey of the Constitutions and Interests of the Empire, Sueden, Denmark, Spain, Holland, France, and Flanders; with their Relation to England, in the Year 1671. II. An Essay upon the Original and Nature of Government. III. An Essay upon the Advancement of Trade in Ireland. IV. Upon the Conjuncture of Affairs in Octob. 1673. V. Upon the Excesses of Grief. VI. An Essay upon the Cure of the Gout by Moxa* (London, 1680; *ESTC* R223440, R733).

[12] *Miscellanea. By Sir William Temple Baronet. The second edition, corrected and augmented* (London, 1681; *ESTC* R38800).

authorship and his desire to be recognised as author of his own work (and no other) had evidently been resolved in favour of the latter, although it still left Gellibrand mired in deferential awkwardness – or at least in the print performance of such awkwardness. In future Temple would take his publishing elsewhere, put his name to his works, and seek active control over the texts in which his works were transmitted to posterity.

Part of Swift's role had been to support the elderly Temple in enforcing this control by making transcriptions of Temple's manuscripts into which his final changes could be inserted. (The process is demonstrated in a surviving transcription of Temple's letters by a previous secretary, which Temple has corrected in his own hand; Swift would give his own account of it some years later, when Temple's sister attacked the authenticity of his edition of her brother's memoirs.[13]) Although the results understandably gave rise to suspicions that Temple had suppressed and invented material in order to enhance his reputation, the detailed analysis by K. H. D. Haley concludes largely in Temple's favour.[14] For Swift in print, however, Temple's emphasis on his last lifetime intentions may well have been influential, coming to bear in time on his revision of his own previously published works for later reprinting.

As Temple's secretary, Swift evidently knew his way round the London book trade: Treadwell suggests that he probably delivered copy to the printing-house and read proofs.[15] Even in 1693, between his two periods with Temple, he was displaying a sophisticated relation to the trade, referring casually to Richard Simpson as 'my bookseller' (more properly, one of Temple's booksellers), and displaying his knowledge of the potential 'difference' between copies of the same publication.[16] Although Temple's only directly documented bequest to Swift, in a codicil to his will dated 1697, is a legacy of £100, Swift later recorded that 'that great Man' had also 'left him the care and trust and Advantage of publishing his posthumous Writings'.[17] Swift's formulation marks here the interplay of three factors: editorial effort, reputational benefit and financial benefit, all three of which

---

[13] *CWJS Tale*, p. lxxxii; *Corr.*, vol. I, pp. 270–74; see Chapter 3.

[14] Haley, *An English Diplomat*, Appendix, pp. 319–27; cf. A. C. Elias, Jr, *Swift at Moor Park: Problems in Biography and Criticism* (Philadelphia, PA: University of Pennsylvania Press, 1982), chapter 1, pp. 1–47.

[15] Treadwell, 'Swift's Relations', pp. 4–5; *Corr.*, vol. I, p. 118.

[16] *Corr.*, vol. I, p. 118. *BBTI* has two entries for Richard Simpson, which, taken together, suggest he was apprenticed in 1653, freed in 1661 and inactive soon after 1716.

[17] *PW*, vol. V, p. 194.

The Shock of the Normal (1693–1705)   39

came under threat very soon after Temple's death, necessitating a decisive printed response.[18]

Temple died in January 1699, and later that year appeared *Letters written by Sir W. Temple, during his being Ambassador at the Hague, to the Earl of Arlington and Sir John Trevor, Secretaries of State to K. Charles II. Wherein are discovered many Secrets hitherto concealed. Publish'd from the Originals, under Sir William Temple's own Hand: And Dedicated to the Right Honourable Sir Thomas Littleton, Speaker of the House of Commons. By D. Jones, Gent* (London, 1699).[19] It carried the imprint 'Printed and are to be Sold by A. Baldwin' (widow of Dunton's collaborator Richard Baldwin); and, in line with the Baldwins' Whig associations and the nonconformist background of the editor, the self-proclaimed spy and Whig historian David Jones (active 1675–1720), its Preface asserted a blunt contrast between the admired Temple and the corruption of politics under Charles II: '*our Learned Author will be found to be ever constant to himself, and to retain the same English Spirit in this, as in all his other Negotiations*; *Which is so much the more Glorious to his Memory, when he had so few Cotemporary Ministers either at Home or Abroad of his Temper*'.[20] The collection, in a single octavo volume, was much less handsomely produced than publications by Temple's chosen booksellers, and its title, framed by double rules, picked out Temple's name and that of his editor in emphatically old-fashioned black letter (an attention-grabbing staple of popular print that loomed large in the Baldwins' output). The title, with its reference to original letters, also made clear how radically this edition diverged from Temple's intentions for his work, for the text evidently did not follow the secretarial transcripts of Temple's file copies that he had revised for publication. From a documentary point of view, such a choice of copy text might have had its advantages, but what Temple had organised was a text that expressed his final lifetime intention.

Swift evidently acted without delay, for in November 1699 (after his return to Ireland in August) his riposte was published in London in two volumes, both postdated 1700.[21] Their title articulated not only the scope of the collection, but also its authority: *Letters written by Sir W. Temple, Bart. and other Ministers of State, both at Home and Abroad. Containing, An Account of the most Important Transactions that pass'd in Christendom from 1665 to 1672. In Two Volumes. Review'd by Sir W. Temple sometime before his*

---

[18] Cf. *CWJS Tale*, pp. lxxxi–lxxxii.

[19] Cf. the account in N. F. Lowe and W. J. McCormack, 'Swift as "Publisher" of Sir William Temple's *Letters* and *Miscellanea*', *SStud*, 8 (1993), 46–57 (pp. 52–4).

[20] *ODNB* ('David Jones').   [21] TS 469, *ESTC* R14603; Treadwell, 'Swift's Relations', pp. 8, 31.

Death: and Published by Jonathan Swift Domestick Chaplain to his Excellency the Earl of Berkeley, one of the Lords Justices of Ireland. Authorial revision was supplemented by the prominent display of Swift's own credentials: he never made a secret of his involvement with Temple's works, which he apparently regarded as a means of recommending himself to potential patrons. Indeed it was to one such, the future dedicatee of the 1704 *Tale*, Lord Somers, that he would later be said to have attributed advice that is highly suggestive in relation to his contrasting practice with his own work: 'never to own or disown any writing laid to my charge . . . because whatever I did not disown afterwards, would infallibly be imputed to me as mine'.[22] There was no such problem about owning his respectful and efficient curation of Temple's work.

Despite Swift's absence from London, established arrangements for Temple's authorised editions facilitated prompt, high-quality publication of the *Letters* by the booksellers Jacob Tonson, A. and J. Churchill and Richard Simpson. Their octavo volumes (including some presentation copies on large paper) were more elegant and substantial than Jones's, with clearer print and ampler margins throughout.[23] Their titles were attractively restrained in typography, deploying full capitals, large and small capitals and lower case. Although the double-ruled frame was retained, and roman was varied with italic, there was no black letter. The first volume was also dignified by a frontispiece engraved from a portrait of Temple by Peter Lely, adorned with a ribbon bearing Lucan's praise of Cato: 'Servare modum finemque / tueri Naturamque sequi' ('to observe moderation and hold fast to the limit, and to follow nature').[24] It is a sign of the editorial and typographical care that Swift and his booksellers brought to the project that these volumes also provided translations of the foreign-language material (which Jones's edition did not), and that they presented it in such a way as to invite close comparison: letters in foreign languages were set in two columns, in slightly smaller type than the rest, with the English translation, in roman, on the left-hand side, and the original language, in italics, on the right. Although this entailed copious

---

[22] Thomas Sheridan, Jr, *The Life of the Rev. Dr. Jonathan Swift, Dean of St. Patrick's, Dublin. By Thomas Sheridan, A.M. Vol. I.* (London, 1784), pp. 439–40.

[23] For large-paper copies among this (and other) Swift publications, see David Woolley, 'Swift's Copy of *Gulliver's Travels*: The Armagh Gulliver, Hyde's Edition, and Swift's Earliest Corrections', in Clive T. Probyn (ed.), *The Art of Jonathan Swift* (London: Vision Press, 1978), pp. 131–78 (p. 133), citing copies belonging to Lords Halifax and Shrewsbury.

[24] Lucan, *The Civil War (Pharsalia)*, II. 381–2.

The Shock of the Normal (1693–1705) 41

column-edge hyphenation, it was neatly executed, making clear to readers the pains that had been taken to allow parallel inspection of the texts.

In line with this dignity and scrupulosity, the title formulation (which M. Walsh suggests 'was probably given by Swift, following Temple's instructions') was more temperate than Jones's, offering, instead of '*many Secrets hitherto concealed*', the more dispassionate '*the most Important Transactions that pass'd in Christendom*'.[25] At the same time it emphasised the volumes' textual credentials, not only declaring that the texts were '*Review'd by Sir W. Temple sometime before his Death*', but also stressing that Swift, the editor, had since continued to develop his connections as '*Domestick Chaplain to his Excellency the Earl of Berkeley, one of the Lords Justices of Ireland*'. All this set the scene, following the blank verso of the title, for Swift's full-page dedication to William III.[26] This was set in type larger even than that of the volume's main text, and formed a becoming context for Swift's subscription, which is laid out across the lower part of the page as if in a handwritten letter: 'These Letters of Sir *W. Temple* having been left to my Care, they are most humbly presented to Your MAJESTY by / *Your Majesty's most dutiful* / *and obedient Subject.* / *Jonathan Swift.*'[27] The type used for Swift's name was not the largest (which was reserved for the King's name), nor the smallest (which was used for the humble self-definitions that preceded Swift's name), but something in between – the same size, in fact, as the main text of the dedication. The balance between deference and pride was neatly calibrated, as, for the second time, Swift's formal subscription to a dedication was rendered in print.

His self-presentation was further developed in 'The Publisher's Epistle to the Reader', which began, in italic, on the next recto. This made great play of the deference with which he embraced the role of 'Publisher' (i.e. the person responsible for bringing the work to press): he deferred to the transcript of the letters made by Temple's previous secretary, Thomas Downes, which Temple had corrected; he deferred to the skill in Spanish of Temple's sister, Martha, Lady Giffard (respectfully refraining from naming her), who had provided translations from that language; and he deferred to the memory of Temple himself, stressing the privileged knowledge that he had derived from '*residing in his Family*', and emphasising

---

[25] *CWJS Tale*, p. lxxxii.

[26] For this and other paratexts to Swift's volumes of Temple's works, see Elias, *Swift at Moor Park*, pp. 71–7; see also Lowe and McCormack, 'Swift as "Publisher"', p. 52.

[27] For the perceived decorum of larger print for dedications, see Bronson, *Printing as an Index of Taste*, p. 11; and for a 1755 view of the proprieties, see Smith, *The Printer's Grammar*, pp. 218–19.

that Temple himself had been '*pleased to be at the Pains of reviewing, and to give me his Directions for digesting them into Order*'. Such deference served to ground Swift's own claim to authority, '*he having done me the Honour, to leave and recommend to me the Care of his Writings*', and provided a creditable (if not entirely credible) rationale for publication: '*I could not at present do a greater Service to my Countrey, or to the Author's Memory, than by making these Papers publick.*' This makes a great deal of sense in relation to Temple's own performances of disdain for publication, but is even more revealing in the light of a discarded reading recoverable from Swift's draft: 'But [I] will not stick to confess that I have been a little tempted to it by the Advantage I propose to my self from the Impression of a Book which I have Reason to think will be received with as much and as generall Kindness and Esteem as any Writings that have appeared since those of this Noble Author.'[28] This suppressed reference to 'Advantage' (which would recur in Swift's later recollection of 'the care and trust and Advantage' of editing Temple's works) marked a major turn in the print representation of Swift as author, putting firmly to one side an authorial identity that Temple would have disdained for himself, but might well have thought good enough for an ex-secretary. Such self-promoting insecurity would flow instead into the manic patter of a multitude of fictionalised authorial selves, reaching its climax in the obsequious and ill-founded hopes of place and profit with which, at the end of Swift's creative life, Simon Wagstaff introduced *Polite Conversation*. By suppressing the image of the author that he disdained to be, Swift energised the print performances of the author that he was in process of becoming.

At its close, however, 'The Publisher's Epistle to the Reader' offered a different and more troubling sign of things to come, in a final sentence separated by a space from the foregoing text:

> *I beg the Readers Pardon for any* Errata's *which may be in the Printing, occasioned by my Absence,*

The fact that this excuse concluded with a comma instead of a full stop is just a minor foretaste of the problems to be caused over the years by what was on the face of it a perverse preference on Swift's part, namely his habit of leaving London and returning to Ireland as his works neared publication. Over the years it would disrupt textual transmission in ways that were both keenly resented and entirely predictable, and Treadwell's formulation is suggestive: 'Swift seems always to have arranged for his publications to

---

[28] *PW*, vol. I, p. xix.

The Shock of the Normal (1693–1705)

appear after he had left the country, or at least London, partly for reasons of caution but also, where caution was not relevant, for complex reasons of pride.'[29] By his absences Swift effectively delegated decisions that contributed significantly to the shaping of Swift in print. In the author's absence, 'printers' normal' became even more important.

A Bookseller of His Own (1701)

Before Swift went any further with his edition of Temple he chose a London bookseller of his own to replace the team he had inherited from Temple.[30] In Tooke he selected someone who was both an accomplished operator in London's larger print world and the heir to a prominent link with Dublin, for Tooke's father had held the patent of King's Printer in Ireland until it passed to his nephew Andrew Crooke in 1693: in 1687 the elder Tooke had taken on the treasurership of the Stationers' Company's English Stock, and after he was dismissed in 1702 on account of 'irregularities' he went on to hold the stewardship of St Bartholomew's Hospital from 1705 until his death in 1716.[31] By 1695 his son had set up independently at the Middle Temple Gate, where a family connection may have brought him the execution sermons of the London clergyman Bankes Crooke, and where he also printed, in the same year, a second edition of an anonymous essay by Swift's future dedicatee Lord Somers, and a tract supporting the Society for the Reformation of Manners.[32] Tooke's Dublin connections also brought continuing opportunities: he acted as book-buyer for Henry Moreton, Bishop of Kildare; he published work by Irish divines such as Swift's future Archbishop, William King; and he handled plays by Swift's schoolfellow Thomas Southerne.[33] He had an impressive profile, being named by 1701 in the imprints of at least seventy extant publications, spanning Anglican divinity and apologetics, plays and travel writing, and ambitious collaborations with other booksellers on major works in fields such as history, classics and botany. In

---

[29] Ehrenpreis, *Swift*, vol. II, p. 34; Treadwell, 'Swift's Relations', pp. 12–13.
[30] Treadwell, 'Swift's Relations', pp. 8–9.   [31] Pollard, *Dictionary*, p. 571.
[32] Treadwell, 'Swift's Relations', pp. 9–10. For the range of Tooke's extant publications, see *ESTC*. For Bankes Crooke, see *Two Sermons preach'd before the Condemn'd Criminals, at Newgate, 1695. By B. Crooke, M.A. rector of St. Michael Woodstreet, London* (London, 1695; *ESTC* R24803). For Somers, see *A Discourse concerning Generosity . . . The second edition* (London, 1695; *ESTC* R42482). For the other anonymous tract, see *A Letter to a Gentleman in the Commission of the Peace* (London, 1695; *ESTC* R26782).
[33] Pollard, *Dictionary*, p. 571; Treadwell, 'Swift's Relations', p. 11. For Southerne, see the various editions of *Oroonoko* issued from 1696 onwards.

44   Part II: London

comparison with Brent, who had produced Swift's *An Ode. To the King* in Dublin, Tooke was a major entrepreneur in a market of considerable reach and sophistication; but he shared with Brent the capacity to secure Swift's lifelong loyalty and affection. In the first instance, Swift, as Temple's authorised editor, was gatekeeper to a saleable literary property, but as time went on Swift would figure on Tooke's impressive list in his own right: alongside him stood classical authors such as Virgil, Cicero, Ovid and Terence; older English writers such as Jonson, Herbert and Oldham; recent male writers such as Otway, Dryden and Wycherley; female pioneers such as Behn, Finch and Chudleigh; scientific thinkers such as Bacon, Evelyn and Heylin; continental classics such as Boccaccio and La Bruyère; and even authors who already were – or later became – anathema to Swift, such as David Jones (the rival editor of Temple's letters), John Partridge the astrologer, and the Whig commentators Abel Boyer and John Oldmixon.[34] Although, for Pat Rogers, Tooke's 'list clearly shows that his connections lay chiefly with the Tories', it also shows his openness to work by Whigs – notably the Temple edition itself.[35] Swift's choice of Tooke suggested both shrewdness and ambition.

The publishing habits that Swift now formed reveal a robust (if in part perplexing) integration of travel, finance and publication. Treadwell comments:

> The publishing arrangements which Swift made in the summer of 1701 must have suited him for he stuck to them almost without variation for the next ten years. On each trip to London he would bring over with him one major manuscript, generally a volume of the Temple papers, the publication of which partly justified the trip in Swift's eyes and the sale of which could, in any case, be counted on to cover his travelling expenses.[36]

In choosing pieces to bring to market, the most obvious at first were the remaining instalments of Temple's works; but during his time with Temple Swift had also been writing on his own account, and his most dazzling publication in these years, the 1704 *A Tale of a Tub*, would be drawn from that accumulated hoard. In 1701, however, it was a third volume of Temple's *Miscellanea* that Swift offered Tooke, who with his partner Timothy Goodwin entered his ownership of the copy in the

---

[34] See the advertising leaf at the end of Sir William Temple, *Memoirs. Part III. From the Peace concluded 1679. To the time of the Author's Retirement from Publick Business ... Publish'd by Jonathan Swift, D.D.* (London, 1709; *ESTC* T146548), and, for further examples, *ESTC*.
[35] Pat Rogers, 'The Uses of the Miscellany: Swift, Curll and Piracy', in *JS Book*, pp. 87–100 (p. 93).
[36] Treadwell, 'Swift's Relations', p. 11.

The Shock of the Normal (1693–1705) 45

Stationers' Register on 28 July, and, with Swift, signed off a receipt on the 29th:

> Then received of M[r] Benjamin Took, the sum of thirty Pounds sterl in full for the Originall Copyes of three Essays . . . all writt by S[r] William Temple Bart, and of which s[d] Copyes I am sole Proprietor . . .[37]

Both Swift's property in the work and his profit from its publication are spelled out, and an attached memorandum confirms his agreement with Tooke about complimentary copies:

> M[r] Took is to give Me twenty Coppyes of the s[d] Essays &c: whereof ten are to be gilt in the Leaves, &c; and ten to be in calves Leather: all letterd at the Back; 3 or 4 to be in Turkey work.

David Woolley notes that these luxurious Turkey leather bindings allowed Swift to make a particularly lavish gift of his patron's works to selected dignitaries, who on this occasion included Narcissus Marsh, Archbishop of Dublin.[38] Swift was dealing (probably on a principle not too distant from that which had motivated the printing of *An Ode. To the King*) not only in literary property itself, but also in the patronage networks that publication might help to consolidate. A high-quality Temple edition that fore-grounded the deserts of its editor might well have seemed to offer potential for advancement; and once such prospects failed, remarkably few of Swift's original publications (whether or not in response to Somers's alleged advice) would parallel such a frank display of his own and his booksellers' names. More characteristic would be a play of masks and evasions articu-lated in material as well as verbal forms; and here too Tooke would demonstrate that he had the relevant expertise at his fingertips.

For the moment, however, the Temple volumes presented an increas-ingly confident Swift whose professed disdain for publication echoed to an extent the performances of his late patron. By 1701 the title page of *Miscellanea. The Third Part*, with its new imprint of 'Printed for Benjamin Tooke, at the Middle-Temple Gate in Fleet-street', was giving relatively perfunctory attention to Temple ('By the late Sir William Temple, Bar.') and emphasising instead its editor's new academic and ecclesiastical dignities, now untarnished by connotations of dependency: 'Published by *Jonathan Swift*, A.M. Prebendary of *St. Patrick*'s, *Dublin*'. (His role was similarly dignified when the volume was listed, at the price of

---

[37] *SCEBC* (1695–1708), p. 47; *Corr.*, vol. I, p. 145; Treadwell, 'Swift's Relations', p. 11.
[38] *Corr.*, vol. I, p. 146, noting three extant presentation copies.

46   Part II: London

4*s*., in the distributor John Nutt's union catalogue for the year.[39]) Swift assured prospective readers that the principal contents had been revised by Temple, that even his notes towards uncompleted projects should be of interest to them, and also (in a move that recalls Temple's disparaging acquiescence to the publication of the first *Miscellanea* in 1680) that printing his youthful translations would be useful to discredit spurious attributions. By the time that Swift had brought a third volume of Temple's letters to London in 1702 (which Tooke bought for £50 and published in 1703 as *Letters to the King, the Prince of Orange, the Chief Ministers of State, and other Persons*), the title notice that this was '𝕿𝖍𝖊 𝕿𝖍𝖎𝖗𝖉 𝖆𝖓𝖉 𝕷𝖆𝖘𝖙 𝖁𝖔𝖑𝖚𝖒𝖊. Published by *Jonathan Swift*, D.D.' proclaimed, as well as his mastery of the edition, the new dignity of Doctor of Divinity that would mark his print identity long into the future.[40] (Although Swift's involvement and dignities were not noted in what appears to be a preliminary notice for this volume, priced at 3*s*., in Nutt's annual catalogue for 1701, his name did appear, complete with D.D., when it was listed again for 1702–3 at the substantially increased price of 5*s*.[41]) The imprint of *Letters to the King* again declared Tooke's agency, this time in partnership with Goodwin, and its Preface, set in italics significantly larger than the roman type of the letters that follow, articulated a relaxed exercise of editorial authority:

> *The following Papers are the last of this, or indeed of any kind; about which the Author ever gave me his particular Commands. They were Corrected by Himself; and fairly Transcribed in his Life time. I have in all Things followed his Directions as strictly as I could: But Accidents unforeseen having since intervened; I have thought convenient to lessen the Bulk of this Volume. To which End I have Omitted several* LETTERS *Addressed to Persons with whom this* Author *Corresponded without any particular Confidence, farther than upon account of their Posts . . .*

When Swift came to focus on the challenge of rival editions, he contrasted his own selective approach to Temple's letters with the less discriminating completeness that might more thoroughly have circumvented competition:

---

[39] *Bibliotheca Annua, 1701–1703*, English Bibliographical Sources, Series I, No. 4 (London: Gregg Press, 1964), p. 45 (first pagination series).

[40] TS 472, *ESTC* T136603. For the formula 'Jonathan Swift, Doctor of Divinity, Dean of St Patrick's, Dublin', represented by its initials on the title of the 1735 Dublin *Works*, see Chapter 7.

[41] *Bibliotheca Annua, 1701–1703*, pp. 43 (first pagination), 64–5 (second pagination). The disparity may reflect an error, revised costings, or an enhanced sense of the price the market would bear.

The Shock of the Normal (1693–1705)

Because great Numbers of such LETTERS, *procured out of the Office; or, by other means (how justifiable I shall not examine) have been already* Printed: *But running wholly upon long dry Subjects of Business, have met no other Reputation than meerly what the Reputation of the* Author *would give them. If I could have foreseen an End of this Trade, I should upon some Considerations have longer forborn sending these into the* World. *But I daily hear, that new Discoveries of* Original LETTERS *are Hasting to the* Press: *To stop the Current of which, I am forced to an earlier Publication than I designed. And therefore I take this Occasion to inform the* Reader; *that these* Letters *ending with the* Author's *Revocation from his Employments abroad (which in less than two Years was followed by his Retirement from all publick Business) are the last he ever intended for the* Press; *having been Selected by himself from great Numbers yet lying among his Papers.*

If I could have been prevailed with by the Rhetorick *of* Booksellers, *or any other little Regards; I might easily, instead of* Retrenching, *have made very considerable* Additions; *and by that means have perhaps taken the surest Course to prevent the Interloping of others. But, if the* Press *must needs be loaded; I had rather it should not be by my means. And therefore I may hope to be allowed one Word in the Style of a* Publisher, *(an Office lyable to much Censure, without the least pretension to Merit or to Praise) that, if I have not been much deceived by others and my self; the* Reader *will hardly find* one Letter *in this* Collection *unworthy of the* Author, *or which does not contain something either of Entertainment or of Use.*

The role of 'Publisher' is here a suspect one, which Swift takes on only briefly and with a grave playfulness, as he concludes with a discreet allusion to Horace's classic formulation of writerly purpose: 'Poets aim either to benefit, or to amuse, or to utter words at once both pleasing and helpful to life.'[42]

Contests and Dissensions (1701)

In fact, by the time *Letters to the King* was presented to the public in 1703, Swift had already published a political intervention that bid fair to satisfy Horace's criteria. This was *A Discourse of the Contests and Dissensions between the Nobles and the Commons in Athens and Rome, with the Consequences they had upon both those States* (1701).[43] Now at last, after scanty, poorly produced publications of original verse and an editing project fraught with connotations of dependency, *Contests and*

---

[42] 'Aut prodesse volunt aut delectare poetae / aut simul et iucunda et idonea dicere vitae' (Horace, *Ars Poetica*, ll. 333–4).

[43] TS 478, noting two printings (see below).

Dissensions inaugurated Swift's contribution to a print genre that would bring him both contemporary notoriety and abiding fame. *Contests* is a significant first for Swift in print: it was his first published political work, his first original publication in prose, and, at sixty-two numbered pages, by far his most substantial publication to date.[44] As an exercise in parallel history characterised by Ian Higgins as 'patrician in tone, pitched above the Grub Street vulgar', it was very differently conceived from some of the edgier and less imposing propaganda pamphlets for which Swift would later be known: *Contests* instead seems calculated to engage classically educated Whigs in decoding 'the innuendo applying the classical instances to topical persons and proceedings in 1701'.[45]

Swift had arrived in London with Lord Berkeley on 15 April 1701, at the height of a controversy between a Tory-dominated House of Commons and a Whig-dominated House of Lords.[46] By his own later account, he had discussed his response with Berkeley en route:

> returning with the Earl of Berkeley from Ireland, and falling upon the subject of the five great Lords, who were then impeached for high crimes and misdemeanors, by the House of Commons, I happened to say, that the same manner of proceeding, at least as it appeared to me from the news we received of it in Ireland, had ruined the liberties of Athens and Rome, and that it might be easy to prove it from history. Soon after I went to London; and, in a few weeks, drew up a discourse, under the title of *The Contests and Dissentions of the Nobles and Commons in Athens and Rome, with the Consequences they had upon both those States*.[47]

This was an affair of pressing personal relevance for Swift, since the Whig grandees who found themselves under attack included two formerly powerful contacts whom he had met through Temple: Robert Spencer, second Earl of Sunderland (1641–1702), and John Somers, Baron Somers (1651–1716).[48] The hopes he had formerly placed in Sunderland are indicated by a letter of 1698 from Swift to his successor at Kilroot: 'I think I told in my last that 10 days before my resignation My L^d

---

[44] Treadwell, 'Swift's Relations', p. 11.

[45] Ian Higgins, 'Swift's Whig Pamphlet: Its Reception and Afterlife', in *Münster* (2019), pp. 553–72 (p. 554); and for an overview of Swift's political alignment in these years, see Introduction to *CWJS English Political Writings, 1701–1711* (forthcoming).

[46] Ellis, *Discourse*, pp. 1–79; Higgins, 'Swift's Whig Pamphlet', pp. 553–62.

[47] *Memoirs relating to that Change which happened in the Queen's Ministry in the Year 1710*, *PW*, vol. VIII, p. 119.

[48] For Sunderland, see Ellis, *Discourse*, pp. 14–15, 180, and *ODNB* ('Robert Spencer, second earl of Sunderland'). For Somers, see *ODNB* ('John Somers, baron Somers'), and, for the ambiguities of Swift's attitude as it developed over time, *CWJS Tale*, pp. 327–9.

The Shock of the Normal (1693–1705)

Sunderland fell and I with Him.'[49] But Somers's stock would again be on the rise when Swift dedicated the *Tale* to him in 1704.[50]

Print was newly central to the debate, as the Licensing Act had lapsed in 1695, leaving both houses of parliament free to print as they wished.[51] Accounts of their respective proceedings, with counter-claims on both sides, staged appeals to extra-parliamentary opinion in papers, pamphlets and books, introducing Swift to a mode of controversy that was very much of the moment – but one in which he did not wish to appear under his own name. He recalled that 'This discourse I sent very privately to the press, with the strictest injunctions to conceal the author, and returned immediately to my residence in Ireland.'[52] Treadwell reasons that, along with the current instalment of the Temple edition, *Contests* 'must also have belonged to Tooke' – who provided the concealment that Swift required by arranging for a different name, that of John Nutt, to appear in the imprint.[53] Like the vogue for the political pamphlet, the emergence of professionals like Nutt was peculiarly timely for Swift in print.

Nutt exemplified a new specialisation in the London book trade, that of the trade publisher, a phenomenon crucially illuminated in the 1970s by the researches of David Foxon, D. F. McKenzie and Michael Treadwell.[54] Typically beginning their careers as printers rather than booksellers, the trade publishers, whose role developed in London only in the late seventeenth century and had no equivalent in Dublin, were in Treadwell's words 'a very small group of men and women known to their contemporaries in the trade as "publishers"', whose function was that of 'a distributor rather than a producer': 'although these trade publishers' names appeared in imprints, they did not own the copyright to the works they printed, but acted on behalf of those who did'.[55] There were several reasons, Treadwell argues, why authors and booksellers might use trade publishers; but in the not unusual case of *Contests* the most obvious motive was concealment: the substitution of Nutt's name for Tooke's obscured the real agencies behind the publication, and made it less likely that the real bookseller would be asked about the author's identity – and as Tooke had identified himself as Swift's bookseller in the imprint of *Letters to the King*, this was a useful

---

[49] *Corr.*, vol. I, pp. 131–3.   [50] Ellis, *Discourse*, p. 180; Ehrenpreis, *Swift*, vol. II, pp. 121–2.

[51] Ellis, *Discourse*, pp. 7–8.

[52] *Memoirs relating to that Change which happened in the Queen's Ministry in the Year 1710*, PW, vol. VIII, p. 119.

[53] Treadwell, 'Swift's Relations', p. 11.

[54] For the timing and contexts of their respective contributions, and unfulfilled hopes of a collaborative study, see Treadwell, 'London Trade Publishers', first footnote.

[55] Treadwell, 'London Trade Publishers', pp. 99–100.

50   Part II: London

precaution.[56] Reflecting on the prevalence of trade publishers' names in the imprints of Swift in print in these early London years, Treadwell concludes that 'I take it as almost certain that all of Swift's separately published works from the period 1701 to 1709 were published (in our modern sense) by Benjamin Tooke Jr', and cites in evidence the fact that 'Tooke claimed the copyright to all of them when entering Swift's *Miscellanies* in S[tationers'] R[egister] on 10 April 1710 and again on 24 February 1711.'[57]

   Contests thus appeared, without its author's name, as 'Printed for *John Nutt* near *Stationers-Hall*'. In the case of *Contests*, there was not even a dedication or preface to align the work with the defence of the Whig lords. (Indeed, the fact that Nutt had a particular association with the Tories added further to the diversionary effect.[58]) The title-page epigraph is from Lucretius: 'Si tibi vera videtur / Dede manus; & si falsa est accingere contra' ('If it seems to be true, own yourself vanquished, or, if it is false, gird up your loins to fight').[59] Such a pose, with its connotations of face-to-face contention, sits awkwardly with such double concealment, setting the precedent for a long career in which print would figure both as medium and mask. Tooke's own imprint seems in contrast to have appeared only on isolated publications for which Swift wished to highlight his personal responsibility, as in the case of his edition of Temple. The works on which Tooke's name appears are few, and those on which Swift's own name appears are even fewer, highlighting not only the distance between Swift in print and the assertion of intellectual property central to later models of authorship, but also Swift's particular reluctance to own the works that we now regard as most quintessentially Swiftian. Those that he would go on to publish under Tooke's imprint, and the one that he went so far as to sign with his own name, proved to be some of the most earnest and unengaging in the canon.[60]

   The quarto pamphlet form of *Contests* marked not so much a diversion from the octavo trend of this phase of Swift in print as a significant supplement to it. Quarto was emerging as a pamphlet format well suited to the cut and thrust of the political moment: Swift in print had lighted on a growing trend that would in time instantiate a major strand of its author's work, a potential that is perhaps already signalled in the variation among

---

[56] *Ibid.*, pp. 113–14, 119–23; Treadwell, 'Swift's Relations', pp. 13–14.
[57] Treadwell, 'Swift's Relations', p. 13; for Treadwell's source in Liber G of the Stationers' Archive, see Chapter 4.
[58] Treadwell, 'Swift's Relations', p. 11; *JSA*, Introduction; Treadwell, 'London Trade Publishers', p. 108; Higgins, 'Swift's Whig Pamphlet', p. 553.
[59] Lucretius, *De Rerum Natura*, ll. 1042–3.   [60] See Chapters 3 and 4.

The Shock of the Normal (1693–1705)

surviving copies. As Teerink realised, there came a moment during or after the initial printing when part of the original setting of type was reset. (It may already have been partially distributed, or left standing and accidentally disturbed.) When reconstituted it was used to print what Teerink called 'another issue or edition', identifiably different from the first.[61] This is certainly consistent with Swift's later boast that 'The book was greedily bought, and read', and since *ESTC* reports forty extant copies of the second printing and only twenty-two of the first, it may be that demand so far outran expectation that it was decided to print twice as many copies as before. This was the first time that Swift in print had engaged effectively with a compelling current controversy, and the contrast with the single surviving copy of Swift's *An Ode. To the King* is striking. (Indeed, it was *Contests*, not the *Ode*, that Swift would later think of as 'the first I ever printed'.[62]) Similarly, Ellis comments on the breadth and significance of the printed rebuttals prompted by *Contests*. Again, this contrasts with the lack of any extant response to *An Ode. To the King*, and with the disappointing fact that Gildon's *History of the Athenian Society*, which carried his notice of his *Ode to the Athenian Society*, had turned out to be no more than another cog in Dunton's self-advertising machine.[63]

Although *Contests* is an appropriately unshowy pamphlet, its material form still marked a significant advance on the kinds of inadequacy variously shown by Brent and Dunton. It was, for example, more substantial and better printed than the twenty-one-page quarto *A Letter from some Electors, To one of their Representatives in Parliament. Shewing The Electors Sentiments, touching the Matters in Dispute between the Lords and Commons the last Session of Parliament, in Relation to the Impeachments. And giving some Advice to their Member, How to demean himself in Parliament for the future*, a piece of uncertain authorship that carried an even more evasive imprint, '*London*: Printed, and sold by the Booksellers of *London* and *Westminster*. 1701'.[64] Both this and *Contests* were, however, dwarfed in scale by the octavo *Essays upon I. The Ballance of Power. II. The Right of Making War, Peace, and Alliances. III. Universal Monarchy. To which is added, an appendix containing the records referr'd to in the second essay* (1701)

---

[61] TS 478, *ESTC* T74617 (the first printing, 22 copies) and T142253 (the second printing, 40 copies); Ellis, *Discourse*, p. 182; R. H. Griffith, 'Swift's "Contests", 1701: Two Editions', *Notes & Queries*, 22 (1947), 114–17; H. Teerink, 'Swift's *Discourse ... Contests ... Athens and Rome*, 1701', *The Library*, 4 (1949), 201–5. The copy described in the present chapter is of the second printing.

[62] *Memoirs relating to that Change which happened in the Queen's Ministry in the Year 1710*, PW, vol. VIII, p. 119.

[63] Ellis, *Discourse*, pp. 177–80; for Gildon's notice of *Ode to the Athenian Society*, see Chapter 1.

[64] *ESTC* T5355.

52 Part II: London

by Charles Davenant, the principal Tory writer in the cause.[65] This ran to
more than 400 pages, and, though anonymous, carried the name and
address of the prominent bookseller James Knapton. A closer parallel to
the scale of Swift's intervention was a sixty-four-page octavo pamphlet also
ascribed to Davenant, *The True Picture of a Modern Whig, set forth in
a dialogue between Mr. Whiglove & Mr. Double, two under-spur-leathers to
the late ministry*, an outstandingly popular piece that went through six
editions in the year, and gave no more information in its imprint than
'*London*: Printed in the Year, 1701' – although it was allegedly printed for
£50 by Swift's own future printer John Barber (1675–1741), suggesting
considerable initiative for a printer who was still a mere journeyman.[66]
All in all, *Contests* was by no means the least substantial, presentable or
eagerly read of the smaller-scale interventions in the controversy – and
a trade publisher's name at least avoided the furtiveness of giving no name
at all.

The full title of *Contests* is, in the manner of the time, a relatively long
one (*A Discourse of the Contests and Dissensions between the Nobles and the
Commons in Athens and Rome, with the Consequences they had upon both
those States*), but the title page centres it effectively on an uncluttered page,
pointing the sense by variation of type. Unlike *The True Picture*, *Contests*
has no recourse to the old-fashioned, eye-catching device of black letter: it
confines itself for the most part to roman, varying capitals with lower case,
using italic lower case to pick out '*Contests*' and '*Dissensions*', and italic
capitals to distinguish '*ATHENS*' and '*ROME*'. In terms of size, however,
the key word on the title is none of these, but 'STATES', with
'DISCOURSE' coming a close second. These two large, centred words
in full capitals emphasise, first, the larger perspective of the state itself –
and, second, the efforts of the anonymous author in discoursing upon it.[67]
The overall design of the pamphlet is equally efficient: chapters are indicated by headings in italics with reverse roman for names; and where
chapters end and begin on the same page, a rule marks the transition,
reconciling economy with clarity. There is, however, in both printings of
this pamphlet, one oddity that slightly mars the poise of the performance:
the first four sheets do not have additional spaces between paragraphs, but

---

[65] *ESTC* T66825.
[66] See *ESTC* for multiple editions of *The True Picture* in 1701. Treadwell points out that Davenant was
uncle to Swift's cousin Thomas, and draws attention to the claim that it was Davenant who first
introduced Swift to Barber ('Swift's Relations', p. 22; *An Impartial History of the Life ... of Mr. John
Barber* (London, 1741), p. 2). For Barber, see Chapter 4.
[67] For considerations of emphasis in setting a title page, see Moxon, *Mechanick Exercises*, pp. 212–15.

The second four do. Otherwise, the styling of the text is, as McLaverty notes, 'typical of Swift's early period: capitals for the beginning of nouns; full capitals for some names; extensive use of italics, particularly for quotation; and side notes, chiefly for references'.[68] Margins are ample, and the text is clear and well spaced. The marginal notes, placed alongside the relevant text, are in smaller roman type, using standard abbreviations which assume the reader's familiarity with classical authors. All in all, it is a sober and decent presentation.

Swift's later recollection was that the anonymous publication of *Contests* facilitated some gratifyingly erroneous attributions, which came to his attention during his next visit to London in 1702: it was, he claims, 'charged some time upon my Lord Sommers, and some time upon the Bishop of Salisbury; the latter of whom told me afterwards, that he was forced to disown it in a very public manner, for fear of an impeachment, wherewith he was threatened'.[69] Print publication had drawn in a large readership, but in Swift's later recollection it was still the flattering excuses of a distinguished inner circle of potential patrons that loomed largest:

> Returning next year for England, and hearing of the great approbation this piece had received, (which was the first I ever printed) I must confess, the vanity of a young man prevailed with me, to let myself be known for the author: Upon which my Lords Sommers and Hallifax, as well as the Bishop above mentioned, desired my acquaintance, with great marks of esteem and professions of kindness: Not to mention the Earl of Sunderland, who had been of my old acquaintance. They lamented that they were not able to serve me since the death of the King, and were very liberal in promising me the greatest preferments I could hope for, if ever it came in their power. I soon grew domestic with Lord Hallifax, and was as often with Lord Sommers, as the formality of his nature (the only unconversable fault he had) made it agreeable to me.[70]

Another factor, Higgins suggests, may have been that Swift's antipathy to dissent was already in evidence in his defence of the Whig lords.[71] Although Somers would receive the dedication of the *Tale* in 1704 (probably in a turkey-bound presentation copy), in the longer term it was to be Robert Harley, leader of the Commons' campaign, who proved the more

---

[68] *JSA*, Introduction.

[69] *Memoirs relating to that Change which happened in the Queen's Ministry in the Year 1710, PW*, vol. VIII, p. 119. The Bishop of Salisbury was Gilbert Burnet (1643–1715); for corroborating evidence see Introduction to *CWJS English Political Writings, 1701–1711* (forthcoming).

[70] *Memoirs relating to that Change, PW*, vol. VIII, p. 119.

[71] Higgins, 'Swift's Whig Pamphlet', pp. 556–62 (p. 560).

54 Part II: London

significant patron (if ultimately an even more disappointing one).[72] A correspondent reported to Harley, soon after publication, that the 'author pretends to much reading and great sincerity, but towards the end there are pretty bold reflections'.[73] Within a few years Swift's advancement in the favour of a new Tory ministry would make it inadvisable to reprint *Contests* without substantive changes.[74]

A Tale of a Tub and the Limits of Material Parody (1704)

In a decade of firsts for Swift in print, *A Tale of a Tub . . . To which is added, An Account of a Battel between the Antient and Modern Books in St. James's Library* (1704) was the outstanding event.[75] For Swift in print it was a watershed, the first publication that stimulated a wide and impassioned response, and the first to sustain its staying power down to the present.[76] At the most basic level, this was Swift's first published satire; it was his first publication of any kind that was incontrovertibly a book and not a pamphlet; and it was the first of the substantial octavos that would mark the upper end of the material ambition of lifetime Swift in print. It was also the beginning of a problem whose repercussions would afflict Swift (psychologically) and his booksellers (practically) for the rest of his life, for, having written and published the *Tale of a Tub*, Swift obsessively refused to own it. While other parts of his almost entirely anonymous published canon might be gathered into collections that in different ways came close to admitting his authorship, the *Tale* remained uncompromised, nominally at least, by any such association.[77]

Publication was again managed by Tooke, who in this instance, as James May has shown, worked with the printer Benjamin Motte the elder (*c.* 1653–1710).[78] Motte, who had an established reputation for scholarly and illustrated work, would also go on to print succeeding editions of the *Tale*, apparently including the expanded and illustrated fifth edition of 1710: his involvement suggests a concerted plan to produce the *Tale* in

---

[72] Ellis, *Discourse*, p. 180; David Woolley, 'The Textual History of *A Tale of a Tub*', *SStud*, 21 (2006), 7–26 (pp. 11–12).
[73] Ellis, *Discourse*, p. 174, quoting Thomas Thynne, first Viscount Weymouth.   [74] See Chapter 4.
[75] TS 217, *ESTC* T49832. For details of early editions, see *CWJS Tale*, pp. 275–90.
[76] For the reception history of the *Tale*, see *CWJS Tale*, pp. xlvi–liv.
[77] See Chapters 3, 4, 7 and 8.
[78] James E. May, 'Re-Impressed Type in the First Four Octavo Editions of *A Tale of the* [sic] *Tub*, 1704–5', in Kirsten Juhas, Patrick Müller and Mascha Hansen (eds.), *'The First Wit of the Age': Essays on Swift and his Contemporaries in Honour of Hermann J. Real* (Frankfurt am Main: Peter Lang, 2013), pp. 85–108 (pp. 87–90).

The Shock of the Normal (1693–1705)

a more impressive form than any original work of Swift's so far published.[79] The neatly printed (if not entirely error-free) octavo *Tale* of 1704, which runs to more than 300 pages, brings together three works of progressively diminishing length (*A Tale of a Tub, The Battel of the Books, A Discourse concerning the Mechanical Operation of the Spirit*), accompanied by diverse paratexts: in effect it is the single-author miscellany of Swift's Temple years.[80] As such, as Pat Rogers notes, it anticipates not only 'the extent to which Swift's literary identity was forged by the miscellany', but also 'the practice of issuing the collected or selected "works" of a given author', trends which would both loom large in lifetime Swift in print.[81] As a piece of practical book-making, its robustness was underwritten by the professional competence of Tooke and Motte: its material structure was significantly tested but not radically disrupted by the challenges of Swift's subversively crafted satire.

This claim may at first sight seem to run counter to the critical consensus that the *Tale*, with its multiple sections and digressions, and the asterisks that stand in for supposedly missing words, constitutes a parody of the book as material object.[82] Such readings, developing in the 1960s in the wake of theories that posited the coming of print as splitting type from voice and modernity from everything before it, now tend to accommodate a more nuanced relation between print and its preceding and accompanying technologies; and this includes a welcome recuperation of the potential of typography to render voice – a potential that Swift would later apply to his own experience in his remark that 'When I am reading a Book, whether wise or silly, it seemeth to me to be alive and talking to me.'[83] Yet the way in

---

[79] For Motte's likely printing of the fifth edition, see Bullard and McLaverty, 'Introduction', p. 11, and Chapter 3.

[80] For likely dates of composition, see *CWJS Tale*, pp. xxxvi–xxxix; P. Rogers, 'The Uses of the Miscellany', pp. 87–8.

[81] For crucial miscellanies, see Chapters 3 and 6; for the 1735 Dublin *Works*, see Chapter 7; and for successive posthumous *Works* series, see Chapter 8.

[82] For this and other functions of the asterisk, see Smith, *The Printer's Grammar*, pp. 79–80.

[83] For interpretations from the 1960s to the present, see Hugh Kenner, *Flaubert, Joyce and Beckett: The Stoic Comedians* (London: W. H. Allen, 1964), pp. 37–9; Denis Donoghue, *Jonathan Swift: A Critical Introduction* (Cambridge University Press, 1971), p. 10; Robert Phiddian, *Swift's Parody* (Cambridge University Press, 1995), pp. 127–32; Clive T. Probyn, '"Haranguing upon Texts": Swift and the Idea of the Book', in *Münster* (1985), pp. 187–90, and 'Swift and Typographic Man: Foul Papers, Modern Criticism, and Irish Dissenters', in *Münster* (1993), pp. 25–43 (pp. 26–8); Christopher Flint, *The Appearance of Print in Eighteenth-Century Fiction* (Cambridge University Press, 2011), pp. 113–23; Marcus Walsh, 'Swift's *Tale of a Tub* and the Mock Book', in *JS Book*, pp. 101–18 (p. 102); Claude Rawson, 'The Typographical Ego-trip from "Dryden" to Prufrock', in Claude Rawson, *Swift and Others* (Cambridge University Press, 2015), pp. 11–47 (pp. 19–23). For typographical voicing, see particularly Love, 'L'Estrange, Joyce and the Dictates of Typography', pp. 167–79, and for Swift's comment on the talking book, *Thoughts on Various Subjects* (*PW*, vol. IV, p. 253).

56   Part II: London

which this or any book speaks also depends in part on a less-discussed aspect of its structure: the relationship between the verbal text and the specific sequence of signatures and pages on which it is printed. Despite a degree of expressive disruption, the material *Tale* is for the most part shaped by methodical print routines that testify to the robust practice of a well-run printing-house. It seems unlikely, in effect, that Swift desired from Tooke and Motte anything other than a high-quality presentation of his copy.

Attribution of responsibility for particular decisions necessarily remains speculative, since no records survive of discussions about any aspect of the design and production of the 1704 *Tale*. (Swift's mysterious prevarications in his 'Apology' to the 1710 fifth edition, alleging that 1704 had been printed from 'a surreptitious Copy' and hinting darkly that 'the Bookseller' had 'given a good Sum of Money for the Copy' implausibly transform an amicable long-term relationship with Tooke into a scenario of professional skullduggery.[84]) As with most of Swift's lifetime publications, no printer's copy is extant (it was probably discarded once printing was complete).[85] But Swift's usual practice in preparing fair copy suggests that it would at the very least have been marked up with underlining for italic; and it is reasonable to assume that it also specified the order in which the various sections and components should appear.[86] By making a book so much more 'normal' than its verbal text might suggest, Tooke and Motte produced an artefact that interacts awkwardly (and suggestively) with the eccentricities of its contents.

Since the chosen format was octavo, each sheet for the *Tale* was folded to produce a signature of eight leaves (sixteen pages). Normally, the main body of a book would have begun on the first recto of a signature, constituting page 1 of the main arabic pagination sequence, and the preliminaries would have been allocated to separate signature(s) as required: in the case of the *Tale*, the main body began with signature B and there was just one preliminary part-signature, signed A. But the notorious excess of prefatory items in the *Tale* (which Phiddian interprets as mocking the numerous hard-to-sequence preliminaries to Dryden's Virgil) makes it far

---

[84] *CWJS Tale*, pp. 12–13.
[85] May, 'Re-Impressed Type', p. 86. For correspondence between Swift and Tooke about the design of the 1710 fifth edition of the *Tale*, see Chapter 3.
[86] See, for instance, *A Modest Defence of Punning*, unpublished in Swift's lifetime but extant in his fair copy (*CWJS Parodies*, pp. 161–70, 675).

The Shock of the Normal (1693–1705) 57

from easy to determine, from the verbal text, where anything that could properly be called the main body of the book actually begins.[87] After an advertisement for works supposedly forthcoming ('Treatises writ by the same Author') and an anonymous title page which again, like *Contests*, screened the book's origins behind Nutt's imprint, there followed four discursive items. First was the dedication 'To the Right Honourable, John Lord Sommers', a semi-public tribute on Swift's part, but one here ascribed neither to the author nor to Swift, but to 'The Bookseller'. Second came 'The Bookseller to the Reader', which intensified the mystification by suggesting that whoever this 'Bookseller' might be, he was not a distributor like Nutt, but an active agent in textual transmission. The third piece was a second dedication, 'The Epistle Dedicatory, To His Royal Highness Prince Posterity', this time voiced by the supposed author, and dated, in a spaced-off formal subscription which includes no name, 'December 1697': the reader is teased by the combination of elaborate self-staging and ultimate anonymity, while, from deep inside the role-play, Swift gestures towards the reality of the work's long withholding from publication. Finally, the fourth piece was the 'Preface', in which the voice of this author was more fully established. All four of these pieces preceded Section I of 'A Tale of a Tub' itself (and Section I itself turned out to be only the 'Introduction', leaving the story of the three brothers to begin in Section II).

In the face of this plethora of preliminaries the decision was made to begin the main body of the work with 'The Epistle Dedicatory, To His Royal Highness Prince Posterity', the third of the prefatory items, which duly appeared on the first recto of signature B as the (inferred) first page of the arabic pagination sequence (which then continues to the end of the book). This decision meant that the preliminaries, as materially consti-tuted, now comprised only 'Treatises writ by the same Author', the title page and the two pieces ascribed to the bookseller. Following normal practice, these preliminaries were arranged on unnumbered pages in a separate signature (signed A); and the type was sized and placed to fill the pages comfortably, despite the conventional refinement of beginning each of the small separate pieces on a new recto: in other words, there was nothing like the amount of empty white space at the ends of each of the 1704 preliminaries that readers of modern run-on texts might hypothesise; nor were there, anywhere in the volume, any of the tell-tale reductions in type size that might indicate problems in casting off such a complex

---

[87] Phiddian, *Swift's Parody*, pp. 127–32.

sequence of items. While the multiple preliminaries of the *Tale*, and the multiple texts and introductory pieces in the main body, served to swell a book made up of digressive and fragmentary materials, the printer's skill meant that they did it without an excessive display of empty space.

The division between preliminaries and main body, clearly made by the material structure, meant that any binder faced with the book in sheets would have found it much simpler to assemble than Dryden's Virgil. Since the *Tale* had a single set of signatures and a single pagination sequence running through all but the first signature, there was no need for specific instructions. Yet this very orderliness raises intriguing questions. A main body that begins on the first page of signature B with 'The Epistle Dedicatory, To His Royal Highness Prince Posterity' followed by the supposed author's 'Preface' makes a material distinction between the two pieces attributed to the author and the two attributed to the bookseller (now relegated to signature A), and this arguably made Swift's composition look far more 'normal' than it really was. Presented as a main body of pieces (including introductory ones) by a single author, and introduced by two preliminary addresses from the supposed bookseller, the structure seemed to associate the bookseller with an outer world of print and the author with an inner world of writing. The transition between A and B thus lent itself to an intensifying sense of fictiveness, as a more or less plausible bookseller handed over to a more obviously implausible author (although later in the book even this would be complicated by prefaces to additional items, also attributed to the bookseller). But different decisions as to where the main body begins are at least conceivable. The 'eTable of Contents' provided in *ECCO*, for instance, determines that the 'Main Body' of the book begins only with Section I of the 'Tale' itself: everything before that, including 'The Epistle Dedicatory, To His Royal Highness Prince Posterity' and the Preface, is 'Front Matter'. This is to take the mocking-up of Swift's role-play more seriously than the material book does, for in this classification every item whose verbal text suggests that it belongs with the preliminaries is accepted as such. In effect, given Swift's prefatory excesses, any material resolution will seem arbitrary. But the making of a normal book demands that a decision be made, and, once made, that decision highlights the tendentious relation between Swift's composition and the printer's craft.

Within the preliminaries in signature A, moreover, particular attention was inevitably drawn to the first opening (Figure 2). This set out, first, on the verso of the blank first page, the list of 'Treatises writ by the same Author, most of them mentioned in the following Discourses; which will be speedily published', and, second, on the facing recto, the title page of the

Treatises writ by the same Author, most of them mentioned in the following Discourses; which will be speedily published.

A Character of the present Set of Wits in this Island.

A Panegyrical Essay upon the Number THREE.

A Dissertation upon the principal Productions of Grub-street.

Lectures upon a Dissection of Human Nature.

A Panegyrick upon the World.

An Analytical Discourse upon Zeal, Histori-theo-physi-logically considered.

A general History of Ears.

A modest Defence of the Proceedings of the Rabble in all Ages.

A Description of the Kingdom of Absurdities.

A Voyage into England, by a Person of Quality in Terra Australis incognita, translated from the Original.

A Critical Essay upon the Art of Canting, Philosophically, Physically, and Musically considered.

A

TALE

OF A

TUB.

Written for the Universal Improvement of Mankind.

Diu multumque desideratum.

To which is added,

An ACCOUNT of a

BATTEL

BETWEEN THE

Antient and Modern BOOKS in St. James's Library.

Basima eacabasa eanaa irraurista, diarba da caeotaba fobor camelanthi. *Iren. Lib.* 1. *C.* 18.

——— Juvatque novos decerpere flores,
Insignemque meo capiti petere inde coronam,
Unde prius nulli velarunt tempora Musæ. Lucret.

LONDON:

Printed for *John Nutt*, near *Stationers-Hall*.
MDCCIV.

Figure 2 Jonathan Swift, *A Tale of a Tub … To which is added, An Account of a Battel between the Antient and Modern Books in St. James's Library* (London, 1704), title and facing page.

Tale itself. 'Treatises' famously sets the tone for the *Tale*'s performance of modern ambition and arrogance, and its placing ahead of and facing the title emphasised this. Tooke's publications in the first decade of the century (which included ambitious collaborations) did not favour such placement. Advertisements were more likely to appear at the end of the book, and they typically differ in three crucial ways from 'Treatises'. First, a heading along the lines of 'Some Books lately Printed for Benjamin Tooke' tempers the attraction of novelty with an assurance that these books are indeed finished and ready for sale. Second, the formula also stresses that Tooke, the bookseller, is in charge of their production and marketing. Third, while the lists tend to focus on genres and topics connected to the book in which they appear, they are not usually restricted to works by the same author.[88] In sum, Tooke's advertising offers a salutary contrast. Tucked away at the end of the book instead of flaunting their wares at the threshold, his lists advertise projects accomplished rather than merely aspired to; they highlight the bookseller, not the author, as the entrepreneur driving the process; and they address readers' inferred interests across a range of authors, exposing the combination in 'Treatises' of scattershot miscellaneity and authorial solipsism. It was not that Tooke and his collaborators failed to recognise the potential of the blank verso facing the title: they just preferred to exploit it in a different way. Unlike an advertisement that distracted the prospective reader, a frontispiece portrait, allegory or map both caught the reader's eye and fixed attention on the book in hand. When in 1710 the *Tale* was redesigned with illustrations for its fifth edition, 'Treatises' would indeed be relegated to a slightly more decorous position on the verso of the title, while the famous frontispiece of the ship, the whale and the tub took pride of place as the eye-catcher facing the title. But in 1704 the *Tale* did not rise to the dignity and expense of illustration – and 'Treatises', with its unseemly forestalling of the reader's attention, arguably tells us more about its supposed author than a portrait ever could.

If the placing of the advertisement suggests a modestly parodic disruption to expected decorum, other aspects of the publication highlight the unpretentious but solid quality by which the material book counterpoints its contents. The title page, for instance, much busier than that of *Contests*,

---

[88] An exception is 'BOOKS Published by George Stanhope, D. D. and Chaplain in Ordinary to her MAJESTY', which appears at the end of *The Christian's pattern: or, a treatise of the imitation of Jesus Christ. In four books. Written originally in Latin by Thomas à Kempis. Now render'd into English. To which are added, meditations and prayers, for sick persons. By George Stanhope* (London, 1704; *ESTC* T93905). Stanhope, who was Dean of Canterbury, lists two major translations (from the French of de Charon and the Greek of Epictetus) and four high-profile sermons.

The Shock of the Normal (1693–1705)

is still reminiscent of what Bronson has aptly called the 'Handbill' style (rather than the more refined 'Inscriptional Tablet').[89] But despite its two component titles, associated authorial bragging, imprint and two epigraphs, it nevertheless makes a neat and elegant impression. Without any recourse to the gaudy attractions of black letter, it relies entirely on variation between roman and italic capitals and lower-case type, framing its components within a conventional (even slightly old-fashioned) double-ruled frame, and using additional rules to delineate different segments of the page. Typographical emphasis is clear: 'TUB' appears in the largest full capitals, with 'TALE' (spaced to extend across the full width of the page) slightly smaller; and the word 'BATTEL', distinguished by the largest full capitals in the title of the second item, is smaller still. Everything else, though expressively varied between roman and italic, upper case and lower case and various sizes of type, is significantly smaller; but even the smallest italic type, used for the quotation from Lucretius, is crisp and legible. Whatever potential confusion may lie ahead, the title page is clear: the 'TALE' is the principal item and the 'BATTEL' its supplement. The book appears, on this evidence, more than capable of holding in appropriate suspension such diverse and preposterous materials as arrogant authorial claims ('Written for the Universal Improvement of Mankind') and epigraphs both obscure (Irenaeus) and trite (Lucretius).[90] Its design and execution indicate the high level of craftsmanship now being applied to Swift in print.

Later on in the volume the subordination of eccentricity to normality was again emphasised when an opportunity occurred that might have lent itself to a much more disruptive kind of material parody – but was ignored. This opportunity presented itself after the *Tale* (the first work promised on the title page) and the fragmentary *Battel* (the second and final work thus promised – which turned out also, like the *Tale*, to have its own preface by the supposed bookseller, and another by the supposed author). Up to this point, the single arabic pagination sequence had continued uninterrupted; but now there appeared an additional item that had not been specified on the title page, *A Discourse concerning the Mechanical Operation of the Spirit*.[91] This piece also had its own part-title; but it has an independent, free-standing look about it, being framed and divided with rules, and carrying its own imprint. Indeed, *Mechanical Operation* also had its own

---

[89] Bronson, *Printing as an Index of Taste*, pp. 20–8; *CWJS Tale*, pp. 284, 315–17.
[90] *CWJS Tale*, pp. 316–17.
[91] For possible strategic benefits of the title-page formulation, see A. C. Kelly, *Jonathan Swift and Popular Culture*, pp. 25–6.

62   Part II: London

'Bookseller's Advertisement' in which the bookseller claimed that this piece *was sent me at a different Time, and in a different Hand* from the rest of the contents, and that after holding it back for *'some Years'* he was now finally publishing it, having *'retrench'd those Parts that might give most offence'*.

Had all this been true, the naming of only the *Tale* and *Battel* on the title page would indeed have been consistent with what the Bookseller implies to have been the original plan for the book; but had it *really* been true that the newly redacted *Mechanical Operation* was a late addition (as the quasi-independent title page might suggest), the incomplete *Battel* would have been the intended conclusion to the volume, and might therefore have been expected to peter out near the end of a signature (even, perhaps, an incomplete one). In such a case it would have been necessary to add new signatures to accommodate the ostensible afterthought, perhaps even underlining the disruption by beginning a new sequence of page numbers. But there was no attempt at mocking up anything like this: despite the separate-looking part-title, *The Mechanical Operation of the Spirit* began mid-signature, the printing of its first few pages fully integrated with that of *The Battel of the Books*. Its pagination continued the single arabic sequence that had begun with 'The Epistle Dedicatory, To His Royal Highness Prince Posterity', which now ran on until *The Mechanical Operation of the Spirit* and the book concluded together. To have done otherwise would have imitated all too literally a kind of sloppy, unplanned work with which Tooke and Motte would have had powerful reasons not to involve themselves – and there is no evidence that any such possibility ever crossed their minds – or Swift's either. In comparison with such fundamentally disruptive mimicry, the celebrated typographical effects of the *Tale* work satirically without compromising the robustness of the physical product: even the neat recessing of the famously elegiac tag *'Hiatus in | MS.'* ('There is a gap in the manuscript'; p. 42) into an ironic drift of shimmering asterisks indicates the sharpness and intricacy of its production.

To readers accustomed to reading the *Tale* as material parody, the notion of setting normative limits to that parody may on the face of it seem disappointing; but, to judge by a comment that Swift would make a few years later, the combination of sound book-making with ramshackle verbal composition had a specific satirical force of its own. When in 1710 Swift contributed a letter on the corruption of taste and language to Steele's *Tatler* no. 230, he inveighed against what he claimed to be the recent infringement of traditional material decorums in the print trade:

The Shock of the Normal (1693–1705)

I cannot but observe to you, that until of late Years, a Grub-Street *Book was always bound in* Sheep-skin, *with suitable Print and Paper; the Price never above a Shilling; and taken off wholly by common Tradesmen, or Country Pedlars. But now they appear in all Sizes and Shapes, and in all Places: They are handed about in Lapfulls in every Coffee-house to Persons of Quality; are Shewn in* Westminster-Hall, *and the Court of Requests. You may see them gilt, and in Royal Paper of five or six Hundred Pages, and rated accordingly. I would engage to furnish you with a Catalogue of* English *Books published within the Compass of seven Years past, which at the first Hand would cost you an Hundred Pounds; wherein you shall not be able to find ten Lines together of common Grammar, or common Sense.*[92]

Thus he asserted a distinction between avowedly downmarket publications whose material form was a warning in itself, and more expensive publications marketed to unwary elites. The *Tale* arguably imitated the latter (and, in 1704, fell near the beginning of the seven-year timeframe that Swift indicates). Although Swift in print would indeed at various times impersonate or allude to cheap print, the emphasis in the 1704 *Tale* was much more on consolidating a novel dignity of presentation. Indeed, so great was Swift's apparent commitment to quality printwork that even his outright parodies of cheap print would tend, throughout his career, to be somewhat better printed than their ostensible targets.

Thus, however ironically, it is in the 1704 *Tale* that we for the first time encounter the characteristic look of early Swift, an octavo text executed to a good standard within the normal conventions of early eighteenth-century print (Figure 3). Most nouns, in the style of the time, begin with a capital letter. The main text is set in roman, attractively spaced and accurately printed, with reverse italic contrast for names, quotations and special emphasis. Italic type, however, is not yet in routine use for most punctuation marks: although italic colons and parentheses already follow italicised words, commas, semicolons and apostrophes maintain an upright stance throughout.[93] The 1704 *Tale* also displays two specific refinements on the styling of *Contests*: side-notes are now neatly recessed into the text-block; and paragraph structure is emphasised by setting the first (indented) word in large and small capitals, and by using additional spaces to separate each paragraph from the next. This was Swift's first substantial original book, and in the hands of Tooke and Motte it sustained through the four London

---

[92] *CWJS Parodies*, p. 94.

[93] For the italic semicolon, see M. B. Parkes, *Pause and Effect: An Introduction to the History of Punctuation in the West* (Aldershot: Scolar Press, 1992), pp. 52–3. For later eighteenth-century comment on italic punctuation, see Smith, *The Printer's Grammar*, pp. 93, 101; Philip Luckombe, *A Concise History of the Origin and Progress of Printing* (London, 1770), p. 267.

full and clear in the Point) that they both are Seminaries, not only of our *Planting*, but our *Watring* too? I am informed, Our two *Rivals* have lately made an Offer to enter into the Lists with united Forces, and challenge Us to a Comparison of Books, both as to *Weight* and *Number*. In Return to which, (with License from our *President*) I humbly offer two Answers: First, We say, the Proposal is like that which *Archimedes* made upon a * *smaller* Affair, including an Impossibility in the Practice; For, where can they find Scales of *Capacity* enough for the first, or an Arithmetician of *Capacity* enough for the second. Secondly, We are ready to accept the Challenge, but with this Condition, that a third indifferent Person be assigned, to whose impartial Judgment it shall be left to decide, which Society each Book, Treatise or Pamphlet do most properly belong to. This Point, God knows, is very far from being fixed at present; For, We are ready to produce a Catalogue of some Thousands, which in all common Justice ought to be entitled to Our Fraternity, but by the revolted and new-fangled Writers, most perfidiously ascribed to the

* Viz. About moving the Earth.

the others. Upon all which, we think it very unbecoming our Prudence, that the Determination should be remitted to the Authors themselves; when our Adversaries by Briguing and Caballing, have caused so universal a Defection from us, that the greatest Part of our Society hath already deserted to them, and our nearest Friends begin to stand aloof, as if they were half ashamed to own Us.

THIS is the utmost I am authorized to say upon so ungrateful and melancholy a Subject; because We are extreme unwilling to inflame a Controversy, whose Continuance may be so fatal to the Interests of Us All, desiring much rather that Things be amicably composed, and We shall so far advance on our Side, as to be ready to receive the two *Prodigals* with open Arms, whenever they shall think fit to return from their *Husks* and their *Harlots*; which I think from the * present Course of their Studies they most properly may be said to be engaged in; and like an indulgent Parent, continue to them our Affection and our Blessing.

* *Virtuoso Experiments, and Modern Comedies.*

BUT

Figure 3 Jonathan Swift, *A Tale of a Tub . . . To which is added, An Account of a Battel between the Antient and Modern Books in St. James's Library* (London, 1704), pp. 44–5.

The Shock of the Normal (1693–1705)

editions of 1704–5 a level of quality that materialised its claims to readers' attention. (By contrast, the Dublin so-called 'Fourth Edition Corrected' was a relatively cramped affair, with a third fewer pages, poor type alignment and uneven inking: Carter's printing-house was among the Tory outlets that handled distribution.[94]) In London, the robust normality that Tooke and Motte conferred on the *Tale* was a material rebuke to the Grub-Street excesses of its supposed author. It was also a major precedent for the octavo as format for Swift's most ambitious lifetime publications.

---

[94] *A Tale of a Tub . . . The Fourth Edition Corrected* (Dublin, 1705; TS 221, *ESTC* T1866). Copies were 'to be Sold only at *Dick*'s and *Lloyd*'s Coffee-Houses, and at the Printing-Press in *Fishamble-street*' – the last of which was Carter's address (Pollard, *Dictionary*, pp. 92–3, 367–8, 473–5). Its relative neatness and accuracy, and the use of double-ruled frames of continuous rather than composite rules, weigh against the likelihood of its being his own work.

CHAPTER 3

Material Voices
The Bickerstaff Effect (1705–1710)

Swift's return to Ireland before the publication of the 1704 *Tale* marked a break in new publications that lasted until his return to England in 1707. He came back to London with a commission from Archbishop King to seek a remission of taxation (the First Fruits and Twentieth Parts) for the Church of Ireland, and this occupied him fruitlessly until his return to Dublin in June 1709.[1] He also canvassed various possibilities for personal preferment, but these too eluded his grasp.[2] Yet if Swift's experiences were disappointing, Swift in print, now in the safe hands of Tooke, went from strength to strength. (Swift's letters and account books record their meetings in London taverns and eating-houses, and their letters give an unprecedented insight into their working relationship.[3]) In contrast with the linear progress of earlier, sparser years, Swift in print was now reaching critical mass, expanding in bulk and developing complex relations among the chronological layerings of its material texts.

While the 1704 *Tale* and the Temple edition had shown the potential of the well-produced but unostentatious octavo, these years in London also saw the proliferation of smaller, even shabbier formats. They lent themselves particularly well to projecting identities inaccessible to external verification, as demonstrated in the case of Isaac Bickerstaff, the first named fictitious author of a Swift work, and the protagonist of Swift's first substantial hoax. The resulting print craze also prompted reprints, both authorised and unauthorised, exemplifying a trend which now increasingly shaped the chronological profile of Swift in print. From now on the new works and reprints of any given year would emerge against the background of an accumulating stock of previous publications. Many

---

[1] See Philip O'Regan, *Archbishop William King of Dublin (1650–1729) and the Constitution in Church and State* (Dublin: Four Courts Press, 2000), pp. 145–6; see also Swift's correspondence with King, particularly Swift's letter of 6 December 1707 (*Corr.*, vol. I, pp. 163–5, and n. 2).

[2] *Corr.*, vol. I, pp. 172, 173, 181, 183–4, 213, 215–16, 218, 222, 227, 229, 234, 237, 239, 245–6, 257.

[3] *CWJS Tale*, pp. xxxiv, 213–14; *Corr.*, vol. I, pp. 282–5.

Material Voices: The Bickerstaff Effect (1705–1710)

would still be for sale, whether new or second-hand; and all the time, in coffee houses, homes and libraries, readers old and new continued to pick up copies already purchased by others. In the years ahead someone somewhere would always be printing Swift, and many more would be reading him.

Two Astrologers, a Civil Servant and an Elegist (1708–1709)

Isaac Bickerstaff and his interlocutors were brought into being by Swift and his book-trade associates in the early months of 1708. Bickerstaff, a self-proclaimed astrological reformer, predicted in his *Predictions for the Year 1708* the imminent death of the best-selling almanac-writer John Partridge (1644–1715), thus launching a hoax shaped by the established conventions of Grub-Street controversy. It was, in Ann Cline Kelly's words, 'a hoax that would destroy a cultural icon' and show how 'Grubstreet genres could change cultural realities'.[4]

For Swift, Partridge's extremist Whig invective, his idealisation of William III and his hostility to the alleged popery of the Anglican hierarchy made his *Merlinus Liberatus* London's leading example of the astrological subversion of traditional pieties.[5] Indeed, Partridge's characteristic mode recalled the populist extremism of the Dublin almanacs compiled by his even more vituperative former colleague John Whalley, suggesting that Swift may well have been pre-sensitised by early exposure. Bickerstaff's prediction, itself emerging from an established matrix of printed astrological controversy (by no means all of it to be taken at face value), prompted a babble of published claims and counter-claims. Published fact was difficult to disentangle from published fiction: once professional and political passions were engaged, more and more writers published their interventions, and the effects multiplied exponentially.

It was (and still is) unclear whether some of the contributions were really the work of those whose names appeared on them; and this too was an essential rather than accidental characteristic of astrological satire and controversy. In 1704, for example, Partridge's long-term Tory antagonist John Gadbury had died, prompting publication of *Mr. P——dg's Elegy on the Death of Mr. John Gadbury, the Famous Astrologer*; but its metre and rhymes are provisional in the extreme, and its satire, unsympathetic to astrology of any stripe, is as severe on

---

[4] A. C. Kelly, *Jonathan Swift and Popular Culture*, pp. 30, 34.
[5] Valerie Rumbold, 'Burying the Fanatic Partridge: Swift's Holy Week Hoax', in Claude Rawson (ed.), *Politics and Literature in the Age of Swift: English and Irish Perspectives* (Cambridge University Press, 2010), pp. 81–115.

68   Part II: London

Partridge as on Gadbury.[6] ('R. Longshaw', the bookseller for whom it claims to have been printed, is otherwise unknown to *ESTC*.) In the Bickerstaff affair too, Partridge would be made to voice papers that he did not write, such as *'Squire Bickerstaff Detected; or, the astrological impostor convicted, by John Partridge, student in physick and astrology. Part I*, which voiced his supposed complaints about the inconvenience of being falsely reputed dead.[7] In contrast, his almanac for 1709 insisted 'that I am living, contrary to that base Paper said to be done by one *Bickerstaff*', denounced Bickerstaff as a producer of 'Scandalous Pamphlets' and inveighed against the 'Impudent Lying Fellow' lurking behind the 'sham Name' of Bickerstaff.[8] (Although he was wrong in his first identification of the High-Church writer William Pittis, he clearly grasped the quarter from which the attack originated.[9])

Bickerstaff, on the other hand, was to enjoy a longer and more prolific career than most authors of flesh and blood: by April 1709 Swift had apparently approved his transfer to Steele's *Tatler*, which he conducted as the whimsically judicious Censor of Great Britain; and he later emigrated to America, where he compiled almanacs such as *Bickerstaff's Boston Almanack. For the Year of our Lord, 1772* – although by 1831 'Isaac Bickerstaff, Jr.' had inherited responsibility for *The Hampden Almanac, and Housewife's Companion ... adapted to the meridian of Springfield, Mass.*[10] The media whirl of the original hoax demonstrated some exhilarating – perhaps discomfiting – facts about print: it hardly mattered whether or not the author really existed; it was impossible to insure authors against impersonation; sensational lies spread more easily than dull truths; and complaints by victims only added to the play of claim and counter-claim. This hoax, besides drawing effectively on the established indeterminacies and counterfeits of astrological controversy, was therefore deeply resonant for the future of Swift in print. The 1704 *Tale*, though itself substantial and well produced, had already highlighted Grub-Street aspirations as a central concern of Swift's satire; and the Bickerstaff affair now projected a cast of different voices

---

[6] Foxon M297; *ESTC* N35300.
[7] No further part is known to have been published. For uncertainties of authorship and publication, see *CWJS Parodies*, Appendix D, pp. 565–72. Although the content suggests a date following closely on Partridge's supposed death, a 'this day is published' advertisement from *The Post-boy* for 17–19 August 1710, and a further mention in *Tatler* no. 216 (26 August 1710), may suggest a later date (Bond, *Tatler*, vol. III, p. 135). I am grateful to John McTague for discussion on this point.
[8] *CWJS Parodies*, pp. 66–75.   [9] *Corr.*, vol. I, pp. 189–90.
[10] Bond, *Tatler*, vol. I, p. 23; *ESTC* W14316 (compiled by Benjamin West); Library of Congress AY201. S82 H36 (produced under the aegis of the newspaper *The Hampden Whig*). For further controversial deployment of Bickerstaff, see John McTague, '"There Is No Such Man as Isaack Bickerstaff": Partridge, Pittis, and Jonathan Swift', *Eighteenth-Century Life*, 35.1 (2011), 83–101 (p. 84).

Material Voices: The Bickerstaff Effect (1705–1710) 69

through the direct impersonation of Grub-Street publications – while all the time concealing the shared origin of the material texts.

Five published Bickerstaff papers can be firmly attributed to Swift: *Predictions for the Year 1708*; *The Accomplishment of the First of Mr. Bickerstaff's Predictions*; *An Elegy on Mr. Patrige, the Almanack-maker, who Died on the 29th of this Instant March, 1708*; *A Vindication of Isaac Bickerstaff*; and, following in 1709, the connected but discrete *A Famous Prediction of Merlin*.[11] Swift's choice of the fatal day shows that the campaign was planned to unfold during February–March 1708, reaching its climax in Holy Week. (In 1708, 29–31 March were Monday, Tuesday and Wednesday of Holy Week; and 1 April, the feast of All Fools that Swift loved to celebrate, was Maundy Thursday: to stage Partridge's fictitious death to so sacred a timetable was in itself a condemnation of his perceived blasphemies.[12]) Yet there was also scope for a degree of flexibility, for the posthumously published *An Answer to Bickerstaff*, apparently written to round off the affair, was in the event withheld from the press: it probably seemed a shame to spoil a joke that was still going strong.[13] The last associated paper, *A Famous Prediction of Merlin*, which followed more than six months later in 1709, took a rather different approach, and may not have been part of the original plan – it may indeed have been prompted in part by Bickerstaff's success. Such a publishing programme, unlike a single substantial book, could hardly be abandoned to the printer while Swift set off for Ireland. Indeed, it was only a relatively long stay that could allow such a project to evolve from day to day in the real time of the London print world.

Swift's published Bickerstaff papers derived their effectiveness not only from his literary construction of characters, but also from the specific material characteristics of the printed texts. Approximating tantalisingly (if not in the end convincingly) to plausibility, these were unpretentious artefacts designed to be hawked through the streets, bringing them directly to a wide range of readers and stimulating more and more third-party interventions. Without all five papers laid out for comparison (not a likely scenario at the time) a full appraisal would have been impossible – though sophisticated observers may well have assumed that earnest adjudication of Grub-Street truth claims was probably beside the point. Yet a structured comparison is revealing (see Table).

---

[11] For the *Elegy*, see *CWJS Poems* I (forthcoming); for the other pieces mentioned, *CWJS Parodies*, pp. 35–87, 642–59.

[12] George P. Mayhew, 'Swift's Bickerstaff Hoax as an April Fools' Joke', *Modern Philology*, 61.4 (1964), 270–80; Rumbold, 'Burying', pp. 97–9. For Swift's All Fools' Day hoaxes see *CWJS Parodies*, pp. 527–8.

[13] *CWJS Parodies*, pp. 573–7.

Table *The Bickerstaff Papers*

	Short Title	Imprint	Format	Layout	References
1	*Predictions for the Year 1708 ... By Isaac Bickerstaff Esq;*	Sold by John Morphew near Stationers-Hall	8vo (half sheet; 4 leaves, 8 pages)	Separate title; text begins on verso	TS 483; *ESTC* T124498
2	*The Accomplishment of the First of Mr. Bickerstaff's Predictions ... In a Letter to a Person of Honour*	[Colophon] London: Printed in the Year 1708	4to (half sheet; 2 leaves, 4 pages)	Text begins under title; colophon	Not in TS (see *CWJS Parodies*, pp. 650–1); *ESTC* N29172
3	*An Elegy on Mr. Patrige, the Almanack-maker, who Died on the 29th of this Instant March, 1708*	London: printed in the year 1708	large 2° (single-sheet broadside, printed one side)	Text begins under title; funeral compartment	TS 496; *ESTC* T32515; Foxon S832
4	*A Vindication of Isaac Bickerstaff Esq; ... By the said Isaac Bickerstaff Esq;*	London: Printed in the Year MDCCIX	8vo (half sheet; 4 leaves, 8 pages)	Separate title; verso blank; text begins on next recto	TS 498; *ESTC* T117404
5	*A Famous Prediction of Merlin ... By T. N. Philomath*	[Colophon] London: Printed, and Sold by A. Baldwin, near the Oxford-Arms in Warwick-Lane. MDCCIX	2° half sheet (1 leaf, printed both sides)	Text begins under title and woodcut portrait; colophon	TS 499; *ESTC* T132987

Material Voices: The Bickerstaff Effect (1705–1710)

All these published Bickerstaff papers were printed to a standard somewhat higher than strictly plausible for their target genres, and nos. 1–4 were most probably managed – though not printed – by Tooke. The differences among the material texts supported the fiction that there were four different writers: if they had been too similar, or too clearly connected with Swift, this might have seemed less plausible. Thus, although four of the five papers are made from a single half sheet of paper, the uses of that half sheet are varied: nos. 1 and 4, the papers ascribed to Bickerstaff, are eight-page octavos (consistent with their claim to be the work of the same author); no. 2 is a four-page quarto; and no. 5 is a single folio leaf printed on both sides. No. 3, the odd one out, uses a full sheet in broadside format. Nos. 1 and 4 name the supposed author (Bickerstaff) in the title; no. 5 gives the initials and profession of a different supposed author (T. N. Philomath); the supposed author of no. 2 provides sufficient personal background to distinguish him from both, but offers no name or initial; and no. 3, which also lacks name or initials, betrays nothing about the supposed elegist beyond the fact that he speaks of Bickerstaff in the third person and identifies with Grub-Street authors. Such diversionary variations of format and attribution are further intensified by the play of evasion in the imprints.

Perhaps the least guarded is that of no. 1, which names the Tory trade publisher John Morphew (apprenticed 1695, active to 1720), successor to the business of John Nutt.[14] Nutt had been named in the imprints of *Contests and Dissensions* in 1701 and the *Tale* in 1704, and Morphew would several times be named in further major publications by Swift – but not in any more of this particular set of papers. Instead, no. 2, which purports to be by a different author, gives only place and date, and places this information at the end in a colophon instead of at the front in an imprint. No. 3, probably published the same day, also gives only place and date, this time at the foot of the second column of the broadside. Bickerstaff is back in no. 4, and again only place and date are supplied, although this time the date is given in roman numerals. Finally, in the following year, no. 5 has a colophon giving the name and address of Abigail Baldwin (widow of Richard Baldwin); and the date is once more in roman numerals.[15] (Treadwell has suggested that John Watts might have been the printer; another possibility might be Motte, or Swift's maternal cousin Dryden Leach, who printed a newspaper for the Baldwins.[16]) In the

[14] *BBTI*, drawing on two entries for John Morphew.
[15] See *CWJS Parodies*, pp. 78–87, textual account, pp. 657–9, and Rumbold, 'Merlinus Verax', pp. 392–412. For the Baldwins, see Chapter 1.
[16] Rumbold, 'Merlinus Verax', p. 407; Bullard and McLaverty, 'Introduction', pp. 10–11; Treadwell, 'Swift's Relations', p. 16.

72   Part II: London

context of the whole sequence, what is important is the absence of print-trade names from all but two of the five papers, and the appearance in one only of each name that does appear. The patchiness of imprint information, combined with differences of format and purported author, obscures any sense of a single originating source.

Furthermore, each author and composition is embedded in an appropriate print context. Bickerstaff, whose campaign against the radical Whig Partridge was plausibly initiated under the imprint of the Tory distributor Morphew, began in no. 1, *Predictions*, by contrasting himself with such commercial almanac-makers as Partridge and Gadbury: Bickerstaff was instead a gentleman astrologer, uninterested in profit and intent on reforming the discipline. His name, set in prominent full capitals on the title, was thus accompanied by a claim to superior rank: '*By* ISAAC BICKERSTAFF *Esq;*'. As such, he easily outclassed astrologers like Partridge or Whalley, who had begun their careers as shoemakers, and set himself above the fray of ordinary astrological discourse:

> And I believe no Gentleman, who reads this Paper, will look upon it to be of the same Cast or Mould with the common Scribbles that are every Day hawk'd about. My Fortune has plac'd me above the little Regards of Scribbling for a few Pence, which I neither value nor want: Therefore let not wise Men too hastily condemn this Essay, intended for a good Design to cultivate and improve an ancient Art, long in Disgrace by having fallen into mean unskilful Hands.[17]

The name Isaac Bickerstaff quickly established its own tradition of commentary. The unpublished 'Answer' pointed out that 'it seems, although he [the writer] has joined an odd sirname to no very common Christian one, that in this large town there is a man found to own both the names, though, I believe, not the paper'; and in 1735 a headnote to *Predictions* would introduce the story that Swift had been inspired by a tradesman's sign.[18] (The plausibility of the name would be further tested when in 1733 a John and Jane Bickerstaff of Dublin gave their son, a future librettist, the name 'Isaac' – possibly by way of allusion to Isaac's puff in *Tatler* no. 4 for a benefit performance for a London actor, 'my next Kinsman Mr. *John Bickerstaff.*'[19]) All this recalls Ian Watt's emphasis in *The Rise of the Novel* on plausible combinations of given name and surname in this period as

---

[17] *CWJS Parodies*, p. 57.   [18] *Ibid.*, p. 43.
[19] Bond, *Tatler*, vol. I, p. 36; *ODNB* ('Isaac John Bickerstaff'); Philip H. Highfill, Jr, Kalman A. Burnim and Edward A. Langhans, *A Biographical Dictionary of Actors, Actresses, Musicians, Dancers, Managers and Other Stage Personnel in London, 1660–1800*, 16 vols. (Carbondale, IL: Southern Illinois University Press, 1973–93), vol. II, pp. 109–12.

Material Voices: The Bickerstaff Effect (1705–1710)

a new way of realising 'particular individuals in the contemporary social environment'.[20] Like his younger brother Lemuel Gulliver, Isaac Bickerstaff would join the small elite of fictional authors capable of functioning outside the literary works of which they were part. Yet Swift himself, with characteristic detachment, gave no sign of any ambition to retain his property in Bickerstaff, finally waving him off in the direction of Steele's *Tatler* without, it seems, a second thought.[21]

Like the *Tale*, *Predictions* was a publication ultimately less concerned to mimic parodic shoddiness than to maintain a respectable quality of print. It made no attempt at a full imitation of a standard almanac, which would have required the laborious mocking-up of tables, astrological symbols and rubricated red-letter days – not to mention the expense of the additional paper required to match the forty-eight pages of a typical Partridge *Merlinus Liberatus*. Instead, *Predictions* imitated only the section devoted to monthly prognostications – which might, on occasion, be printed separately, as in the notorious case of Partridge's baleful anticipations for James II in 1688.[22] Print quality was deftly indicated by the design of the title page: instead of an almanac title crammed with black and red text in varied founts, the title of *Predictions* was spacious, restrained and sharply executed: the main title was set in roman full capitals, with lower-case roman for the subtitle; there was relatively little italic; and there was no rubrication or black letter. In addition, the title highlighted a supposedly reforming purpose ('*to prevent the People of* England *from being further impos'd on by vulgar Almanack-makers*'), rather than offering a typically sensational summary of the year's predictions.[23] This octavo pamphlet, unlike some of the other papers in the hoax, also maintained the relative distinction of having a separate title page – though the text began on its verso, rather than the following recto. In sum, the material text nicely marked the ambivalence of Bickerstaff's aspirations: professedly superior to the common almanac-makers, he remained engrossed in recalculating their predictions. Deploying familiar tropes of inter-brand rivalry, Bickerstaff focused on the political and domestic events of the coming months, although the crucial point, for the hoax that followed, was the preliminary prediction that he presented as 'but a Trifle': '*Partridge* the

---

[20] Ian Watt, *The Rise of the Novel: Studies in Defoe, Richardson, and Fielding* (London: Chatto & Windus, 1957), p. 19.

[21] See Appendix G, 'The Attribution to Swift of Further *Tatlers* and *Spectators*', *CWJS Parodies*, pp. 583–601.

[22] Rumbold, 'Burying', pp. 84–5, 111.

[23] For errors, see emendations in *CWJS Parodies*, pp. 647–8.

74   Part II: London

Almanack-maker . . . will infallibly dye upon the 29th of *March* next, about Eleven at night, of a raging Feaver.'[24] Moreover, Swift was alert to normal printing and distribution schedules: since almanacs, postdated for the following year, usually came out in November, Bickerstaff was launching his project far too late; but the omission of any predictions earlier than March was rationalised by making him identify 'the time that the *Sun* enters into *Aries*' as 'the Beginning of the natural Year'.[25] Since unsold almanacs were usually withdrawn at Candlemas (2 February), Bickerstaff's prognostications (somewhat conveniently) came onto the market only when the year's actual predictions were no longer available.

In contrast with *Predictions*, no. 2, *The Accomplishment of the First of Mr. Bickerstaff's Predictions . . . In a Letter to a Person of Honour*, inhabited a genre familiar across all levels of print in this period, namely an epistolary report from first-hand knowledge. Although the author was unnamed, he gave sufficient detail to place himself socially and professionally: formerly 'employ'd in the Revenue', he used to be the recipient of an annual copy of Partridge's almanac 'upon the Score of some little Gratuity we gave him'.[26] Thus established as Partridge's superior, with a professional regard for accurate reporting, he was well placed to testify to Partridge's death, which he undertook to do 'In Obedience to your Lordship's Commands, as well as to satisfie my own Curiosity'. As a small quarto pamphlet of four pages (a half sheet folded once), with text beginning in unpretentious style immediately beneath the title, his report was neatly affiliated to the quarto pamphlet tradition, while achieving a concision consistent with his professional character. Unlike Bickerstaff, however, he would never write again for Swift, whose unnamed voices never return to claim previous authorship of such publications as the *Tale* or the *Accomplishment*.

Very soon afterwards appeared no. 3, *An Elegy on Mr. Patrige, the Almanack-maker, who Died on the 29th of this Instant March, 1708*, a date which suggests that it was published on 30 or 31 March (Figure 4). Its large broadside format (highly unusual for Swift, whose single-leaf publications were usually half sheets), printed on one side in two columns, and framed by a mourning compartment, imitates the memorial poems traditionally issued on the deaths of persons of national or local significance: its division between a long 'elegy' and a brief 'epitaph' at the foot of the second column is also conventional. J. Woolley and Karian additionally point out that Swift's 1711 *Miscellanies* would reprint the poem as *A Grubstreet Elegy*, a characterisation anticipated in the final lines, which implore the newly

---

[24] *Ibid.*, p. 49.   [25] *Ibid.*, pp. 48, 642–3.   [26] *Ibid.*, p. 61.

Material Voices: The Bickerstaff Effect (1705–1710) 75

stellified Partridge to bestow his influence not on 'St. *James*'s End o'the' Town', but on the '*Astrologers* and *Lunaticks*' of '*More Fields*', near Grub Street: 'Hither thy gentle Aspect bend, / Nor look Asquint on an old Friend.'[27] The most visually striking element was the full-width funeral imagery of the upper border of the compartment: Death sits enthroned against a black half-ellipse, attended by skeletons whose darts extend their pennons into the blank upper corners of the sheet, which are flanked in turn by winged (empty) hour-glasses and crossbones.[28] The design centres on Death's motto, 'I Ouercom & Conquer', displayed across a banner to each side of his head; and the funereal tone is carried through into the broad black borders at side and foot, and the narrower bar dividing the two columns.

This compartment was in fact an old one, as witness an elegy on the ejected minister Francis Holcroft, which was 'Printed for Will. Marshall' in 1692.[29] Several uses of a closely related variant in the early 1690s also suggest links with Whig Protestant print, further linking Swift's commemoration of Partridge with the triumphs of his Williamite heyday: indeed, the less than immaculate print quality of Swift's *Elegy* is plausibly reminiscent of the cheap, popular level at which many of Partridge's publications were pitched.[30] In the British Library copy of the *Elegy* the black background of the top border is noticeably fainter on the left-hand side than on the right, and the joining of borders at the lower right-hand corner is misaligned, as is the central division, which sits to the right of the position indicated for it in the lower border, placing it off-centre in relation to the figure of Death at

---

[27] A copy is preserved among the Bagford Ballads collected for Lord Oxford, BL C.40.m.11.(74); see *CWJS Poems* I (forthcoming).

[28] For compartments, see Fredson Bowers, *Principles of Bibliographical Description* (Princeton University Press, 1949), pp. 141–4, particularly no. 3 in his classification of construction methods ('Four or more pieces carved or engraved separately but evidently intended to form part of a single design when assembled').

[29] *An Elegy upon the Death of Mr. Francis Holcroft who dyed the sixth, and interred this twelfth of January, 1691/2* (London, 1692; *ESTC* R36261; 'Printed for Will. Marshall': the plain border at the foot, may not, however, be from the same set).

[30] In the commoner variant, the upper border lacks the pennons in the top corners and adds angel faces above the hourglasses, while the funereal imagery is carried over into the side and bottom borders. For examples, see Richard Ames, *An Elegy upon the Death of that Learned, Pious, and Laborious Minister of Jesus Christ Mr. Richard Baxter* (London, 1691; *ESTC* R226824, 'Printed for *Richard Baldwin*'); *An Elegy upon the Death of Major John Ashton who was Executed for High-treason* (London, 1691; *ESTC* R33412, 'Printed by G. C.' [i.e. George Croom]); *Natura lugens, or, An Elegy on the Death of the Honourable Robert Boyle, Esq.* (London, 1691; *ESTC* R35064, 'Printed for *John Taylor*'); *An Elegy on the Death of Sir William Turner, Knight, and Alderman of the City of London, and President of Bridwell and Bethlem Hospitals* (London, 1693; *ESTC* R36079, 'Printed for *George Croom*'); *An Elegy upon the Most Pious and Incomparable Princess, Mary Queen of England* (London, 1694; *ESTC* R174935, 'Printed by *Richard Smith*').

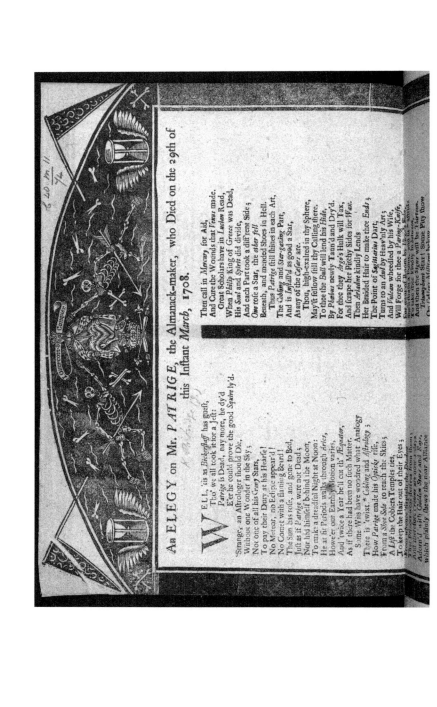

An ELEGY on Mr. PATRIGE, the Almanack-maker, who Died on the 29th of this Instant *March*, 1708.

WELL, 'tis as *Bickerstaff* has guest,
Tho' we all took it for a Jest:
Patrige is Dead, nay more, he dy'd
E'er he could prove the good *Squire* ly'd.
'Strange, an Astrologer should Die,
Without one Wonder in the Sky;
Not one of all his *Crony* Stars,
To pay their Duty at his Hearse!
No Meteor, no Eclipse appear'd!
No Comet with a flaming Beard!
The Sun has rose, and gone to Bed,
Just as if *Patrige* were not Dead;
Nor hid himself behind the Moon,
To make a dreadful Night at Noon:
He at fix Periods walks through *Aries*,
However our Earthly Motion varies,
And 'twice a Year he'll cut th' *Æquator*,
As if there had been no such Matter.

Some Wits have wondred what Analogy
There is 'twixt *Cobling* and *Astrology*;
How *Patrige* made his *Opticks* rise,
From a *Shoe Sole*, to reach the Skies;
A *Last* the Cobler's Temples ties,
To keep the Hair out of their Eyes;

Then call in *Mercury* for Aid,
And Cure the Wounds that *Venus* made.
Great Scholars have in *Lucian* Read,
When *Philip* King of *Greece* was Dead,
His *Soul* and *Spirit* did divide,
And each Part took a diff'rent Side;
One rose a Star, the *other fell*
Beneath, and mended Shoes in Hell.

Thus *Patrige* still shines in each Art,
The *Cobling* and *Star-gazing* Part,
And is *Install'd* as good a Star,
As any of the *Cæsars* are.
Thou, high-exalted in thy Sphere,
May'st fellow still thy Calling there.
To thee the *Bull* will lend his *Hide*,
By *Phœbus* newly Tann'd and Dry'd.
For thee they *Argo*'s Hulk will Tax,
And scrape her Pitchy Sides for *Wax*.
Then *Ariadne* kindly Lends
Her Braided Hair to make thee *Ends*;
The Point of *Sagittarius* Dart,
Turns to an *Awl* by Heav'nly Art;
And *Vulcan* wheedled by his Wife,
Will Forge for thee a *Paring-Knife*.

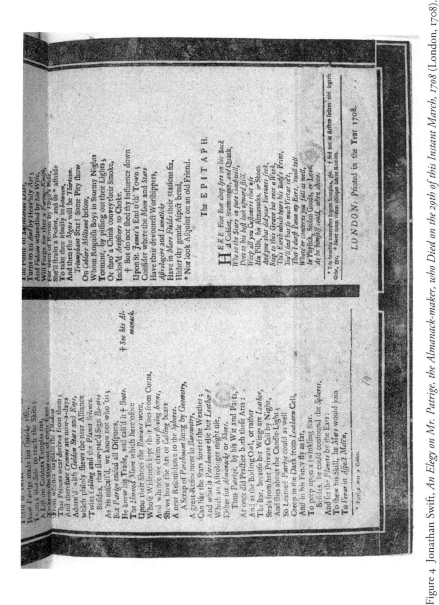

Figure 4 Jonathan Swift, *An Elegy on Mr. Patrige, the Almanack-maker, who Died on the 29th of this Instant March, 1708* (London, 1708).

78 Part II: London

the head of the piece. In addition, a pre-printing fold in the top left-hand corner of the sheet has left an unprinted gap across the left-hand pennon. The verbal text is similarly compromised: the impression is sometimes faint and sometimes over-inked; spacing between words is inconsistent; and errors include a missing capital at the beginning of a line ('which plainly shews'), a missing 't' ('here ofore') and an upside-down '*m*' (in what would have been '*Triumphant*'). Yet there are also signs of sophistication: a side-note and four footnotes, three of them in Latin, are clearly set in small type and neatly separated from the text by rules, and a careful distinction between roman and italic (reversed for the epitaph) is observed throughout. This is far from the worst to be expected in the genre, as was neatly demonstrated by a related example, *An Elegy upon the Death of the Famous Dr. John Partridgd*.[31] This (an entirely different poem) stated that Partridge had died '*This Morning*', which may suggest it was on the streets even before Swift's; but its print quality was far worse. Speedy publication in the wake of the predicted death was important to keep the hoax alive on the streets, but like so many Swift spoofs, *An Elegy on Mr. Patrige* stopped well short of total surrender to Grub-Street standards.

At this point, Swift's *Elegy* might well have seemed to mark the end of the affair, had not the *Accomplishment* now alleged that Bickerstaff had erred in his prediction by 'almost Four Hours', which, in the accustomed manner of astrological disputes, furnished him with an excuse to return to the fray.[32] This he did in no. 4, the *Vindication*, which again appeared as an octavo, this time at a slightly enhanced level, with an ornament on the separate title and a blank verso that allowed the text to begin in style on the next recto. This advance in quality matched the self-regarding rhetoric of this face-saving piece, pitched as a more ambitiously genteel version of the agonistic to-and-fro so familiar from real-life print exchanges between rival almanac-makers. Not only did Bickerstaff gloat over Partridge's denials of his own death and indulge in flagrant logic-chopping to prove him dead, but he also quoted what purported to be glowing testimonials from Europe's scholarly elite. Within the space of two small pamphlets, he had established the combination of whimsical satire and self-undermining conceit that would qualify him – once Swift had released him to Steele – to write the *Tatler* as Censor of Great Britain.

---

[31] Not in *ESTC*, but reproduced at ebba.english.ucsb.edu/ballad/33064/image; see discussion of Swift's *An Elegy on Mr. Patrige* in *CWJS Poems* I (forthcoming).
[32] *CWJS Parodies*, p. 64.

Material Voices: The Bickerstaff Effect (1705–1710) 79

In contrast, no. 5 in the table, *A Famous Prediction of Merlin*, is much harder to weigh up.[33] On the surface it appears to be devised on a similar plan, projecting an author with a recognisable ideology, and imitating a recognisable print genre. This time the author is 'T. N.', who identifies himself as 'Philomath' (lover of learning). He begins by referring back to the Bickerstaff affair, expressing support both for Partridge in particular and for the art of astrology in general. At the core of the performance is a verse prophecy ascribed to Merlin, on which he offers a commentary, deploying the topicality of the events and issues highlighted in the poem to vindicate the possibility of predicting the future. The print genre that embodied this performance, the half-sheet presentation of a supposedly ancient prophecy, was a long-term staple of popular culture; but in this case the printwork is much too good to be true: the two separate printings (distinguished by lineation) use the two sides of a single half sheet to present, beneath a woodcut portrait of Merlin, a complex combination of roman, italic and black-letter type; and they do it with remarkable neatness and accuracy.[34] It is at least possible that some readers took seriously the claims that Merlin had predicted the Act of Union and that the childless and widowed Queen might yet continue the Stuart line by giving birth to a surviving heir.[35] Yet closer attention to the material text suggests that this is something rather more than simply a parody of popular prophecy.

In sum, the half sheet is shaped less by its ostensible target than by two less obvious strands of allusion to print history, one to Partridge's print wars with Gadbury in the early 1690s, and the other to the typography of English incunabula. The Gadbury allusions are focused by the woodcut at the head of the sheet, printed from the very woodblock that Partridge had used to attack Gadbury – although some details specific to that earlier controversy have been excised.[36] Since Partridge's attacks had been handled by Richard Baldwin, his widow Abigail, who now put her imprint to what is ostensibly the work of a Partridge supporter, may have had the block to hand (and it may even be that the mourning compartment used in *An Elegy on Mr. Patrige* was also in her possession, in which – admittedly highly speculative – case she may also have been involved in publishing that associated but much worse printed piece). In addition, Swift's invented author had his own links to Gadbury, whose titles also call him 'Philomath' (usually in Greek characters): the initials 'T. N.' had actually been used by

---

[33] For full discussion, see Rumbold, 'Merlinus Verax'. [34] *CWJS Parodies*, pp. 657–8.
[35] Rumbold, 'Merlinus Verax', pp. 409–10. [36] *Ibid.*, pp. 395–402.

80   Part II: London

a writer who shared his name with a family of Gadbury-supporting almanac-makers.

The second line of print allusion reached much further back in time; for T. N. claimed that Merlin's poem (actually composed by Swift) had been transcribed from 'an Old Edition of *Merlin*'s Prophecies; imprinted at *London* by *Johan Haukyns*, in the Year 1530, *Pag. 39*', which he invited his readers to inspect in person: 'I shall give Orders to have the very Book sent to the Printer of this Paper, with Directions to let any Body see it that pleases; because, I believe, it is pretty scarce.'[37] Only one book printed by Haukyns is in fact extant, a guide to learning French entitled *Lesclaircissement de la langue francoyse compose par maistre Iehan Palsgrave Angloyse natyf de Londres, et gradue de Paris.*[38] Swift had evidently seen a copy, taken Haukyns's name from the colophon, and given its date of 1530 to his imaginary book. Moreover, the typographical distinction in *A Famous Prediction* between black-letter text and roman comment is closer to Haukyns's distinction between black letter for English-language explanations and roman for examples in French than it is to the typographical conventions of ancient prophecy. The practical joke seems calculated to waste Mrs Baldwin's time and send bibliophiles on a fool's errand (Swift's friend Sir Andrew Fountaine perhaps being a particular target).[39] Indeed, of the various questions surrounding *A Famous Prediction*, one of the most intriguing relates to the relation between Swift and Mrs Baldwin. Was *A Famous Prediction* Swift's revenge on Partridge's book-trade supporters? or a stab at the printer of *Ode to the Athenian Society*? Or did it reflect friendlier relations, perhaps mediated through Swift's cousin Dryden Leach?[40] Although it raises more questions than it answers, *A Famous Prediction* demonstrates, in a single half sheet, a remarkable density of book-trade allusion. It suggests how much Swift and his contacts knew about the history and personalities of the print trade – and how little we ourselves know about who decided, and how, the material forms in which his works were published.

A major aspect of the Bickerstaff hoax was the avid reprinting that it provoked in the London book trade, which was for the most part unauthorised. This was the first time that Swift's writings were quickly taken up by a wide range of reprinters, and there could have been no better way of promoting the hoax, or of further mystifying the origins of the affair. The comparison of original Bickerstaff pamphlets with unauthorised

---

[37] *CWJS Parodies*, pp. 83, 87; Rumbold, 'Merlinus Verax', pp. 408–9.   [38] *CWJS Parodies*, p. 80.
[39] *Ibid.*, p. 87.   [40] *Ibid.*, p. 80.

Material Voices: The Bickerstaff Effect (1705–1710) 81

reprints (of which at least seven survive for *Predictions*) further illuminates the nature of genuinely cheap popular print.[41] *An Answer to Bickerstaff,* though in the end withheld from publication, would have drawn attention (had it been published) to some important differences:

> I believe it is no small mortification to this gentleman astrologer, as well as his bookseller, to find their piece, which they sent out in a tolerable print and paper, immediately seized on by three or four interloping printers of Grubstreet, the title stuffed with an abstract of the whole matter, together with the standard epithets of *strange and wonderful,* the price brought down a full half, which was but a penny in its prime, and bawled about by hawkers of the inferior class, with the concluding cadence of *A halfpenny apiece.*[42]

What is striking here (and contributes substantially to the sense that the piece is Swift's) is not only the sensitivity of the supposed commentator to materials, titles and pricing, but his assumption of the shared agency of bookseller and author: both are committed to decent paper and type, a restrained and dignified form of title, and a price appropriate to a quality product. The 'gentleman astrologer' thus has his work published to a standard unattainable by common almanac-makers – and Swift's close and companionable association with Tooke meant that Swift could now assume this quality by default.

Material variation in the unauthorised reprints also puts the comments of the *Answer* into a broader perspective. A case in point is the edition 'Printed for *T. Wise,* near *Fleet-street*' (which also offered the purchaser the delusory reassurance of being '*Licensed according to Order*').[43] This used the same half-sheet octavo format as Swift's original, and, like its original, set aside the whole of the first page for the title; but it used the space to very different effect. At the head, Swift's title was sensationalised as *Esquire Bickerstaff's Most Strange and Wonderful Predictions for the Year 1708,* and most of the remaining space was taken up with a summary of the most striking predictions to be found within. The ordering varied significantly from that adopted in the body of the text, in which Partridge's death (though 'but a Trifle') was announced first: Wise instead prioritised the deaths of the King of France, the Pope and the Dauphin. Only later did he list '*Partridge* the famous Astrologer' and the rest, concluding with 'great

---

[41] TS lists six different reprints (nos. 484–9), and an additional one was offered for sale in 2006 (Maggs Bros. Ltd, *Books and Readers in Early Modern Britain IV: A Selection of Books, Manuscripts and Bindings,* Catalogue 1393 (London: Maggs Bros. Ltd, 2006), p. 198).

[42] *CWJS Parodies,* p. 575.

[43] *Esquire Bickerstaff's Most Strange and Wonderful Predictions* (London, [1708]; TS 486, *ESTC* T69060).

Mischief done in *Bartholomew-Fair*, by the tumbling down of a Booth; with several other strange Things too tedious here to be related'. Wise's implied reader, while by no means indifferent to Partridge's doom or fairground catastrophes, is principally interested in England's prospects in the War of the Spanish Succession, which would have been decisively improved by such an elimination of highly placed Bourbon supporters.[44] Less obviously sensational, in contrast, was the presentation by Henry Hills, a frequent reprinter of Swift in this period, who adopted the same half-sheet octavo format, but laid out the text over all eight pages, replacing the separate title with a brief heading that offered no summary of specific predictions.[45] Like Wise, Hills gave his name and address in full (in this case, in a colophon). In terms of inaccurate text and sloppy presswork, however, it seems that no reprinter outdid the hitherto unknown edition described by Maggs Bros. in 2006.[46] Its title page adopts the sensational summary technique, and the text inside has been described as 'the worst of the lot'. Importantly, its producer, unlike Wise or Hills, seems to have used an imprint very like that of John Morphew (now only partially visible owing to cropping), probably in a deliberate attempt to pass it off as the authorised edition. *A Famous Prediction* also attracted unauthorised re-printings, whose lower quality is betrayed by their substitutions for the woodblock portrait: not having access to the original block, copyists approximated some of the detail and omitted the oddities arising from its previous application to Gadbury.[47]

The enthusiasm with which unauthorised reprinters embraced *Predictions* suggests a high degree of perceived saleability. In Dublin, however, only one reprint is known: it established its right of publication by the declaration '*London* Printed; and Reprinted and Sold at the *Union* Coffee-House on Cork-Hill' – an address which links it to the Whig bookseller, printer and newspaper proprietor Francis Dickson.[48] While it may seem odd to find a committed Whig promulgating a hoax against Partridge (particularly since he made no politically significant alterations), the fact that it was a spoof may have been less immediately obvious than its likely profitability.[49] Like the London editions, the Dublin edition also used half a sheet of paper, but this time in the form of four quarto pages. It

---

[44] For the political implications of the prophecies, see *CWJS Parodies*, pp. 83–6.
[45] TS 485, *ESTC* N012428.   [46] Maggs Bros., Catalogue 1393, p. 198.
[47] Rumbold, 'Merlinus Verax', p. 402.
[48] *Predictions for the Year 1708* (Dublin, [1708]; TS 489, *ESTC* T179431).
[49] For Dickson, see Pollard, *Dictionary*, pp. 152–3; for political readings of *Predictions*, see *CWJS Parodies*, pp. 38–9.

Material Voices: The Bickerstaff Effect (1705–1710)

retained Swift's original title at the head, but set out underneath a summary (if a relatively brief one) of 'all the Remarkable Events that shall happen in *Europe* this Year' – a list in which Partridge retained the first place. The main text then began underneath, in small type scattered with mis-sorted italics, and some longer passages arbitrarily set in italic (perhaps owing to shortage of type). As yet another poor-quality reprint, it added to the degradation which in the *Answer* evoked such fastidious regret; but it also extended the reach of Swift's London hoax across the Irish Sea. As publication slipped beyond the quality control of author and bookseller, what had started as a single small and soberly produced parody had spawned a sensation.

Rather different, however, was the deplorably produced reprint of the *Accomplishment* whose apparently unique extant copy survives in the Armagh Robinson Library, for this displays substantive textual variation which cannot be put down to error or carelessness.[50] Where the authorised *Accomplishment* alleges that Partridge confessed on his deathbed that he was 'a Nonconformist', this reprint calls him '*a true believer*'; and where the original dismissed his chosen 'spiritual guide' as 'a fanatic preacher', the reprint respectfully calls him '*a Zealous Preacher*'. These softened expressions, utterly at variance with Swift's characteristic denigration of dissent, suggest a context in which the nonconformist interest was a force to be reckoned with. Although the piece carries the imprint 'London', it is much more likely to be an Irish reprint, and indeed bears several hallmarks of the work of Cornelius Carter, whose ongoing feud with the Whig almanac-maker John Whalley would have given him a strong personal and ideological motive for ridiculing Whalley's friend and former colleague Partridge. It would also have made it highly inadvisable (given Carter's regular brushes with the authorities for Catholic and Jacobite printing) for him to print Swift's flagrantly insulting references to dissenters (who were pressing for the abolition of the Test that it was Swift's purpose to maintain). Like most of Carter's work, this reprint is also striking for its poor quality, and vividly conjures, by its plethora of errors (including reversed letters, bizarre hyphenation, and random shifts to italic as roman type runs low), the hurry of a meagrely supplied and poorly organised print-shop. On the whole, however, Dublin participation in the hoax was paltry. Comparisons with the annual controversies of Ireland's own astrological community suggest that the predictions of death routinely arising from the drawing of nativities, coupled with

---

[50] *CWJS Parodies*, pp. 650–1.

84 Part II: London

endemic print rivalry among practitioners, meant that unrealised mutual predictions of death on the other side of the Irish Sea excited no particular interest.[51] Only much later, as Swift in the 1720s stood on the brink of his role as Drapier, would Dublin wits relate the Bickerstaff affair to Whalley's claims to have outlived a rival almanac-maker's prediction of his death.

Masks and Performances (1709)

By now, as print continued to stage its various evasions of Swift's responsibility for his works, the effect was often less to conceal his authorship than to flourish his refusal to admit it. At the other extreme from the extremely rare publications to which he openly set his name would be those supposedly written by characters like Isaac Bickerstaff, who, like his younger kinsmen Lemuel Gulliver (*Travels into Several Remote Nations of the World* (1726)) and Simon Wagstaff (*Polite Conversation* (1738)), declares his name, expresses a coherent ideology and recounts his individual experiences.[52] Such figures would do far more (and less) than conceal Swift's agency. Between the two extremes would lie not only the nameless but sharply realised authors of the *Tale, A Modest Proposal* and many smaller works, but also a team of relatively perfunctory stand-ins – nonce-figures whose characteristically earnest writings would tend to prove less than engaging to posterity.

Swift's Preface to the last volume of his Temple edition, which appeared in 1709 under Tooke's imprint as *Memoirs. Part III. From the Peace concluded 1679. To the time of the Author's Retirement from Publick Business. By Sir William Temple Baronet. Publish'd by Jonathan Swift, D.D.* was indeed the occasion for one of his rare performances as Jonathan Swift. Here, however, the role was not that of author but of editor and proprietor (for this final volume of the *Memoirs* was effectively part of his inheritance, and Tooke had paid him £40 for it).[53] The Preface, set in a size of italic type noticeably larger than the body of the work, expresses authority and self-confidence. The covering letter to the *Ode to the Athenian Society* had represented Jonathan Swift as much better placed than he actually was, and his Preface to *Letters written by Sir W. Temple* had

---

[51] For resemblances to established tropes of astrological controversy, see Rumbold, 'Ignoring Swift'.
[52] For the pioneering study, see William B. Ewald, *The Masks of Jonathan Swift* (Oxford: Blackwell, 1954).
[53] *Memoirs. Part III. From the Peace concluded 1679. To the Time of the Author's Retirement from Publick Business. By Sir William Temple Baronet. Publish'd by Jonathan Swift, D.D.* (London, 1709; TS 474, *ESTC* T146548); *Corr.*, vol. I, pp. 250–1.

Material Voices: The Bickerstaff Effect (1705–1710) 85

projected a Jonathan Swift exaggeratedly deferential to his elders and betters; but this 1709 farewell to the Temple edition instead throws down the gauntlet of outright defiance, accusing members of Temple's circle of meddling in editorial matters that they did not understand. The whiff of burning boats is unmistakeable: this was a manifesto with major implications, and as a print performance of authorial voice, it set a new standard for explicitness.

Although Swift had set off for Ireland by the time of publication, Tooke inscribed specially bound presentation copies on his behalf to Lords Pembroke, Somers, Sunderland and Halifax, which suggests that this publication had once again been conceived with an eye to preferment.[54] The volume, another well-produced octavo, has a full but clearly disposed title in roman and italic, divided by rules within a double-ruled frame. 'MEMOIRS' is set in the largest type, but the declaration of Temple's authorship and the ascription of publication to Swift are also set in the same size – although hierarchy is to a degree maintained by setting Temple's name in spaced large and small capitals and Swift's in lower-case italic. Between author and editor, however, is flourished a somewhat barbed epigraph from Pliny: 'Et Ille quidem plenus annis abiit, plenus honoribus, illis etiam quos recusavit' ('He died too when full of years and rich in honours, even those which he refused').[55] Temple's refusal to be further involved in affairs of state is framed as a reproof to those in power, anticipating the potential offence that Swift takes up in the first paragraph of his Preface:

> *It was perfectly in compliance to some Persons for whose Opinion I have great Deference, that I so long with-held the Publication of the following Papers. They seem'd to think, that the Freedom of Passages in these Memoirs, might give Offence to several who were still alive; and whose Part in those Affairs which are here related, could not be transmitted to Posterity with any Advantage to their Reputation. But, whether this Objection be in it self of much Weight, may perhaps be Disputed; at least it should have little with me, who am under no Restraint in that particular; Since I am not of an Age to remember those Transactions, nor had any Acquaintance with those Persons whose Counsels or Proceedings are Condemn'd, and who are all of them now Dead.*[56]

---

[54] *Corr.*, vol. I, p. 257. Rothschild no. 2408 is the copy presented to Sunderland (Nathaniel Mayer Victor, Baron Rothschild, *The Rothschild Library: A Catalogue of the Collection of Eighteenth-Century Printed Books and Manuscripts formed by Lord Rothschild*, 2 vols. (Cambridge University Press, 1954), vol. II, p. 649).

[55] Pliny the Younger, *Letters*, Book II.i, pp. 78–9. For Swift's editorial matter for the Temple edition, see *CWJS Tale*, pp. lxxxi–lxxxv, 189–209.

[56] *CWJS Tale*, p. 207.

Swift's vestigial '*Deference*' is quickly displaced by his own judgement, the justice of Temple's '*Freedom*' is assumed, and Swift, too young to have direct knowledge of the events and personalities concerned, presents himself as sole arbiter of what should now be published. His studied pose would be severely tested by the aggrieved response that followed.

What was at stake was Swift's position in relation to the Temples, his family's long-term patrons: the leading opponent of publication was Temple's sister, Lady Giffard, with whom Swift had exchanged letters (now no longer extant) in August 1709.[57] Having idolised her brother, she resented the publication of a text that differed from the original in her possession, and issued a public reproof on 6 October 1709 in the Baldwins' newspaper *The Post-Man*, declaring on behalf of Temple's 'Relations and Family' that the publication had been undertaken 'without their Consent and Knowledge', and that it was 'an unfaithful Copy' of writings intended only 'for the satisfaction of his Friends'.[58] (David Woolley points out that Swift's volume had previously been advertised in the paper, which was printed by his cousin, Dryden Leach.[59]) From a book-trade point of view, the controversy might have been seen as a further fillip to sales – although Tooke's response is unrecorded.

Despite the publicity of this attack, Swift, alerted by letters from concerned friends in England, replied only in a private letter, in which he averred that Lady Giffard's advertisement had been issued 'in order to ruin my Reputation'.[60] Although the hostile Abel Boyer would in 1714 argue that Swift's failure 'to vindicate himself in Print ... gives but too just ground to believe, that in order to curry Favour with those in Power, he may have *suppress'd, alter'd,* or *interpolated* some Passages', Swift's letter rather suggests exasperation at Lady Giffard's misunderstanding of her brother's editorial practice.[61] In sum, the argument was about choice of copy text, which Temple, and Swift after him, had based on final authorial intention, while Lady Giffard assumed the authority of an early text unaltered by later authorial revision. Swift declared that Temple had never sent original manuscripts to press, but transcripts updated with his later revisions. At the close of his letter Swift went further still, accusing

---

[57] For context, see Swift's letter to Lady Giffard of 10 November 1709 (*Corr.*, vol. I, pp. 270–4).

[58] For the wording of Lady Giffard's advertisement, see *Corr.*, vol. I, p. 266.

[59] *Ibid.*, pp. 251, 272.   [60] *Ibid.*, pp. 270–4.

[61] Abel Boyer (ed.), *Memoirs of the Life and Negotiations of Sir W. Temple, bar. Containing the most Important Occurrences, and the most Secret Springs of Affairs in Christendom, from the year 1665 to the year 1681. With an account of Sir W. Temple's writings* (London, 1714; *ESTC* T171819), pp. 383–4; *Corr.*, vol. I, p. 273.

Material Voices: The Bickerstaff Effect (1705–1710)

Lady Giffard of infringing his literary property by retaining original manuscripts and showing them to others, although 'they justly belonged to me'. She had thus, in his view, increased the danger of 'that uncorrect Original getting abroad', which 'made me publish mine'. Swift, convinced of the author's right to establish a revised text of his own works, and to bequeath the property in those works, asserted the norms of a textual culture of which Lady Giffard had no notion, vindicating the principle of final authorial intention that he would in the longer term apply to his own work.

But it was one thing for Swift to put his name to his performance as editor and proprietor, and quite another to stage his authorship of works that declared his growing political and ecclesiastical resentments. He now understood that the negotiation for the remission of the First Fruits with which he had been charged was going to be impossible without sacrificing the Test on which he believed the survival of his Church to depend, and, brushed aside by the Whig ministry, he moved decisively towards the kind of polemical writing that would in the 1720s find material expression through the deftly realised masks of the Drapier and Gulliver.[62] In *A Letter from a Member of the House of Commons in Ireland to a Member of the House of Commons in England, concerning the Sacramental Test* and *A Project for the Advancement of Religion, and the Reformation of Manners. By a Person of Quality* (both 1709) the Irish MP and the Person of Quality are not so much characters as see-through constructions. They facilitate frame-breaking performances which for the first time put before the public something of the 'saeva indignatio' for which Swift would later choose to be remembered.[63]

Given the expertise of Tooke's printers, there was no problem about producing pamphlets consistent with the status of such supposedly elite commentators. Like *Contests and Dissensions*, the *Letter . . . concerning the*

---

[62] For Swift's letter to Archbishop King of 10 June 1708, describing the meeting with Godolphin at which this was spelled out, see *Corr.*, vol. I, pp. 192–5. See Oliver W. Ferguson, *Jonathan Swift and Ireland* (Urbana, IL: University of Illinois Press, 1962), pp. 32–8; O'Regan, *Archbishop King*, pp. 164–5. For an overview of Swift's writings in defence of the Test, see Ian Higgins, 'A Preface to Swift's Test Act Tracts', in *Münster* (2013), pp. 226–43; Introduction to *CWJS English Political Writings, 1701–1711* (forthcoming).

[63] *A Letter from a Member of the House of Commons in Ireland to a Member of the House of Commons in England, concerning the Sacramental Test* (London, 1709; TS 511, *ESTC* T37830); *A Project for the Advancement of Religion, and the Reformation of Manners. By a Person of Quality* (London, 1709; TS 508, *ESTC* T37830). For 'saeva indignatio' in Swift's epitaph on himself, see Claude Rawson, 'Savage Indignation Revisited: Swift, Yeats, and the "Cry" of Liberty', in Claude Rawson (ed.), *Politics and Literature in the Age of Swift: English and Irish Perspectives* (Cambridge University Press, 2010), pp. 185–217.

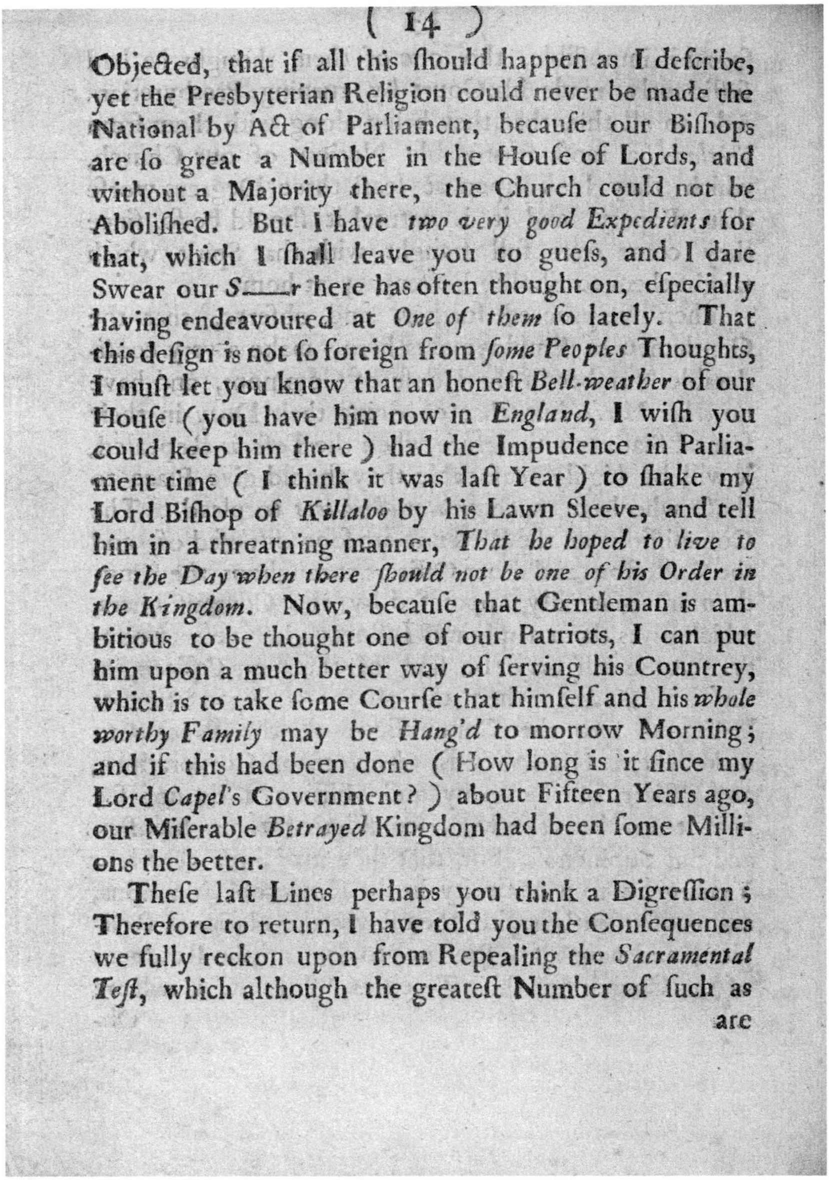

(14)

Objected, that if all this should happen as I describe, yet the Presbyterian Religion could never be made the National by Act of Parliament, because our Bishops are so great a Number in the House of Lords, and without a Majority there, the Church could not be Abolished. But I have *two very good Expedients* for that, which I shall leave you to guess, and I dare Swear our S——r here has often thought on, especially having endeavoured at *One of them* so lately. That this design is not so foreign from *some Peoples* Thoughts, I must let you know that an honest *Bell-weather* of our House (you have him now in *England*, I wish you could keep him there) had the Impudence in Parliament time (I think it was last Year) to shake my Lord Bishop of *Killaloo* by his Lawn Sleeve, and tell him in a threatning manner, *That he hoped to live to see the Day when there should not be one of his Order in the Kingdom*. Now, because that Gentleman is ambitious to be thought one of our Patriots, I can put him upon a much better way of serving his Countrey, which is to take some Course that himself and his *whole worthy Family* may be *Hang'd* to morrow Morning; and if this had been done (How long is it since my Lord *Capel*'s Government?) about Fifteen Years ago, our Miserable *Betrayed* Kingdom had been some Millions the better.

These last Lines perhaps you think a Digression; Therefore to return, I have told you the Consequences we fully reckon upon from Repealing the *Sacramental Test*, which although the greatest Number of such as
are

Figure 5 Jonathan Swift, *A Letter from a Member of the House of Commons in Ireland to a Member of the House of Commons in England, concerning the Sacramental Test* (London, 1709), p. 14.

Sacramental Test inhabited the established print genre of the quarto political pamphlet (though at only half the number of pages). The title, set almost entirely in roman, reserved its largest full capitals for the crucial words 'LETTER', 'IRELAND' and 'ENGLAND', but flourished '*SACRAMENTAL TEST*' in italic full capitals, pointing the controversy's confessional rather than merely political significance. At the foot, beneath a rule, Morphew's imprint complicated the trail of agency in familiar ways. In contrast, *A Project for the Advancement of Religion* adopted the format of an octavo pamphlet, this time running to a substantial sixty-two pages, and its exceptional use of Tooke's imprint connected the work much more obviously with Swift.[64] The title, framed and divided with rules, was elegant and well spaced; and roman full capitals of the largest size placed the emphasis firmly on the word 'PROJECT', while 'Advancement of Religion' and '*Reformation of Manners*' were set in somewhat smaller lower-case with capitalised nouns. The role of projector signalled by such a title, was not, however, an obvious fit for a Person of Quality.

Nevertheless, the issues on which each commentator took his stand were broadly compatible with traditional decorums. The persona of the Irish MP conferred a particular rhetorical advantage; for although extra-parliamentary appeals to public opinion were no longer the innovation that they had been when Swift's *Contests* had joined the paper war over the Tory attack on the Whig Lords, the exchange between the Irish MP and his English counterpart effectively located the discussion where such deliberations traditionally belonged. (Such an author might also be looked to for a view less partial than that of a clergyman defending his vested interests.) In the *Project for the Advancement of Religion* the Person of Quality played a comparable role, pitching his intervention at a social level well above Swift's own – which perhaps imparts a more plausible decorum to his regret that the Societies for the Reformation of Manners 'have dwindled into factious Clubs; and grown a Trade to enrich little knavish Informers of the meanest Rank'.[65] Indeed, the epigraph from Horace suggested that the author might be ambitious of even greater glory for the Queen on whom his plan depended (and indirectly for himself): '*O quisquis volet impias | Cædes, & rabiem tollere civicam: | Si quæret pater urbium | Subscribi statuis, indomitam audeat | Refrænare licentiam*' ('Whoever wants to get rid of unholy bloodshed and the madness of civic strife, if he aspires to having Father of Cities

---

[64] Treadwell, 'Swift's Relations', pp. 13, 15.   [65] *Project for the Advancement of Religion*, p. 44.

90   Part II: London

inscribed on his statues, oh let him have the courage to curb lawless license').[66] Steele's *Tatler* no. 5, supposedly reporting from Will's Coffee House in Holy Week 1709, jested that religion and reformation of manners were topics so unfamiliar to the wits as to make the pamphlet an intriguing novelty: 'The Title was so uncommon, and promis'd so peculiar a Way of Thinking, that every Man here has read it, and as many as have done so, have approv'd it.'[67] Notably, the essay grounded the pamphlet's positive reception in a genteel demeanour that set it above the enthusiastic excesses of 'unseasonable Passions': 'the Man writes much like a Gentleman, and goes to Heav'n with a very good Mien'. Steele's inside knowledge gives his connivance a particular piquancy.

These performances were wilfully intent on breaking the frame. The *Letter . . . concerning the Sacramental Test* was the first of Swift's published works to present an issue of public policy in terms of a High-Church defence of the Anglican establishment in Ireland: it used peculiarly visceral language to denounce the subordination of Irish to English interests ('if your little Finger be Sore, and you think a Poltice made of our *Vitals* will give it any Ease, speak the Word and it shall be done'); and it attacked influential advocates of the repeal in highly personal terms (the lawyer Thomas Brodrick, brother of Alan Brodrick, Speaker of the Irish parliament, was informed that the best contribution he could make to Ireland's well-being 'is to take some Course that himself and his *whole worthy Family* may be *Hang'd* to morrow Morning': Figure 5).[68] Swift had also inserted a prominent compliment to his own Archbishop; and with a characteristic mingling of slander, praise and sheer obfuscation, he dwelt misleadingly on his own situation both as slighted cleric and as triumphant author:

> As for the *other Divine*, we all expected here that He was to be the Person his Excellency would bring over his Chaplain: But since that hath otherwise happened, it may not be altogether improbable that his great Friends have dropp'd him, which Disappointment, if he be a right C—t—r [i.e. Courtier] may chance to cool his Zeal that way, if he had any before, of which I cannot accuse him. However that be, he will find it a difficult matter, with his Skill in Politicks, or Talent at Ridicule, backed by all the Wit he is said to be Master of, to Reason or Laugh us out of the *Sacramental Test*; and will find by the Event that my PREDICTIONS are truer than His.[69]

---

[66] Horace, *Odes*, Book III, no. 24, ll. 25–9.   [67] Bond, *Tatler*, no. 5, vol. I, pp. 47–8.
[68] *Letter . . . concerning the Sacramental Test*, p. 9.   [69] *Ibid.*, pp. 18–19; *Corr.*, vol. I, p. 227.

A Project for the Advancement of Religion similarly manifested a preoccupation with clerical life that was arguably ill-suited to the loftier viewpoint of a Person of Quality. The clergy were criticised for 'affecting so much to converse with each other, and caring so little to mingle with the Laity'; the clerical gown was said to bring scandal on the Church 'as long as any scandalous Persons appear in that Dress'; and supporters of the current administration were decried as merely the kind of Whig who 'rattles it out against *Popery* and *arbitrary Power*, and *Priest-craft*, and *High-Church*'.[70] Suspicions of clerical authorship could only have been strengthened by the dedication to the Countess of Berkeley, whose chaplain Swift had been – which rendered particularly tactless his contemptuous comments on clergy seen 'sneaking out of some Person of Quality's House, where they are hired by the Lady at Ten Shillings a Month'.[71] In fact the whole business of a dedication gave the Person of Quality some difficulty: he told the Countess that he was not seeking 'after the common Form, to desire Your Protection of the following Papers', claimed unconvincingly that they were 'inscribed to Your Ladyship ... without Your Knowledge, and from a concealed Hand', and closed with the compliment that 'I declare this to be no Dedication, but properly an Introduction to a Proposal for the Advancement of Religion and Morals, by tracing, however imperfectly, some few Lineaments in the Character of a Lady who hath spent all her Life in the Practice and promotion of both.'[72] The Person of Quality, it appeared, was not really writing a dedication at all – although Swift clearly was.[73]

Behind-the-scenes correspondence reveals, as the publications do not, the strings that were being pulled by and on behalf of Swift. Both Swift and King, mindful of government surveillance, avoided confirming Swift's authorship of the *Letter ... concerning the Sacramental Test*, and King warned him of the risk of 'warm entertainment'.[74] (A contemporary has indeed recorded on the title of the Rothschild copy: 'Supposed Author – Mr Swift'.[75]) The *Project for the Advancement of Religion*, on the other hand, was evidently seen as a potential step to preferment, and Berkeley seems to have gone so far as to approach the Archbishop of Canterbury on Swift's behalf, though without success.[76] Both pamphlets also contributed to the further proliferation of Swift in print by prompting reprints. In Dublin the

---

[70] *Project for the Advancement of Religion*, pp. 31, 36, 60.   [71] *Ibid.*, pp. 32–3.   [72] *Ibid.*, pp. 6–7.
[73] *Ibid.*, pp. 3–4.   [74] *Corr.*, vol. I, p. 233.
[75] Rothschild no. 1999 (*The Rothschild Library*, vol. II, p. 545).
[76] *Corr.*, vol. I, p. 252. For Swift's opposition to religious dissent as a probable block to his promotion by Whig patrons, see Introduction to *CWJS English Political Writings, 1701–1711* (forthcoming).

Letter ... concerning the Sacramental Test, 'Price One Penny', lacked a separate title page and was crammed onto eight small quarto pages, shifting mid-sentence to even smaller type on the last.[77] The publication information in the colophon, which was squashed in, with the price, right under the final line of text, was distinctly evasive ('Re-printed in *Dublin*, and Sold by the Booksellers'), and ellipses were used to replace dangerous references to the Brodricks, the 'lay Lords' who might take a bribe to vote with the government, and the representative 'C—t—r' to whom Swift would be comparable if he changed sides out of self-interest. Such omissions, while no doubt prudent, implicitly challenged readers to guess the missing words – or, indeed, to seek out the London original. Meanwhile the *Project for the Advancement of Religion* was picked up in London by Hills: cramming the text into a mere three sheets by reducing the format to octavo and the page-count to twenty-four, he tagged his imprint 'For the Benefite of the Poor', probably to encourage bulk purchase for free distribution.[78] The *Project* was also reprinted that year in Edinburgh as a slightly more expansive octavo, 'by the Heirs and Successors of Andrew Anderson, Printer to the Queens most Excellent Majesty', an imprint that associated the piece, if only tangentially, with the Queen on whom the execution of the project relied – since it called upon her to make dubious conduct a bar to her service.[79] Later, when Swift incorporated these two pamphlets into his authorised collections, he would, like Temple, make strategic changes.

Issues of screening and anonymity were also manifested in the printed forms of Swift's poems in this period, as a series of accomplished comic poems began to come to press which proved much more saleable than the earlier Pindaric odes: James Woolley dates to 1709 'Swift's first conspicuous success as a publisher of popular poems'.[80] Typically printed without their author's name, they nevertheless appeared in an impressive major anthology and a ground-breaking periodical, as well as at lower levels of the market. This first efflorescence of Swift's printed verse reflected an energetic and largely positive engagement with London's literary and print networks in these years: as Karian points out, this 'concentration of poems

---

[77] *A Letter from a Member of the House of Commons in Ireland, to a Member of the House of Commons in England, concerning the Sacramental Test* (Dublin, [1709]; TS 512, *ESTC* T1867).

[78] *A Project for the Advancement of Religion, and the Reformation of Manners* (London, 1709; TS 509, *ESTC* T44578).

[79] *A Project for the Advancement of Religion, and the Reformation of Manners* (Edinburgh, 1709; TS 510, *ESTC* T176676). For the work's emphasis on royal rather than parliamentary power, see Introduction to *CWJS English Political Writings, 1701–1711* (forthcoming).

[80] James Woolley, 'Swift's Most Popular Poems', in *Münster* (2013), pp. 367–82 (p. 368).

Material Voices: The Bickerstaff Effect (1705–1710) 93

that Swift quickly published' contrasts markedly with his more usual lifetime habit of retaining verse for long-term manuscript circulation, especially after his withdrawal from London in 1713.[81]

It was indeed Swift's friendship with Steele that facilitated the complimentary presentation in the *Tatler* of *A Description of the Morning* and *A City Shower*: Bickerstaff, now seconded to Steele as writer of his periodical, attributed them to 'an Ingenious Kinsman of mine, of the Family of the *Staffes*, Mr. *Humphrey Wagstaff* by Name', thus further developing a print dynasty which would in 1738 be joined by Simon Wagstaff, the supposed author of Swift's *Polite Conversation*.[82] Swift's standing among literary Whigs also facilitated the publication of two poems, *Baucis and Philemon: Imitated from Ovid* and *On Mrs. Biddy Floyd*, in what would prove to be the landmark anthology of the age, *Poetical Miscellanies: The Sixth Part. Containing a Collection of Original Poems, with several New Translations. By the most Eminent Hands* (1709).[83] While both poems were available in other editions, it was in *Poetical Miscellanies* that they achieved their most elegant material form. Yet, unlike many contributions, Swift's poems predictably appeared without their author's name.

Poetical Miscellanies was the latest addition to 'Tonson's Miscellany', a landmark enterprise by the bookseller Jacob Tonson the elder (1655/6–1736), one of the inherited Temple booksellers whom Swift had in 1701 replaced by Tooke. The project, formerly edited by Swift's cousin Dryden (prime beneficiary of Tonson's innovative crafting of collected reprints as English classics), was now under the care of the Whig poet and playwright Nicholas Rowe; and it is a sign of Swift's insider status that when he wrote to Ambrose Philips on 8 March 1709 he knew both the production schedule and the fact that Philips's pastorals would take pride of place 'at the Head'.[84] The book, an octavo of more than 700 pages, was amply spaced and styled with easy elegance, retaining initial capitals for most nouns, but disdaining intensive italicisation. The title page recalled the

---

[81] Karian, 'Swift as Manuscript Poet', pp. 33–5.
[82] The former appeared in *Tatler* no. 9 (Bond, *Tatler*, vol. I, pp. 80–1), the latter in no. 238 (vol. III, pp. 225–7). See *CWJS Poems* I (forthcoming). For the *City Shower* in its material context, see Janine Barchas, *Graphic Design, Print Culture, and the Eighteenth-Century Novel* (Cambridge University Press, 2003), pp. 1–6 (but for attribution of *Tatler* no. 21, see *CWJS Parodies*, Appendix G, p. 586). For the suggestion that the two poems may have been included in Dublin reprints, no longer extant, by Ann Sandys, see Craig Francis Pett, '"I am no inconsiderable Shop-Keeper in this Town": Swift and his Dublin Printers of the 1720s: Edward Waters, John Harding and Sarah Harding' (PhD dissertation, Monash University, 2015), p. 37.
[83] London, 1709; TS 520, *ESTC* T142876. See also *CWJS Poems* I (forthcoming).
[84] *Corr.*, vol. I, p. 239.

94 Part II: London

volume's illustrious heritage by advertising that at Tonson's shop '*you may
have the Five former Parts*'; and a lavishly engraved frontispiece, depicting
a trumpeting putto waving a palm over the head of a laurel-crowned muse,
celebrated the creativity of the age. Gaining entry to his much-maligned
cousin Dryden's miscellany by a posthumous back door may have been
gratifying in itself for Swift; but even he could hardly have anticipated just
how famous this volume would become. With Pope's *Pastorals* as an
integrated but discrete set of gatherings at the end, more poems by Pope
in the body of the book, and the rival *Pastorals* of Ambrose Philips at the
front, the volume both launched Pope's career and adumbrated its framing
tensions. Soon, as Swift himself turned towards the Tories and former ties
to Whig writers faded, Pope too would become a friend.[85]

The volume's ambitions were underlined by the range of translation
projects represented: Rowe, the editor, contributed samples from Lucan,
Pope from Homer and Chaucer, and Joseph Trapp from Virgil and Ovid.
These took their place among work by other writers destined in various
ways to make their mark on literary culture: Anne Finch, Countess of
Winchilsea; the future Whig Poet Laureate, Laurence Eusden; and
Addison's protégé and future editor, Thomas Tickell. In Tonson's Whig-
dominated array Pope was something of an anomaly, and the crypto-
Jacobite Finch even more so; but both would be important to Swift. For
the moment, however, he earned his place by offering affectionately witty
poems well adapted to the Tonson universe: *On Mrs. Biddy Floyd* even had
the honour of being accompanied by a translation into Latin '*by another
Hand*'.

The material texts of *Baucis and Philemon* and *On Mrs. Biddy Floyd*
illuminate significant issues for the development of Swift in print. The
Poetical Miscellanies text of the former has often been read as demonstrating the (negative) impact of Addison's politely Whiggish mode; and Swift
himself seems to have spread the view that his original had been subjected
to radical correction.[86] Yet J. Woolley and Karian also suggest, from their
wider analysis of his poems' manuscript and printed texts, that Swift's
practice can be seen less as a teleological movement from intermediate to
final intentions than as a pattern of ongoing experimentation, a view that
might also help to contextualise his tolerance of at least some apparently
unauthorised printings of his work. A case in point, in 1710, was an octavo
pamphlet that included both of the *Poetical Miscellanies* poems, published

[85] *Ibid.*, pp. 198–9, 207, 210, 238.
[86] See 'Baucis and Philemon (manuscript version)', in *CWJS Poems* I (forthcoming).

Material Voices: The Bickerstaff Effect (1705–1710) 95

by the disreputable print entrepreneur Edmund Curll.[87] (Never a member of the Stationers' Company, Curll was an effective collaborator with those who were, and would bring to Swift's work a degree of opportunism that Swift at best questionably approved.) Entitled *A Meditation upon a Broomstick, and somewhat beside; of the same Author's*, Curll's 1710 offering was the first edition of the *Meditation* (a mock-devotional work apparently devised to play a practical joke on the Countess of Berkeley).[88] His formula '*of the same Author's*', which raised the issue of attribution without offering to resolve it, nevertheless posited common authorship and consolidated the new with the already familar.[89] He noted on his own copy: 'Given me by John Cliffs Esq; who had them of the Bp. of Kilalla in Ireland, whose Daughter he married & was my Lodger'; and although verification of these details is problematic, Karian concludes that Curll probably did regard his source as authoritative, and may even have hoped (if vainly) 'to curry favour with Swift' – who certainly used Curll's text as copy for later authorised publications.[90]

Alongside Curll, many others would from now on be reprinting, repackaging and responding to Swift poems, confirming their attractiveness to a wide readership: parodies, allusions and imitations were printed in response to *On Mrs. Biddy Floyd*, while *Baucis and Philemon* was issued alongside the work of noted earlier poets.[91] Publishers of unauthorised London texts might take as copy a manuscript that had escaped the author's control, or a printed text whose copy they did not own. An accomplished pirate of the latter kind was Hills, who was in this period persistently drawn to published work by Swift, and in 1709–10 produced a lightly varied sequence of little collections that included poetry. Particularly revealing are the advertised contents of the version haphazardly printed in 1710 as *Bavcis and Philemon: A Poem on the Ever-lamented Loss of the two Yew-Trees, in the Parish of Chilthorne, near the Count-Town [sic] of Somerset. Together with Mrs. Harris's Earnest Petition: and an Admirable Recipe. By the Author of the Tale of a Tub. As also an Ode upot [sic] Solitude: by the Earl of Roscommon.*[92] The attribution to '*the Author of the Tale of a Tub*' (though not immediately fixed on Swift on the work's

---

[87] P. Rogers, 'The Uses of the Miscellany'; Baines and Rogers, *Curll*, pp. 45–7.

[88] *CWJS Parodies*, pp. 635–7; Stephen Karian, 'Edmund Curll and the Circulation of Swift's Writings', in *Münster* (2008), pp. 99–129 (pp. 99, 117–21).

[89] *CWJS Parodies*, pp. 1–15, 635–9; P. Rogers, 'The Uses of the Miscellany', p. 99.

[90] Curll's copy is BL C.28.b.11 (5); *Corr.*, vol. I, p. 391.   [91] *CWJS Poems* I (forthcoming).

[92] Foxon S802; *ESTC* N46570; 'Baucis and Philemon (printed version)', in *CWJS Poems* I (forthcoming).

96   Part II: London

first publication in 1704) by now signalled Swift's fame effectively enough,
at the same time associating him with precisely what he was most reluctant
to own; and in Roscommon he was keeping distinguished title-page
company; but the *Admirable Recipe* is in fact more plausibly ascribed to
his young protégé William Harrison.[93] This is an early instance of the
blurring of the Swift canon facilitated by the author's refusal to own his
work. In future it would be almost impossible to weigh up Swift's contribution to print debate with absolute confidence in the authorship of the
texts involved.

Elaborating the *Tale* (1710)

Swift in print was now being disseminated across a wide range of price and
quality, stretching (if the unpublished *Answer to Bickerstaff* is to be
believed) all the way from halfpenny reprints of penny Bickerstaff papers
to the dignified amplitude of Tonson's *Poetical Miscellanies*. In 1710,
however, in a London market where in Robert Hume's analysis 'relatively
few books were priced above 2s.' and '6s. represented a normal top price for
a book for which substantial sales were anticipated', a volume entirely
devoted to Swift was about to be published at the ambitious price of 8s.[94] It
was necessarily addressed to a very small elite: Hume estimates that 'no
more than about 5 percent of the total population of England and Wales
could have had the discretionary spending capacity to indulge significantly
in the purchase of elite culture', and that 'most of our 5 percent (and
probably a moderate number of others) could indulge in relatively cheap
books or amusements but could not regularly afford expensive ones'.[95]
This, the fifth edition of *A Tale of a Tub*, was definitely one of the expensive
ones. Widely deemed objectionable, the *Tale* had continued to sell through
four editions, and had from 1708 begun to be recognised as Swift's work:
now, with his help, Tooke prepared a much elaborated fifth edition,
featuring an Apology, commentary and illustrations, and including some
copies on large paper.[96] This was another milestone for Swift in print, the
first work to be deliberately upgraded and remarketed by the owner of the

---

[93] The 'Admirable Recipe' is best known from *Tatler* no. 2 (Bond, *Tatler*, vol. I, pp. 23–7). For further
attributions to 'the Author of the Tale', see TS, pp. 189–91. For earlier mistakes about the work's
author, and for the *Admirable Recipe*, see J. Woolley and Karian's introduction to deattributed
poems, and their discussion of the *Admirable Recipe*, in *CWJS Poems* IV (forthcoming).

[94] Robert D. Hume, 'The Economics of Culture in London, 1660–1740', *HLQ*, 69.4 (2006), 487–533
(p. 509), citing data for 1709.

[95] *Ibid.*, p. 497.

[96] Karian, 'Edmund Curll', pp. 113–14. For large-paper copies, see D. Woolley, 'Swift's Copy', p. 133.

Material Voices: The Bickerstaff Effect (1705–1710)   97

copy after first publication, and the first to include commentary and illustration. Tooke and Motte created a sophisticated product of modestly robust quality, very different from Tonson's more obviously aspirational model of the English classic, but far more appropriate to an author increasingly intent on obfuscating the authorship of his most celebrated work.

The Apology to the new edition, although plainly flagged on the title as 'the Author's', now deployed yet another distancing device: this time the author of the Apology spoke of the author of the *Tale* in the third person, flirting repeatedly with a mystery which the author of the *Tale* reportedly regarded as '*no disagreeable Amusement either to the Publick or himself*'; and in the Postscript to the Apology he conjured, as the alleged agent of the '*Chasms*' which '*appear under the Name of* Desiderata', a phantom '*Gentleman*', '*a Friend of the Author*', '*who gave the Copy to the Bookseller*'.[97] It was relatively easy to rebut the suggestion '*that the Author is dead*' (a hint at Temple), or to decline the relatively flattering misattribution of *A Letter concerning Enthusiasm* (actually by Anthony Ashley Cooper, Earl of Shaftesbury); but Curll's *Complete Key to the Tale of a Tub* presented a much more problematic blend of revelation and error.[98] According to Curll, it was reputed that the *Tale* had not one author, but two, 'Generally (and not without sufficient Reason) said to be Dr. *Jonathan* and *Thomas Swift*'. Swift wrote to Tooke of his outrage at Curll's 'publishing names in so bold a manner', exclaiming that 'I wish some lawyer could advise you how I might have satisfaction: For, at this rate, there is no book, however so vile, which may not be fastened on me'; and he advised Tooke to challenge 'that little Parson-cousin of mine' to make good his claim: 'you ought to tell him gravely, that, if he be the author, he should set his name to the &c; . . . And tell him, if he can explain some things, you will, if he pleases, set his name to the next edition.'[99]

Phiddian discerns in this letter 'a surprising and utterly pointless degree of evasiveness' (although Swift, like Tooke, was well aware that the Irish mail was under close surveillance), and judges that his evasions, neither effective nor in

---

[97] *CWJS Tale*, pp. 14–15.

[98] *Ibid.*, pp. 12, 7. For Shaftesbury's *A Letter concerning Enthusiasm, to my Lord* ***** (London, 1708), see p. 321, and *Corr.*, vol. I, pp. 207–8. In addition to some striking if ultimately misleading similarities of approach (Swift described it as 'free Whiggish thinking'), it was, like the *Tale*, dedicated to Somers, and, like *Predictions*, bore Morphew's imprint. For Curll's *Complete Key to the Tale of a Tub* (London, 1710), see *CWJS Tale*, Appendix C, pp. 233–51 (the text here cited), and for the controversy about Thomas Swift's claimed authorship, pp. 236–7; and see also Baines and Rogers, *Curll*, pp. 45–7.

[99] *Corr.*, vol. I, p. 282; *CWJS Tale*, pp. 213–14.

98 Part II: London

all probability seriously intended to be, show Swift 'petulantly determined that the work should not be mis-ascribed even at the same time as he was too nervous even to write its name'.[100] Both in print and in person Swift ostentatiously went through the motions of barring the stable door long after the horse had bolted; the hardest of all voices for Swift to pitch in print was in effect the one closest to the 'psychological uneasiness' that Phiddian discerns around the compulsively unacknowledged *Tale*.[101] Indeed, in the printed volume, the Apology would still be headed 'An Apology / For the, &c.', using the selfsame euphemism that Swift had used in late 1708 or early 1709 in private notes towards a miscellany of his own, and in his letter to Tooke.[102] He also paraphrased that private letter for public consumption, producing what became the Postscript to the Apology.[103] Here he declared that '*certain Names*' assigned in the *Key* were '*utterly wrong*' and that '*the whole Work, is entirely of one Hand*', and concluded with a challenge to anyone '*who will prove his Claim to three Lines in the whole Book*' to '*step forth*', provide '*his Name and Titles*' for '*the next Edition*', and '*be acknowledged the undisputed Author*'. (M. Walsh concludes that any contribution by Thomas Swift was slight: despite early promise, he could no longer compete with his cousin either in terms of advancement or authorship.[104]) Yet compared to the triumphant crafting of Bickerstaff – a relatively joyous, even throw-away *jeu d'esprit* – the difficulty of the performance is obvious. This, after all, was both the work whose author '*hath all along concealed himself from his nearest Friends*', and the one proclaimed to be '*calculated to live at least as long as our language, and our Tast admit no great Alterations*'.[105] It was, and would remain, a problematic conjunction.

Tooke seems once again to have commissioned Motte as printer, and the resulting octavo was well produced: once again the *Tale* presented in its verbal text, but did not substantially mimic in its material construction, the slipshod disorder of the processes that Swift asserted as the modern norm.[106] This was indeed the text that would shape the work's later

---

[100] Phiddian, *Swift's Parody*, p. 177. [101] *CWJS Tale*, pp. xxxix–xli.
[102] Ehrenpreis, *Swift*, vol. II, pp. 768–9. [103] *CWJS Tale*, pp. 14–15.
[104] *Ibid.*, pp. xli–xlvi. Thomas Swift's career seems to have been safe but undistinguished, with only one published work extant: *Noah's Dove. An Earnest Exhortation to peace: Set forth in a sermon Preach'd on the 7th of November, 1710. A Thanksgiving-Day. By Tho. Swift, M.A. formerly Chaplain to Sir William Temple, now Rector of Puttenham in Surrey* (London, 1710; *ESTC* T43126). Swift wryly noted in 1711 that a second edition was being advertised as '*Dr. Swift's Sermon*' (*CWJS Journal*, p. 318): it does not seem to have been published.
[105] *CWJS Tale*, pp. 5, 7.
[106] *Ibid.*, pp. 289–90; Bullard and McLaverty, 'Introduction', pp. 10–11; TS 222; and for Motte's printing of the first four editions, see Chapter 2.

Material Voices: The Bickerstaff Effect (1705–1710)

reception, becoming the routine choice of copy text for succeeding editions – exactly as Temple's former secretary would have expected. Effectively curated for posterity by the Apology (which Swift had formerly considered placing in a miscellany of his shorter works), the volume was now adorned by eight engravings, beginning with the famous frontispiece of the ship, the tub and the whale, facing a title that draws attention to the addition of 'the Author's Apology and Explanatory Notes. By *W. W—tt—n*, B.D. and others'.[107] Yet there were arguably losses too: the positioning of the frontispiece meant that 'Treatises wrote by the same Author', which had formerly faced the title, lost something of its effrontery in its move to the verso; and the gravity of the Apology that now commanded the threshold cast a more sombre shadow over the work's high spirits.

But at least as important as the Apology in its curation of the work was the new commentary, approved and probably compiled by Swift from the publications of his detractors, and presented in the form of footnotes. This allusion to the conventions of the modern learned book constituted a visual as well as discursive appropriation, and the *mise-en-page* now seems so intrinsic to the satire that it might be tempting to assume that Swift had designed it. But when Tooke wrote to Swift in Dublin, asking him to return his corrections to the Apology and 'this Key' (the authorised commentary), he made it clear that the footnotes were his idea, not Swift's:

> What I beg of you at present is, that you would return the Apology and this Key, with directions for the placing it: Although I am entirely of opinion to put it at the bottom of each page; yet shall submit. If this be not done soon, I cannot promise but some rascal or other will do it for us both; since you see the Liberty that is already taken.[108]

Swift evidently accepted his bookseller's suggestion. While the first edition, with its neatly inset marginal references, had adopted a print variant of the marginal commentary of earlier manuscript tradition, this fifth edition embedded the work even more firmly in the culture of scholarly print by adding the newer apparatus of footnotes. Although Bullard and McLaverty note that this was 'a difficult task, with the footnotes added to an already side-noted and complex text', Motte had long experience in manipulating two independent sequences of annotation, as instanced in his reprinting of

---

[107] For 'Subjects for a Volume', see SwJ 437; Ehrenpreis, *Swift*, vol. II, pp. 768–9; *CWJS Parodies*, p. 623. Swift may have suggested the subjects for illustration, and his friend Sir Andrew Fountaine was actively involved; but it is unclear who paid for the engraving (*CWJS Tale*, pp. xxxv–xxxvi; cf. *Corr.*, vol. I, pp. 283–5; Bullard and McLaverty, 'Introduction', pp. 10–11).

[108] *Corr.*, vol. I, pp. 284–5; *CWJS Tale*, p. 214.

Part II: London

Delphin Classics, where marginal 'Interpretatio' was separated from the text by a vertical rule and explanatory notes appeared at the foot.[109] The footnotes to the *Tale* would famously commandeer Swift's would-be critics to frame his satire – in a coup that Pope would imitate in his 1729 and 1743 *Dunciads*.[110] But Tooke's letter is particularly significant, showing that the initiative came not from Swift but from his bookseller; and in this light it seems fully appropriate to the high price and ambition of the new edition – as well as profoundly expressive for readers.[111] On 10 April 1710, the day that the new Copyright Act came into effect, Tooke seems to have been the first bookseller to make a block registration of his holdings with the Stationers' Company.[112] (Tonson, whose long list includes the Temple copies that he had acquired before Swift's move to Tooke, came in second.) The very first item on Tooke's list was the new *Tale*, 'with an Apology and also Annotation, of the Learned D^r. W. W. and others'. Now, in all its elaborated complexity, the *Tale* was officially a piece of literary property; and it was immediately followed on Tooke's list by Swift's *Miscellanies in Prose and Verse*. For this collection, which Tooke had in hand at the same time and would publish in 1711, he also provided a detailed list of contents, further testifying to the importance that he set on his Swift holdings.

Only after the fifth edition of the *Tale* was in print did Tooke produce something closer to what Swift first seems to have had in mind, a pamphlet-style supplement containing the Apology and notes alone – ideal, perhaps, for owners of the first four editions who might have been reluctant to repurchase the whole book.[113] (Unlike the fifth edition itself, which continued to carry Nutt's imprint, this smaller publication properly substituted Morphew's, in recognition that Nutt had passed the business over to him in 1706.[114]) Yet the fact that only a single copy seems now to be

---

[109] For imprints naming Benjamin Motte as printer of texts featuring both side-notes and footnotes, see *M. Valerii Martialis epigrammatum libri XIV. Interpretatione & notis illustravit Vincentius Collesso J.C. jussu Christianissimi Regis, ad usum Serenissimi Delphini* (London, 1701; *ESTC* T94265); *P. Terentii carthaginensis Afri Comoediæ sex. Interpretatione & notis illustravit Nicolaus Camus, J. U. D. Jussu Christianissimi Regis, in usum serenissimi Delphini. Juxta editionem novissimam parisiensem* (London, 1709; *ESTC* T137042).

[110] See, for instance, Phiddian, *Swift's Parody*, p. 111.   [111] *CWJS Tale*, p. xxxv.

[112] This unpaginated sequence of April 1710 registrations is physically separate from the main sequence for 1710–46. The clerk turned upside down a part-used book from the previous century (Liber G) and started using up the blanks from the back, so that the first page of the new entries, on which Tooke's entry begins, is the last page in the book (*SCEBC*, Liber G (unpaginated)). See Karian, *Print and Manuscript*, p. 16; D. Woolley, 'Swift's Copy', pp. 133, 169; and for Tooke's re-registration of *Miscellanies in Prose and Verse* on 23 February 1711, see Chapter 4.

[113] *An Apology for the Tale of a Tub. With explanatory notes by W. W-tt-n, B. D. And others* (London, 1711; TS 223, *ESTC* T196680); *CWJS Tale*, pp. 279–80.

[114] *CWJS Tale*, p. xxxiii, and see Chapter 4.

Material Voices: The Bickerstaff Effect (1705–1710)

extant is far from suggesting a large-scale appeal to readerly parsimony. Instead, Tooke seems to have decided that he could sell at least as many copies of the elaborated fifth edition as he had of the first: *ESTC* records seventy-seven extant copies of the first edition, fifty-four of the second, fifty-six of the third, fifty-six of the fourth, and no fewer than eighty-one of the fifth.[115] All in all, the revised *Tale*, built on the established strengths of the first four editions, remained uncompromised by any parodic disruption of its fundamental structure. The pagination of the fifth edition still began on the first recto of signature B with the 'Dedicatory Epistle to Prince Posterity'; signatures B and C were still devoted to this piece and to the succeeding Preface; the *Tale* proper still started on the first recto of D with the Introduction; and *The Mechanical Operation of the Spirit* still began part-way through a signature.

This new edition of the *Tale* and its companion pieces represented an effective canonisation of Swift's most outstanding work to date, although his lifelong refusal to allow the *Tale* to be grouped with the rest of his works would still pose long-term problems.[116] At the same time Tooke also had in press the *Miscellanies*, another dignified but anonymous octavo, which would set in train the canonisation of the shorter works. The next phase of Swift in print would be increasingly shaped by tensions not only between masking and self-revelation, but also between the demands of the moment and longer-term ambitions.

---

[115] Numbers of copies reflect *ESTC* listings as of 11 October 2016; for *ESTC* numbers and bibliographical descriptions, see *CWJS Tale*, pp. 283–90.

[116] For posthumous consequences, see Andrew Carpenter, 'Reading Swift's *Works* in Dublin in the 1750s', in Kirsten Juhas, Patrick Müller and Mascha Hansen (eds.), *'The First Wit of the Age': Essays on Swift and his Contemporaries in Honour of Hermann J. Real* (Frankfurt am Main: Peter Lang, 2013), pp. 117–31 (pp. 126–7).

CHAPTER 4

Politics and Permanence
Miscellanies, *Politics and a* Proposal *Declined*
(1710–1714)

With Swift's recruitment in London as propaganda writer for the new Tory ministry headed by Robert Harley (1661–1724; Earl of Oxford from 1711) and Henry St John (1678–1751; Viscount Bolingbroke from 1712), Swift in print quickly moved into a context where 'the pamphlets and half-sheets grow so upon our hands, it will very well employ a man every day from morning till night to read them', countering the Whigs by defending traditional views of church and state and pressing for an end to the War of the Spanish Succession.[1] Anonymous papers and pamphlets by Swift, sharply focused on the issues of the day, began to pour in unprecedented numbers from the London press – and even today it is not always clear what was by Swift and what by others.[2] Yet these same years also produced a contrasting handful of Swift publications, not always quite so rigorously distanced from their author, whose greater material ambition suggested longer-term aspirations. From the English deanery or bishopric (ideally supplemented by the post of Historiographer Royal) to which Swift hoped to be preferred by a grateful Queen and ministry, he dreamed of celebrating their virtues to a long posterity – but his hopes came to nothing in 1713–14 as the ministers quarrelled and the Queen died. Meanwhile, authorial anonymity and masking, reinforced by misleading, incomplete or absent imprints, conjured from Swift's single pen an ostensible army of ministerial partisans. Such expedients protected the author in the short term, but they also impeded longer-term consolidation by separating the works both from each other and from their author. In contrast, a few more ambitious publications began to foster the beginnings of an authorial

---

[1] *Corr.*, vol. I, p. 295. For the political issues of these years, see *CWJS Journal*, Appendix A, pp. 543–58; *CWJS English Political Writings, 1711–1714*, pp. 1–43, and (for Oxford and Bolingbroke), Biographical Index, pp. 632, 669–70.

[2] For an important review, see David Woolley, 'The Canon of Swift's Prose Pamphleteering, 1710–1714, and *The New Way of Selling Places at Court*', *SStud*, 3 (1988), 96–117; see also individual works in *CWJS* volumes.

Politics and Permanence (1710–1714)

profile – which even involved, in the exceptional case of *A Proposal for Correcting, Improving and Ascertaining the English Tongue* (1712), setting Swift's name explicitly to his published scheme. Meanwhile, the apparently ephemeral half sheets and pamphlets of this period (into which Swift claimed to the soldier and diplomat Charles Mordaunt, Earl of Peterborough, that 'wit and learning' had 'crumbled') would also make a contribution to Swift's permanent fame, not only by their later inclusion in collected editions, but more immediately by their transmission into Irish print networks.[3] In the future that Swift would actually have (rather than the one he vainly hoped for), it was from this network of Dublin reprinters that the publishers of his Irish tracts would emerge in the 1720s.

All this made 1711–14 a period of tensions. For Swift himself there were tensions between his old identification with the Whigs and his new co-operation with the Tories, between his hope of English preferment and the reality of a Dublin deanery, and between the ministry's immediate needs and his own longer-term aspirations (not helped by Harley's much-resented attempts to give him money).[4] For Swift in print, this quandary played out in the contrast between ephemeral publications whose material origins were obscured, and those that signalled more permanent ambition. Of the two formats that dominated this phase, the half sheet and the octavo, only the octavo lent itself to both.

The material texts of this period are slow to reveal the subterfuges of their making. Swift in print was now entering the London market through two different channels: one was via Tooke, who remained Swift's personal bookseller; and the other was via John Barber (1675–1741), a skilled and ambitious printer (if somewhat aloof from conventional progression through the Stationers' Company), who was recruited by the ministry to print their propaganda.[5] Hence Tooke remained associated with Swift's more conventionally ambitious work, while Barber printed most of the propaganda.[6] Swift saw them both frequently, meeting them for meals as

---

[3] *Corr.*, vol. I, p. 335. For Swift's aspirations to fame, see also A. C. Kelly, *Jonathan Swift and Popular Culture*, pp. 34–7.

[4] *CWJS Journal*, pp. 134–5, 156, 250.

[5] Bullard and McLaverty, 'Introduction', pp. 12–13; *CWJS English Political Writings, 1711–1714*, pp. 328–31. The most detailed biography of Barber remains Charles A. Rivington, *'Tyrant': The Story of John Barber, 1675 to 1741: Jacobite Lord Mayor of London and Printer and Friend to Dr. Swift* (York: William Sessions, 1989); see also *ODNB* ('John Barber').

[6] See James McLaverty, 'Swift and the Art of Political Publication: Hints and Title Pages, 1711–1714', in Claude Rawson (ed.), *Politics and Literature in the Age of Swift: English and Irish Perspectives* (Cambridge University Press, 2010), pp. 116–39 (pp. 121–3); *CWJS English Political Writings, 1711–1714*, p. 329; for partial subsidy of the *Examiner*, see Gadd, '"At Four Shillings per Year"', p. 79.

104 Part II: London

well as spending time at Barber's printing-house. Often in the past he had timed his relatively short visits to England to bring substantial work to press and disappear before publication. Now, in contrast, while he awaited formal acknowledgement of his role in securing the First Fruits, he worked rather as he had done during the Bickerstaff affair, but with much more at stake, producing a succession of smaller publications closely co-ordinated with day-to-day developments. His stay would in the end extend from 1710 to 1714, broken only by a short visit to Dublin in 1713 for his installation as Dean of St Patrick's.

None of the work he was now seeing through the press touched directly on the authorship of the *Tale* (whose fifth edition, along with the *Miscellanies in Prose and Verse*, had already been in production with Tooke before Swift left Ireland for England in 1710). This removed a significant obstacle to involvement with processes that he had often preferred to keep at arm's length. In prudential terms, his close, confidential association with Barber had much to recommend it – and when official investigations threatened, he knew that the ministry was on his side.[7] Barber too needed to be careful: although he generally put his name to his work (as for instance in his role as Printer to the City of London), he withheld his imprint from Swift's propaganda, preferring to use Morphew's instead. Swift's letters home to Johnson and Dingley (the so-called *Journal to Stella*) are also chary of mentioning Barber by name: Swift introduces him, quite late on in their association, only by mentioning that he 'dined with no less a man than the city printer', commenting enigmatically that 'There is an intimacy between us, built upon reasons that you shall know when I see you.'[8] Later, referring also to Barber's companion, Delariviere Manley, he calls them 'people that you never heard of, nor is it worth your while to know; an authoress and a printer'.[9]

Many contemporary purchasers would have understood, when they saw the imprint of John Morphew on the ministry's propaganda, that Morphew was simply the Tories' preferred distributor (just as Abigail Baldwin was the Whigs'); but by the twentieth century it was easy to mistake him for Swift's bookseller – and there was little in Swift's extant

---

[7] See, for example, his response to investigations of *Conduct* (*CWJS English Political Writings, 1711–1714*, p. 343).

[8] *CWJS Journal*, p. 101; Treadwell, 'Swift's Relations', pp. 23, 25; for Barber and Swift, see *CWJS English Political Writings, 1711–1714*, pp. 328–30; for the possibility that Charles Davenant, Swift's relation by marriage, may have introduced Swift to him, and/or recommended him to Harley, see Rivington, 'Tyrant', pp. 8–9, 12; Treadwell, 'Swift's Relations', pp. 22–3; *CWJS Journal*, p. 57.

[9] *CWJS Journal*, p. 112.

Politics and Permanence (1710–1714)

testimony to correct the impression. It was only when Michael Treadwell investigated the trade publisher function in specific relation to Swift that Barber could be restored to his due (if carefully concealed) prominence.[10] In a sense, Barber was only doing consistently what Tooke had done occasionally, for Tooke himself had used the imprint of Morphew's predecessor John Nutt to screen his involvement in the *Tale of a Tub*, and Morphew's to mystify the origins of *Predictions for the Year 1708*. As skilled print-trade strategists, Tooke and Barber had much in common, and Swift delighted in using his ministerial contacts to obtain jointly conferred grants and privileges for them.[11] Yet their contributions to Swift in print were designedly different: Barber's half sheets and octavos, which outperformed Grub-Street standards with consummate ease, provided large-scale production, respectable quality across a wide generic range, and speedy revision in line with evolving emergencies; but Tooke's octavos, which were fewer, more luxurious and less constrained by immediate political horizons, expressed more fully the poignancy of Swift's aspirations towards what was to prove an unrealisable future.

Single Sheets

With the Whigs now out of power, Swift made what seemed to him to have been a successful approach to Harley about the First Fruits on 7 October 1710; and it was probably on 12 October that he was recruited for the ministry's existing half-sheet periodical, the *Examiner*.[12] Timeliness was of the essence, requiring Swift to provide a weekly essay of about 2,000 words: he began in November 1710 with no. 14, and ended in June 1711 with the whole of no. 45 and part of no. 46.[13] He already had

---

[10] Treadwell, 'Swift's Relations', pp. 20–6; cf. Barber's prominence in indexes to *Corr.*, *CWJS English Political Writings, 1711–1714*, and *CWJS Journal*; Bullard and McLaverty, 'Introduction', pp. 12–14.

[11] *CWJS English Political Writings, 1711–1714*, pp. 328–32; *CWJS Journal*, p. 249. For grants in which they shared, notably the reversion of the patent of King's Printer, see Rivington, 'Tyrant', pp. 23–4; Treadwell, 'Swift's Relations', pp. 25–6, 28–30.

[12] *Corr.*, vol. I, pp. 301–3; *CWJS Journal*, pp. 27, 30–1, 45; Introduction to *CWJS English Political Writings, 1701–1711* (forthcoming); Ellis, *Examiner*, p. xxiii (but for suggestions that the paper may have been St John's project rather than Harley's, see Ashley Marshall, 'Swift, Oldisworth, and the Politics of *The Examiner*, 1710–14', in *Münster* (2019), pp. 401–31 (pp. 403–6)). The formal grant of the First Fruits was in fact delayed, and Swift did not receive the credit he felt he deserved (Ehrenpreis, *Swift*, vol. II, pp. 394–405). For his later view of his association with the ministry, see *Memoirs, relating to that Change which happened in the Queen's Ministry in the Year 1710* (*PW*, vol. VIII, pp. 121–8).

[13] Ellis, *Examiner*, p. xxi. Collected editions, which omitted the perceivedly problematic no. 13 (Atterbury on hereditary right), renumbered Swift's contributions accordingly (p. lxx). See Introduction to *CWJS English Political Writings, 1701–1711* (forthcoming).

Part II: London

plenty of relevant experience from his association with Steele (which came under increasing strain with the change of ministry): in happier days he had contributed to the *Tatler* not only the presiding authorial figure of Bickerstaff, but also a variety of hints, an essay and a few poems; and in 1711 he would help the young William Harrison with an attempted continuation.[14] The *Examiner* was in material terms very similar: each number consisted of a half sheet printed on both sides in double columns; the space at the end was filled by advertisements; the imprint was Morphew's; and the price was probably a penny.[15] Indeed, in *Examiner* no. 1 the social commentary of the *Tatler* (unnamed but clearly identifiable) was a prominent feature of the terrain against which the new paper mapped its ambitions:

> *I shall leave the* African *Company and the Coals to the* Review: *I will not touch one drop of the* Observator's October; *he and his Country-man shall bowse it all up the next Elections: All Descriptions of* Stage-Players *and* Statesmen, *the erecting of* Green-Houses, *the forming of* Constellations, *the Beaus* Red Heels, *and the* Furbelows *of the Ladies, shall remain entire to the Use and Benefit of their first Proprietor.*[16]

The tone of derision intensified in no. 5, however, when Bickerstaff was ridiculed for venturing into politics:

> Begin to take care of your self; remember the Fate of one of your Predecessors, and don't gaze at your *Stars*, 'till you fall into a *Ditch*. No more of your *Politick Lucubrations*; put out your Candle; favour your Age; and go to Bed sooner.[17]

Like the breach between Swift (his creator) and Steele (his inheritor), contempt for Bickerstaff was a telling index of political change.

Like the *Tatler*, the *Examiner* declared its time-bound character in the very date on its masthead, and no. 11 went so far in its belittling of Steele's project as to undermine the ephemerality of the format that they shared: 'Writers of the first Rank, in Works design'd for Eternity, may be allow'd to have a due Sense of their own Excellencies: But for a weekly Retailer of loose Papers, one of which is still dying before the next is born, to assume

---

[14] For the essay, see *Tatler* no. 230 (Bond, *Tatler*, vol. III, pp. 190–6; *CWJS Parodies*, pp. 89–103); for the poems, *Tatler* nos. 9, 238 (Bond, *Tatler*, vol. I, pp. 80–1, vol. III, pp. 224–7; *CWJS Poems* I (forthcoming)); for the history of further attributions, *CWJS Parodies*, Appendix G (pp. 583–601); for Harrison's continuation, *CWJS Parodies*, pp. 105–20, 589–601. Rivington points out that Swift kept the continuation separate from his work with Barber by placing the printing with Dryden Leach, his cousin on his mother's side (Rivington, 'Tyrant', p. 31).

[15] Gadd, '"At Four Shillings per Year"', pp. 78–80.   [16] *Examiner*, no. 1.

[17] *Ibid.*, no. 5; Bond, *Tatler*, vol. III, no. 229, pp. 186–90; cf. *CWJS Journal*, p. 46.

Politics and Permanence (1710–1714) 107

the same Privilege, is perfectly ridiculous.'[18] None of this, however, prevented purchasers from binding their collections of half-sheet periodicals into folio volumes (sometimes made up with specially printed title pages and reprinted back numbers); nor did it dissuade publishers from reprinting collected volumes, such as *The Lucubrations of Isaac Bickerstaff* (1710), which was offered in two duodecimo volumes for ordinary purchasers or octavo for subscribers.[19] Swift's thoughts on being shown a copy of the duodecimo by his former tutor St George Ashe (now Bishop of Clogher) are recorded in a letter to Addison:

> The Bp shewed me the 1st Volume of the small Edition of the Tatler, where there is a very handsom Compliment to me; but I can never pardon the Printing the news of every Tatler, I think he might as well have printed the Advertism[ts]; I know it was a Booksellers piece of Craft to encrease the Bulk and Price of what he was sure would sell, but I utterly disapprove it.[20]

Steele's compliment was none the less 'hansom' for Bickerstaff's withholding of Swift's name:

> . . . It happened very luckily, that a little before I had resolved upon this Design, a Gentleman had written Predictions, and Two or Three other Pieces in my Name, which had rendered it famous thro' all Parts of *Europe*; and by an inimitable Spirit and Humour, raised it to as high a Pitch of Reputation as it could possibly arrive at.
>
> By this good Fortune, the Name of *Isaac Bickerstaff* gained an Audience of all who had any Taste of Wit, and the Addition of the ordinary Occurrences of common Journals of News brought in a Multitude of other Readers. I could not, I confess, long keep up the Opinion of the Town, that these Lucubrations were written by the same Hand with the first Works which were published under my Name; but before I lost the Participation of that Author's Fame, I had already found the Advantage of his Authority, to which I owe the sudden Acceptance which my Labours met with in the World.[21]

Steele's testimony is both graceful and telling, but Swift immediately dismisses the news items, which Steele believes originally 'brought in a Multitude of other Readers', as 'a Booksellers piece of Craft' to enlarge the book, a ploy as egregious in his estimation (though not necessarily in

---

[18] *Examiner*, no. 11.
[19] Bond, *Tatler*, pp. xxx–xxxii.
[20] *The Lucubrations of Isaac Bickerstaff Esq; Revised and Corrected by the Author*, 2 vols. (London, [1710]; *ESTC* T134469–T134468, corrected as T134471–T134472); *Corr.*, vol. I, p. 287.
[21] *Lucubrations*, vol. I, pp. iv–v.

108 Part II: London

ours) as it would have been to reprint the advertisements. Swift, however, espouses a high view of the distinction between literature and ephemera. In line with the attachment to final lifetime intention that characterised his approach to editing Temple's works (not to mention Steele's provision, in the *Lucubrations*, of a text said to be '*Revised and Corrected by the Author*'), he prioritises permanent value over contemporary context; and it is revealing that in this letter the distinction leads him quickly back to his own aspirations, as he reminds Addison that the two preferments he has in his eye are 'D^r So–th's Prebend and Sinecure; or the Place of Historiogrphr'.[22]

The *Examiner*'s role in relation to 'Works design'd for Eternity' thus posed something of a challenge. It helped, to a degree, that Swift, who was not in any case privy to the ministers' deepest secrets, had been commissioned to provide opinion rather than news (for which the ministry used an already established newspaper, Abel Roper's *The Post-boy*, in which Swift also published occasional notices).[23] But even the *Examiner* needed on occasion to focus on the emergency of the hour, as when Harley was stabbed by Antoine de Guiscard in 1711:

> I Am diverted from the general Subject of my Discourses, to reflect upon an Event of a very extraordinary and surprizing Nature: A great Minister, in high Confidence with the Queen, under whose Management the Weight of Affairs at present is in a great measure supposed to ly; sitting in Council, in a Royal Palace, with a dozen of the Chief Officers of State, is stabbed at the very Board, in the Execution of his Office, by the Hand of a *French Papist*, then under Examination for High Treason.[24]

The *Examiner*'s weekly timetable, by fostering close collaboration with Barber (whose interest in the periodical was registered by Morphew in the Stationers' Register on 14 September 1710) allowed Swift the luxury of hands-on revision.[25] It also enhanced secrecy and – to judge by such expressions to Johnson and Dingley as 'a little bit of mischief with a printer' – became a pleasure in itself.[26] Indeed, the secret of Swift's authorship remained particularly well kept: to Johnson and Dingley Swift affected to speculate that the author

---

[22] Robert South (1643–1716), was Prebendary of Westminster; Thomas Rymer (1642/3–1713) was Historiographer Royal.

[23] For Swift's notices in *The Post-boy*, see *CWJS English Political Writings, 1711–1714*, pp. 319–24, and for the paper and its production, pp. 510–16; *CWJS Journal*, pp. 460, 464, 489.

[24] For the contentiousness of Swift's published account, see Introduction to *CWJS English Political Writings, 1701–1711* (forthcoming). See also Ellis, *Examiner*, no. 32, 15 March 1711, pp. xxix, 296–8; *Corr.*, vol. I, pp. 336–9; *CWJS Journal*, p. 162 (and for Swift's initial report to Johnson and Dingley, pp. 158–9; for his assistance to Mrs Manley in writing up the event as a pamphlet, pp. 186–7).

[25] *SCEBC* (1710–46), p. 67; Rivington, '*Tyrant*', pp. 22, 31–2. [26] *CWJS Journal*, pp. 258, 418.

Politics and Permanence (1710–1714)   109

might be the poet and diplomat Matthew Prior (1664–1721) or the High-Church clerical controversialist Francis Atterbury (1663–1732), while his own role remained unknown even to some of Harley's inner circle – and for a long time even to Arthur Mainwaring, author of the Whig *Medley*.[27] This was a considerable achievement, presumably helped by the fact that Swift held back from making Mr. Examiner into anything like a second Bickerstaff. Previous writers had done little to develop Mr. Examiner as a character, and Swift, despite taking characteristic steps to ground the persona in a social context by placing him as a country gentleman who speaks of his servants by name and stresses his readiness to converse with men of all parties, did little more. Instead he focused on an aggressive promotion of the ministry's partisan agenda that implied authority rather than playfulness.

Swift also shifted the *Examiner* away from the timely and closer to the timeless by dropping the reactive role imposed by its previous subtitle of '*Remarks upon Papers and Occurrences*'.[28] Answering Whig papers such as the *Medley* was now beneath Mr. Examiner's dignity.[29] Yet the *Examiner* and the *Medley* alike would soon be reprinted in the more permanent form of collected volumes; and it is these, rather than the vulnerable half sheets, that have been most accessible to later readers.[30] The *Examiner* volume appeared in duodecimo in 1712, under the joint imprint of Morphew and Ann Dodd (whose Temple Bar address, Treadwell suggests, gave her particular access to 'the Inns of Court and West End market').[31] Swift, who seems to have been involved in stop-press correction of the new edition, responded to slow sales by invoking the ephemerality of the genre: 'so soon out of Fashion are Party papers however so well writt'.[32] He surmised that the collected *Medley* 'may sell better', which it apparently did – until it was undermined by the false belief that the profits of the subscription were going to Mainwaring.[33] (Swift, in line with his refusal to

---

[27] Introduction to *CWJS English Political Writings, 1701–1711* (forthcoming); Ellis, *Examiner*, p. xxxiii. For Swift's performance to Johnson and Dingley, see, for instance, *CWJS Journal*, p. 156. For his anger at being named as author of the *Examiner* by Steele in 1713, see *Corr.*, vol. I, pp. 483–4, 487, 491–3, 495–7.

[28] Introduction to *CWJS English Political Writings, 1701–1711* (forthcoming).

[29] *Ibid.*; Ellis, *Examiner*, p. lxiv.   [30] Gadd, '"At Four Shillings per Year"', pp. 80–1.

[31] The first volume was *The Examiners for the Year 1711. To which is prefix'd, A Letter to the Examiner* (London, 1712; TS 4 (NB: giving incorrect format), *ESTC* T33670 (giving correct format, i.e. duodecimo); a second and third volume followed in 1714); Gadd, '"At Four Shillings per Year"', pp. 75–80; Ellis, *Examiner*, p. lxiv (and, for *The Medleys for the Year 1711. To which are prefix'd, the Five Whig-Examiners* ([1712]), p. lxviii); Treadwell, 'Swift's Relations', pp. 21, 34.

[32] *CWJS Journal*, p. 416.   [33] Ellis, *Examiner*, p. lxix.

be paid, had turned down such a potentially embarrassing subscription for the *Examiner*, although the volume did take the opportunity to re-advertise what was by then a substantial list of his contributions to ministerial propaganda.[34]) Swift had disapproved of the inclusion of news reports in the collected *Tatler*, and had not routinely featured news even in the original papers of the *Examiner*, rendering its absence from the collected edition a foregone conclusion; but the advertisements to which he had sneeringly compared Steele's old news were another matter. In the original *Examiner* papers they had not only recorded the wider material culture of clothes, fabrics, household equipment and patent medicines assumed to be of interest to its original readers, but had also intensified the essays' propaganda by advertising further publications aimed at Whig targets (notably Richard Bentley, Master of Trinity College, Cambridge, whose edition of Horace and battles with his fellows both came under fire at this time).[35] The purging of advertisements from the collected edition, useful as it was in preparing the essays for a more permanent future, detached Swift's contribution from a printed whole that had been significantly more than the sum of its parts.

Periodicals like the *Tatler* or the *Examiner*, in which the humble half sheet aspired to a new kind of cultural authority, were a relatively recent vogue; but the long-established half-sheet genres of hawkers' verse and prose that Swift was also publishing at this time remained a byword for catchpenny trash. Quick to produce and often priced literally at a penny, they were equally suited to recycle traditional best-sellers or target current excitements. Sometimes they seemed to address their readers in sober seriousness, sometimes to tease them with preposterous inventions – but it was often difficult to tell which, particularly since imprints were typically defective, deceptive or absent. Such half sheets were cheap enough for the poorest purchasers, who might well take an interest in political controversy (Swift's Irish servant Patrick quickly decided that 'the rabble here are much more inquisitive in politicks, than in Ireland'); but, as many of Swift's would show, they could also reach out to elite readers.[36] Soon after his arrival in London in 1710, for example, Motte had printed Swift's *The Virtues of Sid Hamet the Magician's Rod*, a punning satire on the fall of the former Whig minister Godolphin. (McLaverty suggests that Motte's entry of the copy in the Stationers' Register may indicate this was Swift's thank-

---

[34] Gadd, '"At Four Shillings per Year"', p. 80; *CWJS Journal*, p. 312; advertisements illustrated in D. Woolley, 'The Canon of Swift's Prose Pamphleteering', figures 3a and 3b.

[35] *ODNB* ('Richard Bentley').

[36] *CWJS Journal*, p. 10. See also A. C. Kelly, *Jonathan Swift and Popular Culture*, pp. 37–8.

Politics and Permanence (1710–1714)

you to him for his work on the *Tale*, and possibly also for *A Famous Prediction of Merlin*.[37]) Despite its Grub-Street format, Swift found Harley's dinner-guests agog with speculation:

> They began to talk of a paper of verses called *Sid Hamet*. Mr. Harley repeated part, and then pulled them out, and gave them to a gentleman at the table to read, though they had all read them often: Lord Peterborow would let nobody read them but himself: so he did, and Mr. Harley bobbed me at every line to take notice of the beauties. Prior rallied lord Peterborow for author of them; and lord Peterborow said, he knew them to be his; and Prior then turned it upon me, and I on him. I am not guessed at all in town to be the author; yet so it is: but that is a secret only to you. Ten to one whether you see them in Ireland; yet here they run prodigiously.[38]

Swift's actions, in line with his characteristic alertness to issues of price and market placement, suggest his ambivalence towards such lowly products. In 1712 he joined a general rush of pamphleteers to dodge the impending imposition of stamp duty, a 'Bill to limit th Press' that he had long feared: 'They are here intending to tax all little penny papers a half-penny every half-sheet, which will utterly ruin Grubstreet, and I am endeavouring to prevent it.'[39] While the legislation went through anyway, he listed to Johnson and Dingley the fruits of his last-minute endeavours:

> Since Dunkirk has been in our Hands, Grubstreet has been very fruitfull: p^{d}fr has writt 5 or 6 Grubstreet papers this last week. Have y seen Toland's Invitation to Dismal or a Hue & cry after Dismal, or a Ballad on Dunkirk, or an Argument that Dunkirk is not in our Hands Poh, Y^e have seen nothing.[40]

A few days later he added:

> To day there will be anothr Grub; a Letter from the Pretendr to a Whig Ld. Grubstreet has but ten days to live, then an Act of Parlmt takes place, that ruins it, by taxing every half sheet at a halfpenny.[41]

He also reflected on the tax as a potential curb on half-sheet periodicals:

> Do you know, that Grubstreet is dead and gone last Week; No more Ghosts or Murders now for Love or Money. I plyed it pretty close the last Fortnight,

---

[37] *CWJS Poems* I (forthcoming); *SCEBC* (1710–46), p. 76; Bullard and McLaverty, 'Introduction', pp. 10–11. For Swift's 'almost vowing Revenge' for the 'coldness' of Godolphin's reception on his arrival in London, see *CWJS Journal*, pp. 6, 25, 27, 40.

[38] *CWJS Journal*, pp. 40–1, 59.

[39] *Ibid.*, pp. 131, 396, 405. Stamp duty was also a considerable taxation opportunity for a needy administration.

[40] *Ibid.*, pp. 237, 396, 437.   [41] *Ibid.*, p. 439.

112   Part II: London

> and publisht at least 7 penny Papers of my own, besides some of other Peoples. But now, every single half sheet pays a half-penny to the Qu—. The Observator is fallen, the Examiner is deadly sick, the Spectator keeps up, and doubles it price. I know not how long it will hold. Have you seen the red Stamp the Papers are marqued with. Methinks it is worth a halfpenny the stamping it.[42]

All this, though exaggerating the impact of the tax, makes clear Swift's grasp of the varied potential of the half sheet – periodicals included.[43] In his own case, advertising in the *Examiner* helped to bring his writing to the attention of a core group of ministerial supporters: it was structurally crucial that whoever might be writing the *Examiner* at any given moment, Barber would be printing it, foreshadowing the control of in-house publicity that would become even more important for Swift in print in Ireland after 1714.[44]

Swift's lists of his half sheets also make clear their strategic relation to topics of the day: several, for instance, relate to Dunkirk, whose surrender by France was a key issue in moves towards peace; and two attack Daniel Finch, Earl of Nottingham (alias Dismal), a senior Tory and churchman whose defection to the Whigs made him a critical target.[45] The two satires on Nottingham also show how different genres could provide different angles of attack. One of these half sheets, *T—l—nd's Invitation to Dismal, to dine with the Calves-Head Club. Imitated from Horace, Epist. 5, Lib I*, was Swift's first published Horatian imitation (Figure 6).[46] In it, Swift makes the republican deist John Toland invite Dismal to celebrate the execution of Charles I with the supposed republican Calves' Head Club, thus ventriloquising an elite performance of a peculiarly preposterous kind. Printed with provocative blanks for names and priced at a penny, the half sheet confirms its design on a classically trained readership by setting out, in footnotes, substantial passages from the Latin original. But when asking Johnson and Dingley 'How do Y like it?', he commented 'but it is an Imitation of Horace, and perhaps Y don't understand Horace' (which did not stop Johnson from making her own transcription).[47] For an elite male Tory audience, on the

---

[42] *Ibid.*, p. 442. For the hawking of murder reports, see Swift's care to keep the just-widowed Duchess of Hamilton away from street-facing rooms where 'she must have been tortured with te noise of te Grubstreet Screamers, mention her Husband's murder to her Ears', p. 458.

[43] *Corr.*, vol. I, pp. 420–1.

[44] See *Peace and Dunkirk* in *CWJS Poems* I (forthcoming); and for advertising of Swift items distributed by Morphew, D. Woolley, 'The Canon of Swift's Prose Pamphleteering', pp. 106–7 and figure 4.

[45] See also *Corr.*, vol. I, pp. 434–6; David Woolley, *'A Dialogue upon Dunkirk* (1712), and Swift's "7 penny Papers"', in *Münster* (1993), pp. 215–23; *CWJS English Political Writings, 1711–1714*, pp. 418–19. For similar evidence of co-ordination from October 1711, see *CWJS Journal*, p. 297.

[46] *CWJS Poems* I (forthcoming).   [47] *CWJS Journal*, p. 434; SwJ 319.

T--l--nd's Invitation to *DISMAL*, to Dine with the CALVES-HEAD Club.

Imitated from Horace, *Epiſt.* 5. *Lib.* 1.

IF, deareſt **Diſmal**, you for once can Dine
    Upon a ſingle Diſh, and Tavern Wine,
    T——l——*nd* to you this Invitation ſends,
To eat the *CALVES-HEAD* with your truſty Friends.
Suſpend a while your vain ambitious Hopes,
Leave hunting after Bribes, forget your Tropes :
To morrow We our *Myſtick Feaſt* prepare,
Where Thou, our lateſt *Proſelyte*, ſhalt ſhare :
When We, by proper Signs and Symbols tell,
How, by *Brave Hands*, the *Royal TRATTOR* fell ;
The Meat ſhall repreſent the *TTRANT*'s Head,
The Wine, his Blood, *our Predeceſſors* ſhed :
Whilſt an *alluding* Hymn ſome Artiſt ſings,
We toaſt Confuſion to the Race of Kings :
At Monarchy we nobly ſhew our Spight,
And talk *what Fools call Treaſon* all the Night.
    Who, by Diſgraces or ill Fortune ſunk,
Feels not his Soul enliven'd when he's Drunk ?
Wine can clear up *G--d--lph--n*'s cloudy Face,
And fill *J.——ck Sm——th* with Hopes to keep his Place ;
By Force of Wine ev'n *Sc--rb--r--w* is Brave,
Hal-- grows more Pert, and *S--mm--rs* not ſo Grave :
Wine can give *P——rt——d* Wit, and *Cl--v--nd* Senſe,
M--t--g--e Learning, *B--lt--n* Eloquence :
Ch——ly, when Drunk, can never loſe his *Wand*,
And *L--nc--n* then imagines he has Land.
    My Province is, to ſee that all be right,
Glaſſes and Linnen clean, and Pewter bright ;
From our *Myſterious Club* to keep out Spies,
And *Tories* (dreſs'd like Waiters) in Diſguiſe.
You ſhall be coupled as you beſt approve,
Seated at Table next the Men you love.
S——nd——d, Or——rd, B——l, and *R——ch——e*'s Grace
Will come ; and *H--mp--n* ſhall have *W---p--l*'s Place.
Wh——n, unleſs prevented by a *Whore*,
Will hardly fail, and there is room for more :
But I love Elbow-room whene're I drink,
And honeſt *Harry* is too apt to ſtink.
    Let no Pretence of Bus'neſs make you ſtay,
Yet take one Word of Counſel by the way :
If *Gu--rn--y* calls, ſend word you're gone abroad ;
He'll teaze you with King *Charles* and Biſhop *Laud*,
Or make you Faſt, and carry you to Prayers :
But if he will break in, and walk up Stairs,
Steal by the Back-door out, and leave him there ;
Then order *Squaſh* to call a Hackney Chair.   *January* 29.

SI potes archaicis conviva recumbere lectis,
  Nec modica cœnare times olus omne patella :
Supremo te ſole domi, Torquate, manebo.
     *   *   *   *   *
Mitte leves ſpes, & certamina divitiarum,
Et Moſchi cauſam : Cras nato Cæſare feſtus
Dat veniam ſomnumque dies : impune licebit
Æſtivam ſermone benigno tendere noſtem.
   *   *   *   *   *   *   *
Quid non ebrietas deſignat ? operta recludit ;
Spes jubet eſſe ratas ; in prælia trudit inermem :
Sollicitis animis onus eximit ; addocet artes.
Fœcundi calices quem non fecere diſertum ?

Contracta quem non in paupertate ſolutum ?
Hæc ego procurare & idoneus imperor, & non
Invitus ; ne turpe toral, ne ſordida mappa
Corruget nares, ne non & cantharus & lanx
Oſtendat tibi te ; ne fidos inter amicos
Sit qui dicta foras eliminet : ut cœeat par
Jungaturque pari, Brutum tibi Septimiumque,
Et niſi cœna prior potiorque puella Sabinum
Detinet, aſſumam, locus eſt & pluribus umbris :
Sed nimis arcta premunt olidæ convivia capriæ.
Tu quotus eſſe velis reſcribe : & rebus omiſſis,
Atria ſervantem poſtico falle clientem.

Figure 6 Jonathan Swift, *T——l——nd's Invitation to Dismal, to dine with the Calves-Head Club. Imitated from Horace, Epist. 5, Lib I*
(London, 1712).

Part II: London

other hand, primed by his denunciation of Toland in *Examiner* no. 40 as one of the 'Atheistical Writers' given 'publick Encouragement and Patronage' by the Whigs, the comparison rendered all the more piquant Nottingham's transformation from High-Church peer to boon companion of Whiggish bugbears.[48] In contrast, the other half sheet against Nottingham took its rise from a parodic precedent going back to the 1680s, imitating the much lowlier genre of the 'hue and cry' after a criminal on the run.[49] (In a related vein, a missing-person advertisement characterising Nottingham as a vulnerable runaway was placed in *The Post-boy* for 6 December 1711, offering a 10*s*. reward.[50]) Printed on one side only for display as a poster, Swift's *Hue and Cry* makes strategic use of the legal and archaic connotations of a black-letter title. Moreover, the fact that Swift had already in 1711 chosen the popular formula of the 'excellent new song' to satirise Nottingham (*An Excellent New Song, Being the Intended Speech of a Famous Orator against Peace*, described to Johnson and Dingley as a 'ballad, two degrees above Grubstreet'), and that he now used the same formula to celebrate the surrender of Dunkirk (*Peace and Dunkirk; Being an Excellent New Song upon the Surrender of Dunkirk to General Hill. To the Tune of, The King Shall Enjoy His Own Again*) underlines the value to the ministry of an author-and-printer team so generically adept at such beguiling pennyworths.[51]

Yet Swift's zest for such masquerades could seriously outrun his understanding of what was useful (or even safe), as demonstrated by his attack on Elizabeth Seymour, Duchess of Somerset, in *The W–ds-r Prophecy*.[52] Apparently sent 'to the printer in an unknown hand', this was a print parody that resembled *A Famous Prediction of Merlin* in its contrast of black-letter verse with roman comment; but this time, as prudence dictated the omission of the bookseller's name and address from the imprint, those eager to see the non-existent manuscript were recommended instead to 'the Ingenious Dr. W——, F.R.S.' (i.e. John Woodward (1665/8–1728), butt of

---

[48] Ellis, *Examiner*, p. 400.

[49] McLaverty, 'Swift and the Art of Political Publication', analyses several publications from this period; for *A Hue and Cry*, see pp. 121–3 (and reproduction, figure 1); *CWJS Poems* I (forthcoming).

[50] See *CWJS Poems* I (forthcoming).

[51] For *An Excellent New Song, Being the Intended Speech of a Famous Orator against Peace* (London, 1711), see *CWJS Journal*, p. 339. For *Peace and Dunkirk; Being an Excellent New Song upon the Surrender of Dunkirk to General Hill. To the Tune of, The King Shall Enjoy His Own Again* (London, 1712), see *CWJS Journal*, pp. 437, 442. For both, see also *CWJS Poems* I (forthcoming).

[52] For *The Windsor Prophecy*, see Margaret Weedon, 'Bickerstaff Bit, or, Merlinus Fallax', *SStud*, 2 (1987), 97–106; Hermann J. Real, '"The Most Fateful Piece Swift ever Wrote": *The Windsor Prophecy*', *SStud*, 9 (1994), 76–99; *CWJS Poems* I (forthcoming); *CWJS Journal*, pp. 152, 223.

the ancient party in the quarrel of the ancients and the moderns).[53] This offensive attack (which ridiculed the Duchess's red hair and accused her of complicity in the murder of her second husband) took its rise from a serious misunderstanding on Swift's part of the Duchess's influence on the Queen; and even when Oxford's confidante Abigail Masham warned Swift to halt publication, his compliance was barely nominal:

> I called at noon at Mrs. Masham's, who desired me not to let the *Prophecy* be published, for fear of angering the queen about the duchess of Somerset; so I writ to the printer to stop them. They have been printed and given about, but not sold.[54]

On the following day Barber came laden with copies to a meeting of the Tory Brothers' Club, and Swift does not seem to have prevented him from passing them round:

> The printer had not received my letter, and so he brought us dozens apiece of the *Prophecy*; but I ordered him to part with no more. 'Tis an admirable good one, and people are mad for it.[55]

Had Mrs Masham seen his statement to Johnson and Dingley that 'I doubt not but you will have the *Prophecy* in Ireland, although it is not published here, only printed copies given to friends', her fears could only have been confirmed (and the Queen's anger cost Swift any remaining chance of the preferment that he so desired).[56] Swift evidently loved being able to boast that 'people are mad for it', and he loved seeing Barber putting his squibs directly into the hands of appreciative Brothers; but such self-absorbed intrigue did not necessarily serve the ministry's agenda or his own. Barber, more prudently in this particular case, may have reduced his own risk by shifting the printing to others; but his private distribution of papers and pamphlets, now an expected part of the entertainment at the Brothers' Club, effectively spearheaded the elite circulation of what was ostensibly mere Grub-street.[57] In 1712, for instance, Swift boasted:

> To day I published th Fable of Midas, a Poem printed in a loose half sheet of Paper: I know not how it will sell. But it passt wondrfully at our Society to

---

[53] *CWJS Journal*, p. 349; *ODNB* ('John Woodward'); Joseph M. Levine, *Dr. Woodward's Shield: History, Science, and Satire in Augustan England* (Berkeley, CA: University of California Press, 1977).

[54] For composition of the *Prophecy*, see *CWJS Journal*, pp. 154, 341–4, 347, 349, 351 and, for the quotation, 353.

[55] *Ibid.*, p. 353. [56] *Ibid.*, p. 360.

[57] *Ibid.*, pp. 339–40, 407; *CWJS Poems* I (forthcoming); Treadwell, 'Swift's Relations', pp. 21–2. For the private circulation of printed material more generally, see Karian, *Print and Manuscript*, pp. 67–70.

116   Part II: London

> night; & Mr Sec^ty [St John] read it before me tothr night to L^d Tr. [Oxford] at Ld Mashams, where they equally approvd of it.[58]

But the existence of only one known edition of this celebration of Marlborough's dismissal suggests that elite enthusiasm did not guarantee popular success.[59]

Swift's zest for the half sheet also presented a problem for the longer term, for this was a cheap format designed for a short life. Only in the distant future would still-surviving copies make the transition from trash to treasure: in the collection of Sir Harold Williams, now preserved in the Cambridge University Library, each penny half sheet has its own stiffened buckram folder; inside, a paper collar folds down to hold the half sheet in place, and a tab of silk ribbon allows it to be lifted with a minimum of handling. Such reverence for a Grub-Street product would probably have surprised even Swift – and his contemporaries more so. For these were material texts that went to considerable lengths to distance themselves from any sense of an emerging canon: rather than routinely appearing under Morphew's imprint, as the *Examiner* had done, many of them gave no name at all. Indeed, as Treadwell points out, some were evidently deemed too ephemeral – or too dangerous – even to be entered in the Stationers' Register.[60] Gadd, moreover, points to *A Letter from the Pretender, to a Whig-Lord* (1712) as an instance of printing so bad ('suggesting – from a charitable perspective – extreme haste') that Barber's involvement seems unlikely: 'indeed, were the evidence for attribution to Swift less robust, it might be considered suspicious for bibliographical reasons alone'.[61] It is a salutary point. Such instantiation of a materially fastidious author's impersonations trades short-term immunity for the long-term risk of not looking like Swift at all.

Pamphlets

Barber was just as capable of working up octavo pamphlets as ephemeral half sheets, and his collaboration with Swift facilitated an agile response to day-to-day developments in that more substantial format.[62] (Indeed, particular circumstances might even on occasion mean taking on a larger format still: *The Publick Spirit of the Whigs* (1714) responds to Steele's

---

[58] *CWJS Journal*, p. 388.   [59] *CWJS Poems* I (forthcoming).
[60] Treadwell, 'Swift's Relations', p. 20.
[61] *CWJS English Political Writings, 1711–1714*, pp. 330, 425.
[62] Bullard and McLaverty, 'Introduction', pp. 12–14.

quarto *The Crisis*, and was produced in quarto and advertised to be bound up with it, giving Swift a very material last word.[63]) Barber's pamphlets, whether exceptional quarto or default octavo, were well produced; and, as McLaverty notes, their allusion to existing print genres was still a vital resource – particularly in relation to the various kinds of material that might be presented in the guise of a letter, routinely deploying 'a double title, one to give the content and the other to give the form'.[64] Yet the pamphlets were much more uniform in design than the half sheets, often being assembled 'in 4s', making four leaves rather than eight to a signature (something like a very small quarto).[65] Their titles typically framed their content in double rules, deployed expressive touches of black letter, and might also include an epigraph. Crucially, McLaverty judges that 'Swift clearly regarded designing the title page as part of the author's responsibility' (as did Barber, to judge by his reported readiness 'to turn an author out of his shop if the frontispiece of his manuscript exceeded the bounds of moderation'); and it may well be that what Swift had in his mind's eye was something like the double-framed titles that had introduced Tooke's volumes of Temple and the *Tale*, but with freer use of 'English' black letter.[66] Inside, the text was set in clear, well-spaced type, with extensive use of italic to highlight the quotations at issue.

For sheer scale of production and political impact, the outstanding example of this body of pamphlets is *The Conduct of the Allies* (1711), whose ninety-six pages (priced at 1s.) presented the largest and most systematic of Swift's arguments for the new peace policy.[67] (By way of

---

[63] *CWJS English Political Writings, 1711–1714*, p. 446. For two further 1714 quarto publications advertised 'to be bound up with the *Crisis*', see *ESTC* N24909 and T135790.

[64] McLaverty, 'Swift and the Art of Political Publication', pp. 127–34.

[65] For imposition and assembly of octavos 'in 4s' (including the 'work and turn' method), see Gaskell, *A New Introduction*, p. 83 and figure 53.

[66] McLaverty, 'Swift and the Art of Political Publication', pp. 120–1, 123–4; John Nichols, *Literary Anecdotes of the Eighteenth Century; Comprizing Biographical Memoirs of William Bowyer, Printer, F.S.A. and many of his Learned Friends; an Incidental View of the Progress and Advancement of Literature in this Kingdom during the Last Century; and Biographical Anecdotes of a Considerable Number of Eminent Writers and Ingenious Artists; with a Very Copious Index*, 9 vols. (London, 1812–15), vol. III, p. 508. There is no black letter in Tooke's titles to the *Tale* (1704–10), nor to *Memoirs. Part III* (1709), and little in those to *Miscellanea. The Third Part* (1701) and *Letters to the King* (1703). Although Moxon does discuss title-page design as a task for the compositor, he also advises an author in general 'to examine his *Copy very well e're he deliver it to the* Printer, *and to Point it, and mark it so as the* Compositor *may know what Words to* Set *in* Italick, English, Capitals, &c.' (*Mechanick Exercises*, pp. 212–14, 250). Smith, wary of excesses of 'fancy' in title-page design, concludes that 'Titles should have the revisal of one that is allowed to have a good judgment in gracing one' (*The Printer's Grammar*, pp. 217–18).

[67] For the unusual structure of this first octavo edition in comparison with the more conventional octavos that followed, see *CWJS English Political Writings, 1711–1714*, pp. 344–5.

Part II: London

comparison, the next largest would be *Some Remarks on the Barrier Treaty* (1712), at forty-eight pages, which sold for 6*d.*, others had as few as sixteen pages and sold for 2*d.*) The setting of the title highlights the satire: within the double-ruled frame the 'ALLIES' are highlighted in the largest full capitals, the '𝕷ate 𝕸inistry' in smaller black letter, and the 'Present War' in lower-case with initial capitals – and a second glance at these capitals confirms that these words, despite their less flamboyant appearance, are in fact set in the largest type of all. Thus the past actions of Allies and Whig ministers are typographically set up for a fall, ready to be laid low by Swift's reflection on their present consequences. The same agenda is then spelled out (to elite readers at least) by a substantial block of Latin verse in neat italics, set off by rules above and below. It comprises three unattributed quotations (one suggested by Oxford) from Lucan, Ovid and Juvenal.[68] Taken together, they suggest that English troops are dying across Europe to no good end, that warmongering is despicable, and that England's victories are actually cause for tears.[69] By invoking such authorities the *Conduct* signals that it sets a high value on its intervention, an impression underlined by the format-based sally with which its Preface begins, in which the Whigs are accused of resisting peace '*without offering one single Reason, but what we find in their* Ballads'.[70] Thus the anonymous Swift, throwing a veil over his equally anonymous political half sheets, dignifies *Conduct* as the triumph of Tory substance over Whig trash.

Yet for all its aspirations, *Conduct* achieved what Swift called its 'most prodigious run' in part by responding deftly to changing risks and opportunities. Crucially, Barber had enough type to allow large quantities to be left standing, and Swift attended closely on the press to revise and check subsequent editions.[71] Gadd, estimating that *Conduct* 'probably ranks as Swift's most immediately influential and popular work, with 11,000 copies sold within two months', shows in compelling detail how each new edition

---

[68] *CWJS Journal*, pp. 331–2.

[69] For reproduction of an early title, see *CWJS English Political Writings, 1711–1714*, figure 1, p. 46. The three quotations are: Lucan, *The Civil War*, V. ll. 264–8: 'partem tibi Gallia nostri / Eripuit, partem duris Hispania bellis, / Pars iacet Hesperia, totoque exercitus orbe / Te vincente perit. Terris fudisse cruorem / Quid iuvat Arctois Rhodano Rhenoque subactis?' ('Some of us were snatched from you by Gaul, others by the hard campaigns in Spain; others lie in Italy; all over the world you are victorious and your soldiers die. What boots it to have shed our blood in Northern lands, where we conquered the Rhone and the Rhine?'); Ovid, *Ars Amatoria*, II. l. 147: 'Odimus accipitrem, quia vivit semper in armis' ('We hate the hawk because he ever lives in arms'); Juvenal, *Satires*, I. l. 50: 'victrix, provincia, ploras' ('you, Province, the winner of the case, are in tears').

[70] *CWJS English Political Writings, 1711–1714*, p. 47; cf. *CWJS Journal*, p. 308.

[71] *CWJS English Political Writings, 1711–1714*, pp. 344–6.

Politics and Permanence (1710–1714)

responded to ongoing developments.[72] The ministers, intent on pressing their point without incurring prosecution, gave the text close attention in advance of the first edition; then, as it began to sell out, Swift worked with Barber to strengthen and supplement the second; and they made further small corrections and tactful rephrasings in the third.[73] More significant textual changes were prompted in the fourth by the news that the Whig Lords had taken exception to references to the succession: intriguingly, the emended passage was supplemented by what Gadd aptly calls 'a lofty post-script' (promising substantive responses that were never carried through), suggesting that the practicable limits of substantive revision had now been reached.[74] Swift prided himself, meanwhile, that the vast sales of this 'dear twelve-penny book' had rested 'purely upon it's own strength', and not on being 'bought up in numbers by the party to give away, as the Whigs do'; but its material quality was soon to be degraded for precisely this purpose.[75] Although Oxford was content to order 200 copies of one of the first four-shilling editions from Barber (at trade prices), the fifth edition was expressly designed 'to be taken off by friends and sent into the country', being set in smaller type, on half the number of pages, and at half the cost.[76]

Morphew's distribution network was evidently well able to shift copies in bulk while enthusiasm was at its height. But his imprint was by now a rather over-familiar screen – and it is suggestive that *A Short Character of His Ex. T. E. of W. L. L. of I—* (1711), an attack on Lord Wharton, former Lord Lieutenant of Ireland, which Swift described to Johnson and Dingley as 'a damned libellous pamphlet', seems first to have been privately printed so that 'nobody knows the author or printer' in order to be 'sent by dozens to several gentlemen's lodgings' before being published under the fictitious imprint of the supposed 'William Coryton, Bookseller, at the Black-Swan on Ludgate-Hill'.[77] (This may have been a teasing allusion to the Tory MP Sir William Coryton, a leading critic of the previous Whig administration.[78]) Swift's role as ministry spokesman meant that there

---

[72] *Ibid.*, p. 327.   [73] *Ibid.*, p. 342; *CWJS Journal*, pp. 320, 328, 330, 332–3, 336–7.

[74] *CWJS English Political Writings, 1711–1714*, p. 343; *CWJS Journal*, p. 338.

[75] *CWJS Journal*, pp. 338–40.

[76] *CWJS English Political Writings, 1711–1714*, pp. 329, 343, 347, 389; *CWJS Journal*, p. 340.

[77] For an overview of Morphew's career and significance, see *CWJS English Political Writings, 1711–1714*, pp. 330–2. For *A Short Character*, which appears to have been privately printed before publication of the 'Coryton' edition, see *CWJS Journal*, pp. 83, 106–7; for the likelihood that the contents 'probably deterred both Barber and Morphew', see Ian Gadd, 'Leaving the Printer to his Liberty: Swift and the London Book Trade, 1701–1714', in *JS Book*, pp. 51–64 (p. 54), and TS 527–30, *ESTC* T48134; and further account in *CWJS English Political Writings, 1701–1711* (forthcoming).

[78] Private communication from James McLaverty. See textual account in *CWJS English Political Writings, 1701–1711* (forthcoming).

Part II: London

was now far more at stake in his anonymity; but neither Morphew's known alignment with the Tories, nor the repeated use of his imprint on anonymous works widely (and in many cases correctly) believed to be Swift's, was as genuinely obfuscatory as before. Indeed, Morphew's connection with Barber, and implicitly with Swift, was on record in the Stationers' Register, where in 1712 Morphew signed on Barber's behalf for *Some Remarks on the Barrier Treaty* and *The New Way of Selling Places at Court* (which, supplemented by entries made by Barber himself, confirms Barber's financial stake).[79] Twice at least, Morphew was pursued by the authorities: in 1711 the provocation was Swift's remarks on the succession; and in 1714 it was his bitter account of the Union (featuring a contemptuous diatribe against the Scottish peers) in *The Publick Spirit of the Whigs*.[80] In the latter case there were two different investigations, one by the Scottish peer Lord Mar (in Gadd's words 'himself a member of the government on whose behalf Swift was writing'), and another by the House of Lords. Although Mar was able to arrest Barber without any apparent need to learn his identity from Morphew, the House of Lords did question Morphew, who apparently gave them Barber's name. (Gadd indeed holds out the possibility that Mar's action may have been intended as 'protective – by thwarting the investigation by the House of Lords – rather than aggressive'; but although Barber quickly reprinted the work without the offending passage, the Lords proceeded to examine both him and his employees.[81]) Now, for the first time but not the last, Swift had a price on his head; but he apparently took the view that Queen Anne's proclamation of £300 'to any Person who shall discover, and make due Proof against the Author or Authors' actually showed that the authorities had no real desire to see him apprehended – which, given his utility to the ministry, seems not unlikely. Despite one unsuccessful attempt to claim the money (which did not name Swift), and rumours that a scapegoat had been appointed to step in if necessary, Swift himself escaped unscathed. But such encounters suggest that the diversionary power of the trade publisher was now being tested to its limit. The resulting alarms and excursions continued to foreground transient emergency rather than long-term ambition.

---

[79] *SCEBC* (1710–46), pp. 146, 153; *CWJS English Political Writings, 1711–1714*, pp. 387, 329, 402; Treadwell, 'Swift's Relations', p. 20.

[80] Rivington, *'Tyrant'*, pp. 42–9; *CWJS English Political Writings, 1711–1714*, pp. 5, 111, 341–3, 449–54; *Corr.*, vol. I, pp. 589–90, 602–3.

[81] *Corr.*, vol. I, p. 589, details the financial support provided by Harley, via Swift, for the affected printers.

Politics and Permanence (1710–1714)

This was also the case with the authorial masks deployed in many of the pamphlets: though weakly protective at best, and problematic for the overall consolidation of his work, each of the voices in Swift's chorus spoke to precise rhetorical effect. *Some Advice Humbly Offer'd to the Members of the October Club*, appropriately for an address to such a die-hard Tory faction, is 'a Letter from a Person of Honour'; *The New Way of Selling Places at Court* frames its exposure of an attempted fraud against an aspirant for high office as 'a Letter from a Small Courtier to a Great Stock-Jobber'; and *Some Reasons to Prove, that no Person is Obliged by his Principles, as a Whig, to Oppose Her Majesty or her Present Ministry* is clearly attributed, as 'a Letter to a Whig-Lord', to a supporter of the ministry.[82] Ironic claims of benevolent intent introduce both the anti-deist satire *Mr. C—ns's Discourse of Free-thinking, put into Plain English, by way of Abstract, for the Use of the Poor* (London, [1713]), which is attributed to '*a Friend of the* AUTHOR', and *The Importance of the Guardian Considered*, a damaging attack on Steele, which purports to be 'a Second Letter to the Bailiff of *Stockbridge*. By a Friend of Mr. *St—le*' (which, all the more poignantly, Swift had recently been).[83] Some of these voices are more individualised: as well as commandeering Lord Wharton for *A Letter of Thanks from My Lord W*****n to the Lord Bp of S. Asaph, In the Name of the Kit-Cat-Club*, there are also two new named authors.[84] One is a French valet who goes by the pompous title of the Sieur de Baudrier (he presumably affects to carry a sword like a gentleman): Swift's secondary creation, an unnamed English translator and annotator, discerns in de Baudrier's pretentions '*the Vanity of That Nation*', and dismisses him as '*a mean Man, giving himself the Airs of a Secretary, when it appears, by several Circumstances, that he was receiv'd only as a menial Servant*'.[85] The pamphlet, in Swift's words 'a formal grave lie' that 'makes a two-penny pamphlet', describes a fictitious

---

[82] See textual accounts of these three works in *CWJS English Political Writings, 1711–1714*. For *Some Advice Humbly Offer'd* (TS 557, *ESTC* T49240), see McLaverty, 'Swift and the Art of Political Publication', pp. 127–30, reproducing the title as figure 3; for *The New Way of Selling Places* (*ESTC* T43045), *ibid.*, pp. 129–30, reproducing the title as figure 4; for *Some Reasons to Prove* (TS 578, *ESTC* T49355), and the possibility that the 'Whig-Lord' may have been understood to be an identifiable individual, *ibid.*, pp. 129–32, reproducing the title as figure 5, and *CWJS English Political Writings, 1711–1714*, pp. 17–18.

[83] For *Mr. C—ns's Discourse* (TS 587, *ESTC* T117701), see *PW*, vol. IV, pp. xvii–xx, 23–48; *CWJS Journal*, pp. 484–5, 488. For *The Importance of the Guardian Considered*, see *CWJS English Political Writings, 1711–1714*; McLaverty, 'Swift and the Art of Political Publication', pp. 132–4, reproducing the title as figure 6.

[84] Note that there is some doubt about the attribution to Swift of *A Letter of Thanks from My Lord W*****n to the Lord Bp of S. Asaph, In the Name of the Kit-Cat-Club* (London, 1712; TS 585A, *ESTC* N10918). See D. Woolley, 'The Canon of Swift's Prose Pamphleteering', pp. 105–6; *PW*, vol. VI, pp. 147–55, 212; *CWJS Journal*, p. 427.

[85] See also Introduction to *CWJS English Political Writings, 1701–1711* (forthcoming).

Part II: London

journey to France by Matthew Prior, usefully diverting attention from embarrassing leaks about Prior's real negotiations: the printer quickly sold the first thousand and immediately 'printed five hundred more'.[86] At dinner with Oxford, Swift evidently enjoyed the guests' teasing as to whether he might be the author.[87] The other newly invented author was much more transparent, namely Gregory Misosarum ('hater of [the bishop of] Salisbury'), whose *Preface to th B—p of S—r—m's* Introduction *to the Third Volume of the History of the Reformation of the Church of England* (1713) warned readers against the Low-Church Whig polemic of Bishop Burnet.[88]

Strikingly, no such games were played in this period's three major pamphlets of political exposition and argument, *The Conduct of the Allies, Some Remarks on the Barrier Treaty* and *The Publick Spirit of the Whigs* (the second, indeed, in a rare gesture of consolidation, was straightforwardly ascribed to the author of the first).[89] There is something more straight-facedly anonymous about these crucial interventions, an air of disdaining the prop of an assumed identity while nominally withholding the true one. Yet Swift's ingenuity could still get the upper hand, and in 1712 he 'made Ford copy out a small pamphlet, and send it to the press, that I might not be known for author'.[90] This was *Some Advice Humbly Offer'd to the Members of the October Club*, which close collaborators failed to recognise as his (although Swift reported that Oxford 'said, This is Dr. Davenant's style; which is his cant when he suspects me'); and when sales proved disappointing he reflected that 'if I had hinted it to be mine, every body would have bought it, but it is a great secret'. Unknown intermediaries would later be vital to his safety in Ireland; but in these London years, even while he could write to Johnson and Dingley that 'I propose writing controversies to get a name with posterity', such wilful disruption of material transmission rather suggests, like the affair of the *Windsor Prophecy*, a misalignment of immediate and longer-term

---

[86] *A New Journey to Paris: Together with some Secret Transactions Between the Fr—h K—g, and an Eng— Gentleman* (London, [1711]; TS 536, *ESTC* T5344); Rivington, 'Tyrant', p. 32; *CWJS Journal*, pp. 270–1, 273, 277–9, 285; Bullard and McLaverty, 'Introduction', p. 13; Ehrenpreis, *Swift*, vol. II, p. 476–80. For relations among the various early texts, see textual account in *CWJS English Political Writings, 1701–1711* (forthcoming).

[87] *CWJS Journal*, p. 297.   [88] TS 592, *ESTC* T122519; *PW*, vol. IV, pp. xx–xxviii, 51–84.

[89] For print genre and *The Conduct of the Allies*, see McLaverty, 'Swift and the Art of Political Publication', pp. 134–6, reproducing the title of the fourth edition as figure 7.

[90] *CWJS English Political Writings, 1711–1714*, pp. 380–2; *CWJS Journal*, pp. 370–3, 377, and, for Swift's assessment of the threat posed by the October Club, pp. 145–6. For Swift's spelling out of comparable instructions to his friend Charles Ford in 1714, see *Corr.*, vol. I, pp. 627–8.

Politics and Permanence (1710–1714)

perspectives.[91] Inventiveness and agility in meeting the demands of the moment had transformed the scale and impact of Swift in print, but issues of anonymity meant that, rumours and assumptions apart, the canon was neither united in itself nor unambiguously anchored to its author.

Ironically, Swift's contribution to the official responses to the Queen's announcement of the Peace, imposingly commemorated in the only folio pamphlet of the period, *The Humble Address of the Right Honourable the House of Lords . . . with Her Majesties Most Gracious Answer* (1713), came just as the ministry that had brought it about approached its final collapse.[92] Such a folio, the standard serial format for such official business, said much less about Swift than about the elevated circles in which he had fleetingly played a part. But from 1713, as the ministers quarrelled and the Queen's health declined, Swift reluctantly settled for the Deanery of St Patrick's in Dublin (spending his last night in London with Barber, who rode with him as far as St Albans), subsequently returning in a last doomed attempt to support the ministry. His late attempts at intervention now found themselves stalled on the path to publication: when they finally appeared in print they would be read by the children and grandchildren of those for whom they were written.[93] But these frustrations were not the whole story: Swift's next network for topical political engagement was beginning to emerge within the Dublin trade, and in London his long-established collaboration with Tooke had already produced a select group of octavos that gave material form to his claims on posterity.

Material Aspiration

Tooke's well-produced octavos were much better suited to long-term aspiration than Barber's more workaday half sheets and octavos. In this period three were particularly important. The first was the 1710 fifth edition of the *Tale*, reframed for the future with illustrations, Apology and footnotes. The second, sent to press at the same time but published later, was *Miscellanies in Prose and Verse* (London, 1711), the collection that

---

[91] *CWJS Journal*, p. 456, possibly referring to the work published in 1758 as *The History of the Four Last Years of the Queen* (see also, for example, p. 463).

[92] *CWJS English Political Writings, 1711–1714*, pp. 211–15, 431–41; *Corr.*, vol. I, pp. 646–8.

[93] Rivington, 'Tyrant', p. 37, and for works composed towards the end of this period whose publication was substantially delayed, pp. 62–8; Karian, *Print and Manuscript*, pp. 18–19; *Corr.*, vol. I, pp. 610–11, 613–14, 618–19, 627–8, 634–6, 639–40, 643–5; *CWJS English Political Writings, 1711–1714*, pp. 477–509. For the work published in 1758 as *The History of the Four Last Years of the Queen*, see Chapter 8.

Part II: London

first assembled a proto-canon of Swift's smaller works.[94] The third, a pamphlet in the form of a signed letter, was *A Proposal for Correcting, Improving and Ascertaining the English Tongue* (London, 1712), in which Swift solicited Oxford's support for an academy: thus purified and stabilised, English was to provide the medium for Swift's celebration of Queen and ministry to posterity.[95]

The relation between the first two of the three is suggestive: they came to press together, but emerged with marked differences, which supported Swift's insistence on not owning the *Tale* (although its authorship was already an open secret).[96] Although he had first thought of placing the Apology in what became *Miscellanies in Prose and Verse*, its final inclusion with the *Tale* avoided making what would have been an incontrovertible link between the two volumes.[97] As they now stand, it is striking how unrelated they seem: though both are octavos (including some large-paper copies), comparison suggests two entirely separate enterprises.[98] Most obviously, the copious title page of the *Tale* still contains its variegated elements within the double-ruled frame of the earlier editions, while *Miscellanies in Prose and Verse* achieves a sparer, more contemporary effect with a briefer title on an unframed page.[99] It also bears Morphew's imprint, while the *Tale* retains that of his predecessor John Nutt, who had given up the business in 1706: while this might look like a mistake, it serves remarkably neatly to blur the fact of shared distribution.[100] The two title pages are also differentiated by ornamentation: the *Tale*, once more printed by Motte for Tooke (though neither name is given), has, as before, no decorations; but *Miscellanies in Prose and Verse*, printed for Tooke by William Bowyer the elder (1663–1737) (again without the mention of either name), displays a basket of flowers on an elaborate pedestal.[101] Instead of signalling the

---

[94] TS 2 (1a) and (1b), distinguishing first and second states, corresponding to *ESTC* T39454 and *ESTC* N44669. For further details, see *CWJS Parodies*, pp. 623, 628; and for a pioneering exploration of the meanings of the material text, see Ann Cline Kelly, 'The Semiotics of Swift's 1711 *Miscellanies*', *SStud*, 6 (1991), 59–68. Having registered the copy on 10 April 1710 alongside that of the 1710 *Tale*, Tooke entered it again on 24 February 1711, once more itemising the contents (*SCEBC* (1710–46), p. 106; see Chapter 3).

[95] TS 577, *ESTC* T42805; *CWJS Parodies*, pp. 121–56, 669–74.   [96] *CWJS Journal*, p. 31.

[97] For 'Subjects for a Volume', see SwJ 437; Ehrenpreis, *Swift*, vol. II, pp. 768–9; *CWJS Parodies*, p. 623.

[98] For large-paper copies of *Miscellanies* (1711), see D. Woolley, 'Swift's Copy', pp. 133, 169.

[99] For the gathering trend towards unframed titles from mid-century, see Bronson, *Printing as an Index of Taste*, pp. 24–6.

[100] The resulting differentiation may explain what otherwise seems a puzzling mistake (Treadwell, 'Swift's Relations', p. 34).

[101] For the careers and business of William Bowyer the elder and (from 1722) his son William Bowyer the younger, see *Bowyer Ledgers*, p. xvi. For *Miscellanies in Prose and Verse*, see no. 60, p. 114, noting ornament no. 118.

Politics and Permanence (1710–1714)

consolidation of a canon, the two volumes proclaimed their disconnection by a range of minor differences. Even if this was simply the result of passive carry-over from previous features of the *Tale* on the one hand and the delegation of *Miscellanies in Prose and Verse* to a new printer on the other, it was usefully consistent with Swift's attitude to the *Tale*. From this point of view, Bowyer would have had two outstanding recommendations for *Miscellanies in Prose and Verse*: his work was of high quality (here exemplified in a particularly graceful deployment of white space), and it was different from Motte's. Although the *Tale* volume was itself, as Pat Rogers points out, a kind of miscellany, its contents would be kept separate from the tradition begun by *Miscellanies in Prose and Verse* for as long as Swift was capable of managing his own affairs, and it was only later that they appeared as part of collected Works.[102]

While considering his new collection, Swift was struck by a rather different example recently published by William King (1663–1712), one of Oxford's Christ Church wits: Swift reported to Philips in March 1709 that 'D.r King has reprinted all his Works together, and the Volume begins with his Answer to M.r Molesworth's Book of Denmark' (where Philips was currently posted).[103] Swift's alertness to King's activities was understandable, for on publication of the *Tale* in 1704 King had been misidentified as '*the Author of A Tale of a Tub*', on which he had published *Remarks* in 1709 (and was forgiven in the 1710 Apology).[104] As J. Woolley and Karian point out, he was in 1704 the better-known writer of the two. Yet he had difficulty establishing himself, and his hopes of living by his pen were reflected in strategic differences between his *Miscellanies in Prose and Verse* and Swift's: King's, published by subscription, necessarily declared his name, along with the names of the booksellers, Bernard Lintot and Henry Clements; but Swift's did neither. This underlines the strategic omission, in Swift's *Miscellanies in Prose and Verse*, of any name but Morphew's, and the accomplished performance of prevarication about authorship that marks

---

[102] See Chapter 8.   [103] *Corr.*, vol. I, pp. 239, 241.

[104] This was William King of Christ Church, Oxford (1663–1712), not Archbishop William King of Dublin (1650–1729), nor William King of St Mary Hall, Oxford (1685–1763). Author of *Some Remarks on the Tale of a Tub. To which are annexed Mully of Mountown, and Orpheus and Euridice. By the Author of The journey to London* (London, 1704; *ESTC* T49383), and of *Miscellanies in Prose and Verse* (London, [1709]; *ESTC* N10990 (the *ECCO* entry of the same number dated '[1708]' is the proposal)), he would be one of the early writers of the *Examiner* (*CWJS Tale*, pp. 5, 323; Ellis, *Examiner*, p. xxv). Shortly before King's death Swift helped him to become editor of the *Gazette* (*CWJS Journal*, p. 358; *Corr.*, vol. I, p. 411; Rivington, 'Tyrant', pp. 24–5). For his early misidenti-fication as author of the *Tale*, see introduction to deattributed poems in *CWJS Poems* IV (forth-coming); A. C. Kelly, *Jonathan Swift and Popular Culture*, pp. 28–9.

126   Part II: London

'The Publisher to the Reader'. (The introduction was originally to have been written by Steele, but by 1710 Swift was instead telling Tooke to expect 'some hints, which I would have in a preface, and you may get some friend to dress them up'.[105]) It constructed, for the anonymous Swift, an indifference to fame and fortune that King had visibly sacrificed.

Indeed, the supposed Publisher of Swift's *Miscellanies* does not even seem to have the author's consent, but attempts to palliate his action by invoking the '*Universal ... good Reception*' the works have received from '*Men of Wit and Taste*', the dangerous enthusiasm of '*the* Booksellers' to obtain '*other of these Tracts in Manuscript in some Gentlemen's Hands*', and the authority of the friends '*in whose Hands I have reason to believe the Author left them, when his Affairs called him out of this Kingdom*'.[106] He also claims that as '*there is no Person Named*', '*the supposed Author is at Liberty to Disown as much as he thinks fit*'. Moreover, if the author resents publication he may still not '*know where to place his Resentment*' – and the publisher can at least be sure of '*the Thanks of every Body else*'. As to who this author might be, he is introduced as '*the Person who is generally known to be the Author of some; and, with greater Reason than I am at present at Liberty to give, supposed to be the Author of all the other Pieces*'. It is also claimed that he '*excels too much not to be Distinguished, since in all his Writings such a surprizing mixture of Wit and Learning, true Humour and good Sence does every where appear, as sets him almost as far out of the Reach of Imitation, as it does beyond the Power of Censure*'.

This preface thus encouraged readers to focus on Swift's rumoured authorship of '*some*' of the contents, but refused to confirm it. Prominent among the '*some*' were the previously published *Contests* (which came first) and *A Project for the Advancement of Religion* (which came second). The prose papers in the Bickerstaff hoax were grouped together in the prose section, and *A Grubstreet Elegy on the supposed Death of Patrige the Almanack-Maker* appeared with the poetry. Some of the material also contained obvious internal evidence: it was no secret, for instance, that Swift had been Berkeley's chaplain, so when the poem *To their Excellencies the Lords Justices of Ireland. The Humble Petition of Frances Harris* (previously published by Curll) identified the chaplain as a possible object of the speaker's marital ambitions, or when *Lady B— B——finding ... some Verses Unfinished* (here published for the first time) referred directly to 'Dr. S–', it was not hard to guess that the writer was Swift (and

---

[105] *Corr.*, vol. I, pp. 266, 282; *CWJS Parodies*, p. 579.
[106] *CWJS Parodies*, Appendix F, pp. 579–81.

Politics and Permanence (1710–1714) 127

the finder Lady Betty Berkeley).[107] As J. Woolley and Karian note, Swift seemed to take it for granted that his authorship of *Miscellanies in Prose and Verse* was an open secret – just as his affected complaint to Johnson and Dingley took for granted their interest in its price, publication details and sales figures:

> Some bookseller has raked up every thing I writ, and published it t'other day in one volume; but I know nothing of it, 'twas without my knowlege or consent: it makes a four shilling book, and is called *Miscellanies in Prose and Verse*. Tooke pretends he knows nothing of it, but I doubt he is at the bottom. One must have patience with these things; the best of it is, I shall be plagued no more. However, I'll bring a couple of them over with me for MD, perhaps you may desire to see them. I hear they sell mightily.[108]

But the Publisher as performed in the book took the pretence to another level, exhibiting a degree of vigilance against misattribution that served only to draw added attention to two particular pieces, '*before both of which I have in the Book expressed my Doubtfulness*'. One was a work that would be repeatedly invoked in representations of Swift as defender of the Test Act, the *Letter ... concerning the Sacramental Test*, which had previously appeared as a quarto pamphlet in 1709. Exceptionally, its part-title had its own facing Advertisement, assuring readers that it '*is supposed by some judicious Persons to be of the same Author*'. The note to the other, which appeared at the end of the poetry sequence, declared: '*The Following Poem being judged by some to be after the Authors manner, I have ventured to Print it.*' This was *The Virtues of Sid Hamet the Magician's Rod*, previously published as a half sheet in 1710.

The Publisher's scrupulosity both emphasised the collection as the work of a single author and insisted on the anonymity of that author, bringing together works that Swift had already published, works now published for the first time, and works previously published without his authority (but possibly with his connivance). In the first category appeared items such as the separately published *Contests*, the sequence of Bickerstaff papers published in 1708–9, and the poems *Baucis and Philemon* and *To Mrs Biddy Floyd*, both included in Tonson's *Poetical Miscellanies* in 1709. The second category revealed a variety of previously unpublished pieces. *A Description of a Salamander*, a verse satire on the soldier, poet and politician John Cutts (1660/61–1707), had apparently been composed in 1705 or 1706, had been included in Swift's 1708 list of

---

[107] For the publishing history of these poems, see *CWJS Poems* I (forthcoming).
[108] *CWJS Journal*, p. 152.

128   Part II: London

'Subjects for a Volume', and now came out in print for the first time after the subject's death (prompting a complaint to Oxford from his sister – who had no doubt at all that *Miscellanies in Prose and Verse*, like the *Tale*, was by Swift).[109] *A Tritical Essay upon the Faculties of the Mind* (its date of composition given as 1707) presented an act of self-undoing by an inane commonplacer that looked backward to the *Tale* (and would also, by the close of Swift's career, look forward to *Polite Conversation*).[110] Swift's profile as a defender of the Church and satirist of the campaign against the Test was also further developed by *The Sentiments of a Church of England-Man* and *An Argument to Prove that the Abolishing of Christianity in England, may . . . be attended with some Inconveniences* (with composition dated to 1708). Still more intriguing, perhaps, was the third category, exemplified by *A Meditation upon a Broom-stick*, which had previously been published only in unauthorised editions by Curll – on the strength of which Curll issued, immediately following the publication of *Miscellanies in Prose and Verse*, the made-up volume *Miscellanies by Dr Jonathan Swift*, not the least of whose offences was its open use of his name ('some trash ... with the name at large', as Swift characteristically noted).[111] While Curll's text of *A Meditation* seems to have been one that Swift in some sense approved (since he does not seem to have acted in 1711 to prevent its being used as copy), its inclusion in *Miscellanies in Prose and Verse* framed it for the first time as a quasi-acknowledged work.[112]

The collection's aspirations to the timeless over the timely are clear. Dates are supplied at the head of each work, but they are dates of composition, not of publication, emphasising the writer's development over time rather than his published interventions at particular moments. (Indeed, except in the special case of *A Letter ... concerning the Sacramental Test* there is no indication of which works had been published before and which were appearing for the first time.) Early Pindaric poems were understandably not included, and the author's all-round accomplishment was emphasised by separating the prose (at the beginning of the volume) from the verse (at the end), and by the increasing size of the type used for 'MISCELLANIES',

[109] For 'Subjects for a Volume', see Ehrenpreis, *Swift*, vol. II, pp. 768–9; *CWJS Parodies*, p. 623. For *A Description of a Salamander*, see *CWJS Journal*, p. 308; *CWJS Poems* I (forthcoming).
[110] *CWJS Parodies*, pp. xliii–xlv, 17–34, 604–40.
[111] *Ibid.*, pp. 636–7; *Miscellanies by Dr Jonathan Swift* (London, 1711; TS 3, *ESTC* T039444); *CWJS Journal*, p. 207; Karian, 'Edmund Curll', pp. 99, 117–21.
[112] Karian, 'Edmund Curll'; *CWJS Parodies*, p. 636; and for printers' preference for '*Printed Copy*', see Moxon, *Mechanick Exercises*, p. 203, and Smith, *The Printer's Grammar*, pp. 209–10.

Politics and Permanence (1710–1714)

'PROSE' and 'VERSE' on the title. This design weighted the inscription effectively on the unframed page by extending the largest capitals ('VERSE') across the full measure to match the span of the smallest ('MISCELLANIES'), while balancing the medium size ('PROSE') between them; and it also served to direct particular attention to the poems (perhaps by way of compensation for the dominating bulk of prose works at the beginning of the volume). The division between prose and verse also made it harder to reconstruct the relation of the contents to their originating contexts and to each other: for example *A Grubstreet Elegy on the supposed Death of Patrige the Almanack-Maker* was separated from the prose in the Bickerstaff affair (a division that would be influential for the future). Visual elements that had originally signalled allusions to cheap print, now out of scale (and arguably out of keeping) with the new octavo presentation, gave way to a blander dignity: the folio broadside *Elegy* is stripped of its elaborate funeral compartment, the half sheet *A Famous Prediction* of its woodcut of Gadbury *alias* Merlin (though the verse does retain its black letter).[113]

But one element of opportunist timeliness remains very clear. By the time this long-planned collection was actually published, the Tory ministry was in power and Swift was its propagandist: newly published pieces that had missed their chance to intervene in print while the debates they addressed were at their height could now document his commitment to once unfashionable causes. *An Argument to Prove that the Abolishing of Christianity in England, may … be attended with some Inconveniences* had been written in response to a former Whig ministry's attempts to repeal the Test, but now, as the headline date of 1708 emphasised, it proclaimed the High-Church loyalty that Swift had articulated (if not published) in the face of government hostility.[114] The reprinting of *A Project for the Advancement of Religion* under the date of 1709 also confirmed that his reverence for the Queen and concern for public morality predated the new ministry.[115] The previously published *Contests*, with its 1701 date of composition (but without any explicit reminder that the Lords it defended had actually been Whigs), now occupied first place in the volume and nearly a quarter of its pages; but Higgins argues that it 'now just read as a work of anti-populist political-philosophical reflection and historical meditation on the traditional Tory theme of "a *Dominatio Plebis*, or Tyranny of the People"'.[116] (He also notes that its placement parallels that of Temple's *An*

---

[113] For the *Elegy*, see *Miscellanies* (London, 1711), pp. 392–8; for *A Famous Prediction*, pp. 305–12.
[114] *PW*, vol. II, pp. xvii–xix.   [115] *Ibid.*, pp. 278–9.
[116] Higgins, 'Swift's Whig Pamphlet', pp. 554–6.

Part II: London

Essay on Popular Discontents at the beginning of *Miscellanea. The Third Part*, which Swift had edited in 1701, further insinuating a continuity between Tory and patrician Whig attitudes.) Indeed, only after printing had been completed does Swift seem to have realised how inappropriate the original conclusion of *Contests* might now appear: a late cancellation (perhaps motivated by St John's characterisation of bribery as the necessary recourse of the Whigs) removed Swift's suggestion that 'it will be safer to trust our Property and Constitution in the hands of such, who have pay'd for their Elections, than of those who have obtained them by servile Flatteries of the People'.[117]

Even more pervasive changes were made to *A Letter ... concerning the Sacramental Test*, which had previously been published in 1709: a separate 'Advertisement' explained that '*I have taken leave to omit about a Page which was purely Personal, and of no use to the Subject.*' This referred to a passage reflecting on the author and two of his clerical colleagues; but it would also have been striking, to anyone who recalled the original, that in this revised text the Brodricks were no longer invited to go hang themselves.[118] The amended text eschewed such personal distractions in favour of a loftier perspective, and its full-page 'Advertisement' constituted the most blatant commendation of the Tory Swift in the entire volume: '*it will be no disadvantage to him to have it here revived, considering the Time when it was Writ, the Persons then at the Helm, and the Designs in Agitation, against which this Paper so boldly appeared*'. This is the only instance in the collection where a paratext specifically recalls a past political context, and it does so by partisan insinuation, not by providing information. The editorial voice confidingly adds: '*I have been assured that the Suspicion which the supposed Author lay under for Writing this Letter, absolutely ruined him with the late M—stry.*' To recall Swift's former loss of favour was to underline his present claims.

Up to this point the octavos so discreetly handled by Tooke had not specifically named Swift as a deserving object of preferment; but this changed in 1712 with *A Proposal for Correcting, Improving and Ascertaining the English Tongue*, a publication with explicit designs on distant posterity. (Even so, it did not altogether escape association with the propaganda matrix from which it had emerged: in the Stationers' Entry Book it was entered to Tooke at the foot of a page on which Morphew had

---

[117] BL 838.g.1 contains both versions; see also Bodleian Library Vet.A4.e.811 (*CWJS Parodies*, p. 628). See Ellis, *Discourse*, pp. 127, 185–7; Higgins, 'Swift's Whig Pamphlet', p. 562; Introduction to *CWJS English Political Writings, 1701–1711* (forthcoming).

[118] *PW*, vol. II, pp. xxiii–xxiv, 283–4.

already entered for Barber two of the 'John Bull' pamphlets by Swift's Scriblerian friend John Arbuthnot, an attack on Bentley's Horace, and Swift's *The New Way of Selling Places at Court*.[119]) In terms of content, Swift's *Proposal* drew on the defensive attitude to language change that he had outlined in 1710 in a 'long letter to Bickerstaff' printed in *Tatler* no. 230, but its material form also brought to bear an unusual degree of refinement, as it put on record Swift's aspiration to commemorate in imperishable language the triumphs of the Queen and her Tory ministry.[120] His only precedent to date for such explicit self-disclosure in an original work had been in the dedicatory letter to his *Ode to the Athenian Society*: the *Proposal for Correcting ... the English Tongue*, effectively the covering letter to his unsuccessful application for the post of Historiographer Royal, was incomparably superior in print quality and intellectual ambition, but no less futile. Indeed, its exceptional pomp of presentation – not to mention its parading of Swift's closeness to the ministry – made its failure all the more conspicuous.

The *Proposal for Correcting ... the English Tongue* takes the form of a letter to Oxford, and Swift's name appears not only on a half-title describing the work as 'Dr. *SWIFT*'s LETTER TO THE *Lord High Treasurer*', but also, as in the covering letter to the Athenian Society, in a formal subscription.[121] Following a final paragraph that artfully repudiates the role of projector implicit in Swift's proposal for an Academy, the subscription is elaborately presented: a humbly deferential address to Lord Oxford, deploying large and small capitals to invoke his rank and lower-case italic for the rest, is centred as a block further articulated by differential indentation; the signature 'J. SWIFT', set in large and small capitals of a larger size, is set out to the right-hand margin; and the address and date, 'London, / Feb. 22. / 1711, 12', are set out to the left in a block of smaller type. Such an elaborately calibrated flourish of deference is all of a piece with the careful printwork displayed throughout, and with the rhetorical decorum of the letter form itself. Beginning 'MY LORD, / What I had the Honour of mentioning to Your LORDSHIP some time ago in Conversation ...', the pamphlet establishes from the outset the intimate yet respectful terms on which author and Lord Treasurer discuss matters of

---

[119] *SCEBC* (1710–46), p. 153.

[120] For *Tatler* no. 230, see *CWJS Journal*, pp. 14, 18, and *CWJS Parodies*, pp. 89–103, 660–2; for the *Proposal* (TS 557, *ESTC* T42805), pp. 121–56, 669–74; for Swift's ambitions, Ann Cline Kelly, *Swift and the English Language* (Philadelphia, PA: University of Pennsylvania Press, 1988), pp. 97–100.

[121] Swift apparently gained Oxford's approval in advance: he then told Johnson and Dingley that 'I will send it him to morrow, and will print it if he desires me' (*CWJS Journal*, pp. 228, 392).

132   Part II: London

mutual interest – which extend far beyond the political emergencies of the moment into the remote history and long-term future of English culture, here assimilated, in partisan terms, to the policies of the Queen and her Tory ministry. (Indeed, to judge by a scribal transcript apparently closer to Swift's original handwritten letter, coverage of Oxford's subsequently imparted insights has been amplified in the printed text, while a long compliment to Addison has been shortened.[122]) Even at a time when Swift was daily engaged in pamphlet warfare, it was on the more elevated ground of linguistic connoisseurship, and a more distinguished piece of pamphlet-making, that he chose to rest his claim to advancement.

Swift's name does not, however, appear on the title page, although Tooke's does.[123] As with the *Project for the Advancement of Religion*, this unusual frankness about Tooke's role marks it, Treadwell argues, as one of the few works 'worthy and humourless' enough for Swift to relax his defensive instincts, an impression seconded by the wholly exceptional disclosure of his identity in the subscription.[124] (Swift commented to Johnson and Dingley – apparently forgetting the covering letter to the *Ode to the Athenian Society* – that 'I suffer my name to be put at te End of it, wch I nevr did before in my Life.'[125]) The name highlighted on the title is instead that of the addressee, 'ROBERT / *Earl of* Oxford *and* Mortimer, / *Lord High Treasurer* / OF / GREAT BRITAIN.' The largest full capitals of all, larger even than those of 'PROPOSAL' or '*LETTER*', are indeed reserved for 'ROBERT'; but equally large, and more distinctive, is '𝕰𝖓𝖌𝖑𝖎𝖘𝖍 𝕿𝖔𝖓𝖌𝖚𝖊', set in the black letter tellingly known to printers as 'English'.[126] The language is figured as an heirloom to be passed down to distant ages, one that can be entrusted only to a Tory ministry and its propagandist: John Oldmixon, in a Whig critique, aptly noted that 'he has put his Name to his letter, and a Name greater than his own, as if he meant to Bully us into his Methods for pinning down our Language'.[127]

The title page of this octavo pamphlet, with its double-ruled frame and touch of black letter, looks at first glance not unlike the pamphlets that Barber was producing in the same format. Like them, this performance could readily be construed as political in its cultural vision – not to mention self-serving in its quest for influence and preferment – and presumptuous in brushing aside an impressive body of Old English

---

[122] *CWJS Parodies*, pp. 669, 672–3.   [123] For reproduction, see *ibid.*, p. 130.
[124] Treadwell, 'Swift's Relations', p. 15.   [125] *CWJS Journal*, p. 423.
[126] McLaverty, 'Swift and the Art of Political Publication', pp. 123–4.
[127] John Oldmixon, *Reflections on Dr Swift's Letter to the Earl of Oxford about the English Tongue* (London, 1712; *ESTC* T46548), p. 2.

scholarship.[128] Yet if the pamphlet's basic design is familiar, its quality and amplitude is not: although its forty-eight pages sit comfortably in the upper size range of the pamphlets executed by Barber, it contains far less text per page, deploying larger type and ampler spacing to articulate aspirations that transcend Barber's price-sensitive imperatives. Tooke's text begins with a decorated initial, uses full capitals for the first word of each paragraph, separates each paragraph from the next with an added space, and sets the running head across both pages of the opening, between well-printed rules. Yet even in this luxury presentation, the notions of correctness and permanence that Swift strove to promote refuse to be entirely captured in print – possibly because Swift himself did not always recognise conventional departures from the pamphlet's declared doctrines when he saw them. There is a degree of self-reflexive irony, therefore, in a material text that fails to eliminate the abuses of which it complains. Two of Swift's bugbears were the abbreviated past tense in ''d', where mute 'e' was conventionally replaced by an apostrophe, and the abbreviation 'tho''; but the condemned forms still make a few appearances in the first edition.[129] Someone, probably Swift, successfully reduced their number in the second, but still failed to catch every instance. Such supposed faults, actually second nature to contemporary printers, may not have been as noticeable (even to Swift) as he claimed; but in later life their elimination from collections of his works would become a marked preoccupation. This, ironically, would be the most tangible outcome of the ambition embodied in the *Proposal for Correcting … the English Tongue*; for Oxford, while ostensibly favouring Swift's scheme, had still taken no decisive action by the time Swift left London in 1713 in despair over the ministry's prospects.[130]

Dublin

Meanwhile, a range of Swift's political writings from these years was quickly reprinted not only in Scotland, but also, and much more prolifically, in Dublin, where Tory booksellers and printers formed a relatively small but

---

[128] For political responses by John Oldmixon and Arthur Mainwaring, see *CWJS Parodies*, pp. 125–6; for linguistic critique see Elizabeth Elstob, *An Apology for the Study of Northern Antiquities* [as prefixed to her *Rudiments of Grammar for the English-Saxon Tongue*, London, 1715], ed. Charles Peake, Augustan Reprint Society, 61 (1956); *CWJS Parodies*, pp. 127–8, 131–6.

[129] *CWJS Parodies*, pp. 139–41, 669–70, 672–3. For a printer's view from 1755, see Smith, *The Printer's Grammar*, pp. 106–8.

[130] *CWJS Parodies*, pp. 123–7; Rivington, *'Tyrant'*, pp. 54–61.

Part II: London

very active group.[131] Swift himself constantly speculated to Johnson and Dingley as to whether or not particular pieces would be reprinted there (promising, as fall-back, 'If you have them not, I'll bring them over'); and he is unlikely to have been merely a passive observer (he comments that *The Conduct of the Allies* had been 'sent over to Ireland, and I suppose you will have it reprinted').[132] Of the printers who took up such opportunities, one would be prevented by death and one apparently by emigration from contributing further to Swift in print, and another was probably disqualified on grounds of quality; but the other two would play a vital part in the revival of Swift's publishing career when, after his disappointed return to Dublin in 1714, he finally began once more to send new work to press.

Sadly, it was John Henly, the Dublin bookseller whom there is most reason to associate directly with Swift, who was in 1714 removed from the scene by death – while under investigation for a tendentious publication not by Swift.[133] While Swift was in Dublin in 1713 for his installation as Dean of St Patrick's, Henly published and progressively corrected what appears to have been the first edition of Swift's Horatian address to Oxford, *The Seventh Epistle of the first Book of Horace Imitated. And Address'd to a Noble Lord*, apparently intended as a jocular reminder of a substantial payment that Oxford supposedly owed him.[134] The quarto pamphlet's four pages are clearly and accurately printed in appropriately large type, with italics for names and full capitals for 'WINDSOR'; the couplets are kept together at page turns, and neat marginal notes are cued by in-text asterisks. (Swift did not, apparently, provide Henly with the Latin footnotes that featured in the London reprints.) Henley also produced, in 1714, a reprint of *The Publick Spirit of the Whigs* which gave the original unexpurgated text, complete with sneers against the Scottish nobility. Following the unusual quarto format of the London edition (designed to be bound with Steele's quarto *The Crisis*), Henly imitates its markedly clean, modern title page (no frame; no black letter; neat large and small capitals for emphasis). The main body of the text is also sharply printed, with a careful conventional application of italics, full capitals for such terms as 'QUEEN' and 'HIGH TREASON', and italic full capitals to point a final query as to whether Steele is really 'a *HUMAN CREATURE*'. In the same year Henly also commissioned Daniel Tompson, a London-trained printer (alleged by Whalley to have changed his name

---

[131] For Scottish reprints, see *CWJS English Political Writings, 1711–1714*, pp. 333–4. For the relatively restricted Tory network in the Dublin print trade, see May, 'False and Incomplete Imprints', pp. 72–3.

[132] E.g. *CWJS Journal*, pp. 44, 137; p. 338.   [133] Pollard, *Dictionary*, pp. 283–4.

[134] *CWJS Poems* I (forthcoming); *CWJS Journal*, p. 536.

Politics and Permanence (1710–1714)

from 'Dring') who had been active in Dublin since 1702, to reprint for him *A Preface to the B—p of S-r-m's Introduction*.[135] This text was sprinkled with errors, blotches and mis-sorted type, but it found its mark by introducing one '*M...... t h*' as one of those who, like Burnet, spoke slightingly of the lower clergy: taken (as Swift presumably intended) to refer to the anti-clerical Whig Robert Molesworth (1656–1725), the new reading caused a parliamentary furore in Dublin, which was widely reported in London.[136]

Tompson had in fact commenced his service to Swift in print by republishing the *Examiner* in 1710, which makes him, whatever his short-comings, the first to publish Swift's London propaganda in Dublin.[137] But he did not continue the *Examiner* for long, and an advertisement at the end of no. 10 suggests that jobbing work may have suited him better:

> At Daniel Tompson's, *next Door to the Tom of Lincoln, in West-Church Street in Smith-Field, where there's a Rouuling-Press, ready to Print all sorts of Copper-Pleats, as Tobacco Bills, and This Indenture, of different Sizes of Text-Hand, and Lottery Pictures, at reasonable Rates.*[138]

Whatever the reason, Tompson soon relinquished the *Examiner* and (according to Whalley) fled to England in 1714 to avoid prosecution for printing *A Long History of a Short Session of Parliament*.[139] The new under-taker of the *Examiner* was none other than Cornelius Carter, celebrated by Munter (despite his notorious shortcomings in other respects) as 'perhaps the most energetic and enterprising printer of his time' in the development of Irish newspapers, who had identified in the *Examiner* an opportunity which, to judge by the variations among surviving copies, would 'support not just one local reprint edition but several'.[140] Carter seems to have catered to collectors by reprinting some of Tompson's numbers with his own imprint, and advertised at the end of no. 12 that '*All Gentlemen and others may be furnished' d with this Paper for 4 shill. per Year, paying one*

---

[135] For Tompson, alias Dring, see Gadd, '"At Four Shillings per Year"', pp. 85–6; Pollard, *Dictionary*, p. 570. For the Dublin *A Preface to the B—p of S-r-m's Introduction* (1714; TS 539, *ESTC* T119945), see *PW*, vol. IV, pp. xxiv–xxviii.

[136] The representation of the name (including the additional space before and between the final letters) is transcribed from p. 23 of the Dublin edition.

[137] Pollard, *Dictionary*, p. 570; the present account of the Dublin *Examiner*s is based on TCD 'Copy A', 95.TT.l.73, a continuously paginated set of Tompson and Carter numbers. For full analysis of Dublin *Examiner*s, with a listing of extant copies, see Gadd, '"At Four Shillings per Year"', pp. 81–93.

[138] 'Copy A', p. 40.

[139] For two editions of the offending work, attributed to Patrick Delany and Richard Helsham, see *ESTC* T2069, T1888.

[140] Munter, *The History of the Irish Newspaper*, p. 111; see also pp. 57, 77–8; Gadd, '"At Four Shillings per Year"', p. 89.

Quarter in Hand, and shall have 'em sent to their Houses or Lodgings', although he raised doubts that the project would attract sufficient 'Encouragement' to continue (as support was currently 'but very indifferent').[141] This made the quarterly subscription look like a better bet for the printer than the subscriber, but demand was evidently deemed sufficient for the project to go forward. Immediate commercial advantage was obviously an overriding consideration: although the *Examiner*s are far from Carter's worst work, the last two pages of no. 45 are squashed into smaller type to make room for a long (and no doubt profitable) advertisement for a pewterer.[142] Literal errors were both frequent and flagrant ('ublin' in imprint of *Examiner* 1; 'Exaimner' in heading of no. 6); there are arbitrary shifts from larger to smaller type; and Carter's distinctively botched composite rules made their expected appearance.[143] Indeed, such distinctive presswork suggests that Carter may also have been behind a reprint of the 1710 *A Short Character of His Ex. T. E. of W. L. L. of I—*, suspected, despite bearing the London imprint of the fictitious Coryton, of being a Dublin product.[144] Its compressed twenty-four pages (as against the original twenty-nine), which feature mismatched type, uneven composite rules, misspellings, misaligned type and poor spacing (not to mention a substantial section of smaller type in the main text resulting from misunderstanding the status of a London footnote) would all be consistent with his involvement. Given the special interest for Dublin readers of such a scandalous denunciation of Lord Wharton, their former Lord Lieutenant, a speedy reprint probably looked like an opportunity worth taking.

Carter's known reprints of Swift's pamphlets, which, like other Dublin reprints, retained the octavo format of the London originals, show little regard for consistency and accuracy. In 1712 his *The New Way of Selling Places at Court. In a Letter from a Small Courtier to a Great Stock-Jobber* again featured arbitrary changes in type size and introduced literal errors. It also presented one substantive change ('were' for 'could be'), of which Gadd concludes, in the light of the edition's evident setting from the London original, that 'it is difficult to account for this different reading' – and the difficulty is the greater in the context of such a high level of

---

[141] Gadd, '"At Four Shillings per Year"', p. 88.

[142] Munter, *The History of the Irish Newspaper*, pp. 48, 173–6.

[143] For the use of composite rules in Dublin, see May, 'False and Incomplete Imprints', p. 61.

[144] TS 530, *ESTC* T48135; it is particularly well represented in Irish collections. However, for evidence that the text was substantially corrected during printing, see *CWJS English Political Writings, 1701–1711* (forthcoming).

Politics and Permanence (1710–1714)

background error.[145] In the same year Carter also printed *Some Reasons to Prove, that no Person is obliged by his Principles as a Whig, to Oppose Her Majesty or her Present Ministry. In a Letter to a Weig-Lord* [*sic*].[146] Gadd is eloquent on its shortcomings: 'misaligned lines and extremely poor inking', failure to act on the errata note in his London copy, and a particularly severe case of type size reduction towards the end, which, even so, leaves Carter 'having to use the whole of the direction line on the final page to set the last line of text'.[147] Tellingly, the reader of a copy at the Royal Irish Academy has not only corrected the errant 'e' to 'h' on the title, but also underlined with an emphatic flourish the '*FINIS*' so nearly elbowed off the page by Carter's incompetence.[148] In 1713, in *Some Advice Humbly Offer'd to the Members of the October Club; in a Letter from a Person of Honour*, [*sic*], Carter managed, for once, to set a whole pamphlet in the same size of type, and even to correct a few literal errors in the London copy; but his title, with its stray final comma, was still framed by poorly managed composite rules, and the impression was characteristically fuzzy, with some letters failing to print at all. Although he prudently omitted his name from his 1714 reprint of *The Publick Spirit of the Whigs* (which had proved dangerously controversial in London), it contained all his familiar hallmarks: a wobbly double-ruled title frame composed of differently sized short rules; similarly composed rules throughout; mis-sorted type in the imprint ('*DUBLIN*') and in the heading to the main text ('PUBLICK'); several shifts of type size; frequent literal errors; capitals for some verbs as well as nouns; and the use of a different paper, now strongly discoloured, for signature B.[149] More substantively, this text (which may have been taken from Henly's) had not been censored, unlike later London editions, to remove Swift's reflection on the Scottish Lords. The 'probable errors' reported by Gadd are well within Carter's norms – although it remains possible, as Gadd suggests, that the reprint could have been set from a manuscript copy. Although Carter would continue to print occasional pieces by or in support of Swift, he would never in any sense be his printer.

Operating at a somewhat better level of workmanship, and destined for a much more significant future in Swift in print, was the frequently prosecuted Edward Waters (active from 1707, *d.* 1751), who printed two different editions of *The Conduct of the Allies* and two of the *Barrier*

---

[145] *CWJS English Political Writings, 1711–1714*, pp. 407–8.   [146] *Ibid.*, pp. 410–13.
[147] *Ibid.*, p. 410.
[148] Royal Irish Academy, HP 20 (3). 'Weig-Lord' remains uncorrected in the TCD copy, RR. mm.53 (10).
[149] *CWJS English Political Writings, 1711–1714*, pp. 458–9, 468–9.

Treaty.[150] His work, though more accurate than Carter's, betrays at this stage a somewhat similar scrappiness (although he does at least deploy long rules rather than Carter's haphazard composites); but a key difference was that Waters was demonstrably capable of doing better, as he would show when he printed Swift's *Proposal for the Universal Use of Irish Manufacture* in 1720.[151] When printing *Conduct* in 1712, however, he included apparently random pages in italic, and, even more surprisingly, in black letter; and he also resorted to 'vv' for 'w', reinforcing the suspicion that he was working with a very limited quantity of type.[152] His first reprint of *Some Remarks on the Barrier Treaty* in 1712 features among its errors and inelegancies a particularly cramped presentation of the final 'Representation of the English Merchants at Bruges', run on with the preceding text without any additional spacing or distinction of type to pick out its headings. This hard-to-follow presentation is apparently the price of packing the whole pamphlet into thirty-two pages. Similar economy also marks his second edition; but here he does manage to correct some literal errors, which suggests at least the capacity for better work. (Gadd even surmises that he may have been motivated in part by 'embarrassment at the number of mistakes'.) Waters's potential for Swift in print, however, arose in large part from his close association with a more cautiously ambitious Dublin printer and bookseller, John Hyde.[153]

Hyde operated in a wider sphere than Waters or Carter, as instanced by his 1712 reprint of *Conduct of the Allies*, which apparently derives from printed sheets (or perhaps a manuscript) acquired on a visit to London.[154] As bookseller and printer he was capable of producing textually accurate work with relatively clear visual impact, and often worked with the accomplished printer Aaron Rhames (active 1703–34).[155] In reprinting Swift he was notably more generous with paper than Waters: Hyde's *The*

---

[150] For *Conduct*, see *CWJS English Political Writings, 1711–1714*, pp. 349–50, 366–8; for *Barrier*, pp. 388, 394–6.

[151] See Chapter 5.

[152] See Waters's comparable struggles with insufficient type in his Dublin reprint for Hyde of Swift's 1711 *Some Remarks upon a Pamphlet, Entitl'd, [A Letter to the Seven Lords of the Committee Appointed to Examine Gregg]* (TS 535, *ESTC* N22908), and see textual account in *CWJS English Political Writings, 1701–1711* (forthcoming).

[153] *ESTC* records four publications printed by Waters 'for' or 'sold by' Hyde, ranging from 1711 to 1721.

[154] For John Hyde and his wife Sarah, daughter of the distinguished printer Joseph Ray, see Pollard, *Dictionary*, pp. 304–7; *CWJS English Political Writings, 1711–1714*, pp. 348–9; May, 'False and Incomplete Imprints', pp. 60–6, 70, 72, 75–6, 83, 86, 89, 92, 95.

[155] For Rhames, see Pollard, *Dictionary*, pp. 488–9; May, 'False and Incomplete Imprints', pp. 60–1, 63, 67, 70, 72, 75, 80–1, 83, 86–7.

Conduct of the Allies runs to seventy-two octavo pages against Waters's fifty-four, and his *Some Remarks on the Barrier Treaty* to thirty-six against thirty-two.[156] The impact on the reading experience can be judged by comparing their respective presentations of *Some Remarks on the Barrier Treaty*: Hyde uses clear, comfortably sized type throughout, and lays out the final 'Representation of the English Merchants at Bruges' in a much more user-friendly format than Waters. In Hyde's edition its supplementary status is signalled by presenting it as a two-page appendix in smaller type, beginning, with appropriate headings, on a new recto. Admittedly, both works were even more generously presented by Barber in London (where *The Conduct of the Allies* had at first run to ninety-six pages and *Some Remarks on the Barrier Treaty* to forty-eight), but Hyde, foreshadowing the decent but unpretentious work he would later do for Swift, had struck a realistic balance between what a pamphlet might achieve with Barber in London and what it might suffer at the lowest levels of the Dublin trade.[157] It hardly seems a coincidence that Carter, the only one of the Tory printers old enough to have figured in Dunton's late seventeenth-century survey, was also the only one of those still active in the Dublin trade after 1720 to whom Swift does not seem to have entrusted new work. Hyde (and even Waters) could provide a more attractive and accurate product; and in the later 1720s, when the Dublin reprinting of Swift's *Travels* required a scaling-up from pamphlets to book, this too would prove to be within Hyde's capacity. After Swift's brief heyday in London's political dazzle, it was these Dublin printers, rather than Tooke or Barber, who would carry Swift in print forward into a future increasingly shaped by commitment to Ireland.

Meanwhile, did we not know the political disappointments that beset Swift in 1713–14, the appearance in early 1714 of a second London edition of Tooke's *Miscellanies in Prose and Verse*, dated 1713 and once more priced at 4s., might have seemed to mark a moment of triumph (although he could scarcely have been pleased to see it baldly attributed to 'Dr. *Swift*' in *The Monthly Catalogue*).[158] On its title page two putti, replacing the former basket of flowers, flourish palms and laurel crowns

---

[156] *CWJS English Political Writings, 1711–1714*, pp. 355–6, 365–8; 390–1, 393–6.
[157] The fifth and sixth London editions, set in smaller type on forty-eight pages, took up only half the number of sheets. Priced at sixpence, they were ideal for bulk purchase for free distribution (*CWJS English Political Writings, 1711–1714*, pp. 343–4).
[158] TS 2 (2) and 3 (3), corresponding to *ESTC* T39455 and T170386 (for details, see *CWJS Parodies*, pp. 628–9); *The Monthly Catalogue, 1714–17*, English Bibliographical Sources, Series I, No. 1 (London: Gregg Press, 1964), August 1714, I. 29.

Part II: London

in celebration of the still anonymous author (who is not represented). Echoing the imposing frontispiece of volume six of Tonson's *Poetical Miscellanies*, in which a trumpeting putto waves his palm over the head of a laurel-crowned muse, the motif also anticipated the frontispieces that Swift's future Dublin bookseller George Faulkner would commission for volumes II (*Poetical Works*) and IV (*A Collection of Tracts relating to Ireland*) of his 1735 Dublin *Works*, compositions in which the author would be not only represented but also readily identifiable.[159] But first, in the wake of the Hanoverian succession and Swift's return to Ireland as Dean of St Patrick's, Swift in print had a long and difficult transition to negotiate.

[159] See Chapters 3 and 7.

PART III

Dublin

CHAPTER 5

The Irish Patriot in Print (1720–1725)

There now intervened a gap of half a decade in the growth of the printed canon. After a relatively late, slow start, Swift's tally of published works had grown towards its London climax of 1710–14, when he was in his forties: there could hardly be a starker contrast with what followed, as he entered his fifties in Ireland in the aftermath of the Hanoverian succession and the triumph of the Whigs. Yet out of this silence would emerge a crucial reconfiguration, as Swift in print, regrounded in the Dublin print trade, refocused decisively on Irish grievances. Swift's attempts to work with the London trade would from now on involve slow and unsatisfactory delegation; but Dublin's print-shops were so close to St Patrick's that the more pressing problem was how to maintain a safe distance. It was these print-shops' relatively unpretentious products, in a market where pamphleteering was still more a matter of individual expression than a commercial livelihood, that would in the 1720s make Swift in print synonymous with Irish patriotism.[1]

Swift's letters show that he remained keenly interested in London's world of print, noting to Atterbury in 1717 that he was being 'torn to pieces by pamphleteers on that side the water' (i.e. in England), and routinely asking to be remembered to 'Ben and John' (i.e. Tooke and Barber).[2] In January 1719 he noted a report 'that poor Ben Took grows ill an[d] spleenatick'; and he jested about Barber's by now considerable wealth.[3] After years of book-trade conviviality in London, he may have sought comparable company in Dublin: he retained Mrs Brent, the

---

[1] James Kelly, 'Political Publishing, 1700–1800', in Raymond Gillespie and Andrew Hadfield (eds.), *The Oxford History of the Irish Book*, vol. III: *The Irish Book in English, 1550–1800* (Oxford University Press, 2006), pp. 215–33 (pp. 215–24); Sabine Baltes, *The Pamphlet Controversy about Wood's Halfpence (1722–25) and the Tradition of Irish Constitutional Nationalism*, Bernfried Nugel and Hermann Josef Real (eds.), Münster Monographs on English Literature, vol. 27 (Frankfurt: Peter Lang, 2002), pp. 6, 23–5.

[2] *Corr.*, vol. II, pp. 253–4, 280.   [3] For Tooke, see *ibid.*, pp. 291–2; for Barber, pp. 343, 347–8.

Part III: Dublin

Presbyterian widow of his first bookseller, as his housekeeper; and he thought of the shop of the bookseller Thomas Kendall (active by 1729, *d.* 1766) as a place where 'one might pass 3 or 4 hours in drinking Coffee in the morning, or dining tête à tête, and drinking Coffee again till 7'.[4] In Dublin he helped Prior manage the Irish subscriptions for his *Poems on Several Occasions*, which Tonson was producing to sumptuous effect in London, and Prior suggested that such refinements might be a useful distraction in times of political adversity, writing of the 'pretty kind of Amusement' that he found in 'Commas, Semicolons, Italic and Capital, to make Nonsense more pompous and Fabbelow bad Poetry with good Printing', and in 'contriving Emblems such as Cupids, Torches and Hearts for great Letters'.[5] Such a project could hardly have presented a greater contrast with the next phase of Swift in print.

The old tension between time and eternity was about to be reconfigured in terms very different from the material ambition that had marked Tooke's successive editions of the *Tale*, the *Miscellanies in Prose and Verse* and *A Proposal for Correcting, Improving and Ascertaining the English Tongue*. Ironically, the Irish controversial pamphlets of the coming decade, which prioritised cheap distribution for wide and immediate impact, would be reinterpreted by later progressive movements with a passion for which the English Tory writings would find no equivalent. But for the moment Swift found himself in a nation and city he would not have chosen, confronting a hostile regime without the kind of book-trade support he had enjoyed in London: it was clear that techniques that had worked in London could not simply be transferred to Dublin. In the coming years it became more vital than ever to protect his anonymity, but there were in Dublin no trade publishers to screen him – although it was easy enough to issue small pieces with false or incomplete imprints.[6] Yet the open (but unadmitted) secret of Swift's authorship, already so familiar in relation to the *Tale* and some at least of the London propaganda, was soon to become a matter of life and death; and most of the risk (as well as profit) would fall to Dublin printers whose courage and ingenuity now loomed larger than the sophistication and conviviality of Tooke and Barber. The Dublin printers' cheap, risky, popular pamphlets not only secured Swift's permanent celebrity as Irish patriot, but also helped to provide, in the view of Bullard and McLaverty, a 'stimulus to

---

[4] Pollard, *Dictionary*, p. 338; *Corr.*, vol. II, p. 421 (suggesting Kendall's shop as a venue for meeting Esther Vanhomrigh).
[5] *Corr.*, vol. II, pp. 264, 268.   [6] For overview, see May, 'False and Incomplete Imprints'.

The Irish Patriot in Print (1720–1725)

Dublin book culture' that may help to explain the 'very high rise in Dublin's productivity in the 1720s'.[7]

Vital to this new turn was the wider context of poor harvests and depression in the Irish woollen trade, combined with an accumulation of political challenges, including the Declaratory Act of 1720, that heightened Irish resentment.[8] Between 1720 and 1725, alongside relatively innocuous social verse reflecting Swift's renewed friendships in Ireland, his new publications protested against English curbs on Irish trade, opposed the scheme for an Irish bank, decried threats to the Church of Ireland, and, most notably of all, mounted a major campaign against the Englishman William Wood's patent for a new Irish copper coinage.[9] Unlike the propaganda printed by Barber in London, this Dublin campaign against Wood's halfpence would not refract Swift into an endlessly diversified and diversionary troupe of commentators, but focus instead on a single fictitious character, the Dublin woollen-draper M. B. Drapier. As controversy deepened, restaging the dynamics of the Bickerstaff affair on a larger scale and at a higher pitch of intensity, the letters of M. B. Drapier circulated as part of a mass of mostly anonymous or pseudonymous publications constituting what James Kelly has called 'the single greatest effusion of domestically generated political print yet witnessed in Ireland'.[10] It was not easy either then or now to draw a clear line between Swiftian and non-Swiftian contributions, but it was undeniable that Swift in print was shaping much larger issues, both commercially and politically.[11]

Henly and Tompson, who had produced Swift's *The Seventh Epistle of the first Book of Horace Imitated. And Address'd to a Noble Lord* in 1713, were no longer available to take up this new campaign, for Henly was dead and

---

[7] Bullard and McLaverty, 'Introduction', p. 8. For cautions about 'the alleged pre-eminence of his ideas and uniqueness of his rhetoric', however, see Baltes, *The Pamphlet Controversy*, pp. 4–5, 129, 136, 303–4.

[8] Connolly, *Divided Kingdom*, pp. 218–25; Ehrenpreis, *Swift*, vol. III, pp. 108–318; Ferguson, *Jonathan Swift and Ireland*, pp. 7–23, 45–6; Baltes, *The Pamphlet Controversy*, pp. 86–101.

[9] Ehrenpreis, *Swift*, vol. III, pp. 108–318; *PW*, vol. IX, pp. xv–xxii; Davis, *Drapier's Letters*; *PW*, vol. X, pp. ix–xxxi; *CWJS Poems* II (forthcoming). For financial contexts, see Patrick Walsh, *The South Sea Bubble and Ireland: Money, Banking and Investment, 1690–1721* (Woodbridge: Boydell, 2014; see index, 'Swift, Jonathan'); Patrick Kelly, 'Swift on Money and Economics', in Christopher Fox (ed.), *The Cambridge Companion to Jonathan Swift* (Cambridge University Press, 2003), pp. 128–45.

[10] J. Kelly, 'Political Publishing', p. 223.

[11] See headnotes to Sabine Baltes-Ellermann (ed.), *Swift's Allies: The Wood's Halfpence Controversy in Ireland, 1724–1725*, 2nd revised and augmented edition, Bernfried Nugel and Hermann Josef Real (eds.), Münster Monographs on English Literature, vol. 38 (Frankfurt: Peter Lang, 2017), which reprints Swift's contributions as part of a compilation of 108 items in the controversy; for attribution of Wood-related poems to Swift, see *CWJS Poems* II and deattributed poems in vol. IV (forthcoming).

Part III: Dublin

Tompson had apparently fled to England. Carter, on the other hand, though still active and long-inured to official investigation, was notorious for his slapdash work. Hyde and Waters, however, had already shown that they could make a decent job of reprinting Swift's London works; their collaboration and methods of evading official investigation were well established; and Hyde, by comparison with his Dublin generation, had useful London contacts.[12] Yet in the 1720s, when continued involvement in Swift's Irish controversies had probably become too dangerous for Hyde and Waters, Swift's work passed into the hands of John Harding (active from 1718, *d.* 1725) and his wife Sarah (active 1721–9), who worked to a quality that was lower than theirs, but still superior to Carter's. Younger than Hyde and Waters, and much younger than the generation of Crooke, Brent and Carter commemorated by Dunton in his *Dublin Scuffle*, the Hardings belonged to the same print generation as George Faulkner, who would subsequently emerge as Swift's late-life bookseller.[13] But John Harding, who had been Waters's apprentice, would barely outlive the Drapier affair; and his widow Sarah Harding, despite printing for Swift in the later 1720s, soon remarried – and even had John survived, they could not have competed in the long term with Faulkner's strategic ambition, which far exceeded the previous norms of the Dublin trade. In the later 1720s Faulkner sought out work experience in London, not only honing his skills as a journeyman in the Bowyers' printing-house, but also establishing a long-term collaboration with William Bowyer the younger (who joined his father's business in 1722).[14] Only Faulkner approached the London trade with such dynamic aspiration.

What Hyde, Waters and the Hardings did have in their favour was their dauntless persistence in printing on behalf of Tory and High-Church causes. Notably, all three of the men had been investigated in relation to the same seditious reprint of 1715, *English Advice to the Freeholders of England* (Hyde was the bookseller, Waters the printer and Harding the apprentice – the author was Atterbury).[15] All, over the coming years, would

---

[12] For the much-investigated Waters's tactics, see May, 'False and Incomplete Imprints', pp. 68–9, 73, 77–82, 87.

[13] Pollard, *Dictionary*, pp. 198–205 (and her slightly fuller article 'George Faulkner'), updating Ward, *Prince of Dublin Printers*, pp. 6–34.

[14] Pollard, *Dictionary*, p. 199; *Bowyer Ledgers*, p. xvi; Keith Maslen, 'George Faulkner and William Bowyer: The London Connection', in *An Early London Printing House at Work: Studies in the Bowyer Ledgers* (New York: Bibliographical Society of America, 1993), pp. 223–33.

[15] James Woolley, 'Poor John Harding and Mad Tom: "Harding's Resurrection" (1724)', in Charles Benson and Siobhán Fitzpatrick (eds.), *That Woman! Studies in Irish Bibliography: A Festschrift for Mary 'Paul' Pollard* (Dublin: Lilliput Press, 2005), pp. 102–21 (p. 102).

The Irish Patriot in Print (1720–1725)

undertake considerable risks in printing new work by Swift – but all also operated well below the highest level of workmanship; all contributed to the blurring of the Swift canon by disputed attributions; and none, despite the work of the widows Sarah Harding and Sarah Hyde for Swift after the deaths of John Harding in 1725 and John Hyde in 1728, was well placed to carry forward any longer-term project of consolidation. Yet it was these booksellers and printers whose impressive if imperfect work culminated in the triumph of the Drapier over Wood's halfpence, a print campaign that as part of its claim to mobilise a nation projected a notably self-referential construction of print. In turn it was these pamphlets, collected into a subscription volume by George Faulkner in 1725, that laid the foundation for the career-defining *Works of J. S, D. D, D. S. P. D.* that he published ten years later, the first multi-volume collected works of Swift to be published in either nation.

A Proposal for the Universal Use of Irish Manufacture (1720)

In 1720 Swift in print once more claimed the limelight with a new pamphlet of explosive force.[16] In April Swift wrote to Ford, anticipating by a few days the Declaratory Act, which, despite Archbishop King's determined opposition, would establish the English House of Lords as the ultimate court of appeal in Irish cases: Swift's assessment was that 'the Question is whether People ought to be Slaves or no', and his treatment of that question was to prove supremely provocative.[17] O'Regan indeed sees it as 'an early indication that it was he, and not King, who would henceforward champion the patriot cause', and that his method would rely on 'linking the economic and political grievances of the Anglo-Irish' and drawing on 'notions of natural right'.[18] The inflammatory pamphlet that first made this clear bore the imprint of Waters, who had recently printed three other defences of the rights of Ireland, and, earlier in 1720,

---

[16] Ian McBride has also argued that *Some Considerations upon the late Attempt to Repeal the Test Act* (1719) should be attributed to Swift ('Renouncing England: Swift's *Proposal for the Universal Use of Irish Manufacture*', plenary lecture at Swift350 conference, Trinity College, Dublin, 9 June 2017). Its claim of London origin, 'Printed for *H. Clements*, and sold by *J. Hyde*, Bookseller in *Dublin*, 1719', is clearly fraudulent, since the pamphlet features a lion headpiece used by the Dublin printer Aaron Rhames, which would also be used in Hyde's 1726 Dublin reprint of the *Travels* (May, 'False and Incomplete Imprints', p. 60; Pollard, *Dictionary*, pp. 488–9).

[17] *Corr.*, vol. II, pp. 327–8; and, for Archbishop King's opposition to the measure, O'Regan, *Archbishop King*, pp. 261–83.

[18] O'Regan, *Archbishop King*, p. 285.

148 Part III: Dublin

the provocative *Hibernia's Passive Obedience*, which included, alongside more Whiggish objections to Ireland's subjection by Thomas Burnet, extracts from Swift's *Contests and Dissensions*, *The Sentiments of a Church of England-Man*, and *A Letter ... concerning the Sacramental Test*.[19]

Like Hyde, for whom he sometimes printed, Waters had been active as a Tory printer and bookseller since 1707. Having apparently served his apprenticeship with Brent's former associate John Brocas, he succeeded to Brocas's address, type and ornament stock and used his Dutch type.[20] Like Hyde, Waters had also married within the trade: his wife Sarah was daughter of the bookseller Matthew Gunne.[21] Waters, who had worked closely with sympathetic Lords Lieutenant under Queen Anne, specialised in relatively well-produced cheap print and newspapers. He also specialised, on the frequent occasions when his publications gave offence, in ingenious dodging with the authorities – which on occasion included turning evidence against his associates. In 1708, when taken up 'on suspition of Printing and Vending Popish Prayer-Books contrary to Law', he got off by testifying against Malone and Carter; and on other occasions he was reported to have 'leapt out of a Window', or left a message that he had 'gone fishing'. None of his previous defiances, however, came anywhere close to the pamphlet that he now printed for Swift, *A Proposal for the Universal Use of Irish Manufacture, in Cloaths and Furniture of Houses, &c. Utterly Rejecting and Renouncing every thing wearable that comes from England* (Dublin, 1720): in the context of disease, famine and a downturn in trade, the pamphlet not only called for a boycott of English imports, but also mounted a tendentious review of the respective constitutional rights of Ireland and England.[22]

Waters can hardly have been unaware of the risk; but, as Swift would explain in 1732 to a different bookseller, in a different situation:

> I have writ some things that would make people angry[.] I always sent them by unknown hands, the Printer might guess, but he could not accuse me[,] he ran the whole risk ...[23]

---

[19] *Hibernia's Passive Obedience* (Dublin, 1720; *ESTC* N32884); Ferguson, *Jonathan Swift and Ireland*, pp. 53–4 and n. 81.
[20] For Waters's career, see Pollard, *Dictionary*, pp. 589–91.   [21] *Ibid.*, pp. 263–4, 589.
[22] TS 612, *ESTC* T125407. See also Ehrenpreis, *Swift*, vol. III, pp. 123–30; Ferguson, *Jonathan Swift and Ireland*, pp. 53–8; O'Regan, *Archbishop King*, pp. 289–90; Baltes, *The Pamphlet Controversy*, pp. 99–101.
[23] J. Woolley, 'Poor John Harding', p. 102; *Corr.*, vol. III, p. 556 (writing to Benjamin Motte the younger).

The Irish Patriot in Print (1720–1725)

All such considerations would be set aside, however, in the performance of wide-eyed innocence that was played out in 1724, when the Drapier, in the very first of his letters, purported to describe what happened next:

> About three Years ago a little Book was written to advise all People to wear the *Manufactures of this our own Dear Country*. It had no other Design, said nothing against the *King* or *Parliament*, or *any Man*, yet the POOR PRINTER was prosecuted two Years, with the utmost Violence, and even some WEAVERS themselves, for whose Sake it was written, being upon the JURY, FOUND HIM GUILTY. This would be enough to discourage any Man from endeavouring to do you Good … when he must expect only *Danger to himself* and *Loss of Money*, perhaps to his Ruin.[24]

Yet it was hardly unusual for a 'POOR PRINTER' in Dublin at this time to use a defective or misleading imprint – indeed an anonymous collaborative satire in which Swift was involved, *An Elegy on the much lamented death of Mr. Demar, the famous rich man, who died the 6th of this inst. July, 1720* (which has also been claimed for Waters) was a recent case in point.[25] Authorial requirements on Swift's part, as well as commercial considerations on Waters's, may well have made the difference, as James Woolley suggests in positing a three-point plan on Swift's part for sustaining authorial 'deniability':

> a) avoiding direct contact with the bookseller; b) giving the bookseller no assurances as to authorship; and c) expecting that the bookseller would absorb the risks of prosecution or other legal harassment rather than passing such risks back to him.[26]

This implied that the printer would identify himself but the author would not; and Woolley further suggests that by choosing a bookseller like Waters, who did his printing himself, rather than contracting it out like Hyde, Swift 'could more efficiently control production and could limit the circle of those who had even indirect knowledge of the source of what was being published'.[27] Bullard and McLaverty also point out that Waters was well connected in the trade, that 'his business was possibly in some way a subsidiary of Hyde's', and that placing *A Proposal for the Universal Use of*

---

[24] *A Letter to the Shop-keepers, Tradesmen, Farmers, and Common-People of Ireland, concerning the Brass Half-Pence coined by Mr. Woods, with a Design to have them Pass in this Kingdom . . . By M. B. Drapier* (Dublin, 1724; TS 636, *ESTC* T71495), pp. 2–3.

[25] For overview see *CWJS Poems* II (forthcoming), 1720. Pett considers the work below Waters's usual standard ('"I am no inconsiderable Shop-Keeper"', p. 145).

[26] James Woolley, 'Sarah Harding as Swift's Printer', in Christopher Fox (ed.), *Walking Naboth's Vineyard: New Studies of Swift* (University of Notre Dame Press, 1995), pp. 164–77 (p. 165).

[27] *Ibid.*, p. 165.

150 Part III: Dublin

Irish Manufacture with Waters instead of Hyde may have been 'a cautious step down one rung, which protected Hyde'.[28] Taking on the risk on Swift's behalf was probably the price Waters had to pay to get the work at all.

Waters's *A Proposal for the Universal Use of Irish Manufacture* is not particularly accomplished. Besides a prominent error ('UTERLY') on the title of some copies, the printing is somewhat uneven.[29] Yet the overall look of the pamphlet was much more accessible than Swift's previous Dublin publications, with larger, better-spaced, more legible type, and readier recourse to italics for emphasis. A large if slightly fuzzy ornament on the unframed title page shows a putto looking to the right through a spyglass; and 'ENGLAND', which anchors the long and typographically varied title by deploying its largest type almost to the full measure of the page, wittily (if perhaps accidentally) indicates the object of his eastward gaze. (Indeed, given the proposal's focus on the King's impending birthday, a telescope might have come in particularly handy for scrutinising the notoriously opulent attire of his London guests.) As well as the title ornament there is also a narrow (but inaccurately assembled) composite headpiece to the main text. Such decorations, along with easy legibility and expressive typography, may well have helped to engage the relatively wide audience that the *Proposal* had in its sights – for the challenge of this particular piece extended to everyone whose purchasing power put English imports within their reach.

This was the pamphlet that gave rise to the first legal test of Swift's Dublin publication strategy. From May 1720, when Waters was presented for trial by Grand Jury and subjected to the repressive zeal of Lord Chief Justice Whitshed, Swift worked hard to mobilise his contacts on his printer's behalf. Notably, he approached Lord Grafton, the incoming Lord Lieutenant, through his step-father, Sir Thomas Hanmer; but it was not until August 1721 that the prosecution was finally dropped.[30] Swift had complained to Hanmer that even though at Waters's trial the jury had been 'the most Violent Party men', they had 'brought him in not guilty, but were sent back nine times' by Whitshed, finally leaving the printer 'to be tryed again next Term'.[31] He was careful to assure Hanmer that the *Proposal* had the support of 'Whigs in generall', specifying 'all the Bishops except the late ones from Eng^{ld}, the Duke of Wharton, Lord

---

[28] Bullard and McLaverty, 'Introduction', p. 15.

[29] TS 612, *ESTC* T125407. For a possible late addition to page 10, see Pett, '"I am no inconsiderable Shop-Keeper"', pp. 98–9.

[30] Pollard, *Dictionary*, p. 590; *Corr.*, vol. II, pp. 345–6, 349–50.   [31] *Corr.*, vol. II, p. 345.

The Irish Patriot in Print (1720–1725)

Molesworth, and many others'.[32] (Swift's numbering of the radical Whig Molesworth on the side of the angels indicates the changed priorities of the gathering campaign.[33]) Swift also noted to Hanmer, as if in passing, that 'it may be inconvenient, because I am looked on as the Author' – which he certainly was, as testified by the anonymous *An Answer to the Proposal* (Dublin, 1720).[34] A more trenchant account of the prosecution, which Swift drafted but did not publish, alleged that 'The Grand Juries of the county and city were practiced effectually with to present the said Pamphlet with all aggravating Epithets, for which they had thanks sent them from England, and their Presentments publish'd for several weeks in all the news-papers'; it detailed how 'The Printer was seiz'd, and forced to give great bail'; and it further claimed that, even after 'the Jury brought him in Not Guilty ... the Chief Justice sent them back nine times, and kept them eleven hours, till being perfectly tired out, they were forced to leave the matter to the mercy of the Judge, by what they call a special Verdict'.[35] Swift also recalled that Whitshed had 'sworn, that I designed to bring in the Pretender'. After long delays arising from what Swift calls the 'very odious and impopular' nature of the case, it was, in this unpublished account, only the telling concurrence of 'mature advice, and permission from England' that finally prompted Grafton to relieve Waters from the suspense that Swift had solicited so hard to bring to a close.

Meanwhile, in December 1720, Swift also demonstrated that London publication was still within his power: with Ford as intermediary, he now

---

[32] Robert Molesworth had in 1716 become Viscount Molesworth. For his contact with Swift in relation to the *Proposal*, see Ferguson, *Jonathan Swift and Ireland*, p. 58, and for his wider political views and opposition to Wood's patent, see Ehrenpreis, *Swift*, vol. III, pp. 286–7; Baltes, *The Pamphlet Controversy*, pp. 185, 258.

[33] For the 1714 Dublin reprint of *A Preface to the B—p of S-r-m's Introduction*, see Chapter 4; for milder treatment of Molesworth in Swift's 1723 *Some Arguments against Enlarging the Power of Bishops*, see Ferguson, *Jonathan Swift and Ireland*, pp. 809–82. Pett suggests that the Molesworths may have directed patronage to the Hardings ('"I am no inconsiderable Shop-Keeper"', pp. 198, 299–300).

[34] *An Answer to the Proposal* (Dublin, 1720; TS 1661, *ESTC* N42971). The imprint gives no name. For a London reprint which implausibly attributes the piece to Swift, see *A Defence of English Commodities. Being an Answer to the Proposal for the Universal Use of Irish Manufactures, and Utterly rejecting and renouncing every Thing that is Wearable that comes from England ... To which is annexed, An elegy upon the much lamented death of Mr. Demar, the famous Rich Man, who Died at Dublin the 6th Day of July, 1720. Written by Dean Swift* (London, 1720; TS 614, *ESTC* T146390). The imprint is that of the trade publisher James Roberts, whose name also appears on reprints of Hyde's Dublin publications which had originally appeared anonymously, but were in London attributed to Swift (see also Bullard and McLaverty, 'Introduction', p. 6).

[35] The quotation is taken from *A Letter from Dr Swift to Mr Pope*, a pamphlet-style apologia apparently written in 1720, passed to Pope in 1737 and first published by him in a collection of letters in London in 1741 (Ehrenpreis, *Swift*, vol. III, pp. 136–7; *Corr.*, vol. II, pp. 354–64; *PW*, vol. IX, pp. xii–xvi, 25–34).

Part III: Dublin

sent to press a long poem on the South Sea Bubble.[36] Unusually, both the manuscript and Swift's instructions (dated 15 December 1720) are extant, in the form of a letter sent to Ford in London: the poem, in two columns, occupies the first and second pages of the folded sheet; the third page concludes the poem, with the covering letter at its foot; and the fourth page bears the address to Ford at his London lodgings.[37] Since printers' copy for Swift's works was usually discarded after publication, this manuscript offers an unusual glimpse of Swift's preparation of copy: in this example he punctuated carefully, provided clearly differentiated capitals for most nouns, underlined words to be set in italic, indented the first line of each new stanza, and tucked notes neatly into margins. This would have provided the printer with most but not all of the information he needed: decisions were subsequently made (whether by Ford or by the printer) to insert line spaces between stanzas (not present in the closely packed manuscript), to mark alternate rhyming lines by indenting the third as well as the first line of each quatrain, to move the notes to the foot of the page, to add a decorative headpiece at the beginning and 'FINIS' at the end, and, in the absence of a manuscript title, to call the piece *The Bubble. A Poem.* Thus trimmed out, it made an elegant twenty-four-page octavo pamphlet, amply justifying the sixpence charged: a preliminary title page with blank verso bears the price; the title page proper is also graced with a blank verso; and a blank verso at the end forms a back cover. The decorations (an eagle with open beak flourishing its wings on the title; and, at the head of the poem, two peacocks, tails retracted, looking over their shoulders at a double horn of plenty) seem commonplace enough; yet in context they may also seem to suggest a proud empire's alarmed retrospect on baseless promises of abundance.

Particularly interesting in this transformation of manuscript to print is Swift's covering note to Ford:

> I here send you the Thing I promised, as correct as I can [ma]ke it, and it cost me Pains enough, whether it be good or no. The Way to pub[lish] it will be to send it by the peny Post or an unknown Hand to some [oth]er Printer, and so let him do what he pleases: onely tear out this prose P[art an]d blot out the Subscription; and then there can be no other Inconvenience than the Loss of the Copy. When it comes out, buy one & send it franked and inclosed, immediatly, and I will send it to the Printer here.[38]

---

[36] For the crisis and proposals for a bank, see P. Walsh, *The South Sea Bubble and Ireland.* The poem will be edited in *CWJS Poems* II (forthcoming). See also Ehrenpreis, *Swift,* vol. III, pp. 152–5; O'Regan, *Archbishop King,* pp. 290–1; *Corr.,* vol. II, pp. 353–4.

[37] The autograph is Rothschild MS 2265: for textual discussion, see *CWJS Poems* II (forthcoming).

[38] *Corr.,* vol. II, p. 353.

The Irish Patriot in Print (1720–1725)

Much of this is not new, resembling the instructions he had sent Ford in 1712 about *Some Advice Humbly Offer'd to the Members of the October Club*, and in 1714 about *Some Free Thoughts upon the Present State of Affairs.*[39] (The former went through smoothly, the latter not.) In the context of those previous arrangements, three elements here are noteworthy. First, Swift specifies that the work should be done by 'some [oth]er Printer' – i.e. not Barber, whose decision to show the copy of *Some Free Thoughts* to Bolingbroke had caused delays that aborted publication altogether. (Ford understandably chose Tooke.) Second, while Swift wants Ford to send the poem to the printer by the post or an unknown messenger, he does not this time ask that a copy should be made in a different hand – even though he understands that this will probably mean losing his original copy. (To judge by its survival, Ford made a transcript for the press anyway.) Third, Swift is here seen deliberately routing a Dublin publication through London: the copy that Ford is asked to post to Swift for reprinting in Dublin is to be one that he has bought in the normal way, just like any other purchaser.

The Dublin reprinting of *The Bubble* was probably given to Waters by way of compensation for his sufferings over *A Proposal for the Universal Use of Irish Manufacture*. (Similarly, David Woolley argues, Swift had allowed Waters to publish the Dublin original of *A Letter from a Lay-Patron to a Gentleman, designing for Holy Orders*, subsequently reprinted as Swift's in London; and Pett suggests that Waters may also have been responsible for a Dublin reprint of *The Run upon the Bankers*.[40]) Waters's ornaments, though not his name, identify both Dublin reprints of *The Bubble*: an eagle, cruder and more obviously denunciatory than its London cousin, presides over the title, and at the end reappears the fuzzy putto with spyglass whose eastward scrutiny had figured on the title of *A Proposal for the Universal Use of Irish Manufacture*. The fact that Swift appears to have passed Waters his own corrections for use in one of these reprints suggests that even amid the stress of legal proceedings there could still be a degree of mutual benefit in their carefully distanced relationship. Yet as Pollard laconically notes in relation to *A Proposal for the Universal Use of Irish*

---

[39] For the former, see Chapter 4; for the latter, *CWJS English Political Writings, 1711–14*, pp. 480–5.

[40] *CWJS Poems* II (forthcoming); *Corr.*, vol. II, p. 354. For Waters's Dublin edition of *A Letter from a Lay-Patron*, see TS 619, *ESTC* N470938. The London reprint is *A Letter to a Young Gentleman, lately enter'd into Holy Orders. By a person of quality. It is certainly known, that the following treatise was writ in Ireland by the Reverend Dr. Swift, Dean of St. Patrick's in that Kingdom* (London, 1721): its two editions, both TS 618, are *ESTC* T723 and T146254. See also *The Run upon the Bankers* in *CWJS Poems* II (forthcoming); Pett, '"I am no inconsiderable Shop-Keeper"', pp. 143–4.

Part III: Dublin

Manufacture, 'How E[dward] W[aters] fared during this prolonged affair is not known.'[41] Bolingbroke commented in July 1721 that Waters had been suffering as 'yr Proxy, who had needs have iron ribs to endure all the drubbings you will procure him', and later, in a posthumous diatribe against the judge who had tried Waters, Swift alleged that the prosecution had brought Waters 'to Ruin'.[42] Although Waters continued printing until 1746, his output as represented in *ESTC* suggests that in the wake of his prosecution he was reluctant to use his imprint in Irish controversy: in 1722 *ESTC* lists no Waters imprints at all, and although they reappear in 1723 they seem to have played no part in the 1723–4 campaign against Wood's halfpence.

Hyde, however, showed himself ready to step into the breach, putting his imprint to Swift's *Some Arguments against Enlarging the Power of Bishops, in Letting of Leases*: '*DUBLIN*: Printed for J. Hyde, 1723'.[43] He was the most ambitious of the booksellers who worked with Swift in this period: having been active in the trade only since 1707, he had shown a commercial interest in Swift as early as 1711, when he seems to have obtained in London the copy of *The Conduct of the Allies* that he reprinted in Dublin.[44] In 1714 he married Sarah Ray, daughter of Joseph Ray, a distinguished bookseller, printer and campaigner against the King's Printer's monopoly: her father had printed for Trinity College and published scholarly works of divinity and geometry, collaborating effectively both within the Dublin trade and in London; and by 1719 Swift was recommending her husband as 'an honest man' qualified to manage the distribution of Dublin subscribers' copies of the London-printed *Poems* of Matthew Prior.[45] Indeed, the only downside of Hyde's networking in the London trade was the persistent reprinting there, under Swift's name, of works that Hyde had published anonymously in Dublin. In some cases this

---

[41] Pollard, *Dictionary*, p. 590.

[42] *Corr.*, vol. II, p. 387; *CWJS Irish Political Writings after 1725*, p. 38; *An Answer to a Paper, called A Memorial of the Poor Inhabitants, Tradesmen and Labourers of the Kingdom of Ireland* (Dublin, 1728; TS 665, *ESTC* T21996), p. 15.

[43] TS 633, *ESTC* T1831; *PW*, vol. IX, pp. 43–60. For context and discussion, see Ehrenpreis, *Swift*, vol. III, pp. 166–86.

[44] Goldgar and Gadd, reviewing D. Woolley's earlier account, which posited a possible meeting between Swift and Hyde during this visit, suggest that Hyde's copy for his reprint may have been a printed proof rather than a manuscript, making it less likely that his reprint's variants were authorial, and weakening arguments for a personal meeting at this point (*CWJS English Political Writings, 1711–14*, pp. 348–9; D. Woolley, 'Swift's Copy of *Gulliver's Travels*', p. 142; Pollard, *Dictionary*, pp. 304–6).

[45] The subscription for Prior was explained to Swift in January 1717 in a letter from Erasmus Lewis (*Corr.*, vol. II, pp. 212–13; and, for Hyde, pp. 292, 297–8).

compromised Swift's anonymity; in others it gave currency to misattributions.

Although the title page of Hyde's *Some Arguments against Enlarging the Power of Bishops* said nothing explicitly about the author's rank or identity, an epigraph from Cicero made an implicit appeal to an elite readership by invoking the importance of law in defending heritable property, in this case the lands whose rents sustained the church: 'Mihi credite, major haereditas venit unicuique vestrum in ijisdem bonis a jure & a legibus, quam ab ijs a quibus illa ipsa bona relicta sunt' ('Believe me, the property which anyone of us enjoys is to a greater degree the legacy of our law and constitution than of those who actually bequeathed it to him').[46] Towards the end, however, the author's constitutional outrage burst out in a flurry of full capitals, italic full capitals and black letter: a single page displayed 'WHIG', 'CHURCH' and 'GOD'; '*GEORGE*', '*HANOVER*' and '*WILLIAM*'; and, most strikingly of all, '𝕿𝖔𝖗𝖎𝖊𝖘', '𝕵𝖆𝖈𝖔𝖇𝖎𝖙𝖊𝖘', '𝕻𝖔𝖕𝖎𝖘𝖍 𝕾𝖚𝖈𝖈𝖊𝖘𝖘𝖔𝖗𝖘', '𝕻𝖔𝖕𝖊𝖗𝖞', and '𝕾𝖑𝖆𝖇𝖊𝖗𝖞' (Figure 7).[47] Black letter, although increasingly obsolete, still retained traditional connotations of authority and offered an eye-catching source of emphasis in popular print. Conceivably specified along with the italics and capitals that Swift habitually indicated in printers' copy, it encoded an expressively explosive irruption into an otherwise restrained visual discourse. But it was in the work of John and Sarah Harding that the violent emphases of Swift in print would be carried to their highest pitch.

The Drapier's Letters (1724)

The Hardings' shop was the scene in which the letters ascribed to the Drapier became the shabby, nondescript little pamphlets that proved so crucial to the campaign against Wood's patent. Given the scholarship devoted on the one hand to the letters' political and literary strategies, and on the other to the game of cat and mouse played between Swift, his printers and the authorities, it is easy to overlook the letters' original flimsiness and poor execution – and correspondingly important not to.[48] For these are the

---

[46] Cicero, *Pro Caecina*, in *Pro Lege Manilia. Pro Caecina. Pro Cluentio. Pro Rabirio Perduellionis Reo*, pp. 170–1.

[47] *Some Arguments against Enlarging the Power of Bishops, in Letting of Leases* (Dublin, 1723; TS 633, ESTC T1831), p. 18.

[48] Biographical and political accounts include Davis, *Drapier's Letters*, pp. ix–lxvii; Ehrenpreis, *Swift*, vol. III, pp. 187–318; Baltes, *The Pamphlet Controversy*, passim; Ferguson, *Jonathan Swift and Ireland*, pp. 88, 96–7; O'Regan, *Archbishop King*, pp. 302–32; Pollard, *Dictionary*, p. 275. Davis, *Drapier's Letters*, though earlier than the same editor's *PW*, vol. X, gives fuller bibliographical analysis.

(18)

𝕮𝖔𝖗𝖎𝖊𝖘 and 𝕵𝖆𝖈𝖔𝖇𝖎𝖙𝖊𝖘, who charge us with being Enemies to the Church. If I bear an hearty unfeigned Loyalty to his Majesty King *GEORGE*, and the House of *HANOVER*, not shaken in the least by the Hardships we lie under, which never can be imputable to so gracious a Prince ; If I sincerely abjure the 𝕻𝖗𝖊𝖙𝖊𝖓𝖉𝖊𝖗 and all 𝕻𝖔𝖕𝖎𝖘𝖍 𝕾𝖚𝖈𝖈𝖊𝖘𝖘𝖔𝖗𝖘; If I bear a due Veneration to the Glorious Memory of the late King *WILLIAM*, who preserved these Kingdoms from 𝕻𝖔𝖕𝖊𝖗𝖞 and 𝕾𝖑𝖆𝖛𝖊𝖗𝖞, with the Expence of his Blood, and hazard of his Life: And lastly, if I am for a proper Indulgence to all *Dissenters*; I think nothing more can be reasonably demanded of *Me* as a WHIG, and that my Political Catechism is full and Compleat. But whoever under the Shelter of that Party-Denomination, and of many great Professions of Loyalty, would Destroy, or Undermine, or Injure the CHURCH Established, I utterly disown him, and think he ought to chuse another Name of Distinction for himself, and his Adherents. I came into the Cause upon other Principles, which, by the Grace of GOD, I mean to preserve as long as I live. Shall we justifie the Accusations of our Adversaries? *Hoc Ithacus velit.*——— The 𝕮𝖔𝖗𝖎𝖊𝖘 and 𝕵𝖆𝖈𝖔𝖇𝖎𝖙𝖊𝖘 will behold us with a malicious Pleasure determined upon the Ruin of our *Friends:* For is not the present Set of Bishops almost intirely of that Number, as well as a great Majority of the Principal Clergy? And a short time will reduce the whole, by Vacancies upon Death.

An Impartial Reader, if he pleases to examine what I have already said, will easily answer the bold *Queries* in the Pamphlet I mentioned; he will be convinced, that *the Reason still strongly exists for*

which

Figure 7 Jonathan Swift, *Some Arguments against Enlarging the Power of Bishops, in Letting of Leases* (Dublin, 1723), p. 18.

material texts that readers first received as part of the increasing surge of anti-Wood publications in these years, some issued under their authors' names, some under pseudonyms and some anonymously. (Even today, the boxes and bound volumes of Wood-related material in the Early Printed Books department at Trinity College, Dublin give a vivid sense of the controversy's baffling variety.) An identifiable core of publications – the letters themselves and some associated verses and papers – can be confidently identified as Swift's, but many others have at various times been attributed to him on slenderer grounds: all such material, whatever its authorship, kept the issues constantly in agitation before the public.[49] Yet it was the Drapier's letters themselves, in the format and sequence available to readers at the time, that constituted the heart of the campaign. The printed Drapier's letters combined three strikingly interlinked features: a material expressiveness that inhered to a large degree in their oddities and imperfections; a persistent rhetorical foregrounding of the processes of their production; and an associated idealisation of print as medium of national unity.

John Harding, formerly Waters's apprentice, had been in business on his own account since 1718, specialising in cheap print such as half-sheet squibs and newspapers.[50] Whalley, always keen to discredit the Tory printers, had listed him in suspicious company in 1719: 'I am told that Cornelius Carter, John Harding and Richard Pew', under suspicion of giving news of the Pretender 'in their Jackish News-*P*apers . . . have thought fit to play at *Boo-peep*, so that they can't be found.'[51] In Harding Swift could certainly rely on the resilience of a committed Tory printer, but his print quality was poor, and James Woolley points out that (unlike the other booksellers most closely associated with Swift), Harding 'was not highly literate or cultivated'.[52] Although he advertised that he took on jobbing work 'at Rates as Reasonable as any Printer in Dublin can afford', he also somewhat brusquely repudiated any expectation that he would 'force Trade or become a porter by pasting up Bills and advertisements in the Coffee-houses'.[53] When Swift described him as 'an Ignorant *Printer*' in *Seasonable Advice* (1724) he was rebutting the suspicion that Harding had knowingly connived with sedition; but it may also have been his considered opinion.

---

[49] See these years in *CWJS Poems* II and in list of deattributed poems in *CWJS Poems* IV (both forthcoming).
[50] Pollard, *Dictionary*, pp. 274–6.
[51] *Whalley's News-Letter containing an Impartial Historical Account*, no. 692, 4 April 1719; Pollard, *Dictionary*, p. 274.
[52] J. Woolley, 'Sarah Harding', p. 166; 'Poor John Harding', pp. 108, 110.
[53] J. Woolley, 'Sarah Harding', p. 166, citing *Harding's Weekly Impartial News Letter*, 11 April 1721.

158   Part III: Dublin

The Hardings, however, had much else to offer. For one thing, theirs was a resilient partnership: Sarah, apparently born into the Sadleir family of printers and type founders, was well able to run the business when John was in prison or hiding from the authorities.[54] They had also worked for Swift before. In 1721 John Harding had printed, on the two sides of a half sheet, a prologue by Sheridan and an epilogue by Swift for a weavers' benefit performance; and he also printed attacks apparently by Swift and his associates on the abortive project for a Bank of Ireland (for *The Last Speech and Dying Words of the Bank of Ireland*, sometimes attributed to Swift, Harding was ordered into custody).[55] When in 1721 Sarah used her own imprint for what was apparently the first time, it was to publish another work sometimes laid at Swift's door, the anonymous *The Present Miserable State of Ireland. In a Letter from a Gentleman in Ireland to his Friend in London* (Dublin, 1721).[56]

John Harding was also open to producing the dark kind of parody that Swift had explored when, in the Bickerstaff hoax, he both predicted and then pretended to lament the death of Partridge the almanac-maker. Since genuine elegies and the last dying words of condemned criminals were staples of Harding's business, his fakes were impressively plausible. Indeed, when in 1722 he produced for Swift a spurious *The Last Speech and Dying Words of Ebenezor Ellison* (Ellison being a distressed weaver, allegedly of dissenting stock, who had turned to crime), it seems that he had first allowed Swift to see the genuine *The Last Farewell of Ebenezor Elliston to*

---

[54] For John Harding, see Pollard, *Dictionary*, pp. 274–5; for Sarah Harding, pp. 275–6; for the Sadleirs, pp. 506–7.

[55] For overview, see Ehrenpreis, *Swift*, vol. III, pp. 152–65; for Swift and the weavers, see Ferguson, *Jonathan Swift and Ireland*, pp. 58–9, 63–4; *PW*, vol. IX, pp. xix–xxi. For Swift's epilogue, see *CWJS Poems* II (forthcoming). For Swift and the bank, see *The Last Speech and Dying Words of the Bank of Ireland, which was Executed at College-Green, on Saturday the 9th Inst.* (Dublin, 1721; TS 910A, *ESTC* T231076). *PW*, vol. IX, prints this piece in the Appendix under the heading 'Attributed to Swift and his friends' (pp. 306–7). For Swift's ostensible non-involvement, see *Corr.*, vol. II, pp. 398, 404 (and for his actual involvement, p. 399 n. 4); for anti-bank tracts later published in collections authorised by Swift, see Ferguson, *Jonathan Swift and Ireland*, p. 69; for Archbishop King's opposition to the bank, O'Regan, *Archbishop King*, pp. 291–300.

[56] For the argument and attribution of *The Present Miserable State* (TS 1583, *ESTC* N20957), see Ferguson, *Jonathan Swift and Ireland*, pp. 60–1, noting connection with Mist's *The Weekly Journal or Saturdays-Post, with freshest Advices Foreign and Domestic*, 30 September 1721. *PW* rejects Swift's authorship, but does not explicitly consider Sarah Harding's imprint (vol. XII, pp. xv–xvi; J. Woolley, 'Sarah Harding', p. 170). Ferguson considers Swift's authorship 'extremely unlikely' (*Jonathan Swift and Ireland*, p. 62 n. 8). When the piece was reprinted in 1735, without a name in the imprint, as *The Present Miserable State of Ireland. In a letter from a gentleman in Dublin, to his friend S.R.W. in London. Wherein is briefly stated, the causes and heads of all our woes* (Dublin, 1735; TS 750, *ESTC* T179270; and cf. the undated TS 749), it was signed 'J. S.', and bore a crude woodcut apparently intended to represent Swift, with the title updated to suggest that it was addressed to Sir Robert Walpole.

The Irish Patriot in Print (1720–1725)

this Transitory World, which he was also printing.[57] Nor does it appear that Swift was his only source of such hoaxes, for at some point before February 1723 Harding had printed *The Last Speech and Dying Words of Captain Collins who was executed at Kingston in Surry, the 4th, of October inst.* – the only problem being, according to Whalley, that 'that Gentleman is still Living'.[58] Since the occasion of Whalley's complaint was the appearance of a printed elegy on his own supposed death (now lost, but probably an altered version of Swift's 1708 *Elegy on Mr. Patrige* such as would be printed on Whalley's actual death in the following year), it is tempting to wonder also whether that too might have been a Harding product.[59] In sum, Harding was an efficient operator in a popular culture that had few inhibitions about such trifling with death. (Almanac-makers routinely prophesied their rivals' deaths; and the campaign against Wood would also include a mock-execution, commemorated by Swift in a punning handbill.[60]) With Harding at the ready, the stage was now set for the materialisation of Bickerstaff's Irish successor, M. B. Drapier.[61]

Wood's patent, granted in 1722, was soon an established target of print opposition; and by early 1723 Archbishop King, along with the anti-Walpole Whig politician Alan Brodrick, Viscount Midleton, was pressing Swift to contribute.[62] (This was the same Brodrick whose whole family the supposed author of *A Letter . . . concerning the Sacramental Test* had in 1709 wished to see hanged – but, as Ehrenpreis suggests, Swift was probably sought out for his specific skills in pamphlet warfare, and perhaps for his presumed ability to reach 'a sub-literary audience' whose attitude to Wood's small change might make or break the boycott.[63]) By early 1724 Swift – or someone alluding to his mock-elegy on Partridge – wrote Harding an anonymous poem of congratulation on his release from one

---

[57] *CWJS Parodies*, pp. 199–210, 680–2; Ferguson, *Jonathan Swift and Ireland*, pp. 75–80.

[58] *Whalley's News-Letter. Containing an Impartial Historical Account*, 3 February 1723; Rumbold, 'Ignoring Swift', pp. 35–7.

[59] Rumbold, 'Ignoring Swift', p. 38.

[60] For Dublin print-trade hoaxes and satires relating to deaths predicted or commemorated, see Rumbold, 'Ignoring Swift'; for the mock-hanging of Wood, see Baltes, *The Pamphlet Controversy*, pp. 188–9, citing *A Full and True Account of the Solemn Procession to the Gallows, at the Execution of William Wood, Esquire, and Hard-ware-man*, printed as Swift's in *PW*, vol. X, pp. 143–9, and also included in Baltes-Ellermann, *Swift's Allies*, pp. 241–5. In the absence of a contemporary source, text and attribution derive from its 1735 reprinting by Faulkner.

[61] For poems by Swift relating to the Drapier affair, see 1724–5 in *CWJS Poems* II (forthcoming); for publications by others, see Baltes-Ellermann, *Swift's Allies*.

[62] Ehrenpreis, *Swift*, vol. III, p. 207; Ferguson, *Jonathan Swift and Ireland*, pp. 88, 96–7; O'Regan, *Archbishop King*, pp. 313–14; Baltes, *The Pamphlet Controversy*, p. 135.

[63] For Swift's animus against the Brodricks, see Chapter 3; Ehrenpreis, *Swift*, vol. III, p. 206, and, for the wider context of Midleton's politics, pp. 267–8.

160   Part III: Dublin

of his many spells in custody.[64] *Harding's Resurrection from Hell upon Earth*, which Harding printed in his newspaper, voices the printer's predicament in a parody of the 'mad' discourse of 'Tom o'Bedlam' in a popular song; and Wood's patent is introduced right at the beginning:

> By long Confinement poor *John Harding*
> Has hardly left a single Farthing;
> He's brought to such a wretched Pass
> He'd almost take the *English Brass*.

In his poverty, Harding 'Begs that his *Customers* will use / His *Pamphlets, Elegies* and *News*', an allusion to Swift's mock-elegy on Partridge, which had mocked its subject's background in patent medicines, astrology and cobbling ('*Weep, all you Customers that use / His* Pills, *his* Almanacks, or Shoes').[65] The shadow of contempt for a lowly artisan would not be altogether absent from Swift's ensuing collaboration with Harding.

In the poem Harding's type promptly adopts battle formation, playing repeatedly on the structures of rank, party and print hierarchy. The uppercase/lower-case distinction prompts puns equivocating between size and rank, as well as between the printer's fount and the font of baptism:

> The CAPITALS, as being Great,
> Before the Font advance in State.[66]

The different founts are compared to political parties:

> *Italick, Roman*, and *Long Primer*,
> Diff'ring like *Tory, Whig* and *Trimmer*.[67]

Punctuation is likened to the prison from which Harding has just been released:

> For *Stops* and *Points* I take to be
> To *Them*, what is a *Gaol* to Me.[68]

And the half-sheet elegy, one of Harding's staple products, points the way to the grave:

> And when we've met our *Final Doom*,
> Don't they pursue us to our *Tomb?*[69]

---

[64] *Harding's Resurrection*, ll. 2–8; for the poem as printed in *Harding's Weekly Impartial News Letter*, 18 February 1723, see J. Woolley, 'Poor John Harding', pp. 104–5, and for 'Tom of Bedlam', pp. 106–8. See also Rumbold, 'Ignoring Swift', p. 38.
[65] Lines 7–8; *An Elegy on Mr Patrige*, ll. 107–8 (and see *CWJS Poems* I (forthcoming)).
[66] *Harding's Resurrection*, ll. 13–14.   [67] *Ibid.*, ll. 17–18.   [68] *Ibid.*, ll. 29–30.   [69] *Ibid.*, ll. 41–2.

But in the end, Harding laments, his letters have done him no good at all, 'For ALL I *Got* by them I *Lost*', leaving him no option but to throw himself on the mercy of 'my *Old Customers* and *Friends*'.[70] Harding, in effect, is a cobbler who has no option but to stick to his last – and the next substantial piece of work to come his way would be the Drapier's letters, at prices adapted to the poorest readers. This was an opportunity on a scale far beyond Waters's work on *A Proposal for the Universal Use of Irish Manufacture*, but it brought with it even greater dangers.

Expressive Print

The Drapier's stock in trade, as imaged in the letters, was woollens; but in reality it was paper and ink, and the particular way in which Harding brought ink and paper together demonstrated his qualifications right from the start. The Drapier's first letter focused squarely on a mass audience for whom handling small change was a daily concern: *A Letter to the Shop-keepers, Tradesmen, Farmers, and Common-People of Ireland, concerning the Brass Half-Pence coined by Mr. Woods, with a Design to have them Pass in this Kingdom. Wherein is shewn the power of the said Patent, the value of the Half-Pence and how far every person may be oblig'd to take the same in payments, and how to behave in case such an attempt shou'd be made by Woods or any other person. [Very proper to be kept in every family] By M. B. Drapier* (Dublin, 1724).[71] An unpretentious pamphlet was not only accessible and unthreatening to such a readership, but also attractive for bulk purchase by wealthy supporters who might wish to distribute it free of charge (as Swift himself apparently did).[72] The writer was himself supposed to be no more than a tradesman (though, as Ehrenpreis notes, 'a superior member of the class he addressed'), a dealer in the same Irish woollens foregrounded in *A Proposal for the Universal Use of Irish Manufacture*; and one of his master-strokes in this first letter was to set out a step-by-step scenario of what might happen if the occupational groups listed in his title accepted the new small change in their everyday transactions.[73] The Drapier's forceful expression and surprising confidence about constitutional matters may to an extent have undermined his rhetorical plausibility, but the material

---

[70] *Ibid.*, ll. 45–7.

[71] For successive editions of the first letter, see TS, pp. 313–16 (nos. 635–637B). Quotations in the present account are from TS 636, *ESTC* T71495.

[72] For the 2,000 copies that Swift told Ford 'have been dispersd by Gentlemen', see *Corr.*, vol. II, p. 494; Ehrenpreis, *Swift*, vol. II, p. 215; Baltes, *The Pamphlet Controversy*, p. 139.

[73] Ehrenpreis, *Swift*, vol. III, p. 207; *A Letter to the Shop-keepers*, pp. 6–9.

Part III: Dublin

decorum of these small octavo pamphlets (the first comprising a single sheet, and none more than two) maintained an entirely plausible fit with the address in Francis Street from which most of the letters are dated.[74] Francis Street was at the heart of the Dublin weaving trade; and at its southern end, only a few steps from the west end of St Patrick's Cathedral, it passed teasingly close to Swift's own place of work.[75]

The typographical design of the Drapier's first letter, noisily emphatic but patchy in execution, was a crucial aspect of its address to a less sophisticated readership (Figure 8). For McLaverty, the passionate expression and poor quality go hand in hand:

> The typography of this fiercely polemical work is appropriately violent. Harding was not an elegant printer, and his types are worn, but he uses a great variety of them. The title-page, like many others of Swift's, is very lively, with 'Brass Half-Pence' in a kind of bold upper- and lower-case (they're probably not worthy of capitals), while Wood's own name (here 'Woods') is in black letter, marking him out as something strange and dangerous. The text is very varied (perhaps too varied for comfortable reading) with heavy use of italic and also of words in full capitals. Capitals are used for Wood, his coinage, and his majesty, but also for evaluative terms, both ironically positive ('A FAIR STORY') and negative ('A WICKED CHEAT', 'BLOOD-SUCKERS'). Harding is almost certainly following copy and this pamphlet is one of Swift's most interesting exercises in typographical self-expression.[76]

The text is crammed onto the octavo pages of a single sheet, and, to save space, begins directly on the verso of the title. It has no ornaments, and several times uses capital VV for lack of sufficient capital Ws – although it does manage to recess Swift's citations of statute law into the margins. Whereas Barber or Tooke typically produced print parodies that materially outclassed their target genres, Harding (who, McLaverty infers, would have been working from a copy marked up with Swift's crudely violent emphases) produced a much more convincing product. With hindsight, this seems exactly right for the declared readership, but it probably irritated Swift, for Harding evidently felt under pressure to incorporate corrections in a continuous cycle of stop-press interventions.[77] This resulted in what he sometimes called new editions, but were more probably the material evidence of his unflagging persistence in correcting an original setting of type.

---

[74] For variant copies in folio and quarto format, see TS 635.

[75] Francis Street runs north towards Merchants Quay from a point just west of St Patrick's Cathedral: it can be accessed from the west end of the cathedral via Dean Street.

[76] *JSA*, Introduction; see also Higgins, 'Censorship', pp. 187–8.   [77] See discussion, TS 642.

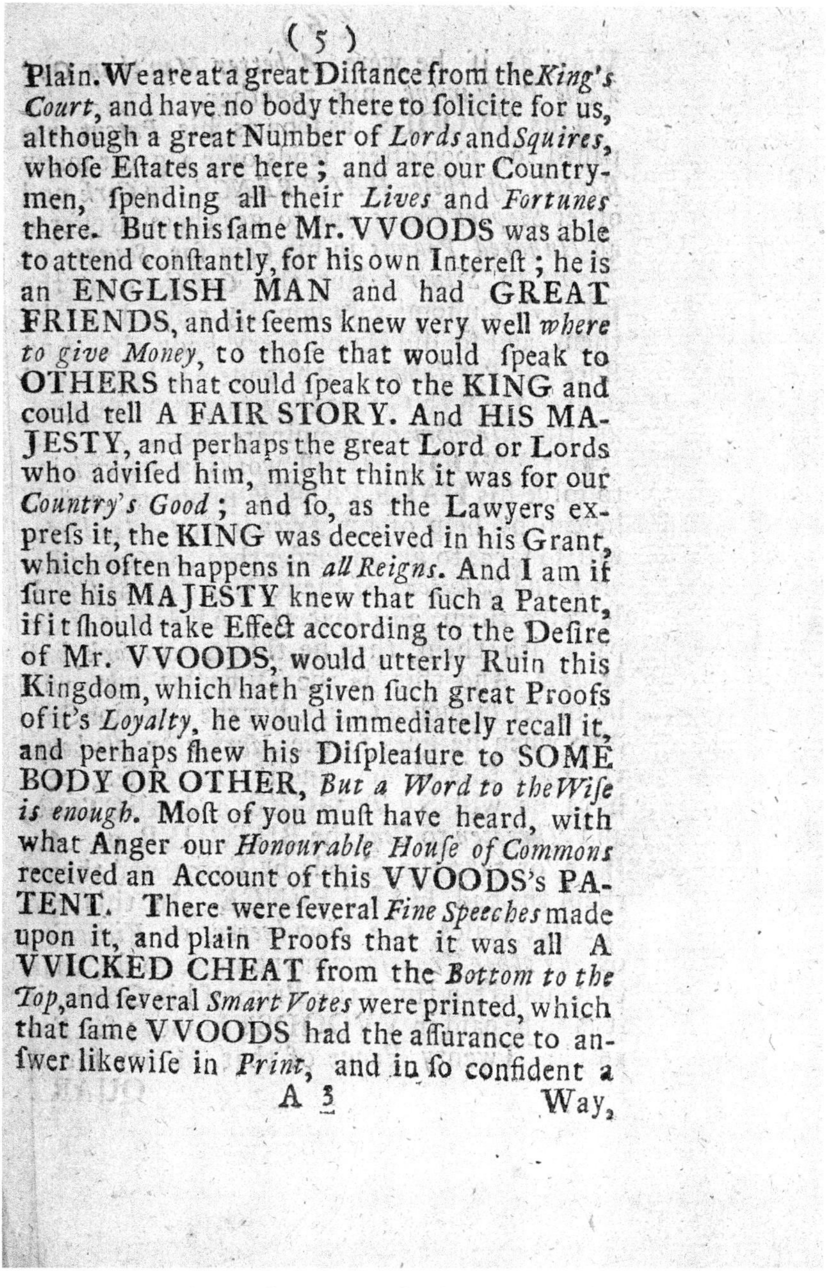

(5)

Plain. We are at a great Diſtance from the *King's Court*, and have no body there to ſolicite for us, although a great Number of *Lords* and *Squires*, whoſe Eſtates are here; and are our Country-men, ſpending all their *Lives* and *Fortunes* there. But this ſame Mr. VVOODS was able to attend conſtantly, for his own Intereſt; he is an ENGLISH MAN and had GREAT FRIENDS, and it ſeems knew very well *where to give Money*, to thoſe that would ſpeak to OTHERS that could ſpeak to the KING and could tell A FAIR STORY. And HIS MA-JESTY, and perhaps the great Lord or Lords who adviſed him, might think it was for our *Country's Good*; and ſo, as the Lawyers ex-preſs it, the KING was deceived in his Grant, which often happens in *all Reigns*. And I am if ſure his MAJESTY knew that ſuch a Patent, if it ſhould take Effect according to the Deſire of Mr. VVOODS, would utterly Ruin this Kingdom, which hath given ſuch great Proofs of it's *Loyalty*, he would immediately recall it, and perhaps ſhew his Diſpleaſure to SOME BODY OR OTHER, *But a Word to the Wiſe is enough*. Moſt of you muſt have heard, with what Anger our *Honourable Houſe of Commons* received an Account of this VVOODS's PA-TENT. There were ſeveral *Fine Speeches* made upon it, and plain Proofs that it was all A VVICKED CHEAT from the *Bottom to the Top*, and ſeveral *Smart Votes* were printed, which that ſame VVOODS had the aſſurance to an-ſwer likewiſe in *Print*, and in ſo confident a

A 3   Way,

Figure 8 Jonathan Swift, *A Letter to the Shop-keepers, Tradesmen, Farmers, and Common-People of Ireland, concerning the Brass Half-Pence coined by Mr. Woods . . . By M. B. Drapier* (Dublin, 1724), p. 5.

164 Part III: Dublin

It may be that buoyant sales of the early letters helped to finance enhancements to later ones.[78] Although the second letter, *A Letter to Mr. Harding the Printer, upon occasion of a Paragraph in his News-Paper of Aug. 1st. relating to Mr. Woods's Half-Pence*, was similar in appearance to the first (with the addition of a single ornamented capital at the beginning of the text, and a brief and businesslike epistolary subscription at the close), the third, *Some Observations upon a Paper, call'd, The Report of the Committee of the Most Honourable the Privy-Council in England, relating to Wood's Half-pence*, which was addressed instead 'To the NOBILITY and Gentry of the Kingdom of IRELAND', looked significantly different.[79] Although the text still begins directly on the verso of the title, it now runs to thirty-two octavo pages, filling two sheets of paper. By way of ornament it deploys not only an initial decorated capital at the beginning, but also a large arrangement of leaves and flowers at the foot of the final page, and, above it, a lavishly spaced formal subscription suited to the dignity of 'your Lordships and Worships'. This final flourish takes up space that Harding would normally have filled with closely packed text, which may be why, on pages 27–9, a substantial passage is set in smaller type, suggesting that space for the closing formalities had not been factored into the initial casting off.[80] A more lavish use of space was also required by the respectfully laid-out subscription to 'My Dear Country-men' that featured at the end of the fourth letter, *A Letter to the Whole People of Ireland*; and this letter also for the first time sacrificed a whole page to provide a blank verso to its title.[81] Even so, once its main text was under way, the typical exuberance of italics and capitals continued unabated, contributing to a blend of respect and popular appeal that figured the dignity of a 'Whole People' in its visual design as well as its verbal rhetoric.

---

[78] For an unfulfilled scheme along similar lines in relation to the *Intelligencer*, printed for Swift and Sheridan by Sarah Harding in her widowhood, see J. Woolley, *Intelligencer*, p. 4, and Chapter 7.

[79] The second letter is *A Letter to Mr. Harding the Printer, upon occasion of a Paragraph in his News-Paper of Aug. 1st. relating to Mr. Woods's Half-Pence. By M. B. Drapier. Author of the Letter to the Shop-Keepers, &c.* (Dublin, 1724; TS 638, *ESTC* T38169). The third is *Some Observations upon a Paper, call'd, The Report of the Committee of the Most Honourable the Privy-Council in England, relating to Wood's Half-pence. By M. B. Drapier. Author of the Letter to the Shop-Keepers &c.* (Dublin, 1724; TS 641–2, *ESTC* T155571). Harding produced four so-called editions in this year.

[80] Davis suggests that the smaller type 'may possibly mean that additions were made while it was being printed', but notes that 'this section is still retained unaltered' in later editions (*Drapier's Letters*, p. lxxxv).

[81] *A Letter to the Whole People of Ireland. By M. B. Drapier. Author of the Letter to the Shop-Keepers, &c.* (TS 644; *ESTC* N10952). The so-called second edition is a corrected reprint from the same setting, with the (corrected) errata printed at the back on a separate leaf, to facilitate removal for insertion into the uncorrected first edition: see TS 645, *ESTC* T124767.

As might have been expected, the noble addressee of the final letter in the published sequence, *A Letter to the Right Honourable the Lord Viscount Molesworth*, received a material text that was produced to a slightly higher standard than its predecessors. (Indeed, its production in the months between Harding's release from gaol and his death in 1725 may suggest that others assisted in the work.[82]) This is the nearest approach to typographical elegance in the series, with much less use of full capitals (although their expressive force is retained, for example, to cite the charge that the Drapier 'WENT TOO FAR').[83] Furthermore, on the very brink of the campaign's success, the title page now presented no fewer than seven epigraphs (six biblical, one classical). First, from Psalm 109 (headed in the King James Bible 'A Psalm of David') come three complaints of the soon-to-be vindicated Psalmist against his enemies, all readily applicable to the Drapier himself; and these are followed by three warnings from Ecclesiastes aimed at Wood and his supporters: 'Seek not to be Judge . . . lest at any Time thou fear the Person of the Mighty' offers a particularly delicious application to Whitshed, and the implications are reinforced by injunctions to 'Offend not against the Multitude of a City' and 'Bind not one Sin upon another', which carry their own threats of punishment and disgrace.[84] Separated from these by a rule, and differentiated by italic type, come two lines from Virgil in which the hero Mnestheus exhorts his crew in a boat race: 'No longer do I, Mnestheus, seek the first place, no longer do I strive to win; yet oh! – but let those conquer to whom you, Neptune, have granted it.'[85] Here Swift's quotation stops short, teasing the classically educated to supply the following line-and-a-half, which finally urges the crew into action: 'It would be shame to return last! Win but this, my countrymen, and ward off disgrace!' The fact that no reference is supplied for these lines (in contrast with the chapter and verse given for the Bible passages more accessible to lowlier readers) effectively passes a wink of mutual recognition to Swift's peers and superiors – including Molesworth – over the heads of 'the Shop-keepers, Tradesmen, Farmers, and Common-People of Ireland'.

Yet the material text is ambivalent. Although the letter to Molesworth is dignified by the use of a headpiece, it is a shoddily composed one.

---

[82] Pett, '"I am no inconsiderable Shop-Keeper"', pp. 290–1.

[83] *A Letter to the Right Honourable the Lord Viscount Molesworth. By M. B. Drapier, Author of the Letter to the Shop-keepers, &c.* (Dublin, 1724; TS 647, *ESTC* T38422). For 'I WENT TOO FAR', see, for instance, p. 7.

[84] Psalm 109, 3–5; Ecclesiasticus, 7. 6–8. Cf. Ehrenpreis, *Swift*, vol. III, pp. 289–90.

[85] Virgil, *Aeneid*, V. ll. 194–5.

166   Part III: Dublin

Comprising two rows of twelve fleurons, each a quadrant of an ellipse, some are from a different set, and the pattern is also broken by haphazard rotation.[86] Moreover, although the subscription at the end of the letter is appropriate to the addressee's rank, it is followed by almost half a page of empty space that could have been graced by a final ornament.[87] Molesworth is important, it seems, but not quite important enough to compel consistent attention to detail. In comparison, the first five pages of the pamphlet are set in slender, well-spaced type, larger and more graceful than anything else in the pamphlet or its predecessors. The text presented with such panache, which also boasts a decorated initial at its head, is not a tribute to Molesworth but 'Directions to the Printer'.[88]

Self-Reflexive Print

This visual disproportion between dedicatee and printer is just one of the ways in which the Drapier's letters highlight a self-reflexive discourse of print – an emphasis heralded by the attention to type and its expressive force in *Harding's Resurrection*. The Drapier emphasises commercial practicalities in the very first paragraph of the first letter, *A Letter to the Shop-keepers, Tradesmen, Farmers, and Common-People of Ireland*, announcing that 'I have ordered the Printer to sell it at the lowest Rate.'[89] He then goes on to recall Waters's prosecution for printing *A Proposal for the Universal Use of Irish Manufacture* (of which he gives a wilfully evasive summary). The second letter, *A Letter to Mr. Harding the Printer*, already gives the printer the unusual distinction of being named in the title, and declares itself to be a response to a notice in Harding's *Weekly Impartial News Letter* (which, like Barber's *Examiner*, provided Swift with in-house publicity), where it was advertised in the issue for 4 August. There is therefore something of the pot and the kettle about the Drapier's indignant complaint that 'I am informed that *Woods* is generally his own News-Writer'; but his performance of outrage works effectively to widen the focus on the various print genres across which the controversy is being conducted.[90]

This emphasis is further developed when, towards the end of this second letter, the Drapier suggests that Harding should undertake a further

---

[86] *A Letter to the Right Honourable the Lord Viscount Molesworth*, p. 1.   [87] *Ibid.*, p. 22.

[88] These pages are numbered [iii]–vii. For the suggestion that 'Directions to the Printer' (and perhaps the whole pamphlet) was not printed by the Hardings, see Pett, '"I am no inconsiderable Shop-Keeper"', pp. 290–1.

[89] *A Letter to the Shop-keepers, Tradesmen, Farmers, and Common-People of Ireland*, p. 2.

[90] *A Letter to Mr. Harding the Printer*, p. 2.

publication of a different kind: 'Let some Skilful Judicious Pen draw up an ADVERTISEMENT to the following Purpose', namely a declaration against Wood's coins for landlords to circulate to their tenants, to 'give Courage to the meanest Tenant and Cottager'.[91] Yet at the end of the letter the Drapier has no hesitation in getting down to brass tacks with his printer:

> I must tell you in Particular, Mr. *Harding*, that you are much to blame. Several Hundred Persons have enquired at your House for my *Letter to the Shop-Keepers*, &c. and you had none to Sel them. Pray keep your self provided with that Letter and with this; you have got very well by the former, but I did not then Write for your Sake, any more than I do now. Pray Advertise both in every News-Paper, and let it not be YOUR Fault or MINE, if our Country-Men will not take Warning. I desire you likewise to Sell them as Cheap as you can.[92]

Such brusque reproof is by no means the least Swiftian aspect of the letter; but it also serves to reinforce perceptions of the campaign's reach and urgency.

When print is again foregrounded in the third letter, *Some Observations upon a Paper*, the discussion is again framed as a response to an existing publication, and repeats the rationale for a printed declaration. The Drapier also discusses issues of textual dissemination between London and Dublin, suggesting that it would actually be helpful if Dublin printers would reprint Wood's London pamphlets, because 'they would convince you of his wicked Design more than all I shall ever be able to say', although, as things stand, he laments that 'no *London* Printer dare publish any Paper written in Favour of *Ireland*, and here no body hath yet been so *bold* as to Publish any thing in *Favour* of *him*'. Thus he implies – more wishfully than realistically – the potential for print to put a balanced statement of the case before both nations. This theme is again pursued in the fourth letter, *A Letter to the Whole People of Ireland*, in which the Drapier summarises the offensive statements made in 'A Pamphlet sent me of near 50 pages' in order to show his readers 'how this Case is represented in *England* by *Wood* and his Adherents'.[93] Furthermore, when the Hardings were arrested, Swift also focused on print-related issues in his half-sheet *Seasonable Advice. Since a bill is preparing for the Grand Jury, to find against the printer of the*

---

[91] *Ibid.*, pp. 14–16. [92] *Ibid.*, p. 16.
[93] For the pamphlet thus summarised, *Some Farther Account of the Original Disputes in Ireland*, which Swift assumed to have been printed in London but has also been suspected to have originated in Dublin, see Baltes, *The Pamphlet Controversy*, pp. 203–6, 219.

Drapier's last letter, there are several things maturely to be considered by those gentlemen, before whom this Bill is to come, before they determine upon it (which bore the name neither of its author nor of its printer).[94] The publication warned that 'a *Bill* is preparing for the *Grand Jury*, to find against the Printer of the *Drapier's last Letter*', and presented Harding as the innocent victim of a process that he had negotiated prudently and in good faith:

> Lastly, it ought to be considered what Consequence the finding the *Bill*, may have upon a poor Man *perfectly Innocent*, I mean the *Printer*. A Lawyer may *pick* out Expressions and make them Liable to Exception, where no other Man is able to find any. But how can it be suppos'd, that an Ignorant *Printer* can be such a *Critick*; He knew the Author's design was honest, and approv'd by the whole Kingdom, He advised with Friends, who told him there was no harm in the Book, and cou'd see none Himself. It was sent him in an unknown Hand, but the same in which He receiv'd the three former. He and his Wife have offer'd to take their Oaths tht they knew not the Author; and therefore to find a *Bill*, that may bring a Punishment upon the *Innocent*, will appear *very hard*, to say no worse. For it will be impossible to find the Author, unless he will please to discover himself, although I wonder he ever conceal'd his Name. But I suppose what he did at first out of *Modesty*, he now continues to do out of Prudence. God Protect Us and Him.

Harding, meanwhile, persisted in denying any knowledge of the Drapier's identity.[95] His courage, even under imprisonment and threat of prosecution, confirmed yet again that he was ideal for the role.

Finally, as the published campaign began to wind down, the 'Directions to the Printer' set before *A Letter to the Right Honourable the Lord Viscount Molesworth* brought full circle the Drapier's self-reflexive projection of the publishing process:

> When I sent you my former Papers, I cannot say I intended you either *Good* or *Hurt*, and yet you have happened through my Means to receive *Both*. I pray God deliver you from any more of the *Latter*, and increase the *Former*. Your Trade, particularly in this Kingdom, is of all others the most unfortunately Circumstantiated; For as you deal in the most worthless kind of Trash, the Penny Productions of Pennyless Scriblers, so you often venture your Liberty and sometimes your Lives, for the

---

[94] Ehrenpreis, *Swift*, vol. III, pp. 278–9; Baltes, *The Pamphlet Controversy*, pp. 225, 240–1; *Corr.*, vol. II, p. 532 n. 8. For Carteret's failure to persuade King and other members of the Privy Council to condemn the letter as a whole, see also O'Regan, *Archbishop King*, p. 317.

[95] Ehrenpreis, *Swift*, vol. III, pp. 277–8.

The Irish Patriot in Print (1720–1725)

Purchase of Half a Crown, and by your own Ignorance are punished for other Mens Actions.

I am afraid, You in particular think you have Reason to complain of Me for your own and your Wife's Confinement in PRISON, to your great Expense, and for a Prosecution still impending. But I will tell you, Mr. *Harding*, how that Matter stands. Since the Press hath layn under so strict an Inspection, those who have a mind to inform the World are become so Cautious, as to keep themselves if possible out the Way of Danger. My Custom is to Dictate to a 'Prentice who can write in a Feigned Hand, and what is written we send to your House by a Black-guard Boy. But at the same time I do assure you upon my Reputation, that I never did send you any thing, for which I thought you could possibly be called to an Account. And you will be my Witness that I always desired you by a Letter to take some good Advice before you ventured to Print, because I knew the *Dexterity* of *Dealers in the Law* at finding out something to Fasten on where no Evil is meant; I am told indeed, that you did accordingly consult several very able Persons, and even *Some* who afterwards *appeared against you*; To which I can only answer, that you must either change your *Advisers*, or determine to Print nothing that comes from a *Drapier*.

I desire you will send the inclosed Letter, directed to my *Lord Viscount* Molesworth *at his House at* Brackenstown *near* Swords; but I would have it sent *Printed* for the Convenience of His Lordship's Reading, because this Counterfeit Hand of my 'Prentice is not very legible. and if you think fit to Publish it, I would have you first get it Read over carefully by some *Notable* Lawyer: I am assured you will find enough of them who are Friends to the *Drapier*, and will do it without a Fee, which I am afraid you can ill afford after all your Expences. For although I have taken so much Care, that I think it impossible to find a Topick out of the following Paper for sending you again to Prison; Yet I will not venture to be your Guarantee.[96]

The Drapier emphasises the printer's low profit margins and the financial risks of imprisonment, while describing a method of self-protection for the author by which he and his handwriting are kept well away from the printing-house. He also reasserts the need for the printer to take legal advice before publishing. Intriguingly (and unconvincingly), he even represents printing not as a strategy for dissemination, but a courtesy to Molesworth: if Harding wants to publish the work once he has printed it for the benefit of the noble addressee, that is up to him. And even when the Drapier finally signs off, he is soon back with another postscript of complaint about print quality:

[96] *A Letter to the Right Honourable the Lord Viscount Molesworth*, pp. [iii]–vi.

Part III: Dublin

> For want of Intercourse between You and Me, which I never will suffer, your People are apt to make very gross Errors in the Press, which I desire you will provide against.[97]

At one blow he delivers a wounding rebuke and repudiates any suspicion of cosy proof-reading sessions in Harding's print-shop. Even if Swift had been previously acquainted with Harding, there was a major advantage not only in staying well at arm's length for the duration of the campaign, but also in performing that distance in print.

There is, in short, an enormous amount of talk about print in the Drapier's letters, which unavoidably raises the question of the performance's relation to the actual processes by which the letters reached print. David Woolley declares, for instance, that 'Directions to the Printer' had evidently started life as a 'very real, unfictional letter' sent to Harding 'seventeen days after his release from prison', and was published by him 'clearly on Swift's instructions'.[98] Other personal letters, relating to an as yet unpublished additional Drapier's letter, *An Humble Address to Both Houses of Parliament*, further suggest how closely the published accounts may have paralleled the actual process.[99] There is one relevant letter from Swift to Sheridan in June 1725, and two to another clerical friend, John Worrall, in August. To Sheridan Swift wrote:

> Pray remem[br] to leave the[e] Pamphlet with Worral, and give him Directions, unless you have settled it already some oth[r] way. You know it must come out just when the Parlmt meets.[100]

On 27 August he reported to Worrall, revealing in the process his resentment of the prudent censorship exercised by his collaborators:

> I gave Jack Grattan the papers corrected, and I think half spoiled, by the cowardly caution of him and others. He promised to transcribe them time enough, and my desire is they may be ready to be published upon the first day Parliament meets. I hope you will contrive it among you, that it may be sent unknown (as usual) to some printer, with proper directions.[101]

But on 31 August he countermanded the request:

> Since Wood's patent is cancelled, it will by no means be convenient to have the paper printed, as I suppose you, and Jack Grattan, and Sherridan will

---

[97] *A Letter to the Right Honourable the Lord Viscount Molesworth*, p. vii.
[98] *Corr.*, vol. II, pp. 534–7.
[99] Baltes, *The Pamphlet Controversy*, pp. 270–2; cf. Ehrenpreis, *Swift*, vol. III, pp. 308–9.
[100] *Corr.*, vol. II, p. 565.   [101] *Ibid.*, pp. 590–4 (p. 591).

The Irish Patriot in Print (1720–1725) 171

agree; therefore, if it be with the printer, I would have it taken back, and the press broke, and let her be satisfied.

The work is done, and there is no more need of the Drapier.[102]

Since John Harding had died in April, it was Sarah who was setting *An Humble Address*, and who was now to be 'satisfied' for what she had done to date.

The precise cause of John Harding's death remains unclear, but prison fees, combined with loss of earnings, could entail financial ruin; and gaol fever was also a significant risk.[103] Even after his death, however, Harding retained his currency in print. Elizabeth Sadleir (probably Sarah's mother) published *A Poem to the Whole People of Ireland, Relating to M. B. Drapier, by A. R. Hosier*, a fund-raising appeal that suggested Harding had died of a broken heart:

> To hearten him, the DRAPIER sent to him in Jail,
> To tell him, he'd quickly get home to his Wife;
> But, scarce cou'd he find one, to stand for his *Bail*,
> Which struck to his Heart, and depriv'd him of Life.[104]

He was also the subject of an anonymous elegy (poorly printed, without an imprint, on a half sheet with a plain mourning border), which acclaimed 'The Drapier's Printer' as a new star in the heavens; and when Swift in 1728 charged the late Judge Whitshed with 'Prosecuting two *Printers*, one to Death [i.e. Harding], and both to Ruin', it was appropriately the widowed Sarah Harding who printed that verdict.[105] Sarah's loyalty and perseverence (as well as her financial necessity) had also been strategically advertised, in a note to *A Poem to the Whole People of Ireland* that suggested that the 'poor Widow ... might, by a small assistance, from each well-wisher of *Ireland*, be enabled to [print] again for her Country's Service, if it should ever be in Need'. Until her remarriage in 1729, her imprint did indeed continue to appear on writings by Swift in the Irish interest, culminating in 1729 in *A Modest Proposal*.[106] In June 1725, meanwhile, she gave birth to her

---

[102] *Ibid.*, p. 593.   [103] For prison fees, see J. Woolley, 'Poor John Harding', p. 106.

[104] *A Poem to the Whole People of Ireland, Relating to M. B. Drapier, by A. R. Hosier* ([Dublin], 1726; Foxon P675, *ESTC* T202777); J. Woolley, 'Sarah Harding', pp. 167, 175.

[105] *Elegy on the Much-Lamented Death of John Harding Printer, who departed this Transitory Life, this present Monday being the 19th of this instant April 1725* ([Dublin], 1725]; Foxon E143, *ESTC* T403); deattributed poems, *CWJS Poems* IV (forthcoming); *CWJS Irish Political Writings after 1725*, p. 38; *An Answer to a Paper, called A Memorial of the Poor Inhabitants, Tradesmen and Labourers of the Kingdom of Ireland* (Dublin, 1728; TS 665, *ESTC* T21996), p. 15.

[106] Pollard, *Dictionary*, p. 276; *CWJS Irish Political Writings after 1725*, pp. 377–9.

172   Part III: Dublin

husband's posthumous son, who was baptised John Draper.[107] He died in 1727.

Print and Community

The Drapier's evocations of a population united by print were inescapably conditioned by Swift's hierarchical assumptions as a member of an indignant Protestant elite.[108] Even the fourth letter, *A Letter to the Whole People of Ireland*, invoked a relatively circumscribed community by its title's unusual (if not unique) trumpeting of the phrase 'the whole people of Ireland'.[109] In later political contexts it could easily appear that the Drapier's title had conjured into being political identities that Swift himself could neither have imagined nor approved – a much more inspirational reading.

Yet in their original engagement with the threat of Wood's coinage the Drapier's letters repeatedly constructed print as a means of bringing people together for the common good. (And Moyra Haslett further points out that songs printed in support of the campaign, mostly of unknown authorship, 'often pay tribute to the solidarity of Dublin's citizens', using puns and knowing allusions 'to bind singers and audience together in knowing alliance'.[110]) The emphasis on mutual assistance was heralded right at the outset: *A Letter to the Shop-keepers, Tradesmen, Farmers, and Common-People of Ireland* began by exhorting recipients who could not read it for themselves to look to the better educated for help ('get it read to you by others').[111] *A Letter to Mr. Harding the Printer* then emphasised the relation between print and hierarchy by advocating the printing of a declaration 'Drawn up, and Signed by Two or Three Hundred principal Gentlemen of this Kingdom, and Printed Copies thereof sent to their several Tenants'.[112] For this purpose even the landlords' agents could be constructed as figures of trust: '*we have sent them a* Copy *of this* Advertisement, *to be Read to them by*

---

[107] Pett, '"I am no inconsiderable Shop-Keeper"', p. 343.

[108] See Connolly, *Divided Kingdom*, pp. 225–9.

[109] *ESTC* records no previous occurrence of the collocation 'whole people of Ireland' in a title, but it was soon picked up by *The Sixth Letter to the Whole People of Ireland. By an Ancient Patriot* (Dublin, 1724; *ESTC* T1988); the echo may suggest strategic reinforcement by an intimate of Swift's circle, possibly Sheridan. (For pro-Drapier publications possibly attributable to Sheridan, see Baltes, *The Pamphlet Controversy*, pp. 208–12, 265–8, 278–9.) For the 1726 *A Poem to the Whole People of Ireland*, see above.

[110] Moyra Haslett, '"With brisk merry lays": Songs on the Wood's Halfpence Affair', in *Münster* (2019), pp. 199–220 (p. 210).

[111] *A Letter to the Shop-keepers*, p. 2.   [112] *A Letter to Mr. Harding the Printer*, p. 16.

The Irish Patriot in Print (1720–1725)

our Stewards, Receivers, &c.' Alongside the letters themselves, *Harding's Weekly Impartial News Letter* developed a complementary presentation of self-organising urban interest groups. These ranged from the detailed and plausible, such as 'The Declaration of the Town of Galway' signed by merchants of the city (19 September 1724), through the just-about-plausible Brewers' claim that although 'designing Persons' have bought Wood's coins 'at a cheap rate', 'the several Brewers have subscrib'd' to have nothing to do with them (18 August 1724), to the flagrantly improbable 'Advertisement from the *Church-Wardens* of the *City*' that 'Whereas some Persons indiscreetly put some of *Wood's Counters* into the Poor-Boxes last *Sunday*; This is to Caution those who made this Mistake, not to do it again, The POOR of every Parish refusing to except any of them' (5 September 1724).[113] Given Swift's particular concern with parish relief, the joke may well be his.[114] Meanwhile, in the 'Directions to the Printer' prefaced to *A Letter to the Right Honourable the Lord Viscount Molesworth*, solidarity against Wood's coins was represented as so powerful that it could charm lawyers into giving legal opinions free of charge: 'I am assured you will find enough of them who are Friends to the *Drapier*, and will do it without a Fee.'[115] Finally, as the affair came towards its close, the supposed tradesman made an ironically deferential gesture in his fifth letter to his aristocratic ally Molesworth: 'Since your last Residence in *Ireland*, I frequently have taken my Nag to Ride about your Grounds, where I fancy'd myself to feel an Air of *Freedom* breathing round me, and I am glad the Low Condition of a Tradesman did not qualify me to wait on you at your House, for then I am afraid my Writing would not have escaped *severer Censures*.'[116]

Such figurations of print as social connection, though performed from behind the mask of the Drapier, were rooted in the real networks behind the campaign. King, Midleton and Molesworth represented the highly placed clergy and nobility. Friends such as Ford, Sheridan, Worrall, the Grattans and Swift's clerical colleague Patrick Delany (1685/6–1768) – some of them anti-Wood pamphleteers in their own right – provided emotional and practical support, obtaining legal advice, toning down dangerous passages, procuring transcriptions and acting as go-betweens.[117] In the published letters' self-reflexive depiction of print processes, even the blackguard boys of the streets (otherwise routinely vilified by Swift as agents of misrule) serve

---

[113] See also Baltes, *The Pamphlet Controversy*, pp. 184–7, and for comparable declarations in other newspapers, see Ferguson, *Jonathan Swift and Ireland*, pp. 110–12.
[114] Cf. Ehrenpreis, *Swift*, vol. III, p. 237.
[115] *A Letter to the Right Honourable the Lord Viscount Molesworth*, p. vi.   [116] *Ibid.*, p. 21.
[117] *Corr.*, vol. II, pp. 590–4.

174   Part III: Dublin

to bring copy secretly to press, a pattern of delegation which may also have had its counterpart in reality.[118] At the other extreme of the social scale Swift subjected the incoming Lord Lieutenant, his former friend Lord Carteret, to the full force of his print campaign, sending him a copy of the first letter in London and co-ordinating publication of the fourth with his arrival in Ireland.[119] Carteret, after a suitable performance of outraged zeal (in a context that might well have resulted in Swift's arrest and imprisonment), concluded by securing the withdrawal of the patent.[120] The extra-parliamentary print debate that had been a relative novelty in London at the time of *Contests and Dissensions* had visibly reached self-reflexive maturity in Dublin: print in the Drapier's letters was now subject as well as medium.

Faulkner and the Irish Patriot

The Drapier was by now the dominant brand in an energised Dublin print trade, but the long-term benefits would be secured not by the Hardings but by Faulkner.[121] Having set up his shop as recently as 1724, Faulkner would go on to become Dublin's leading literary publisher in the quarter-century after Swift's death, partly on the strength of a strategic collaboration with the Bowyers in London, which enabled Dublin texts of Swift to shape transmission in England as well as in Ireland. Faulkner's publications are particularly difficult to identify from their ornaments, since his stock was, in Pollard's words, 'extensive, variable, and apparently peripatetic', often featuring the stock of other printers, and it may be that earlier in 1724 he had already printed the non-Swiftian anti-Wood pamphlet *A Defence of the Conduct of the People of Ireland in their . . . Refusal of Mr. Wood's Copper-Money*; but his decisive publication was the commemorative anthology *Fraud Detected: Or, The Hibernian Patriot* (Dublin, 1725), which contexualised the Drapier's letters alongside official documentation and additional material by Swift and others.[122] Only weeks after printing his first *Dublin Journal* Faulkner had

---

[118] For blackguard boys, see *A Letter to the Right Honourable the Lord Viscount Molesworth* (p. iv) and *Directions to Servants* (*CWJS Parodies*, pp. 454, 477, 483, 490, 503).

[119] *Corr.*, vol. II, pp. 496–7, 526 (and for a summary listing of their correspondence, p. 501); Baltes, *The Pamphlet Controversy*, pp. 217–18; Ferguson, *Jonathan Swift and Ireland*, pp. 113–34.

[120] Ehrenpreis, *Swift*, vol. III, pp. 219–26, 250–2.

[121] For summary, see Andrew Carpenter, 'Literature in Print, 1550–1800', in Raymond Gillespie and Andrew Hadfield (eds.), *The Oxford History of the Irish Book*, vol. III: *The Irish Book in English, 1550–1800* (Oxford University Press, 2006), pp. 301–18 (p. 314).

[122] Pollard, *Dictionary*, pp. 198, 201 (but for a growing body of Faulkner identifications from ornament evidence, see May, 'False and Incomplete Imprints', pp. 61–4 and Appendix). For *A Defence of the Conduct*, see Baltes, *The Pamphlet Controversy*, pp. 232–3; for *Fraud Detected*, TS 21, *ESTC* T1864.

The Irish Patriot in Print (1720–1725)

announced in the issue for 1 May 1725 a subscription to reprint 'all the Drapier's Letters'.[123] Although Faulkner resembled Harding in combining the roles of printer and newspaper proprietor, he did so at a much more strategic level: Swift, now in his late fifties, was an overwhelmingly popular figure with a large but less than ideally curated back catalogue – an obvious target for an ambitious bookseller. In the event, *Fraud Detected* would be the first of three projects through which Faulkner commemorated the Irish Swift: the second was *The Works of J. S, D. D, D. S. P. D.* published in Dublin from 1735; and the third was the portrait bust now displayed at the south door of St Patrick's Cathedral.[124] All three advertised Faulkner's role in celebrating the great patriot.

Faulkner seems in 1725 to have been acting with Swift's implicit support, if not his active collaboration, and was clearly willing to act boldly.[125] As well as advertising the subscription for *Fraud Detected* in his own newspaper and issuing the book with his own imprint, he also signed a letter asking Midleton's permission to dedicate the collection to him. The letter, which praised the Whig opponent of Wood's patent for 'asserting the dying liberty of your country' (although Midleton had never approved the Drapier's constitutional claims), was presumably drafted or at least approved by Swift, who had also, before Harding's arrest, composed but withheld from publication *A Letter to the Lord Chancellor Midleton* in defence of the fourth Drapier's letter. Midleton firmly refused the dedication: 'I ordered the servant to tell the man who left it, that I would not by any means consent to the dedication of the Drapiers to me, and if done, would complain of the printer.'[126] When the book appeared in October it had no dedication, only a Preface sometimes suspected of being Swift's own – although, teasingly tucked away later in the compilation, appeared the more prudently expressed dedication to Midleton (not by Swift) of *Some Reasons shewing the Necessity the People of Ireland are under, for continuing to refuse Mr. Wood's Coinage.*[127] In a strange visual echo of the

---

[123] Pollard, *Dictionary*, p. 198; Barry Slepian, 'George Faulkner's "Dublin Journal" and Jonathan Swift', *Library Chronicle*, 31 (1965), 97–116.

[124] Robert Mahony, *Jonathan Swift: The Irish Identity* (New Haven and London: Yale University Press, 1995), pp. 1–24.

[125] Cf. the suggestion that Swift and Faulkner 'may have met' in London in 1726 (Pollard, *Dictionary*, p. 204).

[126] *Corr.*, vol. II, pp. 603–4; Baltes, *The Pamphlet Controversy*, pp. 236–40, and, for Midleton's alarm at the fourth letter, p. 224.

[127] For Swift's possible involvement in the Preface, see Ehrenpreis, *Swift*, vol. III, p. 317. For *Some Reasons*, see *Fraud Detected*, pp. i–vi, 170; Baltes, while not suggesting an author, identifies the printer as Harding by his peacock ornament (Baltes-Ellermann, *Swift's Allies*, p. 185).

London edition of *The Bubble*, Faulkner heads the Drapier's first letter with an image very similar to Tooke's deflated peacocks, who again look over their shoulders at a double horn of plenty.[128] Once more an English project has turned out to be a snare and a delusion.

Despite Faulkner's later reputation for standard literary editions, he also maintained a flourishing trade as jobbing printer, advertising his business as one 'where Printing Work is done at Reasonable Rates', and May, who emphasises his extensive resort to false imprints at this early stage of his career, takes the view that 'At least in Faulkner's first decade, his presswork was neither good nor creative.'[129] *Fraud Detected* certainly retains much of the original pamphlets' expressive inelegance, even while suggesting that its undertaker is capable of better: its title page, though still old-fashioned in the quantity of detail displayed within its double-ruled frame, gives a clear overview of the contents and offers a subtly expressive balancing of main title and subtitle: the daring claim of 'FRAUD DETECTED' is highlighted in large and small capitals, while the subtitle hailing the Drapier as 'Hibernian Patriot' is set slightly larger, but in lower case. Yet the book is more a signature-by-signature compilation than an integrated whole, and standards of printing soon start to slip: the Preface has some words tilted backwards; some full capitals for emphasis are out of alignment; and the final line of the Preface concludes with an unnecessarily squashed celebration of the Drapier's 'TRULY,WORTHY PATRIOT'sNAME'. Yet the volume nevertheless cemented a portentous association between Faulkner and Swift in print (and Swift would make a point of presenting a copy to the Bodleian Library, 'Humbly' inscribed 'by M. B. Drapier').[130] In the longer term, Faulkner's development of the Swift brand was to be the foundation of his own success – by which time, partly through the accumulated value of Swift in print, the Dublin book trade would have vastly outgrown the restricted tally of relatively unambitious printers whose premises Dunton had perambulated in the 1690s. Like Dunton in that period, however, Swift was in the later 1720s still alternating his scuffles between London and Dublin. Although his continuing involvement with the London trade would produce material texts that helped transform Swift in print into the global phenomenon that it is today, it also resulted in resentments that complicated textual traditions and brought further opportunities to the Dublin trade – particularly to Faulkner.

---

[128] A count of the small flowers along the short edges confirms the difference.

[129] May, 'False and Incomplete Imprints', p. 61.   [130] For inscription, see *Corr.*, vol. II, plate 16.

CHAPTER 6

Delegating in London, Recouping in Dublin
Travels, Miscellanies, *the* Intelligencer
and A Modest Proposal *(1726–1729)*

The years around 1727, when Swift turned sixty, saw the first publication of *Travels into Several Remote Nations of the World* and *A Modest Proposal*, as well as a new Irish periodical, the *Intelligencer*, and, with Pope, an important set of joint *Miscellanies*. The Swift canon familiar today in syllabuses, anthologies and popular culture was almost complete, and the processes by which Swift in print would be assembled for transmission to posterity were well under way. Yet behind these published achievements lay private resentments which produced variant readings in London and Dublin texts, some explicitly brought to readers' attention, others accessible only to careful collation. In the longer term, as momentum gathered behind a Dublin rather than London collected Works, Swift in print would continue to be shaped by tensions not always apparent to readers.[1]

Swift himself was once again looking to London for the first publication of major projects not specifically related to Ireland. The resulting material texts may well have justified his choice in terms of quality and distribution; but now that he was making only occasional visits to London and reverting to his old habit of turning for home before publication, he was necessarily delegating considerable discretion to intermediaries – and resenting the use that they made of it. His desires for his London publications were crossed not only by the predictable caution of his new London bookseller, Benjamin Motte the younger (successor to Benjamin Tooke and son of the printer of the *Tale*), but also by the professional priorities of his younger English collaborator, Alexander Pope.[2] After a last round of visits in 1727, Swift never returned to England; and despite his persistent

---

[1] For an overview of works published both in Dublin and in London, see Adam Rounce, 'Swift's Texts between Dublin and London', in *JS Book*, pp. 199–213.

[2] For the 'risk-averse' Motte junior, see James McLaverty, 'The Revision of the First Edition of *Gulliver's Travels*: Book-Trade Context, Interleaving, Two Cancels, and a Failure to Catch', *Papers of the Bibliographical Society of America*, 106.1 (2012), 5–35 (p. 14).

177

178 Part III: Dublin

attraction to the reach and sophistication of the London trade, it would be Dublin texts that enabled him to reassert his authority.[3]

At the same time, in contrast to the material aspirations of the London *Travels* and *Miscellanies*, the widowed Sarah Harding continued to publish new Irish tracts in Dublin, culminating in 1729 in *A Modest Proposal*. Such publications further developed the long-established affinity between Swift in print and the lower end of the trade – a market segment that would also offer new opportunities in London with the popularity of the *Travels*. Sarah Harding's tracts, along with the Dublin publication of authorised corrections to the London *Travels* and *Miscellanies*, recalled in part the Irish focus of the Drapier years; but this time it was the ambitious Faulkner, with his carefully nurtured London contacts, who would emerge as major beneficiary. While Swift's personal intentions for his works' publication were often inconsistent, ambivalent and querulous, the development of Swift in print was in this period driven forward, particularly in London, by the brisker and more practical assumptions of others.

Travels into Several Remote Nations of the World (1726)

When *Travels into Several Remote Nations of the World ... By Lemuel Gulliver* was published by Motte in London in 1726, it consisted of two elaborate octavo volumes and was advertised at the high price of 8*s*. 6*d*.[4] McLaverty aptly places it as being 'printed in an expensive if not quite luxurious way'; but it far outclassed anything by Swift that had previously appeared in print. Only the London trade could at this point have combined this level of material quality with the intense reprinting schedule required to meet demand.[5] Alongside the ordinary octavos of the first edition, there were also copies on larger, thicker paper, which further enhanced what was already an impressive visual experience: their margins, taken together, almost equal in breadth the print-block that they serve to

---

[3] For what Womersley calls Swift's 'settled preference for publishing all but trifles and narrowly Irish works in London', see *CWJS Travels*, p. 630. Swift would express both his attachment to English publication and his resentment of English oppression of the Irish book trade in letters to Motte in 1735 and 1736 (*Corr.*, vol. IV, pp. 210–11, 304–6).

[4] Large-paper copies are distinguished as *ESTC* T139454, small-paper as *ESTC* T139451; TS 289 includes both. For pricing, see *CWJS Travels*, p. 635, and for text, publication process and overview of textual scholarship, pp. 627–52.

[5] For evidence that Swift may have told Bolingbroke of his decision as early as 1724, see *CWJS Travels*, p. 630; *Corr.*, vol. II, p. 515; McLaverty, 'The Revision of the First Edition of *Gulliver's Travels*', p. 15.

Delegating in London, Recouping in Dublin (1726–1729)   179

frame.[6] Yet even the ordinary paper copies have ample margins to set off the large, well-spaced type. Significant nouns appear with their conventional capitalisation, and italic is largely restricted to summary headings and proper names. The initial words of each paragraph are distinguished by large and small capitals, and each paragraph is separated from the next by an additional space, helping to structure the narrative in visual as well as verbal terms.

Shef Rogers sets this sparing use of italics (suggestive of 'accuracy and sincerity') and the spacing and typographical distinction between paragraphs ('more common in fiction') alongside a title page whose conservative double-ruled border is typical of a travel book, yet contains a comparatively restrained amount of detail: from this point of view the *Travels* places itself somewhere between the conventions of the travel book (for which it seems unlikely that it was ever really mistaken) and those of the novel – although Rogers also notes that the £200 that Motte paid for the copy 'accords more with the sums expected for a travel book than those for a work of fiction'.[7] In fact both the double-ruled title page and the spaces between paragraphs were well established in Swift in print: they had, for instance, characterised the editions of the *Tale* printed by Motte's father from 1704 onwards.[8] (Indeed, as Bullard and McLaverty note, since the younger Motte had been apprenticed to his father in 1708, 'it is not impossible that he had a hand in printing *A Tale of a Tub*'.[9]) To this extent, the *Travels* builds on the modestly decent printwork that had launched Swift's first outstanding success twenty years earlier; and like the *Tale* it prioritises sound production values above slavish material mimesis.[10] As handled by Tooke and Motte, Gulliver's tales succeeded *A Tale of a Tub* as part of a consistent design strategy, now further inflected by the growing taste for a plainer, sparer style. Grounded in the routines of high-quality printing, it accommodated generic allusion without compromising the status of author or bookseller.

---

[6] For representative measurements, see *CWJS Travels*, p. 635 n. 40.

[7] Shef Rogers, 'Exploring the Bibliographical Limits of *Gulliver's Travels*', in *JS Book*, pp. 135–53 (pp. 135, 138–40 and 148 n. 3).

[8] For the 1704 first edition of the *Tale*, see Chapter 2; and for the 1710 fifth edition, Chapter 3; but for the unframed title of the 1711 *Miscellanies in Prose and Verse* handled by Tooke at the same time but printed by Bowyer, see Chapter 4.

[9] Bullard and McLaverty, 'Introduction', p. 11.

[10] Cf. S. Rogers: 'despite all of the author's and publisher's efforts to present the account as a travel book, Swift's work seems to have fooled no one'; 'The likelihood of being deceived by an early eighteenth-century travel book has been overstated' ('Exploring', pp. 142 and 145 n. 152).

180   Part III: Dublin

Yet the *Travels* are noticeably grander than the *Tale*, as demonstrated by a new proliferation of images and decorations. A portrait frontispiece of Gulliver suggests his resemblance to Swift in age and appearance; Gulliver's destinations are pinpointed on four painstakingly produced maps; and transitions from part to part and chapter to chapter are further marked by a variety of ornaments.[11] These visual enhancements further display the sharpness of the printing, whether in the subtly expressive shading of Gulliver's portrait, the neatly aligned lettering of locations mapped across expanses of ocean, or the head- and tailpieces that adorn the beginnings and ends of chapters. As well as fleuron borders there are elaborate pictorial ornaments: at the head of chapter i of Part I, for example, the sun is seen rising in deep perspective over a river flowing through a city of varied ruins, architectural forms and human activities (Figure 9).[12]

No previous first publication of a Swift work had deployed such a range of effects, and none had filled two volumes. Readers who could afford to buy or contrive to borrow were evidently captivated, and the look and feel of the volumes was calculated to enhance their pleasure. Yet if the ample margins, crisp printwork and lively decoration gave Swift any pleasure at all, he seems not to have left it on record. What he emphasised instead, first in a letter to Pope of 17 November 1726 (which maintains the prudent pretence of having just seen the *Travels* for the first time), was his dissatisfaction with the verbal text. He moved quickly to the declaration that 'I read the Book over, and in the second volume observe several passages which appear to be patch'd and altered, and the style of a different sort (unless I am much mistaken)'; and after some reports on other matters he returned to the theme: 'Let me add, that if I were Gulliver's friend, I would desire all my acquaintance to give out that his copy was basely mangled, and abused, and added to, and blotted out by the printer, for so to me it seems, in the second volume particularly.'[13] Womersley sums up Swift's position with salutary robustness:

> Given the textual complications which arose from Swift's determination to remove himself from both the delivery of the manuscript to the printer and the subsequent checking of proofs, and given also Swift's bitter resentment

---

[11] For analysis and side-by-side comparison of two states of the portrait, see *CWJS Travels*, pp. 567–72; for play between ostensible and actual authors, Barchas, *Graphic Design*, pp. 28–9. Differently placed inscriptions in the two states declare the sitter to be in his fifty-eighth year. For the challenges presented by the maps, see S. Rogers, 'Exploring', p. 138.

[12] *CWJS Travels*, vol. I, p. 1.

[13] *Corr.*, vol. III, pp. 56–7; for bibliographical and other evidence supporting Swift's claim, see McLaverty, 'The Revision of the First Edition of *Gulliver's Travels*'.

TRAVELS.

PART I.
A VOYAGE *to* LILLIPUT.

CHAP. I.

The Author gives some Account of himself and Family, his first Inducements to travel. He is shipwrecked, and swims for his Life, gets safe on shoar in the Country of Lilliput, *is made a Prisoner, and carryed up the Country.*

Y Father had a small Estate in *Nottinghamshire*; I was the Third of Five Sons. He sent me to *Emanuel-Colledge* in *Cambridge*, at Fourteen Years old, where I resided three Years, and applyed my self

PART I.   B   close

Figure 9 Jonathan Swift, *Travels into Several Remote Nations of the World . . . By Lemuel Gulliver* (London, 1726), p. 1.

182   Part III: Dublin

of those complications, it is worth noting that he must have been fully aware
that his self-effacement and geographical estrangement from the press made
such complications more likely.[14]

Swift well knew, from his face-to-face collaboration with Barber and his
carefully detached work with Harding, the dangers of using print to bait
established power; but in the case of the *Travels* there were still further risks
and opportunities. Readers might be happily engrossed (and Motte seems
to have sold something of the order of ten thousand copies in the first three
weeks), but behind the scenes a more private drama was being played out.[15]
Its ramifications help to contextualise the forms assumed by the new work,
even though they were not immediately spelled out to the public – and may
have made a limited impression even when they were.

The outstandingly provocative nature of the *Travels* had presumably
made a speedy farewell to London particularly appealing.[16] As early as
29 September 1725, when Swift wrote to Pope that 'my Travells, in four
Parts Compleat newly Augmented' were 'intended for the press when the
world shall deserve them, or rather when a Printer shall be found brave
enough to venture his Eares', he had signalled the sensitivity as well as the
importance of the project.[17] Moreover, after travelling to London in
March 1726 on his first visit since the death of the Queen, bringing with
him a scribal copy which he seems to have further revised en route, he first
sought face-to-face opportunities to put Ireland's case to Princess Caroline
and to Walpole; and it was only after his failure with Walpole, and just
before his return to Ireland, that on 8 August he approached a bookseller.[18]
His choice of Benjamin Motte the younger was evidently a considered one,
for Motte was not only the son of the printer of the *Tale*, but also successor
to Benjamin Tooke the younger, whose business he had taken over with
financial and editorial support from Tooke's brother, the clergyman,
schoolmaster and press corrector Andrew Tooke (1673–1732).[19] For Swift,
Motte was the nearest available approximation to returning to his old
bookseller, even though Motte himself, not yet active in the trade on his
own account when Swift left for Ireland in 1714, could still usefully be
represented as someone 'whom I never saw'.[20] Such indeed were Swift's

---

[14] *CWJS Travels*, p. 643.   [15] *Ibid.*, p. 635.   [16] *Ibid.*, p. 633.   [17] *Corr.*, vol. II, p. 606.
[18] *CWJS Travels*, pp. 630–1, 633 n. 26 (cf. pp. 485–6); McLaverty, 'The Revision of the First Edition of
Gulliver's Travels', pp. 11–12; *Corr.*, vol. III, p. 11; Ferguson, *Jonathan Swift and Ireland*, pp. 140–2.
[19] Michael Treadwell, 'Benjamin Motte, Andrew Tooke and *Gulliver's Travels*', in *Münster* (1985),
pp. 287–304 (pp. 288–96); McLaverty, 'The Revision of the First Edition of *Gulliver's Travels*',
pp. 8–10.
[20] *Corr.*, vol. III, pp. 9–12.

Delegating in London, Recouping in Dublin (1726–1729)   183

distancing techniques that even these words were ostensibly not his, for his approach to Motte took the form of a letter copied out for him by his Scriblerian friend John Gay (with whom he happened to be staying).[21]

The supposed author of the letter was one Richard Sympson, whose name combined piquant literary and print-trade allusions. During Swift's years as Temple's secretary he had apparently thought of the bookseller Richard Simpson, with whom he dealt on Temple's behalf, as his own 'Bookseller'; and 'R. Simpson', one of the sharers in Temple's copy, had featured in the imprint of Swift's first posthumous Temple volume, *Letters Written by Sir W. Temple* (1700).[22] In addition, a so-called 'Capt. William Symson' had in 1715 appeared in print as author of *A New Voyage to the East-Indies*, a travel book 'Adorn'd with CUTS' that included a frontispiece of the supposed author trading with the inhabitants, a map, and images of local plants and activities.[23] The book, in which Curll was a partner, also featured a preface ostensibly by a third party: its deployment of the William Symson figure confirms the apt fit of Swift's *Travels* with conventions already shaped to toy pleasurably with the gullible and the possibly-not-quite-so-gullible. In Swift's own role-play, the self-proclaimed Richard Sympson presented himself to Motte as Gulliver's cousin and literary agent, placing himself inside as well as outside the frame of what would become the published *Travels* by explaining that he had also composed the Preface. This in-character performance comprises the principal contemporary evidence for Swift's intentions in sending his work to press: all that remains of further negotiations with Motte is a one-sentence postscript from Sympson, in Gay's handwriting, from a few days later.[24]

Sympson's letter looks like an attempt on Swift's part to bounce Motte into buying the copy by showing him an unrepresentative sample, setting inflexible terms and allowing only three days for him to make up his mind.[25] In introducing the *Travels*, Sympson cites 'several persons of great Judgment and Distinction, who are confident they will sell very well'; and although he warns that 'the following Volumes may be thought in one or two places to be a little Satyrical', he also reports that 'it is agreed that they will give no Offence', and leaves the decision to Motte, with the rider that 'you must judge for yourself, and take the Advice of your Friends'. (Womersley points out that Gay and Pope offered a similar

---

[21] *CWJS Travels*, p. 633.   [22] See Chapter 2.

[23] For *A New Voyage* (*ESTC* T113736), see R. W. Frantz, 'Gulliver's "Cousin Sympson"', *HLQ*, 1.3 (1938), 329–34.

[24] *Corr.*, vol. III, pp. 13–14.

[25] For other possible motives for Swift's delay in approaching a bookseller, see *CWJS Travels*, p. 633.

184 Part III: Dublin

assessment in their letters of congratulation once the work was published – though they no doubt bore in mind that their correspondence with Swift was likely to be under surveillance.[26]) Yet if the letter is taken at face value, Motte was being asked to make up his mind on the basis of only a quarter (or perhaps half) of the *Travels* – probably, as Treadwell argues, Part I (and perhaps Part II), thus keeping from him the much more explicitly political risk posed by Parts III and IV.[27] At the same time, Sympson's insistence on secrecy ('I require that you will never suffer these Papers to be once out of your Sight') strengthens the suspicion of sensitivity that he seeks to discount; and although he advises Motte to consult his own judgement and that of his friends, he sets him an extremely tight deadline: the messenger was to return in three days for his final answer, and no counter-proposals would be entertained. Moreover, Sympson set a high price on the copy, allegedly 'because I know the Author intends the Profit for the use of poor Sea-men, and I am advised to say that two Hundred pounds is the least Summ I will receive on his account' – although he concedes that, if sales fall short of his expectations, 'then whatever shall be thought too much even upon your own word shall be duely repaid'. (In the light of Swift's record of charitable giving, and of the allegorical element in Gulliver's voyaging, Sympson's 'Sea-men' may conceivably stand here for beneficiaries – such as the beggars around St Patrick's – who were far from doing business in great waters.) In addition to being compensated for any loss, Motte is further assured that, if he decides to accept, 'you may begin to print them, and the subsequent parts shall be all sent you one after another in less than a week'; but he must still pay in full before he has seen the rest of the copy ('deliver a Bank Bill of two hundred pounds wrapt up so as to make a parcel to the Hand from whence you receive this'). Given the contents of Parts III and IV, Motte is being offered what Treadwell rightly calls 'a pig in a poke', and the point seems to be underlined in the postscript, a few days later, which insists 'I would have both Volumes come out together and published by Christmas at furthest.'[28] It was volume II, containing Parts III and IV, that raised the political stakes, and Sympson seems keen to guard against the possibility that Motte might lose his nerve.

Motte's draft reply is still extant.[29] Though his tone is courteous, he is too astute simply to fall in with Sympson's demands – and it is not clear that he ever believed in the real existence of either Sympson or his cousin. (McLaverty argues that he may already have known Ford, if not Swift

[26] *Ibid.*, pp. lxxxvi–lxxxvii; *Corr.*, vol. III, pp. 47, 52.
[27] Treadwell, 'Benjamin Motte', pp. 296–8.   [28] *Corr.*, vol. III, pp. 13–14.   [29] *Ibid.*, pp. 12–13.

Delegating in London, Recouping in Dublin (1726–1729) 185

himself, and that he would hardly have considered paying such a high price for the copy had he not known it to be by the author of the *Tale* – whose fifth edition the firm had further promoted in December 1724 by issuing a duodecimo reprint.[30]) Certainly, when Sympson wrote to Motte in 1727, it was in the handwriting of a different person entirely; and by December 1728 Motte was consulting directly with Swift as author. From the beginning Motte insisted that he had his own constraints to consider: he could not produce 'so considerable a Sum as 200 *l.*' at short notice in the vacation; and as he had undertaken to go 'into the Country' the following week to keep appointments with 'some Dealers there', 'any further Correspondence' would need to reach him 'as soon as possible'. (McLaverty deduces that, indebted as he was to Andrew Tooke, 'He needed cash from sales to pay for the copyright.'[31]) In the event it was suspiciously convenient that 'The Bearer stays for an Answer so that I can only offer a Proposal without giving a Reason'; and by returning the copy with a counter-offer, Motte got away with doing exactly what Sympson had warned him not to. His counter-proposal balanced speedy publication against delayed payment, offering 'my Promise, that the Book shall be publish'd within a Month after I receive the Copy, and if the Success will allow it, I will punctually pay the money you require in Six Months'. Of the further correspondence that presumably ensued, Sympson's brief stipulation of simultaneous pre-Christmas publication of the two volumes is all that survives, making it impossible to be sure which decisions were agreed between Sympson and Motte, and which were made later, by Motte and his printers. Techniques already tried and tested in Ireland (where Swift's deniability had been protected by pseudonymous authorship, third-party transcription, transmission by unknown messengers and avoidance of contact with booksellers and printers) can be relatively plausibly ascribed to Swift himself; but some new features in the publication of the *Travels* are more difficult to ascribe to individuals.

Some decisions may reflect the input of Swift's pre-1714 Tory friends. Swift joked that Gay, for instance, should have had his post directed 'to Tonson or Lintot, to whom I believe his lodgings are better known than to the runners of the Post office': Gay certainly screened Swift's involvement with the *Travels* by acting as amanuensis, and may well have contributed other now untraceable ideas.[32] Arbuthnot too may have been involved – though presumably not in the manner suggested when in 1725 he declared

---

[30] McLaverty, 'The Revision of the First Edition of *Gulliver's Travels*', pp. 11, 14–15.
[31] *Ibid.*, p. 13.   [32] *Corr.*, vol. III, p. 18.

Part III: Dublin

that 'I will sett the letters myself rather than that it should not be publish'd.'[33] But the most obvious strategic contributions seem to have come from Pope. Already notable for the innovative strategies that shaped his own print profile, he had much more experience than Swift of making a profit from high-quality London publication, and a much greater commitment to active management of the publication process.[34] Swift's testimony in 1735 that 'I never got a farthing by anything I writ, except one about eight year ago, and that was by Mr. Pope's prudent management for me', suggests that it may have been Pope's idea to ask for £200 for the copy – indeed, Shef Rogers points out that Pope's Homer translations were one of very few works in the period 'to have garnered more than £200 for their authors'.[35] Moreover, Pope had already made large-paper copies a central element in his own prestige projects, and his 1717 *Works* had featured an engraved portrait frontispiece of considerable rhetorical finesse, furnishing an intriguing comparison with the engraved frontispieces that model Gulliver so closely on his creator.[36] To judge by Pope's gleeful report to Swift on 16 November 1726, it had probably also been left to him to organise the final delivery of copy: 'Motte receiv'd the copy (he tells me) he knew not from whence, nor from whom, dropp'd at his house in the dark, from a Hackney-coach: by computing the time, I found it was after you left England.'[37] Yet despite Pope's meticulous attention to supervising the production of his own works, it does not seem that Swift asked him – or anyone else – to oversee production once the copy had gone to press; and Womersley judges that 'neither Swift nor anyone connected with him corrected proof'.[38] Motte, who would enter his right to the copy in the Stationers' Register later the same year, was now, like Harding before him, on his own – at least until the recriminations started.[39]

The surviving letters suggest that some decisions at least had already been agreed between Sympson and Motte: the price of the copy, provided sales were adequate, was £200; Motte was to exercise strict security over the copy before publication; the work was to be issued in two volumes, simultaneously published; and the publication deadline (setting aside

---

[33] *Corr.*, vol. II, p. 615.

[34] These aspects of his career are explored in Foxon and McLaverty, *Pope and the Eighteenth-Century Book Trade*, and McLaverty, *Pope, Print and Meaning*.

[35] Although David Woolley reads Swift's remark as referring to the London *Miscellanies* (*Corr.*, vol. IV, pp. 107–8), the consensus is that it refers to the *Travels* (S. Rogers, 'Exploring', p. 139 and n. 24). See also McLaverty, 'The Revision of the First Edition of *Gulliver's Travels*', p. 14.

[36] *CWJS Travels*, Appendix A, pp. 567–72; Barchas, *Graphic Design*, pp. 28–34.

[37] *Corr.*, vol. III, p. 52.   [38] *CWJS Travels*, p. 631 n. 20; p. 635.

[39] McLaverty, 'The Revision of the First Edition of *Gulliver's Travels*', p. 15; *SCEBC* (1710–46), p. 344.

Motte's initial 'within a Month') was to be Christmas 1726. Such aspects as price, format, large-paper copies, margins, ornamentation and the commissioning of the engraved portrait and maps may have been discussed in correspondence now lost. Another important decision was that *Travels*, like the Drapier's letters, but unlike the *Tale* and most other Swift items managed by Tooke, was to be issued over Motte's name, without the screening imprint of a trade publisher. This may have been to facilitate distribution by exchange of copies, which allowed booksellers to diversify their stock without the need for cash outlay: Motte's imprint ensured that wherever a copy of this expensive and fashionable publication might be sold, the buyer would recognise it as his. On the other hand, the presence of Motte's name may also suggest a comparison with *A Project for the Advancement of Religion* and *A Proposal for Correcting, Improving and Ascertaining the English Tongue*, whose Tooke imprints (even where, as in the former, Swift's name is withheld) are generally taken, following Treadwell, to indicate a particularly high degree of authorial commitment on Swift's part.[40] Sympson apparently left such decisions to Motte (and Pope too stood ready to hand, had further advice been required). But only when Swift had set off for Ireland and Motte had finally received the whole copy would he have realised the full extent of the risks and opportunities he had taken on: censoring the copy was one part of his solution, and the complex organisation of its printwork was arguably another.

As to the censorship, Swift would in 1733 write twice to Ford, specifying his objections in more detail: 'Now, you may please to remember how much I complained of Motts suffering some friend of his (I suppose it was Mr Took a Clergy-man now dead) not onely to blot out some things that he thought might give offence, but to insert a good deal of trash contrary to the Author's manner and Style, and Intention.'[41] This was a reference to the recently deceased Andrew Tooke, who had evidently come into his own when Motte realised the danger posed by parts of the *Travels* – a work that was in any case at a considerable generic remove from his established specialisms in mathematics and geometry.[42] Much as Swift resented Andrew Tooke's cuts, substitutions and additions, asking an experienced scholar and press editor to revise the copy was an obvious precaution for a prudent bookseller, and Treadwell's sense that Swift 'was irritated

---

[40] Treadwell, 'Swift's Relations', pp. 13, 15; Karian suggests that a more experienced bookseller like Tooke might have used a trade publisher rather than censoring the text (*Print and Manuscript*, pp. 21–2).

[41] *Corr.*, vol. III, p. 639 (and, to similar effect, p. 708).

[42] Treadwell, 'Benjamin Motte', pp. 299–300.

188   Part III: Dublin

without being really surprised' and retained 'some sympathy for the pub-lisher's position' is persuasive, particularly since, as Womersley points out, the whole affair unrolled to a script already anticipated in 'The Bookseller's Advertisement' prefaced to *The Mechanical Operation of the Spirit* in 1704.[43] But the predictability of an outcome in no way diminished the likelihood that Swift would complain about it.

Production was elaborately organised, by dividing the *Travels* into five work packages and placing them with five different printing-houses (sug-gesting particularly careful design and dissemination of the required layout and typography).[44] The arrangement may indeed have been proposed, at least in outline, in lost letters between Motte and Sympson; but it could hardly have been worked out in any detail by anyone not directly on the spot, and it was Motte, not Swift, who had the contacts and experience to recruit the team.[45] Such distribution was an established way of ensuring speedy first and subsequent printings, and Womersley further suggests, on the grounds of catchword error, that setting by ear rather than by eye may have been involved, in which case the extra cost of using a reader may have been offset against faster work by the compositor.[46] Divided printing was also an effective way of protecting pre-publication confidentiality, for five printing-houses, not just one, would have had to be compromised to get sight of a full text; and it is suggestive that one of the printers, James Bettenham, would in 1728 be chosen by Pope to produce – again under conditions of strict secrecy – the first edition of his anonymous *Dunciad*.[47] Under these circumstances it was unlikely that either official investigators or commercial rivals would be able to take hostile action before publica-tion. But whatever Motte's reasoning, or its relation to discussions with Swift or others, the contrast with the handling of Swift in print by the Hardings and other members of the Dublin print trade is clear: the *Travels* were managed by an accomplished professional with a wide network, astute in managing political risk, prepared to invest substantially, and organised to produce high-quality products at high volume. Having

---

[43] *Ibid.*, p. 300; *CWJS Travels*, pp. 639–40.

[44] For the portions printed by Edward Say, Henry Woodfall, James Bettenham, William Pearsall and Jane Ilive, see Michael Treadwell, 'Observations on the Printing of Motte's Octavo Editions of *Gulliver's Travels*', in *Münster* (1998), pp. 157–77 (pp. 160–77).

[45] Treadwell, 'Observations', p. 175.   [46] S. Rogers, 'Exploring', p. 137; *CWJS Travels*, p. 635 n. 38.

[47] McLaverty, 'The Revision of the First Edition of *Gulliver's Travels*', p. 15. One of Bettenham's apprentices later recalled the arrangements for Pope's proofreading, which required his being 'trusted to go to the author with the proofs in great secresy' (Nichols, *Literary Anecdotes*, vol. III, p. 705; *The Poems of Alexander Pope, vol. III: The Dunciad (1728) and the Dunciad Variorum (1729)*, ed. Valerie Rumbold (Harlow: Longman, 2007), p. 5).

Delegating in London, Recouping in Dublin (1726–1729)   189

taken action to minimise the likelihood of trouble with the authorities, he successfully brought a handsome pair of volumes to market before their contents were widely known. Such a premium service presumably met in part Swift's desires in turning once more to London publication; but in part it obviously did not. As the very particular kind of author Swift had become – daring, oppositional, retaining much of his work for manuscript circulation or no circulation at all, and prioritising the technical deniability of what he did publish – his impulses, at odds even with each other, were demonstrably incompatible with the realities of London publishing as understood by Motte.

As the two delightfully saleable octavo volumes of the *Travels* passed into the hands of an excited readership, the first edition quickly sold out, prompting a further two octavo editions in the same year. Extant copies were evidently made up on occasion from sheets from more than one of these editions, providing exhilarating material evidence of what Womersley calls 'the haste, confusion and pressure of work' of a printing-house at full stretch, as Motte exerted himself to meet demand for his expensive two-volume edition.[48] He would quickly add the option of a cheaper duodecimo format; but it was also becoming clear that there was a market for a material text far more radically calculated for a popular audience. On 25 November 1726 the *Penny London Post* suddenly dropped its serialisation of *Don Quixote* in favour of the *Travels* (Figure 10):

> which have been lately published, and bore so considerable a Share in almost every Conversation both in Town and Country, not only from the Reputation of their suppos'd Author, but the vast Variety of Wit and Pleasantry with which the several Relations are interpos'd; that those who have not the Convenience of reading them at the Price they are now sold, may not be debarr'd so delightful an Entertainment, we shall begin them in this Paper in the Manner following, and continue them till the whole is finished.[49]

Here, on a single folded sheet, badly printed in double columns under a cluttered masthead (a view of London from the south bank across London Bridge, with the arms of the City inset to the left and a postboy with his horn to the right), was an attempt to allure readers who could not easily buy or borrow expensive books; and it frames the *Travels* as fashion and fun, a delightful story that everyone is talking about. As such, it is tellingly

[48] *CWJS Travels*, pp. 635–6.
[49] TS 296; *The Rothschild Library*, no. 2109 (vol. II, p. 570; first two pages reproduced as plates XXXV–XXXVI).

(2)

The Continuation of Cynthia: With the tragical Account of the unfortunate Almerin and Desdemona.

Evidence what I have said O ye Powers Divine' By all this and by your Fairself, I swear a Divinity too precious to be prophan'd.

Oh hold! quoth she, Swear not by that: Cankers may eat that Flower on the Stalk; the scratch of a Pin may soon deface it; Sickness and Mischance may soon ruin it; Age and Time are great Devourers of it; and when in these Cheeks and Lips which you extol so high, shall not be left red enough to blush at Perjury, when you shall make it, what will become of me then?

O Madam! (reply'd I) Cease these Doubts, and dissipate such needless Fears: The Sun shall as soon falter in his Career, the Stars drop from their Places, where they have of old been fixed, the Earth shall remove, Nature shall alter her Course, and all Impossibilities shall be perform'd when I prove disloyal and false in my Love.

These Protestations did give her some Satisfaction; and prevail'd so far with her, that she suffer'd me to enjoy the Privilege to accompany her to her Parents House, which was within the City. When we came thither she gave her Friends to understand the timely Assistance I gave her; as also my Birth and Quality, and Authority in the City. They no sooner received this Relation from their Daughter but they bide me Welcome, and caress'd me with the greatest Endearments. My Entertainment was extraordinary; but the Kindnesses bestow'd on me was not after the lofty Court mode, but most familiarly, as if I had been a near Relation unto them, and gave me Thanks in the most obliging Terms for the Kindness conferr'd on their Daughter, which I could not receive without a Blush. Here it was I learn'd his Name was Philaster, an aged Knight, that had liv'd there many Years; that his Fair Daughter was his only Child, whose Name was Desdemona, in whom the old Knight and his Lady did repose all their Comfort and Joy.

In several Discourses we pass'd away the Time while the Supper lasted, where the chiefest Delicates I fed on, was Desdemona's Beauty: And indeed 'twas she alone made all Things seem pleasant where she came, and set a Lustre on the greatest Enormity.

Supper being ended, and the Evening far spent, I began to prepare for my Departure. After I had bade a Farewel unto the old Knight and his Lady, with many Acknowledgements for the Civilities I had receiv'd, I began to order myself to take my Leave of the fairest Desdemona.

We see by Experience, that the Fire that flames highest trembles most; so is it in Love;
To be continu'd. he

We shall omit for some time the Life of Don Quixote to give Place for the Travels of Captain Lemuel Gulliver into several remote Parts of the World, which have been lately published, and bore so considerable a Share in almost every Conversation both in Town and Country, not only from the Reputation of their suppos'd Author, but the vast Variety of Wit and Pleasantry with which the several Relations are interpos'd; that those who have not the Convenience of reading them at the Price they are now sold, may not be debarr'd so delightful an Entertainment, we shall begin them in this Paper in the Manner following, and continue them till the whole is finished.

Travels into several remote Nations of the World. In four Parts. By Lemuel Gulliver, first a Surgeon, and then a Captain of several Ships.

CAHP. I.

The Author gives some Account of himself and Family, his first Inducements to travel. He is shipwreck'd, and swims for his Life, gets safe on Shoar, in the Country of Lilliput, is made a Prisoner, and carryed up the Country.

MY Father had a small Estate in Nottinghamshire; I was the Third of Five Sons. He sent me to Emanuel College in Cambridge, at Fourteen Years old, where I resided three Years, and applyed myself close to my Studies; but the Charge of maintaining me (although I had a very scanty Allowance) being too great for a narrow Fortune, I was bound Apprentice to Mr. James Bates, an eminent Surgeon in London, with whom I continued four Years, and my Father now and then sending me small Sums of Money, I laid them out in learning Navigation, and other Parts of the Mathematicks, useful to those who intend to travel, as I always believed it would be some time or other my Fortune to do. When I left Mr. Bates, I went down to my Father, where by the Assistance of him and my Uncle John, and some other Relations, I got Forty Pounds, and a Promise of Thirty Pounds a Year to maintain me at Leyden: There I studied Physick two Years and seven Months, knowing it would be useful in long Voyages.

Soon after my return from Leyden, I was recommended by my good Master Mr. Bates, to be Surgeon to the Swallow, Captain Abraham Pannell Commander; with whom I continued three Years and a half, making a Voyage or two into the Levant, and some other Parts. When I came back, I resolved to settle in London; to which Mr. Bates, my Master, encouraged me, and by him I was recommended to several Patients. I took Part of a small House in the Old Jury; and being advised to alter
my

Figure 10 *The Penny London Post*, 25 November 1726, p. 2.

Delegating in London, Recouping in Dublin (1726–1729) 191

contrasted with soberer accounts of foreign nations and more conventional kinds of romance: the first page of the issue is taken up with an instalment of *The Present State of the Empire of China* ('The Western Tartars live in Tents . . .'); the first column on the second page enables readers to catch up with *The Continuation of Cynthia: With the tragical Account of the unfortunate Almerin and Desdemona*; and the second column begins the *Travels*. The *Penny London Post* was sloppily managed: readers were given no help at all in remembering where Desdemona and her admirer had got to in the previous issue before he resumed with 'Evidence what I have said O ye Powers Divine'; and at the foot of the column the extract was left hanging in mid-sentence, concluded only by a semicolon and 'To be continu'd.' The printing was equally slapdash: the *Travels* commences with the unpromising heading 'CAHP. I', and it is unclear, for lack of surviving copies, how far the serialisation actually progressed. Yet its significance for Swift in print is hard to ignore, for this was the first ever work by Swift to be serialised, and its appeal to impecunious lovers of travel and romance was a world away from the prudential reading pressed upon the lower orders in the Drapier's cheap pamphlets.[50] A second serialisation, in *Parker's Penny Post*, took a similar approach, explaining that 'The Travels of Capt. *Gulliver* . . . having for their Variety of Wit and Pleasant Diversion, become the general Entertainment of Town and Country, we will insert here in small Parcels, to oblige our Customers, who are otherwise, not capable of reading them at the Price they are sold.'[51] This gives particular point to Arbuthnot's invocation of that traditional staple of popular reading *The Pilgrim's Progress*, when he prophesied that 'Gullivers Travells' would 'have as great a run as John Bunian'; and also to Gay's claim that 'From the highest to the lowest it is universally read, from the Cabinet-council to the Nursery.'[52] These shabby serialisations were a sign of things to come, repackaging a work that had originally cost 8s. 6d. for those who could only spare a penny: cheap print had launched Gulliver into the travels through popular media that continue to this day.

Swift, who could hardly fail to notice how well his *Travels* were doing, responded in typically backhanded fashion, noting sardonically in February 1727 that 'I hear it hath made a Bookseller rich enough to be an Alderman.'[53] (Perhaps Swift was even regretting the once-and-for-all price he had set on the copy.) He immediately recurred to his substantive complaint against Motte: 'In my Judgment I should think it hath been mangled in the

---

[50] For further evidence of popular impact, see A. C. Kelly, *Jonathan Swift and Popular Culture*, p. 66.
[51] TS 296A; *Parker's Penny Post*, no. 246 (28 November 1726).   [52] *Corr.*, vol. III, pp. 44, 47.
[53] *Ibid.*, p. 73.

Part III: Dublin

press, for in some parts it doth not seem of a piece.' Meanwhile, although it seems that he had neglected to retain a copy of the work as sent to press (having apparently left the autograph manuscript with Gay in London, and taken no action to prevent Motte from destroying the transcription that had served as copy), he watched for opportunities to vindicate his own sense of what a tolerable text would comprise.[54] Most obviously, he had Ford send Motte, in January 1727, a list of detailed smaller corrections, with suggestions in more general terms for larger corrections.[55] While it is unclear to what extent these were revisions and to what extent reconstructions, this letter represents a clear attempt to re-establish control over the London text. Motte, however, whom Treadwell plausibly sees as wishing 'to avoid if at all possible a direct refusal to restore the offending passages', hurried into print in May 1727, while Swift was again in London, a 'Second Edition, Corrected' of his octavo, featuring only minor corrections.[56] Since he still had previously published octavos in stock, as well as a duodecimo that he had not yet issued, this was probably, as Treadwell suggests, a tactful way of countering Swift's demands for the restoration of dangerous passages – meaning that the text of the new edition needed to be irrevocably fixed before Motte met the agent (Erasmus Lewis) whom Sympson had in April 1727 appointed (under the hand of an otherwise unknown amanuensis) to pay the £200 originally agreed.[57] Having received the money (and, Treadwell surmises, a presentation copy of the new edition), Lewis signed Sympson's letter 'I am fully satisfyd.' With so much stock already on Motte's hands and a new edition just published, it was obvious that he could not be expected to bring out yet another edition. Meanwhile, Swift had his money, and made a note 'To ~~sell~~ buy 200^{ll} in some Stock', a task that he later marked as completed; and shortly afterwards he seems to have dropped the Sympson mask.[58] By the end of the year Motte and Swift were corresponding without disguise, as demand for Motte's editions slackened and Swift expressed reservations about adding 'Cuts' that 'will raise the price of the Book'.[59] He ended by adopting a judicious balance: 'The world glutted it self with that book at first, and now it will go off but soberly, but I suppose will not be soon worn out.' In due course the duodecimos would also be adorned with decorations.[60]

---

[54] *CWJS Travels*, p. 640.

[55] *Ibid.*, pp. 605–7, 640–2; *Corr.*, vol. III, pp. 66–9; D. Woolley, 'Swift's Copy', pp. 161–5; McLaverty, 'The Revision of the First Edition of *Gulliver's Travels*', pp. 17–23.

[56] Treadwell, 'Benjamin Motte', pp. 301–3.   [57] *Corr.*, vol. III, pp. 82–3.

[58] 'Memoranda from Forster Ms. 519', *PW*, vol. V, p. 334 and facing image.

[59] *CWJS Travels*, pp. 641–2 n. 68; *Corr.*, vol. III, p. 149.   [60] *Corr.*, vol. III, p. 151 n. 2.

Delegating in London, Recouping in Dublin (1726–1729)   193

Swift, however, had already to a degree brought his textual disputes into the public domain by conniving at an edition printed in 1726 by Hyde in Dublin. (To judge by Motte's willingness to use Hyde as go-between in corresponding with Swift, it is even possible that they had reached a financial accommodation, although Dublin convention would not have required it.[61]) Hyde openly declared that his Dublin edition of the *Travels* was 'Printed by and for J. HYDE in *Dame's Street*' and added the claim that '*In this Impression, several* ERRORS *in the London Edition are Corrected.*' For the first time purchasers were alerted to the possibility that the London text might not be full or correct (but as this was a Dublin edition, the implications were presumably slower to reach English readers). Collation supports the suspicion that Hyde had been supplied with authorial readings (some of which correspond to annotations in a printed copy in the Armagh Robinson Library sometimes claimed to have been Swift's own).[62] Although Herbert Davis concluded, from the poor quality of Hyde's reprint, that 'I find it difficult to believe that Swift had any interest in it', the mixture of new readings with casual errors is of the essence: once Hyde's edition went into production, Swift probably paid it as little attention as he had to Motte's preparation of the first.[63] Besides, errors were hardly surprising in a product so disarmingly frank about its lack of material ambition, for Hyde's is a cramped duodecimo that contrasts sharply with Motte's spacious octavo. The paper is distinctly thin, so that when the two volumes are bound together, as they often are, the compilation is still slenderer than a single volume of the ordinary-paper London edition.[64] Hyde's edition, while loosely copying the London styling, eliminates both the large and small capitals that had distinguished the first word of each paragraph and the additional spaces between paragraphs that had further clarified the visual argument. His printing never achieves anything like the clarity of Motte's, and the maps and frontispiece, copied from the London images, visibly lack the crispness of the originals.

---

[61] *CWJS Travels*, pp. 640–1. Hyde's reprint is *Travels into Several Remote Nations of the World*, 2 vols. (Dublin, 1726; TS 297, *ESTC* T176643). Swift refers in December 1727 to Hyde's passing on of a letter from Motte, and in January 1729 to debts to be recovered by Motte from Hyde's estate after his death (*Corr.*, vol. III, pp. 149, 208); see also Bullard and McLaverty, 'Introduction', p. 16. For Swift's 'conceptually troubled' understanding of copyright, and the complications of reprinting his work in the other kingdom from that in which it had first been published, see James McLaverty, 'The Failure of the Swift–Pope Miscellanies (1727–32) and *The Life and Genuine Character of Doctor Swift* (1733)', in *Münster* (2008), pp. 131–48 (pp. 134–5).
[62] *CWJS Travels*, pp. 640–1, 727–9; D. Woolley, 'Swift's Copy', pp. 132–61.
[63] *PW*, vol. XI, p. 301; *CWJS Travels*, p. 641.
[64] TS 297, *ESTC* T176643. Motte would produce his first duodecimo in 1727 (TS 294, *ESTC* T139027; *CWJS Travels*, p. 665).

194 Part III: Dublin

This is also noticeable in the smaller ornaments. For instance, the lion headpiece that introduces chapter i of Part I, previously used by Aaron Rhames, has sustained visible damage.[65]

Like the still shabbier *Penny London Post*, Hyde's reprint contributed to the growing circulation of the *Travels* at lower levels of the market; and in Dublin, where London copies would have come less readily to hand, it was presumably particularly welcome. At the same time, its very existence, however little observed or understood by ordinary readers, confirms the importance of the Dublin print trade in reasserting Swift's covert authority over works whose London texts had evaded his control. In the longer term, in the lead-up to the Dublin *Works* to be launched by Faulkner in 1735, Swift would prompt the development of a textual archive in the form of handwritten alterations to printed copies of the *Travels*, providing tangible evidence, in Womersley's words, of 'Swift's liminal position between the worlds of scribal publication and print culture'.[66] Yet even while the affair of Motte's censorship of the *Travels* continued to reverberate, Swift had entered into yet another London publication project, one in which Pope was the prime mover. Although the idea of publishing joint *Miscellanies* offered, in theory, the prospect of stabilising and promoting what was by now an extensive and varied canon of Swift's smaller writings, it turned out badly, producing a confusing and (to Swift) infuriating set of volumes. This led in turn to an even more evasive circulation of textual revisions in Dublin; unremarked on any title page, they probably escaped the notice of nearly all readers.

Miscellanies (1727–1732)

The *Miscellanies* project, planned with Pope during Swift's 1726 visit to England, ultimately produced a London set of four octavo volumes: two were published during Swift's visit to London in 1727, another early enough the following year to be dated 1727, and another in 1732.[67] Although Swift had figured in miscellanies before, his representation in these was very

---

[65] Lower left-hand border is broken. For Hyde's acquisition of this ornament in late 1724 or early 1725, see May, 'False and Incomplete Imprints', p. 63.

[66] *CWJS Travels*, pp. 643–6; McLaverty, 'The Revision of the First Edition of *Gulliver's Travels*', pp. 24–35.

[67] TS 25 (1–4); vol. I (1727; *ESTC* T39458); vol. II (1727; T39472); 'The Last Volume' (1727; T39473); vol. III (1732; *ESTC* N62568). See *SCEBC* (1710–46), pp. 353, 362 (Motte, entering vols. I and II and 'The Last Volume'), and p. 425 (Motte and Gilliver, entering vol. III). Swift's own four-volume set, with his annotations, is RW 3.5–8 in the Wren Library, Trinity College, Cambridge (*The Rothschild Library*, vol. I, pp. 367–72).

Delegating in London, Recouping in Dublin (1726–1729) 195

different. In contrast with Tonson's *Poetical Miscellanies: The Sixth Part* (1709), to which many authors contributed a little, in these *Miscellanies* a few authors contributed a lot: apart from contributions by Arbuthnot and Gay, the set was in effect an edition of the smaller works of Swift and Pope. But in comparison with the single-volume, single-author focus of *Miscellanies in Prose and Verse* (1711), Swift was now sharing the limelight with Scriblerian friends from the Queen's last years, principally Pope, but also Arbuthnot and Gay.[68] In a further development, this set made a much more open declaration of Pope and Swift's authorship, not only by a specially designed 'AP/JS' monogram on the title page (probably devised by Pope), but also by a volume I Preface jointly signed by both (although Swift would in 1732 still be annoyed to find 'my name is put at length in some notes' in the final volume).[69] The bookseller too made no secret of his involvement: in contrast with Tooke's use of Morphew's imprint to screen the *Miscellanies in Prose and Verse* of 1711, Motte now displayed his own. Yet alongside these advances in transparency, the volumes' failure to attribute specific pieces to specific authors also provided scope for long-term misattribution.[70]

With the passing of fifteen years since Swift's *Miscellanies in Prose and Verse* – not to mention Pope's own modernising taste in book design – readers encountered in the first volume (principally containing the prose from Swift's 1711 volume) a visual language that was subtly but significantly different from that of 1711, even though the two collections shared the same octavo format and made similarly generous use of white space.[71] As in 1711, the title of 1727 retained the spacious effect of an unframed page, but whereas 1711 had used marked contrasts of type size, 1727 deployed a more restricted range, and instead of the 1711 basket of flowers on a pediment, 1727 boasted the authors' monogram. Inside the book, the italicised Preface of 1711 gave way to a Preface in large, well-spaced roman; and the contents list set aside the elaborate and inconsistently executed scheme of roman, full capitals and reverse italic attempted in 1711 in favour of a simpler, more consistent style: titles now appeared in italics varied with sparing reverse roman, and minimal use of capitals. In short, this was a stylish, modern book; and even its errata leaf provided reassurance that care had been taken to provide an accurate text. Furthermore, unlike 1711, this first volume was gracefully decorated throughout, with headpieces for some of the most substantial items, endpieces in final blanks, ornamental bands between

---

[68] More than half of vol. II comprises work by Arbuthnot.   [69] *Corr.*, vol. III, pp. 556, 558.
[70] See Introduction to deattributed poems, *CWJS Poems* IV (forthcoming).
[71] James McLaverty, 'George Faulkner and Swift's Collected Works', in *JS Book*, pp. 154–75 (p. 169).

196 Part III: Dublin

chapters and decorated capitals to mark the beginnings of works and sections. By comparison with the relatively arid visual landscape of 1711, the reader of 1727 was ushered along the way by a lively company of birds, flowers, animals, angels and arabesques. This was not, however, continued into volume II (which contained items principally by Arbuthnot and Pope, with only small contributions from Swift): once past the monogram on the title, the volume reverted almost entirely to the undecorated condition of 1711. 'The Last Volume' then began more elaborately, launching its first element, Pope's *Peri Bathos*, with decorations of birds, books and shells; but although the part-title of its second element, 'Miscellanies in Verse' (nearly all by Swift) was framed by bands of flowers and knots, the text of his poems, though laid out with ample white space, was entirely undecorated. Finally, volume III, which appeared only in 1732, began with 115 undecorated pages, introduced some small endpieces in its middle section, and concluded with a section of verse in the same undecorated format as in volume II.

Such visual inconsistency was just one sign of a larger disarray, most obviously signalled by a bizarre sequencing of volumes that even today makes *Miscellanies* difficult to discuss without confusion. Over the five years from 1727 to 1732 *Miscellanies* emerged as a four-volume set (with volume-by-volume reprinting further complicating the picture); but as early as 1727 a structural decision on Pope's part caused insoluble problems.[72] In short, after the two first volumes had appeared in June 1727, Pope brought out, in early March 1728, 'The Last Volume'.[73] But then, in 1732, he produced 'The Third Volume' – which might reasonably have been thought to be the fourth (or even the last). There were also internal signs of disarray: although J. Woolley and Karian give a lucid account, it was probably a confusing book for the reader.[74] Consisting of three separately paginated sections, it began with Pope's prose satire *Peri Bathos*, went on, after a new half-title, with Swift's longest poem, *Cadenus and Vanessa* (whose tantalising account of his relationship with the late Esther Vanhomrigh had sold out numerous editions when published in Dublin, Edinburgh and London in 1726), and concluded with a large group of shorter poems, mostly by Swift, but not specifically attributed.[75] Without access to private correspondence

---

[72] For early London octavo reprints, see TS 25, and for duodecimos, 26, 27, 28, 29, 30 and 31.

[73] Since publication of 'The last Volume' preceded the beginning of the year, by the old reckoning, on Lady Day (25 March), this volume usually bears the imprint date 1727 (see TS 25 (3a–e), for details).

[74] *CWJS Poems* I (forthcoming), 'General Textual Introduction'.

[75] See discussion in Griffin, *Swift and Pope*, pp. 143–8. For the transmission of *Cadenus and Vanessa* in manuscript and print, see textual account in *CWJS Poems* I (forthcoming). For its popularity, see A. C. Kelly, *Jonathan Swift and Popular Culture*, pp. 72–3.

Delegating in London, Recouping in Dublin (1726–1729)   197

and collation of multiple copies, much of the process by which this arrangement had been arrived at would have been opaque; and the highly significant absence of Pope's *Dunciad*, long intended for this volume but now withheld for separate publication, would necessarily have passed unremarked: only later would it become clear that the prose satire *Peri Bathos*, whose presence among the verse was otherwise unexplained, had been inserted as a curtain-raiser to the absent *Dunciad*, ostensibly justifying that poem's separate publication as a response to the attacks predictably provoked by *Peri Bathos*.[76] Although a partial acknowledgement of the volume's odd arrangement would, in time, be offered by 'The Booksellers Advertisement' found in some copies of the 1732 'Third Volume', it could only confirm suspicions that editorial strategy was at best haphazard: '*The* Verses *are paged separately, that they may be added to that Volume which wholly consists of Verse, and the Treatise of the* Bathos *placed in their stead in This.*'[77] Moreover, the appearance of this 'Third Volume' laid bare the opportunism of the previous 'Last Volume' formula, which had quickly produced an apparently complete and saleable three-volume set, but also left the way open for Pope to insert subsequent volumes between volume II and 'The Last' – as he had now done. Yet 'The Last Volume' had often contained an 'Advertisement to the Reader' which reasserted, in relation to 'the Verses in particular, That all which we have written of this kind are contain'd in it; and that all others, printed in our Names, are Impositions both on us and on the Publick'. After such protestations, 'The Third Volume' could only look like an afterthought; and although Swift had agreed to list his available recent work to Pope earlier in 1732, when the volume came out he told Motte that he did not 'in the least understand the reasons for printing this'.[78] Its very existence undermined the *Miscellanies* both as material text and as monument to friendship.[79]

It would be hard to overstate the difficulties that Pope's perplexing sequencing of the London *Miscellanies* now posed for binders, purchasers and readers. Given the confusion of volume numbers, and the open invitation to purchasers to break up and recombine parts of different volumes, curation was far from straightforward. What should a complete set comprise? In what order should it be presented? One answer may be inferred from Swift's own set, whose eighteenth-century bindings take Pope's volume numbering at face value. (Later owned by Viscount

---

[76] Pope, *Poems*, vol. III, pp. 3–4.   [77] TS 25 (4b).   [78] *Corr.*, vol. III, pp. 489–2, 563.

[79] Thus, for example, TS notes that in response to 'The Booksellers Advertisement', 'copies of *The Last Volume* are found containing only *Verse* and copies of *The Third Volume* consisting of *Prose* only' (TS 25 (4b)).

198   Part III: Dublin

Powerscourt, this set now forms part of the Rothschild collection in the Wren Library of Trinity College, Cambridge.[80]) Although the number stamped on the spine of the unproblematic first volume is no longer visible, the others run II, 3/III and IIII ('The Last Volume'), and corresponding arabic numerals are stamped on their twentieth-century red cloth protective cases. The status of the set is confirmed by a matching twentieth-century leather storage box whose imposing girth confirms that the four volumes are not to be separated – nor indeed supplemented, as has happened in a much odder set bequeathed by Sir Harold Williams to the Cambridge University Library.

This set comprises no fewer than five volumes, in uniform bindings apparently contemporary with the owner, the Revd William Goodall (1757–1844), the Eton-educated zoological watercolourist whose bookplate they bear.[81] All five volumes are lettered 'SWIFT'S & POPE'S MISCELLANIES' (or as much of the final word as will fit across the spine), but the volumes bound as I–III are I, II and 'The Last': the identification of 'The Last' as 'III' (which, chronologically speaking, it was) obscures the absence of the 1732 volume III, which would have completed the four-volume set as Pope conceived it. Instead, the volume bound as IV is *A Second Collection of Miscellanies. Written by Jonathan Swift, D.D.* (London, 1720), a made-up volume bearing the imprint of the trade publisher J. Roberts (Abigail Baldwin's son-in-law and successor).[82] Roberts's record for blurring the Swift canon is amply borne out by the selection of persistently troublesome dubia lurking within. His small octavo crams in *The Right of Precedence between Phisicians and Civilians Enquir'd Into, A Defence of English Commodities, The Swearers-Bank* and *The Best in Christendom. A Tale* – as well as one substantial piece that is known to be principally by Sheridan (*The Art of Punning*). At the end, for good measure, is incorporated Curll's opportunistic *Letters, Poems and Tales: Amorous, Satyrical, and Gallant which passed between Several Persons of Distinction. Now first Publish'd from their respective Originals, found in the Cabinet of that Celebrated Toast Mrs. Anne Long, since her Decease* ([1718]): the only piece in this collection at all likely to be by Swift is the first, *A Decree for Concluding the Treaty between Dr Swift & Mrs Long*.[83] Roberts's offering thus installed a large body of highly problematic material

---

[80] For description and discussion, see *The Rothschild Library*, no. 1422 (vol. I, pp. 367–72).
[81] Cambridge University Library, Williams.139–43; M. Locke and J. V. Collins, 'Who was W. Goodall?', *The Linnean: Newsletter and Proceedings of The Linnean Society of London*, 17 (2001), 28–47.
[82] TS 16, *ESTC* N61159; *BBTI*, 'Abigail Baldwin'.   [83] *ESTC* T119975.

Delegating in London, Recouping in Dublin (1726–1729) 199

at the heart of Goodall's *Miscellanies*. Finally, the fifth volume of Goodall's set presents yet another twist. This is *Miscellanies in Prose and Verse. Volume the Fifth*, printed by Charles Davis in London – but not until 1735. This did have a good claim to authority, and (as its Advertisement explains) was deliberately produced to supplement the Swift/Pope *Miscellanies*; but its contents represented a looping back of the textual transmission through Dublin, since it was printed from pre-publication sheets of Faulkner's 1735 Dublin *Works*.[84] All in all, Goodall's set is an object lesson in the confusions that Pope had set in train. The long-term problem for Swift in print was that, as Motte would complain when Faulkner produced a Dublin *Works* in 1735, *Miscellanies* was already 'generally known and called by the name of Doctor Swift's Works'.[85]

As with the *Travels*, behind the published *Miscellanies* lay a complex private history of indignation. For McLaverty, the *Miscellanies* 'mark the high point of the relationship between the two satirists and its decline into resentment and veiled hostility'.[86] This time Swift's dissatisfaction was all the more damaging because it was aimed not at a bookseller but at Pope, who had professed to commemorate them as 'friends, side by side, serious and merry by turns, conversing interchangeably, and walking down hand in hand to posterity'.[87] (In retrospect, the dominating central position of Pope's 'A' for Alexander in their elaborately interwoven joint monogram had not boded well.) One issue was that by presenting Swift's contributions without explicit distinction from those of Pope and others, the volumes caused persistent problems of attribution, which were corrected ambiguously at best in 1742 by Pope's retrospective attempts to indicate Swift's contributions on the contents pages.[88] Swift himself recorded his unhappiness – as well as his textual corrections – in his own set of *Miscellanies*, where a note in the front of 'The Last Volume' confirms his resentment of Pope's failure to complement Swift's important work with an equivalent contribution of his own: Swift's aggrieved verdict was '252 Pages of one Author' – namely himself. He had also lamented to Motte in December 1727 that in the 'poeticall Volume of miscellanys', by comparison with the mere 'slight loose papers' left over from the works of Gay and

---

[84] TS 25 (5a; and, for a supplement sometimes bound with it, 5b), *ESTC* N62179, T214350 and (with supplement) T39461; John Irwin Fischer, 'Swift's *Miscellanies, in Prose and Verse, Volume the Fifth*: Some Facts and Puzzles', *SStud*, 15 (2000), 76–87 (p. 79). See also Chapter 7.

[85] Cited by McLaverty, 'The Failure of the Swift–Pope *Miscellanies*', p. 139.   [86] *Ibid.*, p. 131.

[87] *Corr.*, vol. III, p. 76.

[88] See Introduction and 'To My Lady Winchilsea' in the deattributed poems section of *CWJS Poems* IV (forthcoming).

Pope, 'five parts in six at least are mine', comprising 'all the poetry I ever writ [wor]th printing'.[89] To add insult to injury, Pope had also declined some of his pieces on grounds that Swift, writing to Motte in February 1728, found less than convincing.[90] The problem was that Swift, unlike Pope, had not published a Works in which to memorialise the pieces he held most dear. As McLaverty puts it, 'The project of making a monumental "Pope", which Pope had begun so confidently in 1717 with the *Works of Mr. Pope*, was to embrace a subsidiary project dedicated to "Swift-Pope"' – as Swift now found to his cost.[91]

On the face of it, Pope's idea had much to offer Swift. Notably, by delegating the editorial work to Pope, Swift could avoid appearing as his own publisher; and by allowing Pope to incorporate such pieces as Swift was prepared to be associated with, Swift not only paid a graceful tribute to their creative companionship in the days of the Tory ministry, but also stood to benefit from a collection that might in principle have proved to be something more than the sum of its parts. Moreover, by disowning items not specifically included, Swift might reasonably have hoped to combat the persistent accumulation of false attributions by such as Curll.[92] Thus (as represented in the printed volume I) he and Pope put their signatures, at Twickenham on 27 May 1727, to a Preface that promised a 'second (and perhaps a third)' volume, indicated the likely distribution of verse and prose among the volumes, complained against unauthorised publications of false attributions and of genuine but embarrassing 'Sallies of Levity', and closed by declaring that the contents of the present collection, taken together with Pope's *Works* of 1717 and Swift's *Miscellanies in Prose and Verse* of 1711, were '*All* that are *Ours*'.[93]

These concerns, so emphatically presented to readers at the beginning of *Miscellanies*, were by no means imaginary, nor were they Pope's alone. Indeed, Swift had suggested something along the same lines to Ford in 1720:

> I cannot help the usage which honest Mr Curl gives me, I watched for his Ears in the Queens time, and was I think once within an Inch of them. There is an honest humersom Gentleman here who amuses this Town sometimes with Trifles and some Knave or Fool transmitts them to Curl with a Hint that they are mine. There is one about Precedence of Doctors,

---

[89] *Corr.*, vol. III, pp. 150–1.   [90] *Ibid.*, p. 156.

[91] McLaverty, 'The Failure of the Swift–Pope *Miscellanies*', p. 132.

[92] For Curll's 1726 *Miscellanea: In Two Volumes*, which named both Pope and Swift on its title, see McLaverty, 'The Failure of the Swift–Pope *Miscellanies*', p. 133.

[93] Vol. I, pp. 10, 14, 16.

Delegating in London, Recouping in Dublin (1726–1729) 201

we do not know who writt it; It is a very crude Piece, tho not quite so low as some others; This I hear is likewise a Present of Curl to me. I would go into any Scheam you please with Mr Congreve and Mr Pope and the rest, but cannot imagine a Remedy unless he be sent to Bridewell for Life.[94]

Swift not only detects Curll behind James Roberts, the trade publisher who had in 1720 given his imprint to the London reprint of *The Right of Precedence between Phisicians and Civilians Enquir'd Into*, but also seems open to some kind of joint retaliation with friends such as Pope and the retired dramatist William Congreve. Curll also seems to be the unnamed irritant behind a complaint in 1722 of an unauthorised London miscellany, along with other 'Scurvy Things' and 'slovenly Pages' – not quite all of which can be confidently laid at the door of others.[95]

Miscellanies, from one point of view, was just such a 'Scheam' as Swift had envisaged. But it turned out to favour Pope's agenda far more than Swift's, for while the relatively young poet, whose published work was his livelihood, focused his career strategy on the *Works* inaugurated in 1717, the older Swift, who needed no profit from his publications and shrank from appearing as their promoter, hung back in the hope that a bookseller would take the business of a Works off his hands. Pope was a highly experienced editor (though usually of dead rather than living writers), and was increasingly acting as his own bookseller as he prepared the ground for his *Works* of 1735.[96] Both of these capacities were in principle attractive, but turned out to serve Pope's business plan much better than his friend's less easily defined ambitions, as Pope relegated to *Miscellanies* the trifles he judged unfit for his *Works*, and used Swift's contributions to fill the gaps.[97] Notably, Pope decided quite late to withhold the *Dunciad* for separate publication in 1728 – and his expansions in 1729 and 1743 fully confirmed its potential to become the cornerstone of his late-career achievement.[98] The inclusion of its first version in *Miscellanies* would thus have been a powerful tribute to friendship; but its withholding was the reverse (as Swift repeatedly hinted in letters).[99] Even when the poem appeared separately in 1728 it lacked the dedication Swift had long hoped for: he would

---

[94] *Corr.*, vol. II, pp. 372–9. *The Right of Precedence* seems likely to have been written by a physician, making Dr Helsham a possible candidate.

[95] *Corr.*, vol. II, pp. 415–17; and for 'a parcel of Trash ... fathered upon me' in 1724, pp. 518–20.

[96] For his editorial record, see McLaverty, 'The Failure of the Swift–Pope *Miscellanies*', p. 133.

[97] McLaverty compares Pope's use of an earlier self-organised miscellany in advance of his *Works* of 1717 (McLaverty, 'The Failure of the Swift–Pope *Miscellanies*', p. 136; Ault, *Pope's Own Miscellany*).

[98] Pope, *Poems*, vol. III, p. 3.

[99] McLaverty, 'The Failure of the Swift–Pope *Miscellanies*', pp. 137–8; *Corr.*, vol. III, pp. 162, 171, 180, 184, 189.

202   Part III: Dublin

have to wait until 1729 for the verse tribute Pope had shown him in draft in January 1728, which was only in 1736 confirmed by a formal title-page dedication.[100] It is not even clear that Pope passed on to him his share of the payments specified in the contract with Motte – a document more hopefully conceived than sales seem to have justified.[101]

When in 1732 Pope went on to include in the so-called 'Third Volume', alongside lighter prose squibs of his own, papers written by Swift in 1728 for the *Intelligencer* (a short-lived Dublin periodical jointly written with Sheridan) and his 1729 *A Modest Proposal* (a brief masterpiece which neither invited nor accommodated further development), it looked as if Pope, for whom short prose was supplementary to poetic ambition, had no real appreciation of Swift's concisely devastating Irish interventions. In McLaverty's words: 'Always short of copy, in an enterprise that took second place to his own *Dunciad Variorum* (1729) and *Works* (1735), Pope found himself publishing a wide range of Swift's best work while withholding most of his own.'[102] He also turned down the opportunity to reprint Swift's politically tendentious *A Libel on D—— D——and a Certain Great Lord* (first printed in Dublin in 1730) – an unquestionably prudent decision, but nonetheless a snub.[103] Pope seems by this point to have been driven less by old friendships than his new business arrangements with the London print trade, as he shifted business away from Motte towards John Wright and Lawton Gilliver (Motte's name now appears with Gilliver's in the imprint).[104] In sum, *Miscellanies* showed Swift once more misjudging the relation between what he expected other people to do for him and what they might feel entitled to do for themselves. After 1727, the year of the first three volumes of *Miscellanies*, he did not see Pope or England again; and it is to this year that Karian dates the beginning of a 'late period' in Swift's career, when, 'liberated' by putting hopes of English preferment behind him, he became 'even more outspoken than earlier' – though not necessarily readier to put his outspokenness directly

---

[100] Pope, *Poems*, vol. III, pp. 177–9 (*Dunciad Variorum*, I. 17–26); *Corr.*, vol. III, pp. 154 (including Pope's draft tribute), 184, 186 (promising, for 1729, 'the inscription, which makes me proudest'), 201 (announcing that 'The inscription to the Poem is now printed and inserted in the Poem'), 595; Ashley Marshall, 'Pope's Dedication of the "1736" *Dunciad* to Swift', in Kirsten Juhas, Patrick Müller and Mascha Hansen (eds.), *'The First Wit of the Age': Essays on Swift and his Contemporaries in Honour of Hermann J. Real* (Frankfurt am Main: Peter Lang, 2013), pp. 69–82 (pp. 72–4).
[101] *Corr.*, vol. III, p. 156; McLaverty, 'The Failure of the Swift–Pope *Miscellanies*', pp. 136–7, 143–4.
[102] McLaverty, 'The Failure of the Swift–Pope *Miscellanies*', pp. 132, 139; and for what D. Woolley calls Swift's 'tendentious appraisal' of the volume, *Corr.*, vol. III, pp. 556–8.
[103] *CWJS Poems* III (forthcoming).
[104] McLaverty, 'The Failure of the Swift–Pope *Miscellanies*', pp. 139, 140–1.

Delegating in London, Recouping in Dublin (1726–1729)

into print.[105] Although there was no open breach between him and his English friend, their relationship was in future transacted through the indirections of correspondence.

The manuscript revisions by which Swift privately reasserted his textual authority in his own set of *Miscellanies* were reminiscent, in a small way, of the extensive annotations and interleavings that Ford had made in the case of the *Travels* – and so was the publication in Dublin of a corrected text. This time the beneficiary of Swift's dissatisfaction was Samuel Fairbrother, who, as Dublin convention permitted, had already produced a reprint of the *Miscellanies*, making him the obvious channel for putting Swift's revisions discreetly before the public.[106] (Otherwise it seems unlikely that Fairbrother, a Whig stationer and bookseller who held the appointments of King's Stationer in Ireland and Printer to the House of Commons, would have attracted the favour of Swift, whose comments about him are uniformly hostile.[107]) Fairbrother's two volumes were duodecimos rather than octavos like Motte's, but they were neatly if closely printed, with sparing use of fleurons, and made a modestly presentable pair. Yet, unlike Hyde (whose revisions to the *Travels* were of far greater extent), Fairbrother made no title-page claim of textual improvements: although Swift presumably had the satisfaction of re-exerting his authority through a distinct Irish transmission, most readers were unlikely to have been any the wiser.[108] Even less consequential for readers (since it never came to fruition at all) was Swift's more radical scheme for a surreptitious London edition to be printed by Bowyer, a futile attempt in which he would later involve his protégé Matthew Pilkington as go-between.[109]

The *Intelligencer* (1728) and *A Modest Proposal* (1729)

Meanwhile, since John Harding's death in April 1725, Sarah Harding had helped to keep the affair of Wood's halfpence alive for Dublin readers by

---

[105] For the political circumstances of the 1727 visit to England, see Ferguson, *Jonathan Swift and Ireland*, pp. 142–4; for Swift's 'late period', see Karian, *Print and Manuscript*, p. 3.

[106] Pollard, *Dictionary*, pp. 195–7; Fischer, 'Swift's *Miscellanies*', p. 79; A. C. Elias, Jr, '*Senatus Consultum*: Revising Verse in Swift's Dublin Circle, 1729–1735', in *Münster* (1998), pp. 249–67; Karian, *Print and Manuscript*, pp. 37, 40; Karian, 'Edmund Curll', p. 122; *CWJS Parodies*, pp. 623–5, and, for bibliographical description, p. 630. Swift's revisions appear in Fairbrother's revised edition of the reprint first published in 1728, i.e. *Miscellanies in Prose and Verse. In two volumes. By Jonathan Swift, D.D. And Alexander Pope, Esq; To which are added several Poems, and other Curious Tracts not in any former Impression. The Third Edition* (Dublin, 1732; TS 33 (2a), ESTC 207559).

[107] Pollard, *Dictionary*, pp. 195–7; *CWJS Parodies*, p. 625.

[108] Fischer, 'Swift's *Miscellanies*', p. 79; *CWJS Parodies*, pp. 624.   [109] See Chapter 7.

204   Part III: Dublin

issuing further associated items. In May 1725 she published *A Funeral Elegy on the much lamented Death of Robert Lord Viscount Molesworth. Who departed this life, on Sunday the 23d of May*, which commemorated the addressee of the last of the Drapier's published letters: by styling herself 'Widow Harding' she reminded readers of her family's loyalty and suffering.[110] Her most impressive display of principled resolution came in September of that year, when she published a predictably inflammatory satire on the Irish House of Lords' embarrassing deliberations about how to thank the King for revoking Wood's patent, *On Wisdom's Defeat in a Learned Debate* – a poem often misattributed to Swift.[111] Even its condemnation to be burned by the hangman prompted the publication (by the mysterious W. P. in Skinner Row) of a last dying speech for the condemned poem.[112] When examined, Sarah Harding refused to name the author, and in November Carteret issued a proclamation (duly printed by Andrew Crooke) offering a reward of £100; but, like the reward for identifying the Drapier, it remained unclaimed.[113] The widow's steadfastness underlined not only her implicit claim on Swift but also her potential utility to him: the next phase of Swift in print would once again engage with Irish issues in the familiar guise of the Hardings' shabby but expressive octavos.[114]

This phase began in January 1728 with the appearance of *A Short View of the State of Ireland*, which not only achieved the rare distinction of being reprinted outside Dublin (by the obscure Combra Daniell in Cork), but also formed the basis of an article in *Mist's Weekly Journal* in London.[115] In March 1728 Sarah Harding also published a related piece by Swift, *An Answer to a Paper, called A Memorial of the Poor Inhabitants,*

---

[110] Dublin, 1725; *ESTC* T4033; not in Foxon.

[111] Rose Common, shameless woman (pseudonym), *On Wisdom's Defeat in a Learned Debate* (1725) (TS 1172, Foxon O230, *ESTC* T5236). For deattribution, see *CWJS Poems* IV (forthcoming). Ehrenpreis's account is complicated by his acceptance of the poem as Swift's (*Swift*, vol. III, pp. 311–16). The affair is summarised by Baltes, *The Pamphlet Controversy*, pp. 274–5.

[112] See *The Last Speech of Wisdom's Defeat. &c. A scandalous libel, burnt this second day of October, 1725 by the common hangman* (Dublin, 1725; Foxon L59, *ESTC* T37578). For the process as it bore on Sarah Harding, see Pollard, *Dictionary*, p. 276; and for W. P., see p. 446.

[113] *By the Lord Lieutenant and Council of Ireland, a Proclamation. Carteret. Whereas the Lords Spiritual and Temporal in Parliament assembled, have address'd His Excellency the Lord Lieutenant, setting forth the very great indignity offer'd their House and the Peerage of this Kingdom, in a false, scandalous and malicious libel called Wisdom's Defeat, printed by Sarah Harding* (Dublin, 1725; *ESTC* T87780).

[114] For an overview of Sarah Harding's work for Swift in this period, see *CWJS Irish Political Writings after 1725*, pp. 377–9.

[115] *Ibid.*, pp. xxxvii–xliii, 13–26, 392–8, and figure 2, p. 12; TS 663, *ESTC* T1868. For the Cork reprint, see TS 664, *ESTC* T174108; for quotation and summary in *Mist's Weekly Journal*, see 20 April 1728. For the Irish context, see Ferguson, *Jonathan Swift and Ireland*, pp. 144–5.

Tradesmen and Labourers of the Kingdom of Ireland. By the Author of the Short View of the State of Ireland; and later that year she printed, without imprint and possibly for private circulation, the apparently collaborative satire *A Paraphrase on the Seven Penitential Psalms*, an attack on a careerist colleague of Swift in the Church of Ireland; but this was also the year that brought her a new project which promised a more substantial supply of work.[116] This was the *Intelligencer*, an essay periodical conceived by Swift and Sheridan, which she published in octavo pamphlets from May to July 1728, and again from October to December.[117] It did not play to her strengths. Even more striking than its patchy printwork is the lack of consistent design: some issues fill a half sheet, some a whole one; some are dated, most are not; some have separate title pages, some not; some are modestly ornamented, others not. The air of provisionality from issue to issue is further confirmed by different sizes of type: indeed, some individual issues themselves display differently styled variants. The Harding focus on a quick turnover of small, discrete items was not suited to the more polite aspirations of an essay periodical. Swift, indeed, complained (perhaps unreasonably) about 'the continual nonsense made by her printers', which he claimed 'every body who reads those papers, are very much offended with'.[118] Writing in January 1729 from the safe distance of Market Hill, where he was exploring a newly productive vein of domestic verse in the company of Sir Arthur and Lady Anne Acheson, he made pointed reference to 'the Intelligencer himself' (i.e. Sheridan) as the person who should 'look over it'; but by then there were no readers to be offended, as Sheridan had ceased publication. Swift, engrossed in an absorbing late-life 'transition . . . from being primarily a prose author to being primarily a poet', was completely out of the loop.[119]

The *Intelligencer* reached its high point with two numbers by Swift on Irish oppression, nos. 15 and 19, demonstrating the periodical's ability to combine trenchant political critique of Ireland's oppression with cultural commentary reminiscent of the London *Tatler* and *Spectator*.[120] His

---

[116] *CWJS Irish Political Writings after 1725*, pp. 27–39, 399–402; TS 665, *ESTC* T21996. See Ferguson, *Jonathan Swift and Ireland*, pp. 151–3. See also *A Paraphrase* in *CWJS Poems* III (forthcoming).

[117] J. Woolley, *Intelligencer*, pp. 20–34; TS 668, *ESTC* P2223. See also *CWJS Irish Political Writings after 1725*, pp. 40–97, 402–21.

[118] *Corr.*, vol. III, p. 206; for a more balanced view, see J. Woolley, *Intelligencer*, p. 36.

[119] Karian, 'Swift as Manuscript Poet', p. 35, citing Arthur H. Scouten, 'Jonathan Swift's Progress from Prose to Poetry', in *The Poetry of Jonathan Swift: Papers Read at a Clark Library Seminar, 20 January 1979* (Los Angeles: William Clark Memorial Library, c. 1981), pp. 27–51.

[120] J. Woolley, *Intelligencer*, pp. 170–86.

Part III: Dublin

dismissive comments (in response to Pope's request for material for the 1732 volume of *Miscellanies*) need not necessarily be taken at face value:

> the 15th is a Pamphlet of mine printed before with Dr Sh–n's Preface, merely for laziness not to disappoint the town; and so was the 19th, which contains only a parcel of facts relating purely to the miseries of Ireland, and wholly useless and unentertaining.[121]

No. 15 had reprinted *A Short View of the State of Ireland* with an additional preface by Sheridan, while no. 19 was cast in the form of a letter to 'Andrew Dealer, *and* Patrick Pennyless'; but the irony, in a letter to London, of Swift's dismissive phrase 'wholly useless and unentertaining' suggests a bitter awareness of just how useful and compelling they *ought* to have been.[122] Yet he was not prepared to prioritise the project over his new opportunities at Market Hill. It was not that Swift did not know how to run a periodical: he had been an interested bystander and occasional contributor to the *Tatler*, had mentored William Harrison's doomed attempt at a continuation, and had later worked with Barber to produce the *Examiner*. But Sheridan was hardly a reliable manager; and Sarah Harding had neither the expertise nor the resources of Swift's cousin Leach (who had printed for Harrison), let alone the drive of Swift's propaganda partner Barber (who had printed the *Examiner*). Lamenting the lack of 'some ingenious young man to have been the manager', Swift explained:

> But the Printer here could not afford such a young man one farthing for his trouble, the Sale being so small, and the price one half-penny; and so it dropt.[123]

Bereft of strategy and direction, the *Intelligencer* lasted less than a year. As James Woolley points out, it was launched at exactly the wrong time of year, when Dublin's elites were returning to their country estates or to England for the summer. Swift's well-established preference for absence from the scene of publication, now seconded by the attraction of the Achesons' hospitality, kept him away from Dublin for much of the paper's run. Sheridan too was away for the school holidays, and does not seem to have kept Swift up to date with developments after his return. Although publication had ceased in December 1728, in January 1729 Swift sent Mrs

---

[121] *Corr.*, vol. III, p. 489.
[122] For *A Short View*, see above; for *Intelligencer* 19, see *CWJS Irish Political Writings after 1725*, pp. 86–97, 418–21.
[123] *Corr.*, vol. III, p. 489.

Delegating in London, Recouping in Dublin (1726–1729)   207

Harding a further number focused on the Market Hill poem *The Journal of a Dublin Lady: in a Letter to a Person of Quality*.[124] Setting aside Swift's introductory letter, she instead published the poem separately in a form which Swift condemned, not without reason, as 'horridly mangled'.[125] With its emphasis on female dissipation, it prompted considerable interest, and was reprinted several times both in Dublin and in London (though in London, bearing out Swift's suspicions that no one wanted to read about Ireland, 'Dublin' was changed to 'Modern').[126] The unusual speed with which this poem moved from composition to publication perhaps reflects a guilty sense on Swift's part that his absorption in Market Hill had been unfair to Sheridan; for at this stage, to judge by the notice that 'Here several Verses are omitted', and a comment to Pope that he had omitted 'what concerned the family', Swift evidently had reservations about the appropriateness of publishing the intimate domestic poems he had been writing as the Achesons' guest.[127]

With the petering out of the *Intelligencer*, it might well have seemed that Sarah Harding's involvement with Swift in print was dwindling towards its end: she was on the point of marrying again, and as the wife of the printer Nicholas Hussey, who indeed added his own 'well intentioned' but 'frequently nonsensical' readings to '*The Second Edition Carefully Corrected and Amended*' of the *Journal of a Dublin Lady*, she would no longer be the sole support of a one-parent family.[128] Yet she now stood on the brink of a final and incomparably significant contribution to Swift in print, one that would in course of time come to stand beside the *Travels* at the heart of the canon – a fact which would probably have surprised her, for, as David Hayton notes, her new publication 'received a relatively muted reception in Ireland when it first appeared', although it was keenly reprinted in London.[129] This was *A Modest Proposal for Preventing the Children of Poor People from being a Burthen to their Parents, or the Country, and for making them Beneficial to the Publick*, which appeared in Dublin in October 1729.[130] As yet one more of the Hardings' characteristically

---

[124] *CWJS Poems* III (forthcoming); TS 669, Foxon, S863, *ESTC* T124769. For Swift's covering letter, see *Corr.*, vol. III, pp. 205–6.

[125] *Corr.*, vol. III, p. 212.

[126] *Ibid.*, pp. 205–6, 212, 221; for the possibility that one of these 'London' imprints may be false, see *CWJS Poems* III (forthcoming).

[127] *Corr.*, vol. III, p. 212.   [128] Pollard, *Dictionary*, p. 304; *CWJS Poems* III (forthcoming).

[129] *CWJS Irish Political Writings after 1725*, pp. xxiii, 442–3.

[130] *Ibid.*, pp. lxxiv–lxxxvii, 143–59, 379, 442–50, and figure 3, p. 145; TS 676, *ESTC* N5335. For London reprints down to 1730, see TS 677, *ESTC* T70428; TS 678, *ESTC* 41350; TS 36, *ESTC* N5048. For contexts, see Ferguson, *Jonathan Swift and Ireland*, pp. 167–76.

208 Part III: Dublin

downmarket single-sheet octavo pamphlets, it presents a striking contrast with the substantial and elegant form in which the *Travels* had recently been launched in London. Yet, as James Woolley has argued, the unusual mention of Sarah Harding's name in a London reprint suggests that the Harding brand had acquired significant resonance in relation to Swift and Irish affairs; and, as with all the Hardings' work for Swift, the undistinguished material form of *A Modest Proposal* has a rhetorical force of its own.

Despite worn type, poor paper and a few misprints, *A Modest Proposal* is rather more carefully printed than many of its predecessors. Efficient casting off ensures that the text (which begins with a decorated initial) reaches its final 'FINIS' without any giveaway reductions in type size, and allowance has been made for a separate title page, a blank verso to follow, and a blank final verso to serve as back cover. McLaverty plausibly suggests that Swift himself (probably working with an amanuensis to conceal his hand) specified 'its inventive use of typography':

> At the close of the pamphlet itself Swift uses italics for the whole section in which counter-proposals (familiar from Swift's other writings on Ireland) are rejected, but there is a more subtle use of italic running throughout the piece. Some of it is doubtless parodic, underlining the sentimental and patriotic ('*dear native Country*'), but on other occasions it emphasizes the outrageous ('*just dropt from it's Dam*'; '*Gloves for Ladies* and *Summer Boots for fine Gentlemen*'). The italic points up the varied and inconsistent voicing of the proposal.[131]

The text also deploys italic full capitals to underline the ghastly singularity of '*this one individual Kingdom of IRELAND*', and the futility of recommending '*learning to love our Country, wherein we differ even from LAPLANDERS, and the Inhabitants of TOPINAMBOO*'.[132] Such old-fashioned typographical eloquence, recalling John Harding's work on the Drapier's letters, brings the Hardings' contribution to Swift in print to a fitting climax, once more putting before the public a material analogy between the intransigent materials of a downmarket print-shop and the obdurate immiseration against which Swift levelled his rhetoric.

The impending conclusion of Sarah Harding's separate career was noted on the title page of *A Modest Proposal* by an imprint featuring her new marital address: '*DUBLIN*: Printed by *S. Harding*, opposite the *Hand and Pen* near *Fishamble-Street*, on the *Blind Key*'. But more arresting is the presentation of the notorious title itself. Swift published several works that have 'proposal' as the leading title word, and for the most part we

---

[131] *JSA*, Introduction.   [132] *A Modest Proposal*, p. 14.

Delegating in London, Recouping in Dublin (1726–1729) 209

distinguish them by short titles that specify the subject of the proposal. Only *A Modest Proposal*, in popular reception perhaps the most flagrant of Swift's title collocations, requires no further specification for anyone who has read or even heard of it.[133] Yet on the title page the two key terms are visually decoupled: the largest capitals play innocent, foregrounding the apparently uncontroversial words 'PROPOSAL', 'CHILDREN' and 'COUNTRY'; 'POOR PEOPLE' is tellingly demoted to a smaller size; and 'MODEST' and 'PUBLICK' top and tail the composition in even smaller capitals. By emphasising 'PROPOSAL' and minimising 'MODEST' the irony is visually as well as verbally enacted. An unignorable black-letter flourish (which McLaverty sees as underlining the irony of the proposal) is then given to '𝕭𝖚𝖗𝖙𝖍𝖊𝖓 𝖙𝖔 𝖙𝖍𝖊𝖎𝖗 𝕻𝖆𝖗𝖊𝖓𝖙𝖘', and the main body begins with an equally ironic display of royal imagery: the headpiece foregrounds the fleur-de-lys, and the factotum initial features two angels bearing aloft St Edward's crown.

Over the years, the Hardings' vehement typography had provided a medium better fitted to Swift's political interventions than he might have liked to admit (the expectations formed in his collaborations with such well-found businesses as those of Tooke, Barber and Motte were not easily put aside). In Dublin, rather better printwork was available by working with Hyde (or, after his death in 1728, his widow Sarah), or with Fairbrother or Faulkner; and all in different ways enabled Swift to confer his authority on distinctively Irish textual transmissions. But it was Faulkner, the most ambitious and the least compromised by past associations, who now took the lead. His adept publication of *Fraud Detected* in 1725 had demonstrated his credentials, and in 1728, when Swift asked his friend Worrall to get the collaborative *An Answer to the Ballyspellan Ballad* 'printed privatly, and published' as a riposte to Sheridan's poem on the celebrated spa, the work went to Faulkner, who published it over his full name and address, without any mention of its authorship.[134] In London in 1729 he evidently made arrangements, during what would be his last spell of work for Bowyer, for a London edition of *Fraud Detected: Or, The Hibernian Patriot*, cementing a collaboration that would shape Swift in print for decades to come.[135] The collection's original title and subtitle were now provocatively switched, foregrounding Swift's status as Irish patriot, and the title page was blazoned with Pope's compliment to Swift as 'Dean,

---

[133] For possible resonances, see *CWJS Irish Political Writings after 1725*, pp. lxxvii–lxxviii.
[134] *CWJS Poems* III (forthcoming); Pollard, *Dictionary*, p. 204; *Corr.*, vol. III, p. 200.
[135] Maslen, 'George Faulkner and William Bowyer', pp. 226–7, citing *Bowyer Ledgers*, no. 1471.

Part III: Dublin

Drapier, Bickerstaff, or Gulliver!' (a tribute long desired by Swift, which Pope had at long last published in his *Dunciad*).[136] For his part, Bowyer was a printer, not a bookseller, so his books routinely bear the imprints of their distributors; but in this case, as Maslen notes, although Bowyer was undertaking the publication jointly with two well-established booksellers, Thomas Woodward and Charles Davis, the distributor was still prudently declared to be the fictitious A. Moor.

By 1730 Faulkner was taking on more work for Swift, as instanced by *A Vindication of His Excellency the Lord C—T*, where both the ornaments and Bowyer's London reprinting suggest Faulkner's role.[137] Also in that year he seems to have printed, with his relation James Hoey, Swift's widely read *A Libel on D—— D——and a Certain Great Lord*, part of a flurry of verse prompted by Delany's injudiciously expressed aspirations to further preferment.[138] The year 1730 was thus for Faulkner one of decidedly mixed fortunes: on his voyage to England in September he sustained an injury that led to the amputation of his leg; but in London he seems to have found a bride as well as further consolidating business links founded on his association with Swift.[139] As Swift entered his mid-sixties and Swift in print confronted the problems and opportunities of textual transmission across two kingdoms, Faulkner's role was to be an increasingly important one.

---

[136] Pollard, *Dictionary*, pp. 199, 203–4; *The Hibernian Patriot: Being a Collection of the Drapier's Letters to the People of Ireland, Concerning Mr. Wood's Brass Half-Pence* (London, 1730; TS 22, *ESTC* T706). For Pope's compliment, see *Dunciad Variorum*, Book III, ll. 17–26; Pope, *Poems*, vol. III, pp. 177–8.

[137] *CWJS Irish Political Writings after 1725*, pp. 456–62; Maslen, 'George Faulkner and William Bowyer', p. 227; *Bowyer Ledgers*, nos. 1545, 1576; Pollard, *Dictionary*, p. 199. Ehrenpreis, *Swift*, vol. III, p. 780; TS 698, *ESTC* T73031.

[138] *CWJS Poems* III (forthcoming).   [139] Pollard, *Dictionary*, p. 199.

CHAPTER 7

The Works of J. S, D. D, D. S. P. D.
(1730–1735)

Swift in print was now an overwhelming presence in Dublin and London: for the years from 1729 to 1735 *ESTC* records more than 250 separate publications – either by Swift, allegedly by Swift, addressed to Swift or about Swift. A few works and collections proved particularly popular – though not, perhaps, the ones that later readers might expect. By far the largest group comprised thirty items either reprinting or otherwise associated with the London *Miscellanies* of 1727–32. In contrast, some of Swift's most celebrated prose works figured relatively little, with the Drapier's letters, the *Travels* and *A Modest Proposal* accounting for only a handful.

New work continued to appear in print, most remarkably a flurry of outrageous late poems whose material texts frequently mystified their actual origins; but in 1733 Faulkner issued a Proposal for a Dublin collected edition that would radically change the face of Swift in print. This edition, whose first four volumes (all dated 1735) appeared in late 1734 and early 1735, consolidated a shift of momentum away from London and towards Dublin: by tempering aspiration with pragmatism it shaped a memorial for the future on the basis of a print performance of mediated authority.[1] Faulkner's volumes were ambitious but not over-weening, a celebration of Swift's achievement consistent both with the realities of Dublin entrepreneurship and with the complexity of Swift's ambivalence about whether, where and how his writings should be collected. The 'whether' attached at this point mainly to sensitivities around particular pieces, the 'where' to his lingering preference for London publication, and the 'how' to his abiding reluctance to be seen as publisher – or even author – of his own work.

---

[1] For Faulkner's commemorative efforts, both achieved and unachieved, see Mahony, *Jonathan Swift*, pp. 11–12, 16–24. For dating of advertisements and published volumes, see Andrew Carpenter and James Woolley, 'Faulkner's *Volume II. Containing the Author's Poetical Works*: A New Uncancelled Copy', in *Münster* (2019), pp. 47–58 (p. 48).

212   Part III: Dublin

Testing the Limits

In the years between the publication of *A Modest Proposal* in 1729 and the appearance of the first four volumes of Faulkner's *Works* in 1734–5 Swift in print was visibly testing the limits. Alongside prose publications in familiar modes – responses to Dublin politics, polemics against threats to the Church of Ireland, satires prompted by Dublin street life – a range of new poems, now coming much more promptly to press as Swift turned increasingly to poetry towards the end of his career, posed challenges of a different order.[2] In the private sphere they depicted female physicality in the grossest terms; in the public sphere they lambasted George II, his Queen and his Minister as agents of national corruption. The limits of print professionals' ability to protect themselves and their author were also tested. Faulkner gave ample proofs of loyalty, particularly in relation to ecclesiastical tracts; but where the poems were concerned, Dublin printings typically resorted to the traditional evasions of absent, defective and misleading imprints. In London, publishers additionally availed themselves of whatever protections lay ready to hand. Yet the success of such stratagems was mixed, for Swift was now sending to press material so personally offensive that prosecution was a serious risk. And all the time, out of sight of his readers, he was also testing the limits of another set of constraints as, in the face of a tangle of London copyrights and Faulkner's preparations for a multi-volume Dublin *Works*, he continued his wistfully repetitive approaches to Motte in London.

As far as the rights of the Church of Ireland were concerned, May's analysis of the publications to which Faulkner put his name suggests that, in a print trade generally aligned with the conservative position, 'George Faulkner in particular wished to be associated with forces for keeping the Test Act.'[3] (Contributions that concealed his agency were rare.) Notably, after summarising 'Some Queries humbly offered' in relation to *Considerations upon Two Bills* in his *Dublin Journal* for the very day when the bills were presented to (and in the event rejected by) the

---

[2] For political issues, see *Some Considerations . . . in the Choice of a Recorder* and *Advice to the Free-Men of the City of Dublin in the Choice of a Member to Represent them in Parliament*, in *CWJS Irish Political Writings after 1725*, pp. lxxxviii, xcviii, 269–73, 279–87, 476–8, 480–2; for satires of Dublin street life, see *An Examination of certain Abuses, Corruptions, and Enormities in the City of Dublin* and *The Humble Petition of the Footmen in and about the City of Dublin*, pp. xciv, 239–68, 468–76 (noting additional material printed in London as part of the former, on which see Rounce, 'Swift's Texts between Dublin and London', pp. 207–8); for ecclesiastical tracts and poetry, see further below. For the unusually prompt publication of new poems in the early 1730s, see the list in Karian, 'Swift as a Manuscript Poet', p. 33.

[3] May, 'False and Incomplete Imprints', p. 74.

The Works of J. S, D. D, D. S. P. D. *(1730–1735)*

Commons (26 February 1732), Faulkner was summoned by the House of Lords for 'highly reflecting upon the honour of the House'.[4] He staged a dogged display of non-compliance: when he failed to present himself, he was ordered to be arrested; but to judge by a repeated order in October 1733, this was not put into effect; and later that month he was reprimanded and discharged upon petition, having displayed just the kind of resolution that Swift valued in his printers.[5] London publication was far more discreetly handled: one edition of *Considerations upon Two Bills* appeared under the fictitious imprint of A. Moore, and another was passed by Bowyer to John Purser, a printer known for his opposition associations.[6] (In the same year Purser also produced a London reprint of *The Advantages Proposed by Repealing the Sacramental Test*: like his reprint of *Considerations*, it bore Roberts's imprint.[7]) Suspiciously, *The Presbyterian's Plea of Merit ... Impartially Examined* appeared in London in 1733 with an imprint declaring it to be 'Reprinted from the Dublin edition, for G. F. and sold by A. Dodd', which would have implied that Faulkner had paid for reprints to be distributed in London by the pamphlet-seller Ann Dodd; but May points out that a similar imprint appeared in London on the anti-Test *A Vindication of the Protestant Dissenters, from the Aspersions Cast upon Them* (1733), whose Dublin edition, printed 'by S. Powell', was highly unlikely to have been backed by Faulkner.[8] His initials may have been commandeered for their association value.

In contrast with Swift's prose tracts in defence of the Church, Dublin publications of his recent poems were more evasive. In 1730, for instance, only the ornaments would have shown that Faulkner and Hoey had produced the first octavo pamphlet of *A Libel on Dr Delany*.[9] In the light

---

[4] The ecclesiastical tracts of this period, grouped with later Irish tracts in *PW*, vol. XII, will appear in *CWJS Writings on Religion and the Church after 1714* (forthcoming). Examples by Swift published under Faulkner's imprint include *The Advantages Propos'd by Repealing the Sacramental Test, Impartially Considered* (Dublin, 1732: TS 723, *ESTC* N29821); and *The Presbyterians Plea of Merit; in order to take off the Test, Impartially Examined* (Dublin, 1733: TS 743, *ESTC* T1823). For 'Queries humbly offered', see *Dublin Journal*, 26 February 1732 (transcribed in *PW*, vol. XII, pp. xxxvii–xxxviii); Pollard, *Dictionary*, p. 199; Slepian, 'George Faulkner's "Dublin Journal"', pp. 103–4.

[5] *PW*, vol. XII, p. xxxviii.

[6] For the two London editions of *Considerations upon Two Bills*, see TS 716, *ESTC* T73914 (A. Moore imprint, 1732), and TS 717, *ESTC* T145270 (J. Roberts imprint, [1732]); for Purser, see *JSA*, Introduction. For associated material printed by Bowyer in 1731–3, see Maslen, 'George Faulkner and William Bowyer', pp. 231–2; *Bowyer Ledgers*, nos. 1729, 1734, 1735, 1751, 1775.

[7] TS 724, *ESTC* T145105; *JSA*, Introduction.

[8] TS 735, *ESTC* T90339 (and, for a second edition, TS 736, *ESTC* T89518); *JSA*, Introduction; May, 'False and Incomplete Imprints', p. 69, citing *ESTC* T89555.

[9] *CWJS Poems* III (forthcoming).

214   Part III: Dublin

of the poem's reflections on King, Queen and Minister, the imprint prudently gave no place or name; and although the Irish Privy Council and House of Lords considered prosecution, they did not proceed. Although this strategy meant that Faulkner and Hoey could neither defend their copy against rivals nor advertise a sales address, they could still call on hawkers for distribution, and J. Woolley and Karian suggest that *A Libel* came to be 'among Swift's most popular poems during the eighteenth century'. Faulkner and Hoey then toned down the offensive passages in a reprint (and also produced what may have been a single presentation copy in quarto, perhaps for Delany himself). Meanwhile, other printers in Dublin, Edinburgh and London issued further reprints. Later that year Faulkner and Hoey dealt similarly with the two parts of *Traulus*, an attack on Lord Allen, who had agitated for the prosecution of the *Libel*.[10]

Another well-established defence, peculiarly fitted to this late sequence of controversial poems, was to claim to be reprinting a text published on the other side of the Irish Sea. In the case of the 1730 *To Dr Delany, on the Libels Writ against him*, Faulkner and Hoey not only withheld their names from the first edition, but also made the false claim that it had previously been printed in London.[11] (Afterwards, when it really was reprinted in London, as a shared venture between Faulkner and Bowyer, it bore the imprint of T. Warner.) When Hoey and Faulkner ended their partnership, further diversification ensued: in 1732 Hoey stole a march on his former partner by issuing the first (apparently unauthorised) edition of *The Lady's Dressing Room*, not only withholding his own name and using asterisks to stand in for the author's, but also falsely claiming that he was reprinting from a previous London edition.[12] Faulkner, meanwhile, published an associated prose piece (probably also by Swift) entitled *A Modest Defence of a Late Poem by an Unknown Author, Call'd the Lady's Dressing Room*: having staked his claim by giving his name and address, Faulkner seems to have passed it to Bowyer, who reprinted it without place or name.[13] Faulkner then capped Hoey's performance by publishing a third Dublin edition of the poem, apparently the first to be authorised by Swift: this again gave Faulkner's full imprint, as well as somewhat boldly declaring its author to be '*D— n S——t*'. Faulkner probably also sent it to Bowyer in

---

[10] *CWJS Poems* IV (forthcoming).

[11] *CWJS Poems* III (forthcoming); but for the general decline of such claims in Dublin imprints of the 1720s and 1730s, see May, 'False and Incomplete Imprints', p. 68.

[12] *CWJS Poems* III (forthcoming).

[13] *A Modest Defence of a Late Poem by an Unknown Author, Call'd the Lady's Dressing Room* (Dublin, 1732; *ESTC* N35099), reprinted in London by Bowyer; *CWJS Poems* III (forthcoming).

The Works of J. S, D. D, D. S. P. D. *(1730–1735)*

London, where it was issued under the imprint of J. Roberts. In this case, Faulkner's privileged access to Swift's authorised texts, combined with his London contacts, had seen off Hoey's challenge. In the case of *The Grand Question Debated*, a verse discussion about what to do with a redundant building acquired by the Achesons, Dublin and London editions were published at about the same time in 1732.[14] Although Faulkner claimed to be reprinting from a London edition, textual differences suggest other-wise – and he was inaccurate in laying the London edition to the charge of the fictitious A. Moore, since it actually bore the imprint of J. Roberts, acting as distributor for Bowyer. Although there seem to have been some crossed wires between the two collaborators over this poem, particularly about annotation, the overall effect was to compound the elusiveness of the agencies behind the printed texts. By manipulating information about location, agency and textual transmission, publishers protected themselves by misinforming their readers (which is not to say that readers necessarily believed them).

On one revealing occasion Swift wanted to present a poem as if it was by someone else entirely, and accordingly turned to a different Dublin print-er. This was during the 1730 furore about Delany's claims to preferment, and Swift's plan was to ventriloquise *An Answer to Dr Delany's Fable of the Pheasant and the Lark* as an attack on himself by a supposed Whig: he told Gay that he had sent 'the Scrubb libel . . . to a Whig printer'.[15] The imprint gave only place and year, but ornaments suggest that the printer was Aaron Rhames – whose ornaments had also appeared in Hyde's Dublin reprint of the *Travels* in 1726. Faulkner's obituary in the *Dublin Journal* would describe Rhames as 'the first Person that brought the excellent and useful Art of Printing to any Perfection in this Kingdom'; but his successive reprints of work by Gilbert Burnet may have meant that Swift now wrote him off as a Whig.[16] The fictitious character in which Swift voiced the *Answer* tellingly recalls his masquerade as T. N. Philomath in the 1709 *A Famous Prediction of Merlin* (issued by the widow of the London Whig publisher Richard Baldwin, and headed with a woodcut that he had used in the 1690s): the Dublin trade now showed itself perfectly capable of equiva-lent mystifications. Faulkner, for instance, seems to have borrowed orna-ments from Hyde's widow, Sarah, to obscure his responsibility for *Memoirs of Capt. John Creichton. Written by Himself*, which Swift had apparently

---

[14] *CWJS Poems* III (forthcoming). See also discussion in J. Woolley, 'The Circulation of Verse', pp. 141–3.
[15] *Corr.*, vol. III, pp. 327, 335–6. [16] *CWJS Poems* III (forthcoming).

Part III: Dublin

helped to write up from the Jacobite Creichton's recollections.[17] Though the preliminary Advertisement refers to the support of *'generous Subscribers'*, there is no subscribers' list, and the imprint says only 'Printed in the Year, 1731.' (Faulkner certainly knew how to run a subscription, and would later prove to be rather well informed about the *Memoirs*.) Indeed, given the multiplicity of Faulkner's disguises, his importance to Swift in print was probably not obvious to all readers, especially as it was difficult to assemble, either in Dublin or London, a textual archive that comprehensively represented the publications of both.

Although Swift no longer visited England himself, its high-quality print market, legally secured copyright and wide distribution network still appealed to what Carole Fabricant has called 'his never entirely suppressed wish to be a writer speaking from the center of civilization rather than from its margins', and he repeatedly (if unrealistically) wrote to Motte in an effort to square the circle of the London and Dublin copyright regimes in which his copies were entangled.[18] The London Works he still hankered for would have entailed collaboration between the various owners of copy (a difficulty that Faulkner would in due course offer as justification for undertaking a Dublin *Works* instead).[19] In 1732, even while Pope and Motte were preparing 'The Third Volume' of *Miscellanies*, Swift went so far as to promote, through his protégé Matthew Pilkington (chaplain to John Barber, now Lord Mayor of London) a plan for a rival volume of his own, to be printed by Bowyer.[20] Unsurprisingly, it was blocked by Pope and Motte.

Some of the pieces Swift sent Motte turned out to be a mixed blessing. One was a hoax, namely *The Life and Genuine Character of the Rev. Dr. S—t, D. S. P. D. Written by Himself*, which was published in London in April 1733. It purported to be a surreptitiously leaked text of Swift's unpublished *Verses*

---

[17] *ESTC* T113807; *Corr.*, vol. III, pp. 208–9; *CWJS Poems* III (forthcoming: 'Here lies the body of Saint Steel'); May, 'False and Incomplete Imprints', pp. 63–4. See also Higgins, 'Censorship', pp. 189–92.

[18] Carole Fabricant, 'Swift the Irishman', in Christopher Fox (ed.), *The Cambridge Companion to Jonathan Swift* (Cambridge University Press, 2003), pp. 48–72 (p. 70); Karian, *Print and Manuscript*, pp. 23–9; *Corr.*, vol. III, pp. 502–4, 556–9, 563–6; vol. IV, pp. 151–5, 210–11, 304–6.

[19] Faulkner would write in the vol. I Preface that *'such a Collection as we proposed could not be printed in* London; *because several Copies, and some whole Treatises were the Property of different Booksellers, who were not likely to agree in Partnership'*; while *'we offended against no Law in acting as we did; because in this Kingdom, neither Authors, Booksellers, or Printers, pretended any Property in Copies; which in* London *is fixed as certainly as any other legal Possession'*.

[20] Maslen, 'George Faulkner and William Bowyer', pp. 228–9; McLaverty, 'George Faulkner', pp. 156–7; Fischer, 'Swift's *Miscellanies . . . Volume the Fifth*', pp. 78–9.

The Works of J. S், D. D, D. S. P. D. *(1730–1735)*

on the Death of Doctor Swift, crudely put together by 'some very low writer who had heard' that poem.[21] (Swift had indeed allowed friends to read the manuscript, though not to take copies.) In fact it was Pilkington who had approached Motte, who then issued it under the imprint of James Roberts: nevertheless, Swift had involved Motte in publishing a poem that not only aired his current concerns about attempts to repeal the Test Act, but also constituted a satire on editorial insincerity in which Motte himself was implicated.[22] Readers familiar with the Pope/Motte *Miscellanies*, particularly the so-called 'Third Volume' of 1732, probably made the connection for themselves when they saw the poem's dedication to Pope, which was voiced (in tones suspiciously reminiscent of the entrepreneur of the *Tale* and his successors) by a book-trade pilferer happy to parade his lack of concern for publishing ethics. In May, Faulkner denounced *The Life and Genuine Character* as a fraud in the *Dublin Journal*.[23] When he reprinted it in Dublin (probably before he issued his disclaimer) he gave it a false London imprint; and it may have been after this that Edward Waters, resuming a prominence in Swift publishing that he had long laid aside, produced, on thin paper with distracting show-through, an exuberant but low-quality reprint of his own.[24]

In 1733 Pilkington also offered Motte a much more problematic trio of political poems, brought over by Mary Barber.[25] (A Dublin poet and protégée of Swift, she was not related to John Barber.) Motte cautiously redirected two of the political poems to Gilliver, and they were published (and prominently advertised) in November as a folio pamphlet: *An Epistle to a Lady, Who Desired the Author to Make Verses on Her, in the Heroick Stile. Also a Poem, Occasion'd by Reading Dr. Young's Satires, Called, The Universal Passion.*[26] Postdated to 1734 and issued under the imprint of John Wilford, this claimed to have been printed in Dublin and reprinted in London – which was both true and misleading. Faulkner had indeed been

---

[21] This was Swift's disingenuous disclaimer to Carteret (*Corr.*, vol. III, p. 633); *CWJS Poems* IV (forthcoming). See also Slepian, 'George Faulkner's "Dublin Journal"', pp. 102–3.

[22] McLaverty, 'The Failure of the Swift–Pope *Miscellanies*', pp. 144–8; Ashley Marshall, 'Swift on "Swift": From *The Author upon Himself* to *The Life and Genuine Character*', HLQ, 75.3 (2012), 327–63 (pp. 355–9); *CWJS Poems* IV (forthcoming).

[23] *Dublin Journal*, 15 May 1733.

[24] May suggests wider competition between Faulkner and Waters ('False and Incomplete Imprints', pp. 81–2).

[25] John Irwin Fischer, 'The Government's Response to Swift's *An Epistle to a Lady*', *Philological Quarterly*, 65 (1986), 39–59 (pp. 41–2). (Fischer later withdrew his support for the view that Pilkington's consignment included *A Beautiful Young Nymph going to Bed*, *Strephon and Chloe* and *Cassinus and Peter*: see Fischer, 'Swift's *Miscellanies*', p. 79 n. 19; and further below.)

[26] *CWJS Poems* III (forthcoming).

Part III: Dublin

the first to print it; and the London printing does indeed appear to derive from his original (with revisions that appear to be authorial); but the Dublin printing was as yet unpublished, since it formed part of the forthcoming *Works. An Epistle to a Lady* was so outrageous in its satire of King, Queen and Minister that the authorities launched an investigation, and as, in early 1734, each of those involved progressively informed on the others (with Pilkington, in Fischer's analysis, as 'the Government's star blabber'), even Motte was arrested (although, as he told Swift, he had offered to refund half of Gilliver's expenses if he kept quiet).[27] Fischer, working from the records of the government case against Mrs Barber, shows that she was accused of 'intending to . . . scandalize and vilify . . . our said Lord the King and his administration of the Government of this Kingdom and also to scandalize and discredit the Rt. Hon. Sir Robert Walpole', charges which, if sustained, could have led to her being pilloried, whipped, branded and having her ears cropped, as well as being fined and imprisoned.[28] In the event there were no convictions; but the poem was cancelled from volume II of Faulkner's 1735 *Works* and there does not seem to have been a separate Dublin printing.

Motte also needed a strategy for dealing with the third poem in Pilkington's consignment, *On Poetry: A Rapsody*. This was another scathing attack on the King and his administration, and at the end of 1733 it duly appeared under yet another imprint, that of John Huggonson, dated 1734 (Fischer shows that Huggonson was associated with Wilford and Gilliver through the *Grub-Street Journal*).[29] This once again claimed to have been previously printed in Dublin (although no such edition is known); but this time it was the subsequent Dublin reprinters of the poem who were reportedly arrested: the imprint was that of Sarah Hyde, and it was from her text, for which Swift seems to have provided revisions, that Faulkner would print the poem in 1735. It is possible, indeed, that someone in London had already acted to reduce the danger by suppressing passages which Faulkner would print only in 1762 (following first publication in a rival Dublin edition); but they may not have been present in the version that Motte received.[30] While there is no reason to think that Swift had acted with malice, Pilkington's consignment had undeniably given Motte and Gilliver, joint booksellers of the resented 'Third Volume' of *Miscellanies*, considerable

---

[27] Fischer, 'The Government's Response', pp. 43–4; *Corr.*, vol. IV, pp. 151–2.
[28] Fischer, 'The Government's Response', pp. 48–52.   [29] *Ibid.*, p. 41.
[30] For these passages and their transmission, see *CWJS Poems* IV (forthcoming); see also A. C. Elias, Jr, John Irwin Fischer and James Woolley, 'The Full Text of Swift's *On Poetry: A Rhapsody* (1733)', *SStud*, 9 (1994), 17–32.

The Works of J. S, D. D, D. S. P. D. *(1730–1735)*

anxiety and inconvenience (and Pilkington's own role has sometimes been considered suspect).[31] Given the advanced stage that Faulkner had already reached in printing his projected Dublin *Works*, it is striking testimony to the tenacity of Swift's London ambitions that he continued sending new work to Motte for as long as he did.

By the time that *A Beautiful Young Nymph Going to Bed. Written for the Honour of the Fair Sex ... To Which Are Added, Strephon and Chloe. And Cassinus and Peter* was published in London, dated 1734, and claiming (under the imprint of J. Roberts), to reprint a previous Dublin printing, the new, Dublin-driven transmission between Faulkner and Bowyer was soundly established.[32] This time, the claim of previous Dublin printing was correct but doubly misleading: the Dublin printing had once more been part of the as yet unissued *Works*, and the pamphlet had not been copied directly from it, but from an intermediate London reprint made as part of *Miscellanies ... Volume the Fifth*, which would not be published until January 1735. Thus, though first published in London under Roberts's imprint, the pamphlet in which these now notorious poems first went on sale had been printed by Bowyer from Faulkner's *Works*, via a supplementary London collection of its novelties (also printed by Bowyer). Even before the *Works* appeared, Faulkner's Dublin texts were driving London publication.

A Measure of Ambition

Whatever reports and rumours early readers may have heard about the negotiations behind the 1735 *Works*, their crucial experience was of the material texts themselves.[33] Scholarship, on the other hand, has been understandably concerned to tease out the relationships and processes that lay behind them.[34] Direct evidence of active collaboration between Faulkner and Swift is scanty; Swift's own claims to a bare toleration of Faulkner's project are persistent but suspiciously similar to his misleading

---

[31] Fischer, 'The Government's Response', p. 52.

[32] *CWJS Poems* IV (forthcoming); Fischer, 'Swift's *Miscellanies*', pp. 79–80.

[33] For the first publication, in octavo, see TS 41 and commentary (pp. 22–5; *ESTC* T52771).

[34] For authorial involvement in Faulkner's edition, see, in addition to discussions of particular textual transmissions in *CWJS* and *PW*, the following: TS, pp. 22–5 (prefacing nos. 41–8); Ehrenpreis, *Swift*, vol. III, pp. 779–90; Margaret Weedon, 'An Uncancelled Copy of the First Collected Edition of Swift's Poems', *The Library*, 22.1 (1967), 44–56; Pollard, *Dictionary*, pp. 199, 204–5; Ashley Marshall, 'The "1735" Faulkner Edition of Swift's *Works*', *The Library*, 14.2 (2013), 154–98; Karian, *Print and Manuscript*, pp. 22–43; *CWJS Travels*, pp. 447–51; McLaverty, 'George Faulkner' (particularly pp. 164–5). For a compilation of Faulkner's later accounts, see *PW*, vol. XIII, pp. 201–7.

220   Part III: Dublin

claims about previous collections; and, as Karian has shown, Faulkner's 1763 claim that Swift had proofed every sheet was published in the context of particular pressure from rivals within the book trade. Yet Swift's resentment of the 1727–32 *Miscellanies* and the demonstrable impracticability of a London Works gave him good reason to connive at a Dublin alternative – especially after Faulkner had in 1732 demonstrated his loyalty by his silence about the authorship of 'Some Queries humbly offered'. Swift either facilitated or at least did not prevent the incorporation into the *Works* of what appear to be authorial revisions; and he specifically claimed responsibility for a major post-print cancellation of several poems originally printed for volume II; but it is far from clear that he was committed to regular practical collaboration.[35]

Faulkner's subscription was nevertheless a huge success, which changed the direction of Swift in print by opening up a sustainable long-term future for a major Irish edition. The project balanced an expanded and enhanced design against a realistic sense of what was feasible; it reframed Swift's current significance by revising his writings and adding notes; and it staged a shrewd mediation of the vexed questions of authorship and authority. Faulkner showed that he could calibrate an ambitious offer to the relative limitations of the Dublin print trade, extend its reach through a carefully planned English network, and respond with appropriate resilience to the setbacks inseparable from printing the *Works* of a not entirely co-operative author. By no means everyone was impressed; but the volumes sold well enough for Faulkner to continue adding volumes and reprinting for the rest of his career.[36] Even the initial subscription put Faulkner's first four octavo volumes into the hands of an impressively large and varied readership: McLaverty calculates 888 subscribers for 152 sets, with 54 multiple subscribers accounting for 318 of those sets.[37] The volumes appealed to subscribers across a broad social range: Irish and English; nobility and gentry; clergy and office-holders; writers and tradesmen. Faulkner even evaded the ban on exporting Irish books by securing subscriptions from English booksellers: the most prolific single subscriber, John Hopkins, was a Lancashire bookseller who 'took in subscriptions and subscribed for and ordered twenty-five compleat setts'.[38] The edition's reach was then extended by sales to non-subscribers, reprintings in the same and smaller formats (including

---

[35] *Corr*, vol. III, pp. 752–3, and see below.
[36] McLaverty, 'George Faulkner', p. 171; Marshall, 'The "1735" Faulkner Edition', pp. 175–80.
[37] McLaverty, 'George Faulkner', pp. 160–1.   [38] *Ibid.*, pp. 161–2.

The Works of J. S, D. D, D. S. P. D. *(1730–1735)*   221

publications derived from sheets sent to Bowyer in London), and progressive additions of further volumes.[39] What the subscribers who provided the start-up funding received in return was a four-volume set that expressed both the novelty and the awkwardness of the project.

The opportunity was brought to their attention on 10 February 1733 by a Proposal in Faulkner's *Dublin Journal* (a reminder that even this ambitious plan was grounded in his management of cheap print, and his deftness in keeping his principal author in the public eye).[40] The Proposal does not read like the pitch of a confident entrepreneur: indeed, given the subsequent fame of the *Works*, its tone is surprisingly downbeat – which is probably not an accident. Instead of insisting on its own ambition, innovation or monumentality, the Proposal begins in deferentially responsive mode, focusing less on opportunities than problems: the difficulty of discriminating Swift's work from others' in the 1727–32 *Miscellanies*; the existence of Irish tracts not included in *Fraud Detected*; the textual corruption of Motte's *Travels*; the commercial impossibility of a collected London edition. The Proposal's paragraphs are short (often a single sentence), its train of thought apparently halting.

A hint of ambition (but only a hint) emerges only in its third paragraph: 'It hath been long wished, by several Persons of Quality and Distinction, that a new compleat Edition of this Author's Works, should be printed by it self.' The respectful displacement of agency is decorously matched to the role of bookseller; and enthusiasm only breaks through, with a sudden shimmer of positive qualifiers, when the proposer turns to the material specifics of his own business. This is also the topic that elicits the Proposal's first and only substantial paragraph, setting out prices (17s. 4d. for the four volumes, in instalments, with a free set for every six subscribed for), scope ('all the Works that are generally allowed to have been written by Dr. S.'), format ('OCTAVO') and quality ('beautifully printed on a fine Paper', 'neatly bound in Calves Leather, and lettered on the Back'). There is also a money-back offer should sufficient subscribers fail to present themselves within three months. (This turned out to be entirely unnecessary; but Faulkner would later claim that the subscription itself was an expedient for overcoming Swift's scruples that 'the Publisher might be a Loser' by the project.[41]) At the end of the Proposal, after two paragraphs of

---

[39] For the 1735 duodecimo reprint, see TS 49–52 (and commentary pp. 46–59; *ESTC* N30995). For collaboration with Bowyer, see Maslen, 'George Faulkner and William Bowyer', p. 229.

[40] See Slepian, 'George Faulkner's "Dublin Journal"'; A. C. Kelly, *Jonathan Swift and Popular Culture*, pp. 83–4.

[41] *PW*, vol. XIII, p. 202; McLaverty, 'George Faulkner', p. 159.

222   Part III: Dublin

disproportionate detail on the textual problems of the *Travels* and the manuscript materials available for their correction, the proposer again asserts the decent ambition of the proposed volumes, offering specially commissioned 'Cuts' (including portrait frontispieces by George Vertue) and repeating the promise of 'a beautiful Letter and a fine Paper'. This decorous courtship of potential subscribers by a bookseller who knew both his place and his business was further supplemented by Faulkner's personal solicitation (notably during a visit to England for which Swift supplied introductions).[42]

The four 1735 volumes for which subscribers were now invited to put down their money did much by their bulk, quality and contents to suggest monumentality. In 1734 sets were also advertised to non-subscribers in London, priced at a guinea (3s. 8d. more than the subscription price); and the announcement further emphasised their quality and bulk ('in Octavo, in a beautiful new Dutch Type, and a fine Genoa paper, containing upwards of 1700 Pages, with a most beautiful frontispiece prefix'd to each Volume engrav'd by the famous Mr. Virtue'), as well as tempting the connoisseur with the optional luxury of copies 'printed on a Royal Paper for the Curious'.[43] (These large-paper copies significantly enhance the impression of monumentality.) By even the crudest measure, this was the largest set of uniform volumes ever devoted to Swift's writings. It was twice the size of the 1726 London *Travels* (a two-volume set which had itself doubled the previous one-volume maximum for a single-author Swift publication). Yet the choice of octavo, with large octavo as the luxury option, was a measured one: by comparison with the large quarto or folio on which Pope had focused to date, this was a modest format (although Pope himself was by this point turning his attention to its potential for reaching a wider readership).[44] For Swift in print, one of its advantages was its flexibility: it could be as decorative and amply spaced as Motte and his team's *Travels* (which had also adopted large octavo as its prestige option); as neat, intricate and substantial as Tooke and the elder Motte's *Tale*; or as passionately shabby and thin as Harding's Drapier's letters. Faulkner's *Works* octavos, characterised by McLaverty as 'modest rather than luxurious', were incomparably superior to the Drapier's letters, though neither as imposing as the *Travels* nor quite as neat as the *Tale*; and their frontispieces and decorations provided a decided visual flourish, as the series built,

---

[42] *Corr.*, vol. III, pp. 721–2; McLaverty, 'George Faulkner', pp. 159–60.
[43] *London Evening Post*, 12–15 October 1734, transcribed in McLaverty, 'George Faulkner', p. 169.
[44] McLaverty, *Pope, Print and Meaning*, pp. 214–16, 227–41.

The Works of J. S, D. D, D. S. P. D. *(1730–1735)*   223

volume by volume, into an edition of unprecedented bulk and completeness. Yet Faulkner's frugal opportunism is also shown in these years by his purchases of second-hand type from Bowyer, some of whose discarded ornaments can be seen in the *Works*.[45]

In line with changing tastes, the *Works* aligned their title pages with notions of elegance very different from the exuberant double-framed title pages of earlier Swift in print (which still characterised some of Faulkner's humbler offerings).[46] Typographical contrast was restrained but effective, as demonstrated by the series title, which is set entirely in roman, except for a few proper names in italic (Figure 11). It deploys at its head three subtly distinguished sizes of type: the largest full capitals emphasise 'WORKS', the middle size presents the attribution to '*J. S, D. D, D. S. P. D.*', and the smallest size promises 'Four VOLUMES'. The page then continues in the smaller size (with '*DUBLIN*', in the imprint, just a little larger): a contents list for each volume serves to introduce the individual volume titles that follow; and a statement just above the imprint, set off by rules above and below, advertises not only that the edition contains 'great Alterations and Additions', but also that 'each Volume' contains 'Pieces . . . never before published'. There is no ornamentation. In contrast, the individual titles of volumes I and II boast an elaborately mirrored 'GF' monogram, curlicued and breaking out into foliage, a device that Faulkner had used in some of his higher-profile publications since at least 1732. As these volumes had relatively short titles, the ample space around the central monogram both emphasised Faulkner's status and associated his project with a spare, modern aesthetic. Although the titles of volumes III and IV reverted to a busier page containing more information, the restrained scheme of typographical articulation persisted. Modestly but visibly, in the author's home city, Swift in print was approaching a more elegant future. Indeed, although Swift had never been a polite writer, and was in these years explicitly coding politeness as Whiggish sycophancy, Faulkner's design placed the *Works* deftly on the profitable verge of polite production values.[47] Both aspirational and realistic, frugally but respectably drawing on discarded type from a first-class printer, his octavo volumes still resonated with the

---

[45] For Bowyer's sales of type to Faulkner, 1732–7, and for Bowyer ornaments in Faulkner's *Works*, see Maslen, 'George Faulkner and William Bowyer', p. 230.

[46] May notes that in Dublin, 'Double-ruled frames and black letter continued to be used on title-pages by some older printers in the 1730s when they were abandoned by those new to the trade' ('False and Incomplete Imprints', p. 61).

[47] *CWJS Parodies*, p. 694.

THE

WORKS

OF

J. S, D.D, D.S.P.D.

IN

FOUR VOLUMES.

CONTAINING,

I. The Author's MISCELLANIES in PROSE.

II. His POETICAL WRITINGS.

III. The TRAVELS of Captain *Lemuel Gulliver*.

IV. His Papers relating to *Ireland*, confifting of feveral Treatifes; among which are, The DRAPIER's LETTERS to the People of *Ireland* againft receiving *Wood's* Half-pence: Alfo, two Original DRAPIER's LETTERS, never before publifhed.

In this Edition are great Alterations and Additions; and likewife many Pieces in each Volume, never before publifhed

---

DUBLIN:

Printed by and for GEORGE FAULKNER, Printer and Bookfeller, in ESSEX-STREET, oppofite to the Bridge. M DCC XXXV.

Figure 11 *The Works of J. S, D. D, D. S. P. D.* (Dublin, 1735), vol. I, series title.

The Works of J. S, D. D, D. S. P. D. *(1730–1735)*

analogy between unostentatiousness and outrageousness that had long been at the heart of Swift in print. Later in 1735 Faulkner followed up his advantage with a duodecimo reprint, and by 1769 the octavo series had reached twenty volumes.[48]

Faulkner made no secret of the fact that the first four volumes were to be constructed by updating previously published collections (just as the 1727 Pope/Swift *Miscellanies* had built on Swift's 1711 *Miscellanies in Prose and Verse*). *Fraud Detected* was to be supplemented to form volume I, and the 1727 *Miscellanies* would provide a basis for volumes II and III.[49] (There was as yet no equivalent collection of the English political works of 1710–14, which Swift in any case professed to regard as ephemera not worth reprinting: these would appear only later, in the 1738 volumes V–VI.[50]) This sat well with established reader expectation, for Motte testified that the *Miscellanies* were already commonly known as Swift's Works: now it was time to expand and update them.[51] Unfortunately, a post-Proposal change of plan significantly marred Faulkner's original scheme: *A Collection of Tracts relating to Ireland*, volume I in the Proposal, was subsequently held back to become volume IV. (*Miscellanies in Prose* then took its place as volume I; *Poetical Works* was volume II; and *Travels* was volume III.) Such a change, apparently trivial, had serious thematic, commercial and material consequences. Thematically, by giving a more chronological presentation of Swift's career, it prioritised an English rather than an Irish Swift. (Whereas Fabricant suggests that 'The importance of this edition is that it presented Swift's works as part of a consciously and thoroughly Irish production' and that 'Swift recognized and quietly embraced this fact even as he continued to express the desire to have such an edition published instead in England', the *Works*' Irish focus would have been much more obvious if *A Collection of Tracts relating to Ireland* had retained its intended position as volume I.[52]) Commercially, the reordering displaced a prominent celebration of Faulkner's 1725 commitment to Swift in *Fraud Detected*. Materially, the change left the *Works* with a volume IV originally designed to launch a series and a volume I that looked rather ordinary in comparison. It is hard not to suspect Swift's own agency.

---

[48] McLaverty, 'George Faulkner', p. 154; for summary, see TS tables of octavo and duodecimo editions, pp. 47, 60; and, for the octodecimo edition begun in 1762, pp. 59–65.

[49] It was in fact Bowyer's London reprint of *Fraud Detected*, entitled *The Hibernian Patriot*, which provided copy for the projected vol. I (later renumbered IV), *A Collection of Tracts relating to Ireland* (McLaverty, 'George Faulkner', pp. 155, 168).

[50] TS 42; *ESTC* T205439, T205440; *Corr.*, vol. III, pp. 698–99, 708–9; Marshall, 'The "1735" Faulkner Edition', pp. 170–1.

[51] See Chapter 6.   [52] Fabricant, 'Swift the Irishman', p. 69.

226   Part III: Dublin

In the *Works* as published, it was only in the frontispiece of the reordered volume IV, *A Collection of Tracts relating to Ireland*, that readers first encountered a concerted claim, both visual and verbal, for the edition's monumental status. McLaverty rightly comments that the image is 'one that might have preceded the set as a whole', and this is one of several signs that the volume has lost the place of honour for which it was designed.[53] Vertue's composition stages a specific evocation of Swift as Irish patriot: seated in front of St Patrick's Cathedral, he spurns a defeated figure (presumably the now-detected Fraud) who sprawls beneath his feet, scattering his coins across the step beneath. A nursing mother, her elder child beside her, gazes gratefully at Swift while displaying a (presumably genuine) coin in her open palm. Swift gestures with his left hand towards a bound volume and two further written sheets on the table beside him (the bound volume is presumably *Fraud Detected*, flanked by the two additional Drapier's letters that Faulkner now prints for the first time). With his right hand he presents a document to the kneeling Hibernia, neatly coiffed and discreetly but definitely crowned, whose harp lies at her feet. (While the text that passes between them may simply represent the Drapier's letters as originally sent to press, it would be hard to rule out some more portentous confirmation of constitutional right.) The composition is surmounted by putti who reach down to crown Swift with a wreath, while lifting a quill pen towards the sky as if in sign of apotheosis. Finally, at the foot of the engraving, appears a verbal claim that would have appeared much more appropriately in its intended position at the head of the series: 'Exegi Monumentum Aere perennius. Hor.' ('I have finished a monument more lasting than bronze').[54] The effect of the change is double-edged: if the original plan had prevailed, the whole edition could have been launched much more impressively; but it would have been far more obviously an Irish monument to an Irish patriot.

In comparison, volume I as actually published was *Miscellanies in Prose*, which took up the story of Swift's writing at a much earlier point, and thus provided a largely English focus (with a few more recent Irish items towards the back). Its frontispiece is a comparatively simple portrait: '*The Reverend D'. J: Swift D. S. P. D.*' As the reader passes on to volume II, *Poetical Works*, the next frontispiece makes a somewhat muted pitch for monumentality by

---

[53] McLaverty, 'George Faulkner', p. 170. For discussion of the image, see Griffin, *Swift and Pope*, p. 189.

[54] Horace, *Odes*, Book III, no. 30, l. 1. Griffin comments: 'it is for his "Papers relating to Ireland" that Swift looks for his real fame, yet wittily reminding his readers that it was his Drapier's Letters that helped to defeat Wood's *brass* half-pence' (*Swift and Pope*, p. 189).

depicting a framed portrait very similar to that in volume I, now uplifted by putti and surrounded by adoring figures, one of whom presents a laurel crown. This is the first time that the coronation motif appears in the sequence as published, and (like the deferred Drapier frontispiece in which Swift is also about to be crowned) it too enters a Horatian claim: '*Quivis speret idem*. Hor.' The passage from which the tag is taken is aptly chosen to compliment Swift's distinctive familiar style of verse: 'My aim shall be poetry, so moulded from the familiar that anybody may hope for the same success, may sweat much and yet toil in vain when attempting the same: such is the power of order and connexion, such the beauty that may crown the commonplace.'[55] But the boast, though apt, is limited and specific. Volume III also gives a Horatian motto ('*Splendide Mendax. Hor.*') to its frontispiece portrait of Gulliver.[56] Evoking Horace's praise of Hypermnestra, who deceived a murderous father in order to save the life of her husband, the inscription both glances at the conventional scepticism for travellers' tales and casts Swift's fiction as heroic intervention. But it makes no wider claim to memorialise his achievement. Thus, it is only in the published volume IV that the imagery and mottos arrive at what the *Proposal* had conceived as their starting point, in the Horatian 'exegi monumentum' inscribed beneath the Drapier allegory. McLaverty comments: 'Of course, the writer has made the monument, but Faulkner himself must have reflected that he might equally be the speaker of this motto himself.'[57] It is a shrewd point; and Faulkner may also have reflected that both would have made more impact as first designed. Similar thoughts may indeed have occurred when he found himself having to cancel poems that he had already printed for volume II and replace them with new ones.[58] But Swift was by now the most valuable part of Faulkner's stock-in-trade, and he evidently confronted difficulties pragmatically as they arose.

One sign of how seriously Faulkner took the *Works* is their lavish ornamentation: unlike Motte's generously decorated *Travels*, whose figurative ornaments had been substantially supplemented by fleuron composites, Faulkner's *Works* focuses on the former. Enriched by copies and cast-offs from Bowyer and others, the volumes display discrete headpieces, endpieces and decorated initials throughout, tacitly confirming that this is indeed an 'Irish manufacture' fit for a polite home.[59] Yet in addition to the

---

[55] Horace, *Ars Poetica*, ll. 240–43.   [56] Horace, *Odes*, Book III, no. 11, l. 35.
[57] McLaverty, 'George Faulkner', p. 170.   [58] See below.
[59] One of Faulkner's headpieces, used several times, is a lion between cornucopias strikingly similar to the one associated with Rhames that had appeared in Hyde's 1726 reprint of *Travels*: in *Works*, it appears, for instance, on p. 141 of vol. I, heading *A Tritical Essay*, on p. 243, heading *A Letter to a Young Lady on her*

228   Part III: Dublin

ornaments' decorative function, there are numerous instances where their juxtaposition with specific works invites particular reflection. Two ornaments obviously designed to this end are placed in high-profile positions in volume IV, *A Collection of Tracts relating to Ireland*. Apparently purpose-made for what had been planned as the first volume, each appears only once. First comes the apotheosis of suffering Hibernia, in an unusually large headpiece to *A Proposal for the Universal Use of Irish Manufacture* (Figure 12). Abject and dishevelled, with head drooping, bosom partly bared and harp at her feet, her image is framed in flowers and foliage and borne aloft by putti.[60] The *Proposal* dates from 1720, well before Swift had taken on the role of the Drapier; but the headpiece marks it, in retrospect, as his first decisive intervention on Ireland's behalf – one for which Waters had famously been prosecuted, as readers were reminded in a footnote to the relevant passage in the Drapier's first letter.[61] Second, another unusually large headpiece precedes the first letter itself, this time presenting an unmistakeable allegory of Swift as Irish patriot: distinguished by his clerical gown, he turns away from the smartly coiffed Britannia on his left (accoutred with olive branch, shield and spear), and offers a cup to a dishevelled Hibernia on his right.[62] (Clad in rags, her harp beside her, this is a reversed version of the figure that heads the *Proposal*.) With his left hand, Swift holds out towards Britannia the chain from which he has delivered Hibernia, while above his outstretched arm is blazoned the accusatory comment 'detur indigenti' ('it is owed to the poor'). As Davis suggests, the rendering of the two female figures resembles descriptions in the elaborate allegory of the 1725 half sheet *Tom Punsibi's Dream*; but Faulkner's simpler allegory achieves greater force with fewer figures, and is much more explicit about Swift's individual political agency.[63]

Yet there was a complication, for this second oversized headpiece does not appear in all copies. The others have instead a shallower headpiece, used repeatedly in the *Works*, which features an angler on a village riverbank (a reversed copy of a Bowyer ornament).[64] This meant that more space was available for the setting out of the title, which in these copies extends to four lines rather than three: hyphenation of '*Far-mers*' and 'Gen-

---

Marriage, and on p. 281 of vol. III, heading Book II, chapter iv of *Travels*. It is distinguished from Rhames's lion by facial expression and detail of cornucopias, foliage and border. For ornaments in the *Works* earlier used by Bowyer, see Maslen, 'George Faulkner and William Bowyer', p. 230.

[60] Vol. IV, p. 23.   [61] *Ibid.*, p. 65.

[62] *Ibid.*; Davis, *Drapier's Letters*, p. xciii; TS 41, p. 27.

[63] *Tom Punsibi's Dream* (Dublin, 1725; *ESTC* T087763). The pseudonym is Sheridan's.

[64] Keith Maslen, *The Bowyer Ornament Stock* (Oxford Bibliographical Society, 1973), no. 69.

A PROPOSAL
FOR THE
UNIVERSAL USE
OF
Irish MANUFACTURE, &c.

IT is the peculiar Felicity and Prudence of the People in this Kingdom, that whatever Commodities, or Productions, lie under the greatest Discouragements from *England*, those are what they are sure to be most industrious in cultivating and spreading. *Agriculture*, which hath been the principal Care

Figure 12 *The Works of J. S, D. D, D. S. P. D.* (Dublin, 1735), vol. IV, p. 23.

230

Part III: Dublin

eral' is avoided, commas are generously spaced, and '*IRELAND*', in full capitals rather than lower case, sits on a line by itself. Similarly, the opening address to '*Brethren, Friends, Countrymen*, and *Fellow-Subjects*' extends from one line into two, giving a more expansive display. Although Davis took 'detur indigenti' to be the later state, its (reversed) representation of Hibernia is so similar to that in the *Proposal* headpiece as to suggest that the two were conceived together, in which case it is hard to see why both would not have been used from the beginning. It may be that Swift, or Faulkner, had second thoughts about the allegory's explicit identification of Swift as the Drapier, or that this first crucial letter was thought to need a more spaciously conceived title and inscription. Whatever the sequence of the changes and the reasoning behind them, the allegorical headpiece underlines Faulkner's material investment in the volume originally planned to head the series.

These two large Hibernia headpieces were evidently a special case. Yet it was an intriguing characteristic of the *Works* that even stock ornaments might provoke reflection by their teasing relation to a specific verbal text. In the same volume, for instance, *A Proposal for the Universal Use of Irish Manufacture* ends with Faulkner's favourite phoenix tailpiece, whose inscription points its moral with a motto from Claudian's account of the phoenix: 'praebetur origo per cineres' ('Thine ashes give thee life').[65] This ornament seems to have been copied from one of the phoenixes that Bowyer commissioned to celebrate the renaissance of his business after a disastrous fire in 1713.[66] Compared to the disconsolately flustered phoenix often used on titles by Waters, the first printer of the *Proposal* (though not, admittedly, in that particular work), this is a confident and compact version of an emblem well fitted to the risks braved by Dublin's Tory printers, providing an apt tailpiece to Faulkner's presentation of this momentous essay.[67] *Some Arguments against Enlarging the Power of Bishops*, meanwhile, shares with *A Modest Proposal* a narrow headpiece, used several times in the *Works*, which frames Hibernia, with her harp, as a small enclosed figure between rampant lions.[68] When it first appears in volume I, at the head of chapter iv of *Contests and Dissensions*, its iconography suggests no particular application; and when it appears later in that volume at the head of one of the *Intelligencer* essays, that essay is

---

[65] Vol. IV, p. 33; Claudian, *Phoenix*, ll. 102–3 (reading 'cinerem' for 'cineres').

[66] *Bowyer Ledgers*, p. vi; Maslen, *The Bowyer Ornament Stock*, no. 120.

[67] For Waters's phoenix, see title page of Charles Coffey, *Temple-Oagg. A Poem in three canto's ... The sixth edition* (Dublin, 1728; *ESTC* T178007).

[68] Vol. IV, p. 37.

The Works of J. S, D. D, D. S. P. D. *(1730–1735)*   231

concerned not with Ireland but with the *Beggar's Opera*; but when it reappears above *Some Arguments* and *A Modest Proposal* it prompts an irresistible question: are the lions protecting or threatening?[69] In this light, even the fishing scene that replaced the 'detur indigenti' tableau at the head of the Drapier's first letter bears closer inspection: the angler, just lifting his catch from the water with one hand, while with the other he moves his landing net into position, might well provide an emblem for the prematurely triumphant Wood.[70] Indeed, even the ornament of English roses and Scottish thistles which replaced Faulkner's monogram on the title of volume IV begins to look distinctly provocative.

Far beyond *A Collection of Tracts relating to Ireland*, juxtapositions of text and ornament suggest teasing reflections – which is not necessarily to say that they were placed with deliberate intention. The recurrent use of the small headpiece of Hibernia flanked by lions, however, underlines a much more general point: Faulkner has very little Irish national imagery to display, but plenty of English roses and Scottish thistles, in this Irish edition of an Irish defender of Ireland. More specifically, traditional Christian imagery such as the lamb and flag, which might seem to sit appropriately at the head of *On the Irish Bishops* or *An Argument* against abolishing Christianity, but to have less point elsewhere, is also a reminder of a religious heritage that Swift believed to be in need of constant defence against dissent. Traditional topics of piety and prudence were similarly evoked by secular and classical emblems such as the fox and goose, the hopeful angler and the phoenix; and these too might also seem to respond to the pressure of particular contexts.[71] In volume I, for example, the warnings of the 'Church-of-England Man' against dissenters are headed by the image of the ravished goose squawking back at its elderly mistress, who, tucking up her skirts to climb the garden gate, flourishes her broom in impotent rage; and the riverbank scene at the head of *A Letter to a Young Gentleman, lately entered into Holy Orders* again foregrounds, against the background of the parish church, the angler preparing to land his prize.[72]

Such effects are particularly suggestive in volume III, the *Travels*: at the head of Part I, chapter i, where Gulliver '*is made a Prisoner, and carried up the Country*', the fox is seen carrying off the goose; at the head of Part I, chapter v, when '*The* Author *by an extraordinary Stratagem prevents an*

---

[69] Vol. I, pp. 38, 267; vol. IV, pp. 37, 273.   [70] Vol. IV, p. 65.

[71] For lamb and flag, see vol. I, p. 91, and vol. II, p. 426. For reversed fox and goose, see Maslen, *The Bowyer Ornament Stock*, no. 68. Faulkner's *Works* also uses a reversed version of Bowyer's no. 67, a couple on a riverbank with ruins and townscape in the distance.

[72] Vol. I, pp. 56, 208.

232 Part III: Dublin

Invasion', Hibernia once more reappears between rampant lions – in this context recalling the threatened influx of Wood's halfpence); and at the head of Part I, chapter vii, when '*The Author being informed of a Design to accuse him of High Treason, makes his Escape to* Blefuscu', the crown so fatefully assumed by George I appears entwined with roses and thistles.[73] Faulkner's phoenix endpiece also makes some particularly striking appearances. At the end of chapter x ('*The Empress's Apartment on fire by an Accident; the* Author *instrumental in saving the rest of the Palace*'), it arises from the ashes with thematic aptness; and when it appears again, at the end of Part III, chapter x ('*A particular Description of the* Struldbrugs'), its emblematic reflection on the mysteries of ending and beginning points the horror of Swift's alternative.[74] Its final appearance in volume I of the *Travels* is at the end of Part IV, chapter ix, which closes: 'I could with great Pleasure enlarge farther upon the Manners and Virtues of this excellent People; but ... in the mean time, proceed to relate my own sad Catastrophe.'[75] Again, the protagonist is challenged to make a new start. Indeed, the pattern of phoenixes might almost frame a counter-argument to Swift's laments for the balmy days of the Queen's last ministry: perhaps the fall had actually been the making of him, as it had been of Swift in print? Such visual juxtapositions, whether intended or not, opened up to readers new dimensions of interpretative possibility.

Past, Present and Future

Like most monuments, the *Works* most immediately addressed its own present, revealing more about the current preoccupations of its bookseller and author than about either the past of Swift in print or the imagined future into which it was to be projected. Faulkner seems to have focused on memorialising the author on whom his future success was secured, and Swift on combining his posture of independence with the gratification of accumulated textual resentments, while supplying hints for notes expressive of an angry pride in his thwarted ambitions. (McLaverty's suggestion that 'the *Works* appeared in spite of as well as because of him', and that he 'was engaged in the editing of his works in a patchy, truculent, interfering way', seems painfully apt.[76]) But there was one vested interest that both bookseller and author had in common: both in their different ways needed an edition fit for the future, the former to assure his investment, the latter

---

[73] Vol. III, pp. 1, 48, 72.   [74] *Ibid.*, pp. 57, 360.   [75] *Ibid.*, p. 360.
[76] McLaverty, 'George Faulkner', pp. 154, 163.

The Works of J. S, D. D, D. S. P. D. *(1730–1735)*   233

his fame. Once again, tensions between the stable monument and the timely intervention, between the permanent and the topical, were played out in the material text.

One of the crucial attractions held out to subscribers in the Proposal had been the promise of an edition that would be 'compleat' as well as 'new', including additional 'small papers' that had already been published, two Drapier's letters that were 'never printed before', and 'many original Poems, that have hitherto only gone about in Manuscript'.[77] (And readers were artfully nudged to buy all four volumes, since there would be 'Pieces ... never before published' in 'each Volume'.[78]) They were also promised 'great Alterations' to the texts, and were supplied with more headnotes and footnotes than ever before; but despite a few loudly trumpeted changes to text and canon, most additions and changes to the text went unannounced. Although the *Works* looked like a compendium of Swift's varied engagements with the contexts and crises of his career, individual items might well mislead the reader as to how his published interventions had been staged at any specific historical moment. Works that had circulated among relatively small circles in manuscript now appeared alongside works that had been printed in multiple editions; and previously printed works also appeared, without comment, in texts significantly different from their original published forms. In sum, while it was repeatedly impressed upon the reader that Faulkner was offering a new and improved edition of an author distinguished for his heroic defiance, rather little was said about the specific verbal forms or modes of circulation through which that defiance had taken effect. In the light of Marshall's sense that 'Swift is so much an occasional writer that attending to particular provocations is crucial', and her emphasis on reading each work 'in its own specific moment', this might today be seen as a problem.[79] In 1735 it may have looked more like a purging of ephemeral particularity in favour of monumental permanence.

In this context, the fanfare given to a small minority of changes and additions was misleading. The most heavily advertised instance was the text of the *Travels*, where the case for revision was laboured in Proposal and published volumes alike: there is a close match between Swift's private correspondence and the Proposal's emphasis on the 1726 London edition's 'Alterations and Omissions without the Author's Knowledge and much to his Displeasure'. The Publisher's Preface to volume I also noted, in relation

---

[77] *Ibid.*, pp. 155–6.   [78] Series title, vol. I; Marshall, 'The "1735" Faulkner Edition', Appendix.
[79] Marshall, 'Swift on "Swift"', p. 362.

234   Part III: Dublin

to the abandoned prospect of a London Works, the corruption of previous publications by *some very injudicious Interpolations; particularly in the Voyages of Captain* Gulliver'; and the volume III title page also cited the additional damage inflicted by Hyde's careless reprinting ('In this Impression several Errors in the *London* and *Dublin* Editions are corrected'). Faulkner's 'Advertisement' to volume III further set out the issues regarding Tooke's editing for Motte; and it was immediately followed by Swift's prefatory 'A Letter from Capt. Gulliver to his Cousin Sympson', which Faulkner now printed for the first time.[80] (Dated 2 April 1727, it had probably reached Motte – perhaps to his relief – too late to be inserted into his editions.[81]) In a move reminiscent of the self-reflexive foregrounding of print process in the Drapier's letters, Swift's in-character riposte, refracted through Gulliver's post-Houyhnhnm perspective, now made the charges against the original publisher part of the story, prefixing them to a text correspondingly bolder in its satirical challenges.[82] It remains unclear exactly how far the 1735 text restored a previous text and how far it constructed a new one; but for Faulkner to be first publisher both of this revised text and of its fictionalised covering letter was a considerable coup. But to attain a clear understanding of the differences between the printed texts, early readers would still have needed to make their own comparison with the London *Travels* of 1726: it was crucial to the viability of a commercial project like Faulkner's that there was in the 1730s no expectation of anything like a historical collation.

Meanwhile, in volume IV, the Drapier's letters were subtly remodelled by silent changes. Davis notes slight but flagrantly defiant revisions of the letter to Molesworth – but ends by choosing Harding's originals as his copy text.[83] For though Faulkner's readings revealed what Swift had withheld at the time, or what he had thought since, it was Harding's text that had figured in the original crisis. The comparison underlines the *Works'* consistent focus on the author, and the author's updated text, rather than the reconstruction of original controversies. Yet volume IV also contained new works so exciting that Faulkner did, exceptionally, draw attention to them. These were two unpublished Drapier's letters that Swift had composed just as the tide finally turned against Wood's project, *To the Lord Chancellor Middleton* and *An Humble Address to both Houses of Parliament* (here numbered for the first time as Letters VI and VII).[84] They had not figured

---

[80] McLaverty first suggested Pilkington as provider of revisions ('George Faulkner', pp. 166–7), but now considers Ford the more likely.
[81] *CWJS Travels*, pp. lxxxii, 7–14, 641–3.   [82] McLaverty, 'George Faulkner', p. 167.
[83] Davis, *Drapier's Letters*, pp. lxxiv–lxxv, lxxviii–lxxix.   [84] Vol. IV, pp. 168–242.

The Works of J. S, D. D, D. S. P. D. *(1730–1735)*   235

in the print campaign against Wood's halfpence, nor been collected in *Fraud Detected*, and now appeared ten years after the crisis was over. In a special 'Advertisement to the Reader' Faulkner shared his inside knowledge.[85] He testified that the manuscript of Letter VI had the name of the author (self-identified as Dean of St Patrick's) *'subscribed at the End of the Original, although blotted out by some other Hand'*; he surmised that the evident success of the Drapier's campaign and the consequent displeasure of those in power might account for its being withheld from publication; and he suggested a date for Letter VII, as well as commenting favourably on the author's command of financial issues and the originality of his proposals (*'he hath specifyed several important Articles, that have not been taken Notice of by others who came after him'*). This rare instance of detailed comment on newly incorporated items was certainly helpful to readers wanting to understand the process of Swift's participation in the crisis: the separate 'Advertisement' not only trumpeted Faulkner's coup, but also ensured that no careful reader could mistake the new letters for part of the original sequence. Even so, the fact that they were now numbered VI and VII, following in sequence from Harding's original I–V, would make it increasingly difficult for future readers to focus on the Drapier's campaign as it had actually unfolded in time.

Another addition to volume IV, the 1708 *A Letter . . . concerning the Sacramental Test*, was also given unusual prominence in line with Swift's renewed campaign in support of the Test Act. (Already given exceptional attention in the 1711 *Miscellanies in Prose and Verse*, it had in 1733 been published by Faulkner, without his imprint, from the same setting of type as he now used for volume IV.[86]) The current significance of this early intervention was again strongly asserted: rather than being placed with the *Miscellanies in Prose* in volume I, the *Letter* was given pride of place at the beginning of volume IV; and a separate Advertisement, in unusually large type, gave only a brief account of the original context ('a Juncture, when the *Dissenters* were endeavouring to repeal the *Sacramental Test*'; 'The Speaker mentioned in this Letter was *Allen Broderick . . .* and the Prelate was Dr. *Lindsay*'; 'The Author . . . Personates a Member of Parliament here'), before moving on to apply the piece to current agitation against the Test ('as by common Fame, and some Pamphlets published to the same

---

[85] *Ibid.*, pp. 183–5.

[86] *Ibid.*, pp. 1–20. For its treatment in *Miscellanies in Prose and Verse*, see Chapter 4. Faulkner's separate issue was *A Letter from a Member of the House of Commons in Ireland, to a Member of the House of Commons in England, concerning the Sacramental Test. Written in the year 1708* (Dublin, 1733; TS 512A, *ESTC* N19756).

236   Part III: Dublin

Purpose, they seem now again attempting, with great Hope of Success').[87] Although the publisher, in offering 'an Extract' from this work, refers to the pruning of 'some Passages, which relate to certain Persons, and are of no Consequence to the Argument', the *Letter* had long ago dropped its imprudent suggestion that the Brodrick brothers should go hang themselves – which was just as well, given that one of the additional Drapier's letters was addressed to the elder brother, Lord Midleton.[88] Now, however, claims that 'the Author's Way of Reasoning seems at present to have more Weight, than it had in those Times, when the Discourse first appeared' are coupled with a wry footnote to Swift's claim that the Irish bishops 'will be all to a Man against repealing the *Test*': '*N.B.* Things are quite altered in that Bench, since this Discourse was written'.[89] One cost of thus deploying the 1708 *Letter* was its removal from its chronological sequence (its nearest neighbour in volume IV was the 1720 *Proposal for the Universal Use of Irish Manufacture*). The renewed threat to the Test Act had meanwhile been defeated in December 1733.

In contrast, most changes to text and canon were carried out with less fanfare, including the cancelling, at Swift's insistence, of verse that Faulkner had already printed for volume II. In August 1734 Swift wrote in typically evasive terms to Edward, Lord Oxford, apparently referring in whole or in part to this volume:

> As to the Printer, All he has done or will do in the matter is against my Will. Neither have I concerned my self further with him than to let him know that if he should publish any thing offensive or unworthy, as mine, he should have cause to repent it ... I have put the Man under some Difficultyes by ordering certain Things to be struck out after they were printed, which some friends had given him. This hath delayed his work, and as I hear, given him much trouble and difficulty to adjust. Farther I know not; for the whole affair is a great vexation to me.[90]

Readers may perhaps have noticed that the spine of volume II was thicker than the number of printed pages could properly account for, owing to the presence of remaining stubs; but without inside knowledge it would have been difficult to work out what had happened and why.[91]

In addition to Swift's private letter to Oxford, the evidence now available also includes two copies which, exceptionally, contain both the

---

[87] Vol. IV, pp. i–ii; and, for further comment, McLaverty, 'George Faulkner', pp. 168–9.
[88] See Chapter 3.   [89] Vol. IV, p. 12.
[90] Carpenter and J. Woolley, 'Faulkner's *Volume II*', p. 49; *Corr*, vol. III, pp. 752–3.
[91] On the relative thickness of volumes, see Carpenter and J. Woolley, 'Faulkner's *Volume II*', p. 48.

The Works of J. S, D. D, D. S. P. D. *(1730–1735)*   237

replacement poems and the original cancelled poems (one apparently made up by a binder in error, the other deliberately reconstructed at a later date using cancelled poems from Faulkner's stock).[92] This evidence suggests that, as James Woolley has recently concluded, the cancellation (not necessarily carried out as a single operation) 'was designed both to preserve Swift's ethical character as a satirist and to shield Faulkner from prosecution or other governmental harassment'.[93] (On the first point, Weedon cites parallel testimony from Faulkner, who in 1746 excused himself from adding to the *Works* '*a few satyrical Pieces on particular Persons*' on the grounds that '*the Author laid repeated Commands on his Printer, never to publish such Pieces of Private Resentment*'.[94]) Even before the cancellation, Karian argues, Faulkner's planned chronology had been distorted by the addition of 'dozens of poems' not available when printing first began, and cancellation only made things worse.[95] Marshall further emphasises the replacement of trenchant satire (including the disastrous *An Epistle to a Lady*, the two parts of *Traulus* and *A Dialogue between Mad Mullinix and Timothy*) by domestic and sociable pieces.[96] These too could be offensive, if in quite other ways: the politically explosive *An Epistle to a Lady* was replaced by *A Panegyric on the D—n*, whose explicitness about sanitary arrangements was not calculated to enhance the author's reputation.[97] Whatever its prudential and ethical rationale, the cancelled volume was likely to strike readers as both disorderly and problematic. Although Carpenter and J. Woolley suggest that 'with the passage of time, Faulkner probably became willing to cooperate with an interested customer who wanted to preserve the original texts', it seems unlikely that many early readers would have sought or achieved this level of insight.[98]

Meanwhile, another glaring omission from the 1735 *Works* was by now so familiar that it probably passed almost without remark. Faulkner's *Works* was in many ways a supplementation of the long-standing miscellany tradition as reconfigured in London in 1727–32; and it usefully claimed for Swift many pieces whose attribution had not been explicitly stated in those volumes.[99] Yet ever since the publication of the fifth edition of the *Tale* in 1710 and *Miscellanies in Prose and Verse* in 1711 the former had

---

[92] The former of these was identified by Weedon in 1967 in 'An Uncancelled Copy', the latter in 2019 by Carpenter and J. Woolley in 'Faulkner's *Volume II*' (and see pp. 54–8 for the different likely causes of the copies' respective anomalies).

[93] Carpenter and J. Woolley, 'Faulkner's *Volume II*', p. 53.

[94] Weedon, 'An Uncancelled Copy', p. 51.   [95] Karian, 'Swift as a Manuscript Poet', p. 43.

[96] Weedon, 'An Uncancelled Copy', p. 54; Marshall, 'The "1735" Faulkner Edition', pp. 165–8.

[97] Vol. II, pp. 281–94.   [98] Carpenter and J. Woolley, 'Faulkner's *Volume II*', p. 56.

[99] See Introduction to deattributed poems in *CWJS Poems* IV (forthcoming).

238   Part III: Dublin

been kept strictly away from the latter; and the *Works* did not challenge that conventional separation. (In 1763 Faulkner would indeed cite it as a particular mark of his 'Friendship and Intimacy' with Swift 'that he owned to him his being Author of the *Tale* of a *Tub*'.[100]) Yet while this genuine masterpiece was rebuffed, much weaker attributions slipped in. Here, bold as brass, appeared the highly dubious *The Wonder of all the Wonders, that ever the World Wondered at*.[101] Unlike the more securely attributed *The Wonderful Wonder of Wonders*, which preceded it in volume I, it had not been included in the 1727–32 *Miscellanies*. Its inclusion in *Works* implied a status which was almost certainly erroneous; but once in place it would be hard to dislodge.

More general implications of presentation and styling now reinforced the distancing of the *Works* from original print forms. It was, for example, almost thirty years since the Bickerstaff papers had launched their discrete print interventions from their variously occluded points of origin; *A Famous Prediction of Merlin* had long lacked the woodcut that had originally linked it back to Partridge's campaign against Gadbury (though Faulkner still set the verse in the now even more outmoded quaintness of black letter); and even the Drapier's letters were a decade removed from the expressive disorderliness of Harding's blotchy, cramped and varied typography.[102] In these respects the *Works* consolidated a long-visible preference, stretching back through 1727–32 into the 1711 *Miscellanies in Prose and Verse*, for promoting textual dignity over the expressive relation of first printings to their original contexts. Along similar lines, there were also pervasive linguistic changes, as texts were restyled in line with Swift's expressed concern for correcting and future-proofing the English language.[103] Faulkner evidently shared Swift's attraction towards 'formal, old-fashioned' presentation, and further intensified it even after his death: *Tatler* no. 230 and *A Proposal for Correcting, Improving and Ascertaining the English Tongue* provided a clear programme, and Swift himself may have further pressed the case (which would be consistent with the report that he had in 1735 felt moved to 'correct . . . all the abbreviations and elisions which were ordinary in the beginning of the century' before giving a copy of the *Tale* as a present).[104] The changes

---

[100] *PW*, vol. XIII, p. 203.   [101] Vol. I, pp. 257–62 (perhaps by Sheridan).
[102] *Ibid.*, pp. 148–85, 238–42; vol. IV, pp. 59–182.   [103] *CWJS Parodies*, pp. lxxix, 622.
[104] *CWJS Tale*, pp. 281–3; Scott, *Works*, vol. I, p. 90; McLaverty, 'George Faulkner', p. 165; Daniel Cook, 'Publishing Posthumous Swift: Deane Swift to Walter Scott', in *JS Book*, pp. 214–30, pp. 225–6.

The Works of J. S, D. D, D. S. P. D. *(1730–1735)*   239

in part anticipated future directions in standard printed forms (more grammatical punctuation; more consistent spelling; avoidance of abbreviations and elisions); but Swift's preference for the archaic third person in '–eth' (rather than the modern '–s') would only look odder with the passage of time. This increasingly formal style tended to mute the demotic verve of Swift's earlier writings, shuffling his variously preposterous characters willy-nilly towards linguistic hyper-correction: linguistically as well as typographically, Swift in print became more dignified but less incisive.

Faulkner's headnotes and footnotes were a crucial factor in distinguishing the *Works* from preceding collections. They recorded testimony that would soon slip out of living memory; they contributed to Swift's long-term memorialisation; and they shaped interpretation in a direction consistent with his beliefs and commitments. Yet, especially by contrast with the strategic authorial annotation that would distinguish Pope's octavo *Works* of 1735–6, it is striking how erratically they were supplied: although Faulkner made a consistent attempt to give a date of composition for the shorter pieces (thus underlining the emphasis on the author's writing rather than publishing history), many works have no other headnote or footnotes at all.[105] The notes that do appear are scanty and inconsistent in coverage – indeed, their familiarity in modern discussions of particular texts can give a misleading sense of their actual function within the *Works*. Where Faulkner has – or has been given – something particular to say, he says it; otherwise he remains silent. The Bickerstaff papers, which occur nearly 150 pages into volume I, are the first items to have headnotes at all, but these notes are anecdotal, unsystematic, and in part misleading.[106] The first begins with the now-familiar story of how the author had derived the *'somewhat uncommon'* surname from a locksmith's sign. Quickly, however, by way of Steele's later use of the Bickerstaff character in the *Tatler*, the headnote veers off into unhelpful and unsubstantiated hints about the *'considerable Part'* played by *'the Author'* in the *Tatler* and *Spectator*.[107] (Faulkner, who first printed in the body of volume I only Swift's well-attested *Tatler* no. 230, later added to the confusion by sweeping up, into an extra

---

[105] McLaverty, *Pope, Print and Meaning*, pp. 209–41.   [106] Vol. I, p. 148.

[107] For the accumulation of dubious claims about Swift's contributions to these periodicals, see *CWJS Parodies*, Appendix G: 'The Attribution to Swift of Further *Tatlers* and *Spectators*', pp. 583–601. While Swift was clearly generous in sharing ideas for the *Tatler* and contributed some verse to particular numbers, it is far from clear that he composed additional essays.

240   Part III: Dublin

signature that is visibly an afterthought, two numbers written by Swift
for Harrison's continuation, with a headnote wrongly assigning them
to the *Tatler* proper.[108]) Yet the Bickerstaff papers also demonstrated
the potential of a headnote to put on record potentially useful
testimony that might otherwise have passed out of memory: the
headnote to the non-Swiftian *'Squire Bickerstaff Detected*, for instance,
offers the claim that *'The following Piece, under the Name of* John
Partrige, *was written by that famous Poet* Nicholas Row' (whereas 1727
had commented only that it was *'not written by the same Hand'*, i.e.
not by Swift).[109] The Bickerstaff papers also display a scattering of
brief footnotes; and of these, some seem particularly close to Swift,
e.g. *'This is Fact, as the Author was assured by Sir Paul Methuen, then
Ambassador to that Crown'* [i.e. Portugal], or *'The Quotations here
inserted are in Imitation of Dr.* Bentley, *in some Part of the famous
Controversy between him and* Charles Boyle, *Esq; afterwards Earl of*
Orrery.'[110] Yet while such notes provide, in the aggregate, a valuable
archive of privileged information, they are also scanty, unsystematic
and far from uniformly reliable.

In keeping with the preoccupations of the *Works* as a whole, there
was no consistent attempt to place Swift's writings in relation to the
contexts originally addressed. The first item in volume I, for example,
was *Contests and Dissensions*, written and published more than thirty
years previously: following the 1711 *Miscellanies in Prose and Verse*,
Faulkner provided the date of 1701 and remained silent about Swift's
early Whig commitment, leaving Swift's anti-populist agenda to be
silently assimilated to his familiar Toryism.[111] When notes did occur,
they often served as much to vent his pain and prejudice as to furnish
information. In volume II, a brief headnote to the 1713 poem *The
Faggot* echoed the unhappy circumstances in which Swift had left
London before the Queen's death, *'when the* QUEEN's *Ministers were*

---

[108] The headnote reads: *'The Printer and Publisher hereof having been in* London *after the first Volume
was printed off, met with the following* TATLERS, *which are supposed to be wrote by the Author of the
foregoing Works; and as they were never printed in this Kingdom, we hope they will be acceptable to our
Readers.'* In the duodecimo reprint (vol. I, p. 193), which integrates the two essays into the body of
the volume, it is replaced by a differently misleading headnote: *'The two following* TATLERS *are
not in the Volumes published by Sir* Richard Steele' (who would have known better than anyone that
they did not belong). For Swift's involvement in Harrison's continuation, see *CWJS Parodies*,
pp. 663–6.
[109] Vol. I, p. 167; *CWJS Parodies*, Appendix D: ''Squire Bickerstaff Detected', pp. 565–6.
[110] Vol. I, pp. 178–9. For Swift's involvement with notes, see McLaverty, 'George Faulkner', p. 165.
[111] Vol. I, pp. 1–55; see Chapter 4.

The Works of J. S, D. D, D. S. P. D. *(1730–1735)* 241

quarrelling among themselves.[112] A footnote to the 1725 poem *Wood, an Insect* explained its subject's desire to be 'out of Danger' in ignominious (and inaccurate) terms: '*He was in Jayl for Debt.*'[113] A footnote to the 1724 poem *Whitshed's Motto on his Coach* denigrated the subject as '*That infamous Chief Justice, who twice prosecuted the Drapier, and dissolved the Grand Jury for not finding the Bill against him.*'[114] In volume I, *A Proposal for Correcting ... the English Tongue* was introduced to particularly wistful effect. The headnote claimed that '*if the Queen had lived a Year or two longer, the following Proposal would in all Probability have taken Effect*', and stated that '*the Lord Treasurer had already nominated several Persons ... and resolved to use his Credit with Her Majesty, that a Fund should be applyed to support the Expence of a large Room*'.[115] The tone was closer to wishful advocacy than objective analysis: '*this Scheme fell to the Ground, partly by the Dissentions among the great Men at Court; but chiefly by the lamented Death of that glorious Princess*'.[116] Meanwhile other headnotes, altogether bouncier in tone, teased readers with Swift's anonymous shadow-boxing against nonconformists, Whigs and Hanoverians, explaining in a headnote to *On Poetry, a Rapsody* that '*we thought proper to insert it in this Collection: And although the Author be not known, yet we hope it will be acceptable to our Readers*'.[117] The headnote to *On the Words – Brother Protestants, and Fellow Christians* is almost identical.[118]

It was a further sign of the intended but now aborted centrality of the Drapier to Faulkner's plan that the most consistently informative headnotes and footnotes were reserved for volume IV. (This, the volume based on his own *Fraud Detected*, contained the material whose texts and contexts Faulkner knew best.) The tone was predictably partisan. Swift's courage and effectiveness were emphasised, for instance, in relation to the inflammatory Letter IV:

> N.B. *This was the Letter against which the Lord Lieutenant* (Carteret) *and Council, issued a Proclamation, offering three Hundred Pounds to discover the*

---

[112] Vol. II, p. 97; *CWJS Poems* I (forthcoming).

[113] Vol. II, p. 365; *CWJS Poems* II (forthcoming).

[114] Vol. II, p. 279; *CWJS Poems* II (forthcoming). Harsher condemnation of Whitshed had been printed in a note to the cancelled *An Excellent New Song on a Seditious Pamplet*, but was somewhat moderated in subsequent reprinting (Weedon, 'An Uncancelled Copy', p. 49).

[115] Vol. I, p. 186.

[116] For Swift's dealings with Harley in relation to the proposed Academy, see *CWJS Parodies*, pp. 124–7.

[117] Vol. II, p. 433.   [118] *Ibid.*, p. 472.

242   Part III: Dublin

Author; *and for which*, Harding *the Printer was tried before one* Whitshed, *then Chief Justice*: *But the noble Jury would not find the Bill*; *nor would any Person discover the Author.*[119]

Footnotes also named persons referred to, glossed Irish terms, and provided cross-references, making the Irish tracts more accessible for readers who might not be Irish themselves. But the notes also expressed the *Works'* orientation to the present by noting later developments, many unwelcome. A footnote to Letter IV, for instance, noted Walpole's subsequent knighthood ('*Mr.* Walpole, *now Sir* Robert'), and another lamented the weavers' refusal to act on the Drapier's advice to 'contrive some decent Stuffs and Silks for *Clergymen*, at reasonable Rates', a scheme which '*was . . . often urged to the Weavers by the supposed Author*; *but he could never prevail on them to put it in Practice*'.[120] But the spoof *The Last Speech and Dying Words of Ebenezor Elliston*, reprinted towards the end of the volume, had a more encouraging (if scarcely convincing) tale to tell: '*this Speech had so good an Effect, that there have been very few Robberies of that kind committed since*'.[121] In contrast, no headnotes or footnotes were deemed necessary to volume III, the *Travels*, which was now further contextualised, from within the fiction, by 'A Letter from Capt. Gulliver to his Cousin Sympson.'[122]

Authorship and Authority

Given that Swift's publishing had so often been characterised by abdication, ambiguity and evasion, it is not surprising that his role in the 1735 *Works* should be difficult to establish. With Swift's own memorialisation so awkwardly at stake, there was evidently no question of adopting the hands-on collaboration so excitedly pursued with Barber during the political emergencies of the Queen's last ministry. Now, as previously during the Drapier affair, his printer was only half an hour's walk from the Deanery; so the delegate-and-depart routine he had long ago established with Tooke was hardly viable either. Swift never went as far in publicly staging his detachment from Faulkner as he had from Harding, but the difficulty of his complicity seems to have been reflected in the opacity of his dealings.

In publishing terms, Swift was now both an opportunity and a nightmare. He had lived on, somewhat awkwardly, from his late early modern formation in a small Irish print world regulated by royal patent

---

[119] Vol. IV, p. 128.   [120] *Ibid.*, pp. 142, 234.   [121] *Ibid.*, p. 375.   [122] Vol. III, pp. i–vi.

into a period when Pope, in the larger and less commercially constrained London trade, was demonstrating the viability of writing as a profession – and his innovations had not always worked to Swift's advantage. If Pope's shrewdness and confidence had secured Swift £200 for the *Travels*, he had also been deeply offended by Pope's promotion of his own interests in the *Miscellanies*. The writings of a clergyman formed in a diplomatic household of the late seventeenth century were more readily conceptualised within an older framework, either as sociable amusement or as service to nation and establishment; and after 1714, when possessed as Dean of St Patrick's of a full-time occupation and the income and public profile to go with it, Swift had no need of an additional profession. Yet if we turn from behind-the-scenes contention to what was actually published, it is striking how insistently the paratexts staged their own representation of contested authority. Whatever allowance might need to be made for authorial pressure and book-trade self-fashioning, the mediating voice performed as 'the publisher'; and it was plain from the *Works*' Proposal and titles that that publisher was George Faulkner.

As to the identity of the author, things were necessarily more complicated. Faulkner's series title attributed the *Works* to '*J. S, D. D, D. S. P. D.*', a defence by now not so much attenuated as untenable (McLaverty calls it 'a deference to the authorities rather than a disguise').[123] The initials of Swift's name (in italics), his degree of Doctor of Divinity, and his status as Dean of St Patrick's Cathedral, Dublin, were all set out at the top of the title page: Swift's identity would have been obvious even had he been a less conspicuous Dean. Meanwhile the imprint highlighted Faulkner as undertaker of the project: 'Printed by and for GEORGE FAULKNER, Printer and Bookseller, in ESSEX-STREET, opposite to the Bridge.' On the volume titles of volumes I and II this was further emphasised by the GF monogram that occupied the central portion of the page. In contrast, Motte's monogram on the titles of *Miscellanies* (probably designed by Pope) had referred only to the authors ('AP/JS' – although the centrality to the design of Pope's own 'A' might, in retrospect, have hinted at impending difficulties from an author on his way to becoming his own bookseller). Faulkner's monogram, in contrast, pointed openly to himself. Yet he was hardly slighting his author's claims, for he had also impressed Swift's likeness on every volume in the form of a Vertue frontispiece. Two of these images, the emblematic tributes to Swift as Drapier in volume IV and as master of familiar verse in volume

---

[123] McLaverty, 'George Faulkner', p. 168.

244   Part III: Dublin

II, explicitly associated his likeness with his works; the frontispiece to volume I was professedly a portrait of Dean Swift; and the Gulliver frontispiece in volume III was suspiciously like that portrait.

Asserting the authority of the author in the *Works* was crucial; but Swift (so adept at appearing as Bickerstaff, or T. N. Philomath, or the entrepreneur of the *Tale* or *A Modest Proposal*) continued to cling to nominal anonymity. Faulkner addressed the issue primarily in the introductory remarks that he provided for each volume, performing a mediation of authority couched for the most part in the deferential mode of the Proposal, and referring to himself simply as 'the publisher'. Although this self-effacing figure began, in the Preface to volume I, by citing '*great Encouragement from both Kingdoms*' for his publication of '*the Works supposed to be written by the Reverend Dr. S. D. S. P. D.*', he remained strategically silent as to whether any of that encouragement had come from the person whom he now routinely referred to as '*the supposed Author*'. Indeed, he went to the nub of the problem when he identified the 1712 *A Proposal for Correcting . . . the English Tongue* as the author's sole previous publication under his own name.[124] At the same time, by citing Swift's letter to Lord Midleton (which would be incorporated into volume IV) as a signed but previously unpublished piece, he emphasised his familiarity with Swift's manuscripts: '*we found the Name subscribed at Length in the original Manuscript*'. Nevertheless, he still represented himself as no more than '*complying with the general Opinion, which hath fixed certain Writings both in Verse and Prose upon him, whether truly or no we shall not presume to determine*', even while he pinpointed '*the unavoidable Consequence*' of false attributions in the face of the author's refusal to provide '*the least Satisfaction, by owning or denying it*'. Yet he spoke much more assertively, even tartly, when he rested his authority on his own trade: '*many others were vulgarly fixed on him, which a Writer much inferior (at least if Printers and Booksellers were to be the Judges) might have just Reason to complain of*'. The publisher may adopt a guarded and deferential manner; but print professionals know what they know.[125]

The publisher's distancing rhetoric also made considerable use of '*the supposed Author's Friends*' (although McLaverty shrewdly notes that by 1763 these 'intermediaries' had disappeared from Faulkner's account, and suggests that 'little suggestions of exasperation' in the 1735 introductions may

---

[124] This suggests that he did not know of the signed covering letter to *Ode to the Athenian Society* (not included in the *Works*).

[125] Davis indeed notes occasional lapses in volume IV by which Swift's name is given in full (Davis, *Drapier's Letters*, p. xciii).

The Works of J. S, D. D, D. S. P. D. *(1730–1735)* 245

hint at some kind of direct working relationship).[126] In the Preface to volume I a whole range of effects were laid at the door of these '*Friends*': unauthorised publications via leaky coterie circulation; two years' worth of requests to the supposed author to authorise a new edition; and a general supervision by their '*Advice and Direction*' – to which this publisher apparently deferred where others might not. Under allowance, '*the supposed Author's Friends*' also provided editorial and proof-reading services: they '*were pleased to correct many gross Errors, and strike out some very injudicious Interpolations*'; '*the supposed Author was prevailed on to suffer some Friends to review and correct the Sheets after they were printed; and sometimes he condescended, as we have heard, to give them his own Opinion*'; the selection of poems '*generally ascribed to the same Author*' was '*entirely submitted to the Directions of his Friends*'; and '*his Friends in* England' were solicited for '*as many original Pieces as were possible to be got*' ('*which we found a great Difficulty in Procuring*'). The passive voice further distanced the publisher from such sources of authority. He noted that '*we have been advised to observe the following Order*' (which, with its relegation of the Drapier to volume IV, seriously disrupted his original design); and even his Preface was constrained by the short leash on which he found himself – though he hinted at the hope of getting in a few words of his own later on: '*This is all we have been allowed to prefix as a general Preface; but before each of the three ensuing Volumes, there may perhaps be a short Advertisement.*' Even when the publisher spoke in what seemed to be his own voice, it was with the distancing plurality of a corporate '*we*' – and this '*we*' was most confident in its understanding of the bookseller's business, as witnessed by the Preface's final justification of the edition's rising cost and receding publication date.

The deference established in the volume I Preface was equally in evidence in each '*short Advertisement*' that followed. In volume II, *Poetical Works*, the resulting composition read very much as a sandwich in which Swift, by whatever means, had provided the filling. The first of the four paragraphs was the publisher's: he noted the appearance of '*this Author's Writings*' in *Miscellanies in Prose and Verse* (1711), but carefully specified only that the Preface to the 1727 *Miscellanies* was '*signed* J. Swift *and* A. Pope'. As before, it was in his professional role that he spoke most decisively, noting the presence of material '*by the supposed Author's Friends*' in the latter volumes and asserting, in contrast, '*our Intention only to publish the Works of one Writer*'. Yet even in highlighting his expansion of the poetical works '*by above a third Part*' he resorted to the passive voice; and '*the supposed Author's Friends*'

---

[126] McLaverty, 'George Faulkner', p. 164.

246   Part III: Dublin

made their ritual appearance as sources for previously unprinted poems ('*who at their earnest Request were permitted to take Copies*'). The publisher's second and third paragraphs, while acknowledging his commercial interest and paying homage to the '*Writer, from whose Works we hope to receive some Benefit*', also cited '*several Persons of great Judgment*'. What followed were familiar topics of Swiftian self-representation (the absolute originality of his writings, the innocence of satires that aim only '*to reform the Errors of both Sexes*', his solicitation of favours for Whigs from the Queen's Tory ministry, his steady profession of Whig principles), suggesting that, while Faulkner was holding the pen and intermediaries might well be involved, the sentiments were those of the author himself. Only in the short final paragraph did the publisher's active (if still plural) voice break through:

> *Our Intentions were to print the Poems according to the Time they were writ in; but we could not do it so exactly as we desired, because we could never get the least Satisfaction in that or many other Circumstances from the supposed Author.*

Swift, of course, had done far worse than this; for his insistence on cancelling poems already printed had created additional disorder, as well as diluting the volume's intensity. But there was no need to tell readers everything: the Advertisement said enough to acknowledge the imperfect chronology, without specifying further grounds for potential dissatisfaction – still less broaching awkward questions about the precise nature of Swift's involvement.

In volume III the publisher's extremely brief Advertisement almost went so far as to declare itself redundant, since the newly published letter supposed to be written by Gulliver to his cousin would supposedly '*make a long Advertisement unnecessary*'. As before, he avoided naming names and attributed action to others: '*a Person since deceased*' (i.e. Andrew Tooke) was to blame for claiming that '*her late Majesty … governed without a Chief Minister*'; he did not understand '*the Scheme of the Author*'; he was not '*able to imitate his plain simple Style*'. On the positive side, '*a very worthy Gentleman in* London, *and a most intimate Friend of the Authors*' (probably Ford) transcribed original readings, and '*the same Gentleman did us the Favour to let us transcribe his Corrections*'. Meanwhile, the publisher reverted once more to plural passivity ('*We are assured, that the Copy … was a Transcript of the Original*'). The Advertisement to volume IV rounded off the first stage of his project in similar style, although with the professional satisfaction of being able to declare not only that this volume 'compleats the Set', but also that to the Drapier's letters 'we have added two which were never printed before'.

The Works of J. S, D. D, D. S. P. D. *(1730–1735)* 247

For the rest, he loaded the Drapier with praise while maintaining the rhetorical distinction between active agents (the Drapier and his friends) and passive (himself, Harding, and an '*Amanuensis*' rewarded for '*his Fidelity*'). He ends on a note of abdication: '*This is enough for the Information of future Readers, because the Author in the Course of his Letters, gives full Satisfaction upon all Particulars necessary to be known.*' It is almost as if Swift really has, as Drapier, written that 'small portable Volume' that makes all other writing redundant.[127] Whatever had gone on behind the scenes, the probity of Faulkner's respect for his author, and his shrewdness about his own business, were kept continually before the reader's eye.

Faulkner's regular supply of pre-publication sheets to Bowyer now enabled Bowyer's associate Charles Davis to publish, in 1735, *Miscellanies, in Prose and Verse. Volume the Fifth*, soon followed by *A Collection of Poems, &c. Omitted in the Fifth Volume of Miscellanies in Prose and Verse*, which added the poems substituted for those cancelled from Faulkner's volume II.[128] In Dublin, meanwhile, Fairbrother, who had in 1733 added a third volume to his original two-volume *Miscellanies*, now issued a final catch-up volume IV, boldly explaining that having seen the four volumes of *Works*, 'wherein are several Pieces not in my Edition, as there are very many valuable Tracts both in Prose and Verse in my Three Volumes 12°. entirely omitted in the other', he would now complete his set with 'the Works ... that have been Printed since my last Edition of the said Works': by way of balance, he also offered 'several Poems ... taken from the D—ns own Original Manuscripts, never before Printed'.[129] But despite Fairbrother's bravado, he had offended Swift by his politics, by his poor return to Sheridan for supplying Swift material, and probably now also by his undercutting of Faulkner's *Works*. By 1735 he was for Swift 'an arrant Rascal' and 'a Fellow I have never been able to endure', and in 1736 he and Sheridan dubbed him 'Fowlbrother'.[130] Although Fairbrother now brought into the canon manuscript material from 'The Whimsical Medley', and reprinted both the rare Pindaric *An Ode. To the King* (first published 1691) and the

---

[127] *CWJS Tale*, p. 82.

[128] For Davis's volume and its supplement, see Chapter 6. For the registration of copy to Bowyer, Davis and Thomas Woodward, see Fischer, 'Swift's *Miscellanies*', p. 77.

[129] 'The Publishers Preface' , *Vol. IV. of the Miscellanies begun by Jonathan Swift, D.D. and Alexander Pope, Esq. containing all the tracts in prose and verse that have been since done by J. S. D. D. S. P. D. to compleat the three former volumes. To which are added several other poems by the same author, many of which are printed from original manuscripts, not in any former edition* (Dublin, 1735; TS 33 (4), *ESTC* T207623). See J. Woolley, 'The Circulation of Verse', p. 143.

[130] *CWJS Parodies*, pp. 625; *Corr.*, vol. IV, pp. 280–1, 285–7, 293–5, 297–9.

248   Part III: Dublin

punning April fool's joke *A History of Poetry* (first published 1726), this was the end of a reprinting project, not the beginning of a rival Works.[131]

In contrast, back in London, it was not the Dublin *Works* but the English rights in *Miscellanies* that Davis had to worry about: he explained that although 'it would have been injurious to the *English* Buyer, as well as Proprietor, to have reprinted here the *Dublin* Edition of his Works', his new volume V contained only 'such Pieces as are Not in the forementioned Volumes, but contain every thing in the Dublin Edition besides'.[132] This not only made clear that the initiative now rested with the Dublin *Works*, but also emphasised Davis's respect for London copyright. Its enforceability, so attractive to Swift but so obstructive to the London Works he would have preferred, now generated a further irony: one of the reasons we know so much about the publication of the *Works* is that Motte successfully took legal action against its distribution in England (the duodecimo reprint being a particular provocation).[133] Swift's writings had previously been in court because of what they said, but now they were in court because of what they were worth.

---

[131] For the *Ode*, see *CWJS Poems* I (forthcoming); for the *History*, see *CWJS Parodies*, pp. 219–27, 684–7.

[132] *Miscellanies . . . Volume the Fifth*, Advertisement (on verso of title); for transcription, see TS, p. 10.

[133] McLaverty, 'George Faulkner', pp. 162, 171.

PART IV

Into the Future

CHAPTER 8

Ending and Going On (1736–1765)

By 1735 Swift and Swift in print were approaching the brink of their final separation. At first Swift continued to send important new poems and prose to press (while personal letters began to appear through the machinations of Pope and Curll). But Swift's agency diminished as he became increasingly deaf, frail and forgetful, and from 1742 his affairs were managed by guardians: his death in 1745 caused hardly a ripple in the onward progress of Swift in print. *Directions to Servants*, finally sent to Faulkner unfinished and unfinishable, was published only a few days after Swift's death, with a Preface that shifted Faulkner's long-practised performance of mediated authority smoothly into posthumous mode.

Only twenty years later, most (but not all) of the works that we now receive as Swift's would be circulating in print, while major changes had been proposed, and sometimes carried through, in the editing and presentation of collected Works. At first Faulkner maintained his dominance, with Bowyer as his London collaborator; but by 1751 imprints showed Bowyer pooling his resources with Charles Bathurst's associates in the *Miscellanies* tradition derived from Motte, signalling a shift of textual dynamic from Dublin to London. By 1743 the London *Miscellanies* had incorporated the *Tale*; and in 1751, only a few years after Swift's death, the *Tale* and the *Travels* assumed their now familiar place at the head of *The Works of Dr. Jonathan Swift*, an evolution of the London *Miscellanies* which now proclaimed Swift's authorship without prevarication.[1] Old motives for pussy-footing round Swift's insistences lost their force in Dublin also, and Faulkner quickly began to give Swift's name in full; but by the time he formally incorporated the *Tale* into the *Works* in 1762 it was too late for a chronological restructuring of his once-pioneering edition.[2] In this posthumous period the status of editors was also changing, as proposals, titles and paratexts gave increasing emphasis to their

---

[1] TS headnotes, 66 and 82.
[2] For Swift's name, see TS 44 (1746); for Faulkner and the *Tale*, see below.

251

252 Part IV: Into the Future

discrete contributions. Although a personal connection to the author remained the typical editorial qualification down to the end of the century, it was clear by mid-century that an editor of Swift did not need to share Swift's views, nor even, necessarily, to have met him. John Hawkesworth (1720–1773), a freelance man of letters who exemplified a new formation in print culture, was apparently not the booksellers' first choice for the London *Works* of 1755; but his role as editor was nevertheless blazoned across its title. Soon afterwards, in 1758, the first publication of *The History of the Four Last Years of the Queen* was edited by an anonymous commentator whose boasted acquaintance with Swift seemed only to have sharpened his political hostility.

The Swift editions of the later eighteenth century, predating by at least a century the academic study of English literature in universities and schools, continued to court a general book-buying public: it was not expected that editors should print everything, nor that they should distinguish explicitly between pieces printed for the first time and pieces previously printed but uncollected, nor that they should routinely report variant readings over time, nor that they should supply extensive contextual or interpretative commentary (though Hawkesworth did begin the tradition of including a prefatory biography). The issue of how far to extend the printed canon proved particularly troublesome. Swift's habit of circulating (or retaining) unpublished pieces in manuscript, combined with the incapacity of his last years, produced a predictably long tail of first publications. These could in theory enhance the profile of an already compelling author and constitute a unique selling point for a new edition; but once the last two large prose works had appeared in 1745 and 1758 (*Directions to Servants* and *The History of the Four Last Years of the Queen*), much of what was added was slight, repetitive or unfinished.[3] Manuscripts were in any case so widely distributed that a co-ordinated policy was impracticable. Faulkner's appropriations were disapprovingly noted by the clergyman and antiquarian John Lyon (1710–1790), who had acted as Swift's amanuensis and managed his finances in his last years: in 1783 he commented to Swift's cousin Deane Swift (1707–1783) that 'Many things did fall in my way as Executor of Mrs. Dingley ... But Faulkner very easily got everything that he thought fit to take without fee or reward.'[4] Deane Swift himself acquired through his mother-in-law,

---

[3] Cook, 'Publishing Posthumous Swift', pp. 216, 218, 220–3; for examples see *CWJS Parodies* (p. 158), *CWJS English Political Writings, 1711–1714* (p. 335).

[4] *PW*, vol. XIII, p. xi; for Lyon and his manuscripts, see *ODNB* ('John Lyon'); A. C. Elias, Jr, 'Swift's *Don Quixote*, Dunkin's *Virgil Travesty*, and Other New Intelligence: John Lyon's "Materials for a Life of Dr. Swift"', *SStud*, 13 (1998), 27–104.

Ending and Going On (1736–1765) 253

Martha Whiteway, a major collection whose highlights he would add to Hawkesworth's edition in 1765; Delany and Laetitia Pilkington included in their published reflections small items that testified to their intimacy with the Dean; and further material continued to circulate well outside Swift's immediate circle.[5]

But new content was far from the whole story, for one of the major ways in which the London booksellers seized the initiative was by remodelling style and format. At one extreme the impact would be as unignorable as the luxurious large quarto offered as part of Hawkesworth's 1755 *Works*; at the other it was as inconspicuous as the italic semicolon, whose discreet obliquity marked in 1765 the transmutation of Swift's manuscript inscriptions into Deane Swift's published texts, exemplifying the posthumous movement of Swift in print towards modes of typographical expression unthought of in his lifetime.[6] Deane Swift's 1765 expansion of the published canon was itself published as part of the Hawkesworth edition, and Faulkner's immediate reprinting, along with his unfulfilled aspiration to produce a quarto *Works* of his own, confirmed that the Dublin influence established in the 1730s by his transmission of pre-publication sheets to Bowyer had now gone into reverse.

Last Poems (1736, 1739)

Two outstanding political poems were published for the first time in this final period: *A Character of the Legion Club* and *Verses on the Death of Doctor Swift. Written by Himself: Nov. 1731*. Their respective onslaughts on Irish and English elites brought Swift's career as published poet to a climactic conclusion, and, in keeping with the dynamics of that career, the form and manner of their early publication were significantly odd, demonstrating the unavoidable limitations of authorial control under conditions that combined manuscript circulation with legal jeopardy. The first, *A Character of the Legion Club*, was a verse tirade against the Irish House of Commons, prompted in general by its hostility, as Swift saw

---

[5] For the services rendered to Swift by Martha Whiteway (1690–1768), and for her daughter's marriage to Deane Swift in 1739, see Ehrenpreis, *Swift*, vol. III, pp. 806–7, 875–6, 904–5. For the first publication of *On Good-Manners and Good-Breeding* by Patrick Delany in *Observations upon Lord Orrery's Remarks on the Life and Writings of Jonathan Swift* (London, 1754), see *CWJS Parodies*, pp. 677–8; and for Laetitia Pilkington's incorporation of *A Certificate for a Discarded Servant* into *The Third and Last Volume of the Memoirs of Mrs. Laetitia Pilkington* (London, 1754), see *CWJS Parodies*, pp. 615–17, and *Memoirs of Laetitia Pilkington*, ed. A. C. Elias, Jr, 2 vols. (Athens, GA: University of Georgia Press, 1997), vol. II, p. 677.

[6] For italic punctuation, see Chapter 2.

254   Part IV: Into the Future

it, to the claims of Church and clergy, and in particular by its imprisonment of Faulkner for printing Bishop Josiah Hort's *A New Proposal for the
Better Regulation and Improvement of Quadrille*, into which Swift seems to
have inserted a reflection on a particular *bête noire* among the Irish MPs.[7]
The most relevant (but dangerous) place to print such a poem would have
been Dublin, but instead it emerged for the first time in 1736 in London,
where it appeared, alongside *A New Proposal* and two poems not by Swift,
in the provocatively titled collection *S—t contra omnes* ('Swift against
everybody'), which bore the imprint 'Dublin printed: and London reprinted; and sold by R. Amy, over-against Craggs-Court, Charing-Cross;
Mrs. Dodd, at the Peacock without Temple-Bar; and by the book and
pamphlet-sellers of London and Westminster'.[8] The claim of previous
Dublin printing was implausible, and the presentation had several disadvantages: it associated Swift's name with slighter pieces by others; it
brought an important poem to market in the kingdom where it was of
least interest; and it lacked the revisions by which Swift had since tempered
his initial attack.[9] In that sense it had significantly evaded its author's final
intention; yet in creative terms this older version, uninhibited by subsequent moral scruple, was arguably superior.

Behind this divergence lay Swift's recognition of the problems inherent in
moving the poem from manuscript to print circulation: he described it to
Sheridan as 'a very masterly Poem on the *Legion-Club*, which, if the Printer
should be condemn'd to be Hang'd for it, you will see in a three-penny
Book'.[10] In order to make prosecution less feasible, he seems to have waited
until the end of the parliamentary session, and then to have eschewed print
in favour of a clandestine circulation in manuscript, continuing all the while
to throw out diversionary hints.[11] This strategy both favoured forthright
expression and avoided endangering a printer; but it also compromised the
author's power to determine the form in which the poem would first reach
print.[12] Swift's revised version would remain unpublished in London until

---

[7] For *A New Proposal*, *ESTC* T39924, see further below; *CWJS Poems* IV (forthcoming); Karian, *Print and Manuscript*, pp. 134–46, 203–6.

[8] *S—t contra omnes. An Irish miscellany. Containing, I. Some proposals for the regulation and improvement of quadrille. II. The legion club. III. A curry-comb of truth for a certain Dean: Or, The Grub-Street Tribunal. IV. The Scall'd Crow's Nest. A Very Old Tale* (London, [1736]; TS 752, *ESTC* T107920). For the final piece, see the deattributed poems section of *CWJS Poems* IV (forthcoming). Griffin cites Vulgate precedent for the phrase 'contra omnes' (*Swift and Pope*, p. 212).

[9] Karian, *Print and Manuscript*, pp. 134, 156–65.   [10] *Corr.*, vol. IV, pp. 286–7.

[11] Karian, *Print and Manuscript*, pp. 133, 146–7, 162–3; *Corr.*, vol. IV, pp. 286–7, 296, 302, 306, 312.

[12] For Sheridan's (possibly tongue-in-cheek) comments on scribal alterations to the poem, see *Corr.*, vol. IV, pp. 306, 308.

Ending and Going On (1736–1765)

Bowyer printed it in 1738, and in Dublin there would be no published version at all until after he and most of his victims were dead.[13]

Significant problems also attended the London publication in 1739 of what is now one of the most celebrated poems in the Swift canon, *Verses on the Death of Doctor Swift*. Here Swift relied on the agency of William King (1685–1763), Principal of St Mary Hall, Oxford; but in this case the effect was not to publish a stronger attack than the author desired, but a much weaker one.[14] The imprint of the London *Verses* was that of Charles Bathurst (successor to the recently deceased Motte), who produced the poem in a spaciously printed folio pamphlet. (This was a routine presentation in London, but less so in Dublin: Swift had in 1733 told Pope that his recent London-printed poems had been reprinted in Dublin 'in tolerable wealdable volumes, not your monstrous twelvepenny folio'.[15]) But in marked contrast with the laudatory images with which Faulkner had preluded the *Works*, the title-page medallion, borne aloft by putti, displayed a cockerel in mid-swagger – which may have recalled for at least some readers the Senecan proverb of the cock who crows loudest on his own dunghill.[16] Such a reading could only have been further encouraged by the outrageousness of the title page itself: in uniform large capitals (with lower case for 'Doctor'), it gave Swift's name without disguise, followed, in smaller type, by the words *Written by Himself: Nov. 1731*. All this served to underline the poem's subversion of generic pieties, for the phrase 'Verses on the Death of' was a formula with established precedent, which had already been applied to two deaths at the heart of Swift's English network: Charles Beckingham's *Verses on the Death of Mr. Prior, humbly inscrib'd to the Right Honble the Lady Henrietta Cavendish, Holles, Harley* (London, 1721), and Samuel Wesley the younger's *Verses on the Death of Mrs. Morice* (London, 1730: reprinted by Faulkner in the same year).[17] In these published tributes, one to Swift's friend and colleague Prior, the other to Atterbury's daughter, the subject was dead, their praises were sung by a third party, and the poem addressed a grieving survivor. Swift, in contrast (despite occasional false alarms in the press), was

---

[13] Karian, *Print and Manuscript*, pp. 154–6.

[14] *Verses on the Death of Doctor Swift. Written by Himself: Nov. 1731* (London, 1739; TS 771, Foxon S920, *ESTC* T50707). *CWJS Poems* IV (forthcoming) will offer two versions of the poem, of which this edition provides copy text for the second ('William King's compilation'). For the poem's popularity, see tables in J. Woolley, 'Swift's Most Popular Poems', pp. 370–4.

[15] *Corr.*, vol. III, p. 615; the Dublin volumes were octavos.   [16] *ODEP* ('Cock').

[17] *Verses on the Death of Mr. Prior, humbly inscrib'd to the Right Honble the Lady Henrietta Cavendish, Holles, Harley. By Mr. Beckingham* (London, 1721; Foxon B152, *ESTC* T75221); *Verses on the Death of Mrs. Morice* (London, 1730; Foxon W355, *ESTC* T97822); and Faulkner's Dublin reprint, *Verses on the Death of Mrs. Morrice, late wife to Mr. Morrice, high-bailiff of Westminster, and daughter to the Late Bishop of R-ch——r, now in exile* (Dublin, 1730; Foxon W356, *ESTC* T176946).

256   Part IV: Into the Future

still alive, the praises he was singing were his own, and the poem implied that
no one, not even his closest Scriblerian friends, would need much consoling
anyway ('Poor *Pope* will grieve a Month, and *Gay* / A Week, and *Arbuthnot*
a Day').[18] As striking as its generic effrontery was the self-declared incomplete-
ness of the published poem: no reader could fail to notice the asterisks that
stood in for the Queen's title on page 9, or the six lines of asterisks that replaced
most of her ensuing speech.

In one sense, the mixed and mangled London *Verses* manifested the
predictable failure of an impracticably fantastic strategy, heralded in 1733
by the mystification surrounding *The Life and Genuine Character*.[19] King,
bringing *Verses* to press in London via the older London connection with
Motte and his successor Bathurst, had sought safety by censoring the verse,
incorporating material from *The Life and Genuine Character* and suppressing
Swift's extensive notes. (J. Woolley and Karian suggest that King's choosing
to correspond with Mrs Whiteway, as well as with Swift, may imply King's
uncertainty at this point as to whether Swift was still competent to make
appropriate decisions.[20]) It was Faulkner who would to a degree vindicate
Swift's original conception: the Dublin edition, once more adopting the
more usual octavo format, and priced at 6*d.*, reverted to Faulkner's typically
deferential style. It used dashes to obscure all but the first letter of Swift's
name, cited '*the supposed Author's Friends*' for its claim '*that many Lines and
Notes are omitted in the English Edition*', and invited the aid of '*such Persons
who have seen the Original Manuscripts*' to further restore the text.[21] Yet
Faulkner's edition (which generated continuing demand for reprints) offered
an even more flagrant exhibition of censorship, printing some footnotes that
were substantially represented only by lines of spaced rules: like a blank form,
they challenged readers to fill in what the printer could not print; and
manuscripts were evidently circulated to make clear exactly what that was.
On page 41, for instance, note (1), which relates to a passage of verse on the
Irish parliament, consists only of a provocative '*The*', followed by five
invitingly spaced ruled lines: two copies that can now be seen side by side
in Cambridge University Library have been supplied, in different hands,
with the same derisive account of '[*The*] Irish Parliament (as they call it)'.[22]

---

[18] *Verses* (London, 1739), p. 10. For false reports of his death, see Slepian, 'George Faulkner's "Dublin Journal"', p. 114.

[19] See Chapter 7.   [20] *CWJS Poems* IV (forthcoming).

[21] This is the first version of the two presented in *CWJS Poems* IV (forthcoming). Copy text is *Verses on the Death of Dr. S——, D. S. P. D. Occasioned by Reading a Maxim in Rochefoulcault* (Dublin, 1739).

[22] Cambridge University Library, Williams. 4101 and Hib.7.739.11. For a full review of readers' annotations, see Karian, *Print and Manuscript*, pp. 133–65.

Ending and Going On (1736–1765)

As if this were not enough, the pamphlet finally presented, immediately before Faulkner's catalogue, a mock-proposal '*For the Honour of the Kingdom of* IRELAND' reprinted from his *Dublin Journal* of 21 March 1732.[23] This invited readers to send in, from their personal knowledge, '*the most remarkable Corruptions, Frauds, Oppressions, Knaveries, and Perjuries*' as contributions to 'The Author's Critical History of his own Times.' Contributors were promised that (in implicit contrast with the poem they had just read) '*the Names of all the Persons concerned, shall be inserted at full Length*'. This late mock-proposal recalls fantasy libraries going all the way back to the forthcoming titles advertised in the 1704 *Tale*; but now, under George II and Walpole, the extravagance lay simply in imagining a printed book that dared to name names. In this light, the London and Dublin publications of *Verses*, though clearly in a literal sense falling far short of the author's intentions for the work, brought the print trajectory of Swift's verse to a triumphant rhetorical conclusion. By foregrounding the intimidation of print by power, the texts turned purchasers into collaborators: King, in excusing to Swift the omissions in the London text, suggested that 'care has been taken that almost every reader may be able to supply the blanks' in 'the story of the medals' promised by Queen Caroline; and some of Faulkner's readers were evidently told exactly what to write in.[24] These early printed editions of *Verses* make a fitting *envoi* to the two kinds of material text in which Swift's verse had circulated during his lifetime. Print, though more liable to prosecution than manuscript, could also reach more readers; and if it could not so openly speak truth to power, it could still deploy its repertoire of blank spaces, asterisks and dashes to perform a provocative silence – reactivating in the process the safer subversions of private inscription.

Letters (1737)

Although Swift in print had long used epistolary convention to place his variously voiced interventions in appropriate social and confessional contexts, genuinely personal letters were another matter.[25] But when Curll published two letters by Swift (one to Pope, the other to Lord Peterborough) in *Mr. Pope's Literary Correspondence ... Volume the Fifth* (London, 1737) it marked the emergence into print of what would within the next few decades

---

[23] For the relation between this mock-proposal, the poem and its wider contexts, see headnote in *CWJS Poems* IV (forthcoming).

[24] *Corr.*, vol. IV, pp. 553–60, 362–4 (p. 557).

[25] See Abigail Williams, 'Epistolary Forms: Published Correspondence, Letter-journals and Books', in *JS Book*, pp. 119–34 (pp. 123–5 and *passim*).

258   Part IV: Into the Future

become a substantial epistolary canon.[26] What readers first saw in Curll's volume was, in the letter to Pope (from 1723), an account of Swift's Irish exile that quietly but firmly confronted Pope and Bolingbroke's posturings of philosophical detachment: 'I chuse my companions among those of least consequence and most compliance: I read the most trifling Books I can find, and whenever I write, it is upon the most trifling subjects.'[27] This is also, however, the letter in which he famously declared: 'I have often endeavour'd to establish a friendship among all Men of Genius, and would fain have it done: they are seldom above three or four Cotemporaries, and if they could be united, would drive the World before them'; and the elegiac sense of lost potential was caught also in his closing request to be remembered 'with great affection' to Arbuthnot, Congreve and Gay.[28] The 1733 letter to Peterborough, in contrast, showed Swift rallying him on the qualities and accomplishments that had brought it about that 'all your Lordship's undertakings ... only terminate in your own honour, and the good of the public, without the least advantage to your health or fortune', while soliciting a letter in return, 'that I may have the pleasure in this scoundrel-country, of going about, and shewing my depending Parsons a letter from the Earl of Peterboro'.[29] The elegance of Swift's raillery underlined his intimacy with the grandees of a late Stuart past, as well as emphasising his sense of Irish exile.

Curll's decent but not particularly well-printed octavo collection predictably emphasised Swift's association with a discredited political dispensation: on its title the list of correspondents was headed by Bolingbroke and the recently deceased George Granville, Baron Lansdowne, in the early 1720s a leading strategist at the Jacobite court.[30] (In addition, Curll's separate issue of the first part of the volume as *New Letters of Mr. Alexander Pope* bore the provocative imprint 'Printed, *Anno Reformationis*, 1737', insinuating that Pope, a Catholic, had no legitimate part in a Protestant nation.[31]) On the title of *Mr. Pope's Literary Correspondence ... Volume the Fifth* Curll also deployed his favourite monogram, borne aloft by putti, each of whom supports the frame with one hand while flourishing an open book in the other. Seconded by his taunting preface 'To my Subscribers encore', the putti celebrated Curll's triumph over

---

[26] *Mr. Pope's Literary Correspondence ... Volume the Fifth* (London, 1737; TS 56, *ESTC* T5512). The two Swift letters are on pp. 65–8 (to Pope, 20 September 1723) and pp. 222–6 (to Peterborough, probably May 1733). See *Corr.*, vol. II, pp. 468–71; vol. III, pp. 641–2. The first of these letters also appeared in a separate issue of the first part of the volume from the same sheets, entitled *New Letters of Mr. Alexander Pope. And Several of his Friends* (London, 1737; also TS 56, *ESTC* T5516).
[27] *Mr. Pope's Literary Correspondence ... Volume the Fifth*, p. 68.   [28] *Ibid.*, pp. 67–8.
[29] *Ibid.*, pp. 225–6.
[30] *ODNB* ('George Granville, Baron Lansdowne and Jacobite Earl of Albemarle').
[31] *New Letters of Mr. Alexander Pope. And Several of his Friends* (London, 1737; *ESTC* T5516).

a despised coterie; and it was now Swift's fate, as well as Pope's, to find himself thus framed. It is suggestive that Faulkner reprinted only two letters that Swift had received, and none that he had written.[32]

Few ordinary purchasers at the time were likely to grasp the extent of the intrigue that lay behind Curll's publication. Pope was intent on persuading Swift to return his letters so that he could include them in an unprecedented lifetime edition of his own correspondence; and he was equally intent on making his long-term adversary Curll serve his purposes by publishing selections that would appear to justify him in issuing that edition in self-defence.[33] Using disguised go-betweens and misleading statements of all kinds, Pope himself had supplied Curll with material, launching what turned out to be an accelerating print presentation of epistolary Swift – as already threatened by Curll's pugnatiously sardonic address 'To my Subscribers encore' in *Mr. Pope's Literary Correspondence ... Volume the Fifth*: '*Beside, what is here presented to You, I have Several other very valuable Originals in my Custody, which, with these, were Transmitted to me from* Ireland.'[34] Swift, to whom neither Curll nor Pope was an unknown quantity, at first responded to Pope's overtures with straight-faced prevarication; but finally, despite his experience of delegating the London *Travels* and *Miscellanies*, he gave Pope what he wanted. Today the five volumes of David Woolley's *Correspondence of Jonathan Swift, D.D.* and the five volumes of Sherburn's *Correspondence of Alexander Pope* sit side by side as examples of the now long-established convention of collecting and publishing authors' letters. But that idea was originally much more Pope's than it was Swift's.

Last Prose (1736, 1737, 1738)

The most conspicuous part of Swift in print had always been his prose tracts and satires, and in this final phase, much – but not all – of their content took on an increasingly belated air. Though dwindling in number, the material texts of newly published works ranged from tiny to substantial, from shabby to opulent, capitalising on his established fame by

---

[32] *Letters from Alexander Pope, Esq; and the Right Hon. the Lord Bolingbroke, to the Reverend Dr. Swift, D. S. P. D. To which is added Almahide, a poem by the Lord Bolingbroke* (Dublin, 1737; TS 56A, *ESTC* N10954).

[33] For accounts of Pope's intrigue and Swift's responses, see *Correspondence of Alexander Pope*, ed. Sherburn, vol. I, pp. xi–xviii; Maynard Mack, *Alexander Pope: A Life* (New Haven and London: Yale University Press, 1985), pp. 664–71; Ehrenpreis, *Swift*, vol. III, pp. 883–98; James McLaverty, 'The First Printing and Publication of Pope's Letters', *The Library*, 2 (1980), 264–80; Baines and Rogers, *Curll*, pp. 246–73.

[34] *Mr. Pope's Literary Correspondence ... Volume the Fifth*, pp. i–ii.

260   Part IV: Into the Future

deploying a variety of strategies within and between the two book trades of Dublin and London.

The risks and responsibilities of controversial prose had once more been highlighted in the affair of Hort's *A New Proposal for the Better Regulation and Improvement of Quadrille* in 1736, which resulted in Faulkner, its printer, being sent to prison – as was Waters, who had reprinted it (though without declaring his name).[35] Swift, dismayed by Hort's refusal to recompense Faulkner, expostulated that 'He sells such papers to the running-boys for farthings apiece; and is a gainer by each, less than half a farthing; and it is seldom he sells above a hundred, unless they be of such as only spread by giving offence, and consequently endanger the printer both in loss of money and liberty.'[36] Swift, David Woolley infers, had acted more generously towards Waters; and in April 1736 Waters went on to put his name to the octavo pamphlet *Reasons why we should not Lower the Coins now Current in this Kingdom*, an anonymous argument against revaluation of the currency which included, as its final item, a speech by Swift. Most of his writing on economic affairs in these years, increasingly repetitive and out of touch, would remain unpublished until after his death; but Waters's pamphlet is still significant for Swift in print.[37] While Hayton and Rounce correctly note that Waters's printing of the speech 'is not a thing of beauty', it is nonetheless in its own way a joy for ever, a squashed, blotchy, ungrammatical but irrepressible testimonial once again offered to the public by the printer who had in 1720 so notoriously suffered for publishing *A Proposal for the Universal Use of Irish Manufacture*.[38] Not for nothing, it seemed, had the crude device of a phoenix (if a somewhat worried-looking one) so often adorned Waters's publications.

If this was, as it appears, Swift's last lifetime publication of new writing about the Irish currency, it was not quite the last to evoke the reputation of the Drapier, which was now given major emphasis in Faulkner's 1737 printing of *A Proposal for Giving Badges to the Beggars*, the working up of an idea abandoned ten years earlier.[39] This octavo pamphlet broke the habits of a print lifetime by blazoning its author under a trinity of identities. At the end, like *Ode to the Athenian Society* and *A Proposal for Correcting . . . the English Tongue*, it was signed 'J. SWIFT'; at the head of

---

[35] For the *New Proposal*, see Chapter 7. Waters's reprint, not in *ESTC*, is identified in *Corr.*, vol. IV, p. 264. For Swift's involvement, see *Corr.*, vol. IV, pp. 264–5, 291–3, 302; Karian, *Print and Manuscript*, pp. 143–4.

[36] *Corr*, vol. IV, pp. 291–2.

[37] See publication dates in headnotes to *CWJS Irish Political Writings after 1725*.   [38] *Ibid.*, p. 486.

[39] TS 755, *ESTC* N12214; *CWJS Irish Political Writings after 1725*, pp. 305–19.

Ending and Going On (1736–1765)

the title page it was ascribed to 'the Dean of St. Patrick's'; and further down, in cursive type following the outline of a roundel depicting the Drapier (clerically garbed, with pen in hand), it was signed 'M. B. Drapier'.[40] (The pamphlet also reused, at the head of the main text, the 'detur indigenti' headpiece found in some copies of volume IV of Faulkner's 1735 *Works*.[41]) Fittingly, for what Hayton and Rounce describe as 'Swift's last substantial prose intervention in Irish affairs', this was the most insistently authorised of all Swift's authorised texts – which renders particularly poignant the harshness of its vision and the grimness of its close:

> I had some other Thoughts to offer upon this Subject. But, as I am a Desponder in my Nature, and have tolerably well discovered the Disposition of our People, who never will move a Step towards easing themselves from any one single Grievance; it will be thought, that I have already said too much, and to little or no Purpose; which hath often been the Fate, or Fortune of the Writer.[42]

Yet the very next year, 1738, saw publication of *A Treatise on Polite Conversation*, the last major work that Swift lived to see published. Despite a long gestation (some of the sayings had been recorded as far back as 1702–3), it betrayed much less of the belatedness that marked other prose coming to press in this period: instead, particularly in its in-character Introduction by Simon Wagstaff, it drew deeply on the skewering of modern pretence that had announced Swift's satirical gifts in the *Tale*, now applied to the Whig regime of the 1730s. Near-simultaneous London and Dublin editions, prepared from separate manuscripts, addressed noticeably different objectives.

Divergence was evident even from their respective titles: the London edition led with *A Complete Collection of Genteel and Ingenious Conversation*, the Dublin edition with *A Treatise on Polite Conversation*: each then used the other as a section title.[43] Either way round, the provocative application of 'polite' effectively summed up the discursive apocalypse threatened by Wagstaff's offering at the shrine of Whig modernity, but the Dublin edition foregrounded it immediately, while its London equivalent prioritised alternative markers of social pretention.[44]

---

[40] See Clive T. Probyn, 'Jonathan Swift at the Sign of the Drapier', in *Münster* (1998), pp. 225–37 (pp. 229–33); *CWJS Irish Political Writings after 1725*, figure 6, p. 307.
[41] See Chapter 7.   [42] *CWJS Irish Political Writings after 1725*, p. 319.   [43] *CWJS Parodies*, p. 693.
[44] Valerie Rumbold, 'Locating Swift's Parody: The Title of "Polite Conversation"', in *Münster* (2008), pp. 255–72.

262   Part IV: Into the Future

Further material differences highlighted different strategies in the two print trades.[45] The London edition was fashionable and relatively luxurious (some copies were on large paper).[46] It featured a degree of modernised spelling, lighter and more grammatical punctuation, modish typographical effects (extending to large and small capitals for relatively minor emphases), large type and generous white space. (The Introduction was even separated into shorter paragraphs than in Dublin, allowing the text to be spaced out further.) It was also more successful in assigning speeches plausibly to characters (though inconsistencies remained). The separate Dublin edition, meanwhile, made a more traditional, closely printed, thinner book: its spelling was old-fashioned and its punctuation heavily rhetorical; but the longer, blockier paragraphs of its Introduction were more coherent and characteristic. Crucially, Faulkner advertised his volumes not as more beautiful but as better value, setting his price at 'a British Eighteen Pence' rather than the 4s. 4d. charged for the London edition.[47] He also complained of a rival Irish edition 'upon a dark, brown, spungy paper, and an old, blind, battered, unintelligible worn out Letter, which cannot be read without Spectacles and very young Eyes'.[48] Faulkner's path lay between these extremes, producing a setting of type that could be used both for a separate edition and, with minor correction, for volume VI of the *Works*, where it was inserted alongside *The Public Spirit of the Whigs*.

These material differences between London and Dublin texts reflected two separate lines of transmission. *Polite Conversation* was emphatically not part of Faulkner's collaboration with Bowyer, and the London text was not set from Faulkner's sheets. Instead, Swift had made a present to Mary Barber, at her request, of the benefits of the London edition. (Her friends had encouraged her by pointing out that 'you made no advantage for your self by your writings': they understood that Swift's publishing was an adjunct to a career in public service, not part of a strategy for living by the pen such as Barber aspired to.[49]) While Swift retained the manuscript material from which Faulkner's text would derive, Barber was supplied with a manuscript of her own by Swift's acquaintance, the fifth Earl of Orrery (1707–1762): she took it to Motte, whose joint imprint with his current partner, Bathurst, duly appeared on the title. (Thus, when Faulkner advertised against the London edition he was competing not

---

[45] *CWJS Parodies*, pp. 690–3.   [46] D. Woolley, 'Swift's Copy', pp. 133–4, 169, citing TS 761.
[47] *CWJS Parodies*, pp. 691–2.
[48] *Ibid.*, p. 694; cf. *ESTC* N471564, a 1738 Belfast reprint of the Dublin edition.
[49] *Corr.*, vol IV, p. 359.

Ending and Going On (1736–1765)

with a partner, but with the rival who had in 1735 taken him to court over the English distribution of the Dublin *Works*.[50])

Yet the resulting text, whose fashionable design no doubt appealed to Barber's wealthy supporters, also raised uncomfortable questions.[51] At the heart of the work was a satire of London's modish elite, who were shown exchanging, over gargantuan meals, an empty but aggressively vulgar selection of proverbs and catchphrases. The dialogues were prefaced by Wagstaff's Introduction, which presented them not only as the fruit of his life's work, but also as a protection for government against the possibility of public dissent (since everyone would be too busy memorising and repeating his sayings). In effect, in this last lifetime published major work, Wagstaff appears not only as a degenerate outlier of the Staff family (whose efforts for the public good, inaugurated by Isaac Bickerstaff's *Predictions for the Year 1708*, had provided the founding fiction for Steele's *Tatler*), but also as a more elderly version of the author of the *Tale* (making it fitting that the son of the *Tale*'s printer survived long enough to put his imprint to this late-career meditation on the consequences of Whig modernity). Wagstaff, if understandably incommoded by the long-term exigencies of slenderly financed literary aspiration, was only the more convinced, in the age of Cibber and Theobald, of his claims on George II and Walpole ('Must is for the king' being an adage that he took care to introduce at an early stage). The modish luxury volume that Motte and Bathurst produced in London instantiated his text accordingly (and it may also be significant that it lacks the Dublin edition's ridicule of the royal favourite Stephen Duck).[52] As so often in Swift in print, the London edition of *Polite Conversation* alluded materially as well as discursively to the object of satire.

Faulkner's treatment of *Polite Conversation*, meanwhile, heralded problems with the Dublin Works that would only get worse with the passage of time, for when he incorporated *Polite Conversation* into the *Works*, also in 1738, he placed it in the octavo volume VI, *The Public Spirit of the Whigs; and other Pieces of Political Writings, &c. With Polite Conversation, &c.*[53] While a case could certainly be made for reading the two named works together, this is hardly the company in which readers would expect to find them; but *Polite Conversation* on its own made fewer than 100 octavo pages,

---

[50] See Chapter 7.   [51] *Corr.*, vol. IV, p. 564.
[52] *CWJS Parodies*, pp. 256, 267–301. It is possible, however, that Swift had added the reference to Duck after Barber's manuscript had been dispatched.
[53] TS 42, *ESTC* T205440; *CWJS Parodies*, pp. 694–7; Marshall, 'The "1735" Faulkner Edition', pp. 183–4.

264   Part IV: Into the Future

while with the political writings it made a substantial volume of more than
300. If this suggests that the *Works* was developing the momentum of
a literary sausage-machine, it is also striking that the filling, once processed,
had a remarkably long shelf-life, for Faulkner regularly stockpiled unused
sheets for later reissue with updated titles. Orrery, in his 1752 *Remarks on
the Life and Writings of Dr. Jonathan Swift*, would reflect on the (by then)
further expanded *Works* that although they were authoritative ('the
author . . . was in reality the editor'), 'the several pieces are thrown together
without any order or regularity whatever', and 'every scrap was thrust into
the parcel' – including 'idle amusements' bordering on the 'puerile'.[54] Even
by 1738, the roots of the problem were evident.

From a book-buyer's point of view, 1738 might well have looked like
a triumphant year of late harvest; but, as Swift had told Pope in 1734, *Polite
Conversation* was only one of the three major works that he was still hoping
to bring to press (the others were *Directions to Servants* and *Four Last Years
of the Queen*, and both would remain unpublished at his death).[55] The year
1738 also saw the death of Motte. Through him there had been
a continuous succession, back through the printing of the *Tale* by the
elder Motte for Benjamin Tooke the younger, to Benjamin Tooke the
elder and the Crooke relations he had supported as King's Printer in
Ireland in Swift's youth. Bathurst, the younger Motte's successor, would
not long be bound by the taboos on which Swift had so long insisted, and
in 1743, in a consolidation of inherited copyrights, he reunited the distinct
transmissions by which Tooke had in 1710–11 separated the *Miscellanies*
tradition from the *Tale*.[56] By reprinting the *Tale* as a volume in his set of
Miscellanies Bathurst set aside, quietly but decisively, the crucial infra-
structure of Swift's refusal to own it. As of May 1742 it had been officially
determined that Swift was 'of such unsound mind and memory that he is
incapable of transacting any business, or managing, conducting, or taking
care either of his estate or person', and he was in future cared for by
guardians.[57] His authorship of the *Tale* had long been an open secret, his
active involvement was a thing of the past, and there was little reason for
copyright owners to maintain the fiction of separation. Even in the last
years of Swift's life, old habits of deference were beginning to slip.

It was also in these transitional years that Swift's godson, Thomas
Sheridan the younger (1719–1788), having bought his late father's Swift

---

[54] John Boyle, 5th Earl of Cork and Orrery, *Remarks on the Life and Writings of Dr. Jonathan Swift*, ed.
João Fróes (Newark, DE: University of Delaware Press; London: Associated University Presses,
2000), pp. 135–6; Marshall, 'The "1735" Faulkner Edition', pp. 175–6, 183–4.
[55] *Corr.*, vol. IV, p. 8.   [56] See Chapter 4.   [57] Ehrenpreis, *Swift*, vol. III, p. 915.

Ending and Going On (1736–1765) 265

manuscripts from his executors, took to the London printer Robert Dodsley (1704–1764) three sermons (which were published both by Dodsley and by Faulkner around the time of Swift's death), along with various other works (published in London in 1745–6 as *Miscellanies*, volumes X–XI).[58] The elder Sheridan had at various times been allowed to print small pieces for his own benefit, and now his son continued the tradition, although Swift himself seems to have had no interest in seeing his sermons published. Again, Swift's decisions and desires were superseded by the rational self-interest of survivors. Purchasers were informed that the manuscripts of the sermons could be inspected at the publisher's: as Swift faded from the scene it was just as well to offer material evidence that new pieces were indeed genuine.

Directions to Servants (1745)

Swift died on 19 October 1745, as Faulkner reported in his *Dublin Journal* for that day, combining commemoration (on the front page) with an advertisement of his now expanded *Works* (on its verso).[59] But Swift's death figured only in the last of the paper's three columns: the first two were dedicated to the Irish bishops' exhortations to Catholics against supporting 'a Rebellion in North Britain' led by 'a Popish Pretender to his Majesty's Crown'. Even as Swift lay dying, the Jacobite rising heralded the inexorable recession of his political world into the past. Faulkner, setting his face to the future, published later in the same year the auction catalogue that announced the dissolution of Swift's library.[60] But the major new Swift publication of the year was Faulkner's *Directions to Servants*, whose readers were greeted at the threshold with a 'Publisher's Preface' that demonstrated just how far this particular publisher had come since launching his edition in 1735:

> *The following Treatise of* Directions to Servants *was begun some Years ago by the Author, who had not Leisure to finish and put it into proper Order, being engaged in many other Works of greater Use to his Country, as may be seen by most of his Writings. But, as the Author's Design was to expose the Villanies and*

---

[58] *Three Sermons: I. On Mutual Subjection. II. On Conscience. III. On the Trinity. By the Reverend Dr. Swift, Dean of St. Patrick's* (London, 1744). See textual account by Louis A. Landa in *PW*, vol. IX, pp. 139 (reproducing title page), 375. For *Miscellanies*, vols. X–XI, see A. Williams, 'Epistolary Forms', p. 127.

[59] Mahony, *Jonathan Swift*, pp. 8–11 (with reproduction, p. 9); Slepian, 'George Faulkner's "Dublin Journal"', p. 115.

[60] *A Catalogue of Books, The Library of the late Rev. Dr. Swift, Dean of St. Patrick's, Dublin. To be sold by Auction. The Time and Place for the Sale of them will be inserted in the Dublin Journal. N.B. The Books mark'd thus * have Remarks or Observations on them in the Hand of Dr. Swift* (Dublin, [1745]; TS 1326, *ESTC* T162694).

Frauds of Servants to their Masters and Mistresses, we shall make no Apology for its Publication, but give it our Readers in the same Manner as we find it, in the Original, which may be seen in the Printer's Custody. The few Tautologies that occur in the Characters left unfinished, will make the Reader look upon the Whole as a rough Draught with several Outlines only drawn: However, that there may appear no Daubing or Patch-Work by other Hands, it is thought most adviseable to give it in the Author's own Words.

It is imagined, that he intended to make a large Volume of this Work; but as Time and Health would not permit him, the Reader may draw from what is here exhibited, Means to detect the many Vices and Faults, which People in that Kind of low Life are subject to.

If Gentlemen would seriously consider this Work, which is written for their Instruction, (altho' ironically) it would make them better OEconomists, and preserve their Estates and Families from Ruin.

It may be seen by some scattered Papers (wherein were given Hints for a Dedication and Preface, and a List of all Degrees of Servants) that the Author intended to have gone through all their Characters.

This is all that need be said as to this Treatise, which can only be looked upon as a Fragment.

G. F.

Dublin, Nov. 8,
    1745.

The meticulously deferential persona of 1735 is a thing of the past: there is nothing here about 'the supposed Author' and his 'Friends'. The publisher himself, though still retaining the corporate 'we', speaks of his own actions, not only the author's. He takes it upon himself not only to infer the author's intentions for the work, but also to instruct '*the Reader*' what to take from the text, and to advise '*Gentlemen*' on household management. His Preface is initialled and dated.

Faulkner's self-assertion was founded on his claim to have made clear and appropriate decisions about why the work was important, how it fell short of Swift's intentions, and how it should be presented to readers. First, the Preface emphasised the work's moral and prudential credentials, encouraging employers to focus on the dangers constituted by servants' '*many Vices and Faults*'. (While conceding that the work's exhortations were written '*ironically*', the Preface eschewed any hint at subversive role-play.) Second, it outlined Swift's inferred plan, and gave a tactful explanation for his failure to complete it: while he was giving priority to '*Works of greater Use to his Country*', his '*Time and Health*' had run out. (Thus, while passing tactfully over the indignities of his final years, Faulkner reminded his readers of Swift's status as Hibernian Patriot, the figure on whom Faulkner's own investment had been grounded.) Third, continuing to

Ending and Going On (1736–1765)

draw on manuscript material which he had seen and his readers had not, he explained that there were repetitions and unfinished characters in his copy, and that there also existed '*scattered Papers*' of hints for further unrealised elements. Thus he framed his crucial message: he had decided not to have this '*rough Draught*' filled out and revised by a third party, but to present it simply '*in the Author's own Words*'. The alternative – which would have produced a longer and superficially more coherent book – he stigmatised as '*Daubing or Patch-Work by other Hands*'; and given Swift's response to Andrew Tooke's revisions to the *Travels*, he was almost certainly saying what Swift, in his prime, would have wanted him to say (and what readers of Swift today would also want him to say). But the work as he printed it was substantially unachieved, and Faulkner's invitation to readers to inspect his copy was prudent. During Swift's lifetime manuscripts were generally disposed of after printing, but from now on they took on new importance as material proof of his involvement. Today, although Faulkner's copy itself is lost, there are still two extant partial manuscripts of *Directions* (one authorial, the other scribal with authorial corrections).[61] There is nothing like this for the major prose works published in Swift's lifetime, when the priority was more often to conceal than to certify Swift's authorship.

Readers had good reason to be shocked by the unfinished state of *Directions*. If Faulkner had commissioned some latter-day Andrew Tooke to polish the work for publication, it is clear – to an extent from the printed text, and even more so from the manuscripts – that he would have faced three major challenges. The simplest would have been to remove the partial repetitions in which a similar point, perhaps in similar words, was differently developed in multiple paragraphs or segments. More difficult would have been to expand on the bare notes that constituted some of the final chapters: to have brought them up to the length of a chapter would have meant attempting to imitate Swift for page after unsupported page – all without repeating the topics and effects of earlier chapters. Harder still would have been the task of shaping accumulations of separate injunctions into coherent paragraphs (notably the central section of single sentences addressed to the Footman in chapter iii).[62] (Purchasers could not have known that Swift had considered simply sorting the precepts according to whether or not a reason was offered for them: this might have made things tidier, but would hardly have improved coherence.[63]) In a sense, the

---

[61] The earlier, authorial manuscript is Rothschild no. 2275 (Wren Library, Trinity College, Cambridge); the later, scribal but authorially corrected, is Forster MS 528 (National Library of Art at the Victoria and Albert Museum); see *CWJS Parodies*, pp. 720–6.

[62] *CWJS Parodies*, pp. 485–8.   [63] *Ibid.*, p. 550.

268   Part IV: Into the Future

underlying problem was the rhetorical brilliance of the most finished sequences, a brilliance posited on Swift's apparently effortless leading of topic and argument from one paragraph to the next, as his anonymous ex-footman followed Bickerstaff, Gulliver, the modest proposer, Wagstaff and a host of other authorial stand-ins in convicting himself out of his own mouth. So consummate is the perversity with which he advises the butler on how to manipulate barrels, bottles and corks, the cook on how to combine combing her hair with stirring soup, the footman on how to dress for his inevitable hanging, the chambermaid on how to sell her mistress's daughter to the highest bidder, and everyone on how to minimise effort and maximise perks, that, had the author only thought to identify himself by some such name as Hector Bragstaff, his book – had he ever finished it – would have been ideally qualified to take its place with the publications of the rest of the Staff family.

Faulkner's rationalisation that Swift had better things to do and was finally overtaken by illness was not, presumably, the whole story. It may well have been that Swift's ex-footman had already worked his 'hint' almost to exhaustion, and would have become less and less amusing had he attempted a full chapter for every servant. But what the printed text cannot show is the pathos of the manuscript annotations, which testify to Swift's attempts to finish a work that he could no longer remember well enough to reorganise. Mrs Whiteway seems to have given up, by 1740, any hope that it could be completed, telling Pope that it was 'very unfinished and incorrect, yet what is done of it, hath so much humour, that it may appear as a posthumous work'.[64] (The word 'posthumous', five years before Swift's death, is chilling.) By 1 October 1745 Faulkner had the sheets ready to send to Bowyer: 'Fix your day of publication ... that we may both come out the same day. I think the middle of November will do very well.'[65] The letter confirms just how effectively Faulkner's Dublin initiative was driving the consolidation of Swift in print; but its sequel again shows how times were changing. Bowyer had his reprint published by Robert Dodsley, a former footman whose probity, diligence and success as writer and bookseller constituted a standing reproof to Swift's pessimistically elitist creation of the ex-footman delegated to write *Directions to Servants*.[66]

---

[64] *Corr.*, vol. IV, p. 488.   [65] *CWJS Parodies*, p. 722; *Bowyer Ledgers*, no. 3314A.
[66] *CWJS Parodies*, p. 732; for Dodsley's creativity, enterprise and standing in literary society, see *ODNB* ('Robert Dodsley').

Ending and Going On (1736–1765)

Hawkesworth's Edition (1755)

Within a decade the London copy-holders would articulate their challenge to Faulkner's dominance in what is now known as Hawkesworth's edition.[67] The plan seems first to have been put before the public in *Proposals for Printing by Subscription a Beautiful and Correct Edition of the Works of Dr. Jonathan Swift* ([London], 1752: Figure 13).[68] Now represented by only a single known copy and related newspaper advertisements, its three printed folio pages show Motte's successor, Charles Bathurst, joining Davis, Dodsley, Bowyer and others to produce a rival edition to Faulkner's. Gradually the divisions among London copyright holders were beginning to be overcome, as Swift had vainly hoped they might have been during his lifetime.[69]

The booksellers clearly recognised the potential of a radically upgraded Works. Their declared intention '*to prevent the Importation and Spreading of such as are incorrect and imperfect*' plainly impugned the textual integrity and completeness of Faulkner's edition – which at this date still excluded the *Tale*.[70] The *Proposals* also offered additional inducements: 'COPPER PLATES by the best Masters', 'AN / Account of the DEAN's LIFE' and 'HISTORICAL and EXPLANATORY NOTES / upon his Writings annexed in their proper Places'.[71] Of these, the 'LIFE' was the outstanding novelty, but on turning the page readers would have seen another innovation at least equally significant: for the first time they were being offered a quarto. Large quarto, gradually displacing the folio as prestige format, had long dominated Pope's *Works* (at least until the annotated octavos of 1735–6), but Swift's had never been offered in any format more imposing than Faulkner's large octavo.[72] This was still the default option in the *Proposals*, which offered the quarto volumes only in the event that 'a sufficient Number of Subscribers appear to desire them in that Size'; but the *Proposals* were still inviting subscribers to set aside what was by now one of the longest-standing conventions of Swift in print. The pricing model was brisk and simple: there would be exactly twice as many volumes in an

---

[67] *The Works of Jonathan Swift, D. D. Dean of St. Patrick's, Dublin*, edited by John Hawkesworth, 6 vols. (London, 1755; TS 87, and for further development, see TS pp. 80–1030, with summary pp. 80–3 and table p. 104). The 'printed for' list comprised C. Bathurst, C. Davis, C. Hitch and L. Hawes, J. Hodges, R. and J. Dodsley and W. Bowyer.

[68] *Proposals for Printing by Subscription a Beautiful and Correct Edition of the Works of Dr. Jonathan Swift* (London, dated 11 May 1752; *ESTC* T227101): for images of all three pages see the online printed items catalogue of Chetham's Library, Manchester (keywords 'Swift' and 'prospectus'). Booksellers are named on p. 2. For newspaper advertising, see *London Evening Post*, 26 May 1752.

[69] For London copyright divisions, see Cook, 'Publishing Posthumous Swift', pp. 215–16.

[70] *Proposals*, p. 2.　[71] *Ibid.*, p. 1.　[72] McLaverty, *Pope, Print and Meaning*, pp. 47, 209–41.

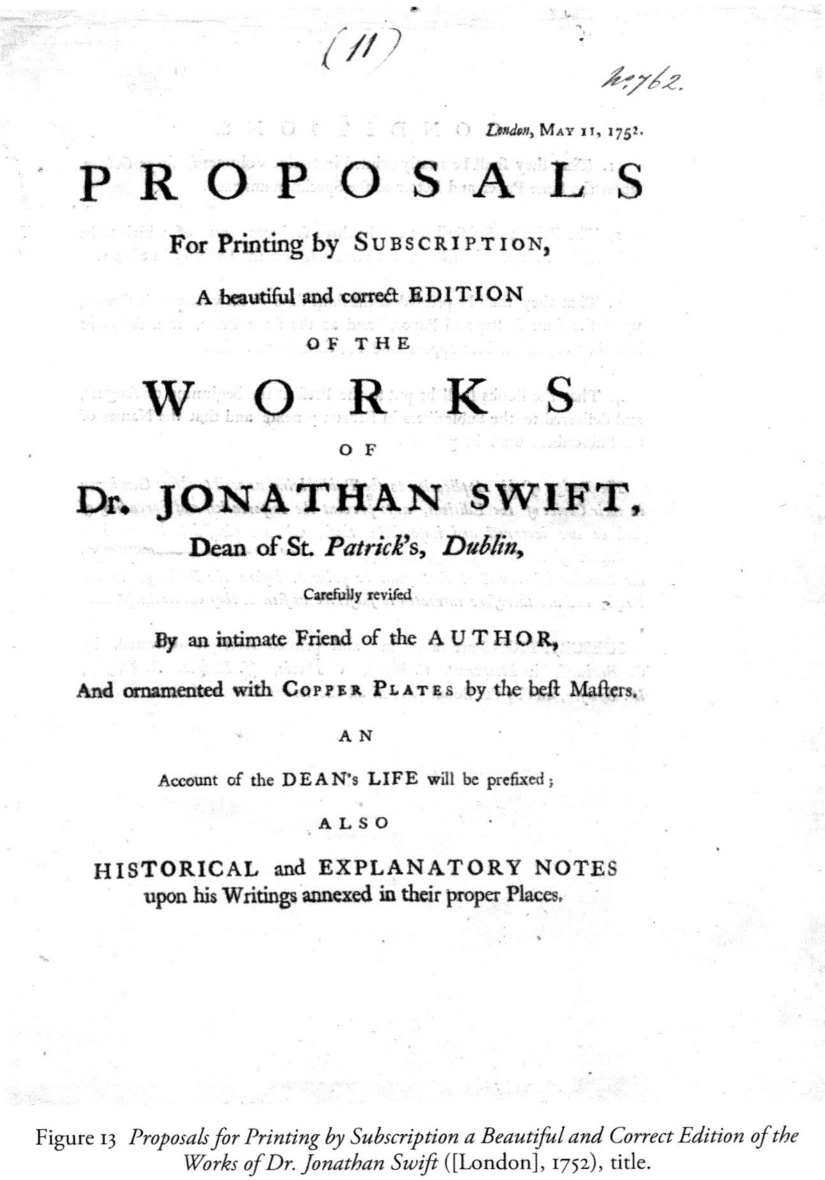

Part IV: Into the Future

(11)

h. 762.

London, MAY 11, 1752.

PROPOSALS

For Printing by SUBSCRIPTION,

A beautiful and correct EDITION

OF THE

WORKS

OF

Dr. JONATHAN SWIFT,

Dean of St. *Patrick's*, *Dublin*,

Carefully revised

By an intimate Friend of the AUTHOR,

And ornamented with COPPER PLATES by the best Masters.

AN

Account of the DEAN's LIFE will be prefixed;

ALSO

HISTORICAL and EXPLANATORY NOTES
upon his Writings annexed in their proper Places.

Figure 13 *Proposals for Printing by Subscription a Beautiful and Correct Edition of the Works of Dr. Jonathan Swift* ([London], 1752), title.

Ending and Going On (1736–1765)

octavo set as in a quarto (twelve as opposed to six), and the price for the set, a very reasonable 'three Guineas', would be the same irrespective of format. A 'Specimen' on the facing page presented, beneath a simple italic heading, a sharply printed page from *Contests and Dissensions*: consisting of a single unbroken paragraph, it was set entirely in roman, with initial capitals for proper names only.[73] The effect, far more modern and elegant than Faulkner's, was of a crisp, clean page uncompromised by footnotes, side-notes, or any variation of emphasis or layout whatsoever (apart from a final catchword). Although this sample from one of Swift's earliest publications still featured the 'wish'd' and 'dream'd' contractions which he had soon come to disapprove (and which Faulkner was progressively eliminating), the effect was impressive.

Subscribers were asked to confirm their choice between the innovative quarto and the familiar large octavo:

> *The Design of this Application to the Public being as well to oblige Gentlemen in their Choice of the Editions, as to prevent the Importation and Spreading of such as are incorrect and imperfect; those, who are pleased to become Encouragers of the Undertaking, are desired to consider, that it is necessary to fix the Number of each Sort that shall be printed, before the Books go to the Press; and are therefore entreated to subscribe as soon as they conveniently can.*[74]

But the booksellers seemed sufficiently confident to ask only for one guinea down and the balance 'on the delivery in Sheets'. In return, subscribers were assured that 'the Books shall be put to the Press at the beginning of August, and delivered to the Subscribers in February next'. All they had to do was deliver their guinea, with a note of their preferred format, to one of the London booksellers listed, who would provide 'printed Receipts' – or they could approach any of 'the Booksellers in all the noted Towns of *Great Britain*'.

The weak link in the chain (for no such edition appeared at the stated time) was most probably the unidentified person whose involvement was blazoned on the title: immediately underneath the author's name the edition was described as 'Carefully revised / By an intimate Friend of the AUTHOR'. There was as yet no mention of Hawkesworth (an entire outsider to Swift's circle), and it is suggestive that he began to publish

---

[73] Smith would in 1755 emphasise the need for 'the Author, or Master' to tell the compositor whether to follow 'the old way, with Capitals to Substantives, and Italic to Proper names', or 'the more neat practice, all in Roman, and Capitals to Proper names, and Emphatical words' (*The Printer's Grammar*, p. 201).

[74] *Proposals*, p. 2.

Part IV: Into the Future

the *Adventurer* in November 1752 and ceased only in early 1754, supporting the inference that he was brought in only after the original plan had stalled.[75] But though the identity of the 'intimate Friend' is not clear, the nature of his qualifications is. There are reasons to suspect that he may have been Deane Swift, whose grandfather was Swift's uncle Godwin Swift, and whose mother-in-law was Martha Whiteway, the cousin who cared for Swift at the Deanery in his old age.[76] This double relationship certainly gave Deane Swift a close family connection with Swift, even though his combination of dependency and resentment made for an awkward relationship, and he had never been as 'intimate' or as much of a 'Friend' as Lyon or Mrs Whiteway.[77] It is striking that in 1755, the year in which the Hawkesworth *Works* was finally published, Bathurst, the first-named bookseller in the 1752 *Proposals*, would also publish (with an advertisement for Hawkesworth's edition at the back) Deane Swift's *An Essay upon the Life, Writings, and Character, of Dr. Jonathan Swift*.[78] The *Essay* may indeed have started life as the 'LIFE' promised in the 1752 *Proposals*. (Cook points out that Hawkesworth's 'Life' cites the *Essay* 'far more frequently' than it does Orrery's *Remarks* or Delany's *Observations*.[79]) Through his mother-in-law Deane Swift certainly had access to manuscripts that could have made the proposed edition fuller and less '*imperfect*', as well as to a corrected copy of the *Tale* given her by Swift, which Hawkesworth, who informed the reader that its 'corrections will be found in this impression', stated to be 'now in the hands of Mr. Dean Swift'.[80] It may even be that Hawkesworth derived from Deane Swift not only information about the annotated *Tale* but also the contempt that he

---

[75] John Lawrence Abbott, *John Hawkesworth: Eighteenth-Century Man of Letters* (Madison, WI: University of Wisconsin Press, 1982), pp. 32, 48.

[76] *ODNB* includes Deane Swift in the entry for his son ('Theophilus Swift').

[77] For Swift's efforts to assist Deane Swift, and their complications, see Ehrenpreis, *Swift*, vol. III, pp. 754, 859, 875–7, 900, 904–7; for Deane Swift's resentments, see letters to Sanderson Miller in Lilian Dickins and Mary Stanton (eds.), *An Eighteenth-Century Correspondence, being the letters of Deane Swift, Pitt, The Lytteltons and the Grenvilles, Lord Dacre, Robert Nugent, Charles Jenkinson, the Earls of Guilford, Coventry, & Hardwick, Sir Edward Turner, Mr. Talbot of Lacock, and others to Sanderson Miller, Esq., of Radway* (London: John Murray, 1910), pp. 37–40, 45.

[78] TS 1345; see *ESTC* for printings in this year; for its commitment to 'polemical Controversy' see Deane Swift's letter to Sanderson Miller, in Dickins and Stanton, *An Eighteenth-Century Correspondence*, p. 62.

[79] Daniel Cook (ed.), *The Lives of Jonathan Swift*, 3 vols. (London and New York: Routledge, 2011), vol. I, p. xvii.

[80] See below for the publication of manuscript material by Deane Swift in 1765. For the corrected copy of the *Tale*, and its possible use by Faulkner, see *CWJS Tale*, pp. 281–3; and for Hawkesworth's discussion, *Works*, vol. I, Preface.

Ending and Going On (1736–1765) 273

would express for Faulkner in his Preface; for although Deane Swift had in 1739 thanked Swift profusely for a gift of Faulkner's *Works*, Sir Walter Scott would in 1824 record that 'The late Mr. Deane Swift used to express great displeasure at Lord Orrery's having insinuated that his distinguished relative had corrected the Dublin edition.'[81] Even so, Deane Swift would in 1778 condemn Hawkesworth's edition itself (conceivably with some personal frustration) as 'the vilest that ever was yet published', since 'he published an edition of an Author whose writings he neither did, nor, for want of opportunities, could understand'.[82] Once again, the implication was that personal knowledge of Swift was the crucial qualification for an editor.

In the event, whoever the 'intimate Friend' was, and however Hawkesworth came to replace him, the 1755 edition was very similar to what had been proposed in 1752, triumphantly fulfilling its offer of quarto luxury. Whereas Faulkner had offered his first four volumes as a set of octavos including 'A few' large-paper copies 'printed on a Royal Paper for the Curious', purchasers of the 1755 London edition were offered either six large quartos or twelve large octavos: what had been exceptional luxury in Dublin in 1735 was the default in London twenty years later.[83] The text block was framed with ample margins, with occasional footnotes in smaller type below. Title pages, unframed and set with elegant restraint in roman throughout, compensated for loss of typographical variety by rubricating titles and key words, and the promised 'COPPER-PLATES' were exemplified in volume I by a frontispiece of the whale, the ship and the tub (confirming the new convention of placing the *Tale* at the head of the series). Having first wooed their premium market with quartos and large octavos, the booksellers then went on to offer smaller formats, right down to the tiny octodecimo (a final innovation which they made in 1765, approximately in parallel with Faulkner).[84]

---

[81] Ehrenpreis, *Swift*, vol. III, pp. 876–7; Scott, *Works*, vol. I, p. 411. For Orrery's testimony, see Boyle, *Remarks*, p. 135.

[82] John Nichols, *Illustrations of the Literary History of the Eighteenth Century. Consisting of Authentic Memoirs and Original Letters of Eminent Persons; and intended as a sequel to The Literary Anecdotes*, 8 vols. (London 1817–58), vol. V, p. 376.

[83] McLaverty, 'George Faulkner', p. 169, citing *London Evening Post*, 12–15 October 1734. TS notes: 'This practice of printing copies on small and thin paper as well as on large and thick paper he continued for the later volumes' (p. 22); Abbott, *Hawkesworth*, p. 48, citing *Public Advertiser*, 7 May 1755.

[84] See table, TS, p. 104, compared with Faulkner's octavos (p. 47), duodecimos (p. 60) and octodecimos (pp. 59–65).

274   Part IV: Into the Future

Hawkesworth was a new kind of print intermediary, a professional whose authority was not that of an author, nor of a bookseller, nor even of an 'intimate Friend' of the author. Already known as editor and author of the *Adventurer*, he would in the following year become literary editor of the *Gentleman's Magazine*.[85] Born into a skilled-manual dissenting background in London, he was largely self-educated and entered literary society partly on the strength of his marriage to a prosperous businesswoman.[86] In his early twenties he had responded to Pope's 1742 *New Dunciad* by condemning his treatment of Shaftesbury and accusing him of plagiarising his ethic epistles from him, while noting with satisfaction the revenge taken by Colley Cibber.[87] The outrage that such theological and literary views would have caused Swift was by now completely irrelevant – which might, perhaps, have opened up the opportunity for a genuinely fresh engagement with Swift's work. Unfortunately, it became instead the occasion for innovations ranging from the derivative, through the desultory, to the damagingly ignorant. But Hawkesworth was at least a businesslike choice, ready to turn his hand to many different kinds of assignments, and well used to meeting deadlines.

Hawkesworth brought three novel features to the editorial tradition. First, his Preface attempted a textual history of the entire canon; second, his 'Account of the Life of the Reverend Jonathan Swift' provided a prefatory biography; and third, his notes included critical and evaluative reflections as well as points of information. Of these, the second contribution, the 'Life' whose 'scheme' Samuel Johnson said he had 'laid before him in the intimacy of our friendship', was the most successful (and it is hard not to remark the contrast between an intimate friend such as Johnson was to Hawkesworth and the 'intimate Friend of the Author' for whom Hawkesworth found himself standing in).[88] Hawkesworth, conferring with the future author of *Lives of the Poets*, heralded a future in which the author, passing out of living memory, would cede the field to the professional biographer. In comparison, Hawkesworth's third contribution, the annotation, was less impressive: even in comparison with Faulkner's, the notes were slight and extremely scattered (although the 'Life' also provided substantial relevant information). A few works had an initial footnote to sketch in a context; occasional words and references were

---

[85] Abbott, *Hawkesworth*, pp. 4–12.   [86] *Ibid.*, p. 13.   [87] *Ibid.*, pp. 11–12.
[88] Lonsdale, *Lives*, vol. III, p. 189; Abbott, *Hawkesworth*, pp. 52–6.

Ending and Going On (1736–1765) 275

explained; a few Swiftian sallies prompted a critical insight or moral reflection, but Hawkesworth showed no consistent view of what to annotate, or how. Far worse was the ill-informed and partisan Preface in which he attempted a textual history of Swift's works.

This new edition, for all its material fanfare and enlarged team of undertakers, was still in part the outcome of Faulkner's long sharing of copy with Bowyer, yet Hawkesworth's textual history commended the new edition by attacking Faulkner's.[89] Hawkesworth took Swift entirely at his word in repudiating involvement with Faulkner's edition, implied that Faulkner had acted in bad faith throughout and accused him of pervasive textual incompetence. Most damagingly of all, Hawkesworth bolstered his argument with ostensibly impressive allegations that only readers with access to the relevant archives could assess. (Such expert readers, though probably few in number, would easily have registered the dissonance between claim and evidence – and might also have questioned, for instance, how many of the Scriblerian writings in volume II were really by Swift, or why the *Ode to the Athenian Society*, first published in 1692, was grouped with the 'Posthumous Pieces in Verse' in volume IV.[90])

It is instructive, in this light, to examine the way in which the series title constructs Hawkesworth's role (Figure 14). Here, in the hierarchy of editorial responsibilities, sequencing and visual impact play tellingly against each other. In terms of sequencing, establishing the text has priority, with the claim that the contents have been 'Accurately revised'; but there is no immediate statement as to who has done this or how, and the declaration is set in lower-case type of the smallest size. Only towards the foot of the title are specific contributions credited to Hawkesworth: 'Some Account of the AUTHOR'S LIFE' is rubricated in medium size, and 'NOTES HISTORICAL and EXPLANATORY' in smaller large and small capitals, while 'By JOHN HAWKESWORTH', though in type of only medium size, is both rubricated and set in full capitals. To judge by visual impact, Hawkesworth matters, and his most important contribution is the biography, with the notes coming a close second. Much more ambiguously presented, first in sequence but subordinate both in visual impact and in closeness of connection to Hawkesworth, is the establishment of the text. In this phase in the evolution of literary livelihoods it was evidently less important to understand the textual transmission than to

---

[89] Abbott, *Hawkesworth*, pp. 56–7.   [90] Vol. II, pp. 69–165; vol. IV, p. 229.

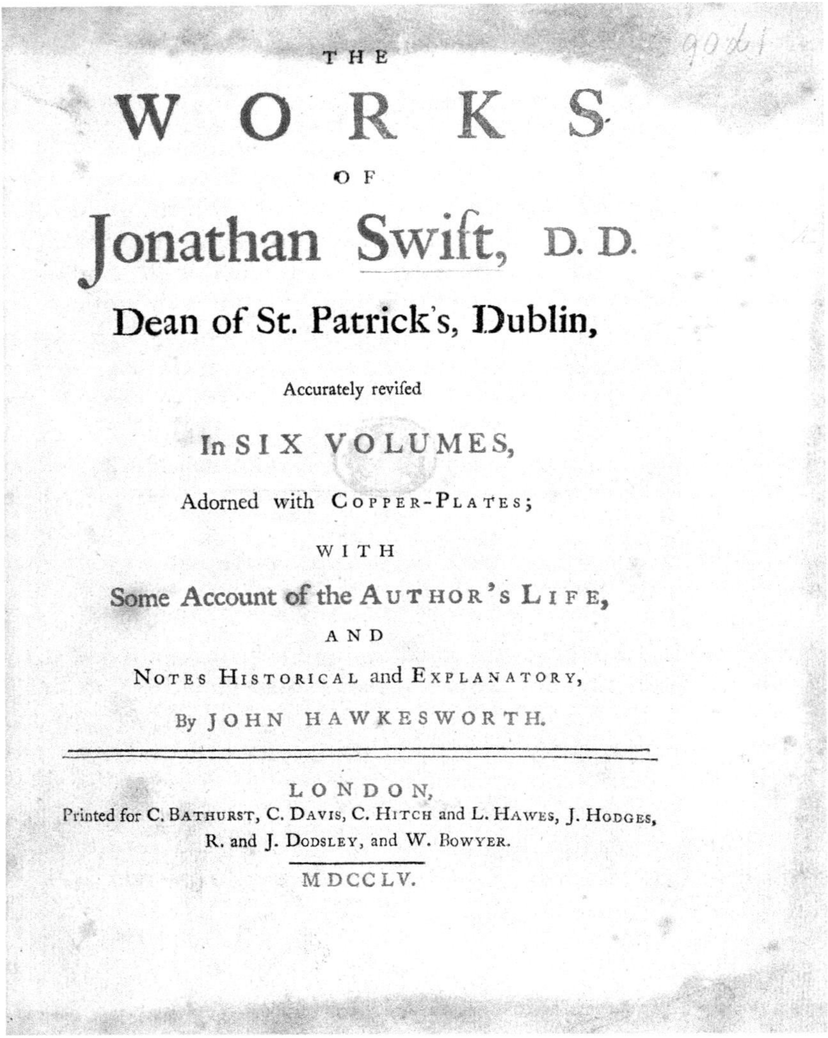

Part IV: Into the Future

THE

WORKS

OF

Jonathan Swift, D. D.

Dean of St. Patrick's, Dublin,

Accurately revised

In SIX VOLUMES,

Adorned with COPPER-PLATES;

WITH

Some Account of the AUTHOR'S LIFE,

AND

NOTES HISTORICAL and EXPLANATORY,

By JOHN HAWKESWORTH.

LONDON,

Printed for C. BATHURST, C. DAVIS, C. HITCH and L. HAWES, J. HODGES,
R. and J. DODSLEY, and W. BOWYER.

MDCCLV.

Figure 14 *The Works of Jonathan Swift, D. D. Dean of St. Patrick's, Dublin*, ed. John
Hawkesworth (London, 1755), vol. I, series title.

promote sales. Luxury formats, stylish typography and novel paratexts
all helped; and to the extent that the text mattered at all, the new
edition's superiority was proclaimed both by the series title and by the
assurance with which Hawkesworth denigrated Faulkner.

Ending and Going On (1736–1765)

Taking Stock

Hawkesworth's edition marks the great posthumous watershed of Swift in print. It achieved for the London copy-holders a product that was far more than the sum of its previously scattered parts, establishing itself as the new standard edition and carrying forward the long-term transmission that would deliver Swift as a household name into the twenty-first century. But it was also overblown, inexpressive, ill-informed and bluntly literal in naming the author whose biography it now established as the routine introduction to a set of Works. The fact that changing contemporary taste made such changes a condition of commercial and cultural survival does not diminish their significance.

Hawkesworth's edition built on the process by which, starting with the 1710 fifth edition of the *Tale* and the 1711 *Miscellanies in Prose and Verse*, Swift's works had been progressively curated for posterity. He effaced any remaining sense of the modestly workmanlike quality that had characterised lifetime Swift in print, calibrated in its own time across the relatively narrow range between respectable octavo and better-than-average half sheet. Despite this unpretentiousness of format, production values had been consistently pitched towards the upper range of practicability; and one result (visible in the design and printwork of the *Tale*, the *Travels* and many smaller spoofs) had been to maintain a crucial distance between parodic allusion and literal materialisation of the preposterousness conjured in the verbal texts. Swift's routine anonymity had often been supplemented by evasive imprints, and many of his publications had been voiced by fictitious characters constructed in part by the generic allusions of the material texts; but all this play of prevarication was now at an end, barred by the plain-as-a-pikestaff placement of his name across the title, and the print standardisation that had progressively stripped away the material allusion of the original texts. Equally muted in Hawkesworth's edition was the demotic force of the genuinely down-market printing represented by the Drapier's letters and the slapdash under-investment of opportunist reprinters like Carter. (Although there is really no one quite like Carter.) Most pervasively of all, Hawkesworth's over-large and blandly chaste page retained almost nothing of the noisily expressive patterning of roman, italic, full capitals, small capitals and black letter by which the reader of lifetime Swift in print (especially in its earlier and cheaper manifestations) had been alerted to the differential force of particular words.[91]

---

[91] For changing taste in the use of italic, see Smith, *The Printer's Grammar*, published, like Hawkesworth's edition, in 1755 (pp. 12–17).

278   Part IV: Into the Future

Reading Hawkesworth is a much quieter experience, ushering the reader away from the labour and ingenuity of the printing-house and into the hush of the library, a trend that would be continued in succeeding late-century editions.

But such reflections are the privilege of hindsight. For any bookseller in the 1750s whose stock in trade was Swift, it was necessary to act (or at the very least to do some market research). To judge by an Advertisement dated 9 March 1754, Faulkner knew exactly what he would be up against when Hawkesworth's London edition appeared (it is hard to imagine that Bowyer would not have kept him informed).[92] The first part of his Advertisement reminded readers that 'GEORGE FAULKNER' was 'the Editor and Publisher of the WORKS of the Rev. DR. *SWIFT*, D. S. P. D.' The doubly articulated claim emphasised that he was not just the bookseller but also the established editor in the city that Swift had made his own (whereas the London publishers had farmed out the editing to a stranger, by whom Faulkner was about to be denounced for ignorance and malpractice). Faulkner further gestured towards his personal connection with the Dean by mentioning that he was about to print 'several original Pieces . . . in the Author's own Hand Writing'. Several of the proposed improvements to the content of Faulkner's *Works* then addressed specific issues to be raised by Hawkesworth's edition. Faulkner, for instance, promised 'several historical and explanatory Notes to the Works already printed', and 'an HISTORY of the Author and Writings, from the most authentic MSS' (which gave him a potential edge over a biography based on secondary sources). Also, as if confronting in advance Hawkesworth's accusations of textual incompetence, Faulkner offered 'a compleat, genuine, and correct Edition of the TALE of a TUB', at the same time accommodating the trend towards placing the work at the head of the set by stating that it 'will make the first, or eleventh Volume of his Works, as the Purchaser shall please to bind them'. The second part of the Advertisement then addressed the crucial issues of format, type quality and illustration: 'He will also print in a short Time, all the WORKS of the said DR. *SWIFT*, in seven volumes in large Quarto, fine Paper, and in a Beautiful NEW TYPE of this Size' (to illustrate the effect, these six words are set, larger than the rest, on a line by themselves), 'with a Set of CUTS designed by the celebrated HAYMAN, of *London*.' Although the price was 'three guineas and a Half' instead of the three guineas

---

[92] The Advertisement appeared at the back of *Brotherly Love. A Sermon, preached in St. Patrick's Church; on December 1st, 1717. By Dr. Jonathan Swift, Dean of St. Patrick's, Dublin* (Dublin, 1754; TS 808, *ESTC* T166834). See also headnote to TS 53, Faulkner's octodecimo edition, pp. 59–60; Elias, 'Swift's *Don Quixote*', pp. 34–7.

Ending and Going On (1736–1765)

mentioned in the London booksellers' 1752 *Proposals*, it was proportionate to the additional volume. Faulkner also announced, in the same Advertisement, an octodecimo edition of 'Pocket Volumes'.

Had all this been achieved, it might in part have forestalled the threat to Faulkner's primacy, but no quarto edition in fact appeared. Indeed, the concession that 'There will be no Subscription Money demanded, until the Works shall be ready to deliver to the Subscribers' may suggest that the aim was principally to test the market. The following years saw several indications of further preparation: Faulkner experimented in his octodecimo edition, inaugurated in 1756, with the reordering of the canon; he advertised in 1759 not only that Trinity College had authorised the printing of his 'very pompous and compleat edition' in quarto at the University Printing Office, but also that Deane Swift had supplied him, in effect, with the same corrections to the *Tale* as boasted by Hawkesworth; and in 1762 he included in his octodecimo volume XI both the *Tale* (this being its first appearance as an integral part of Faulkner's *Works*) and a slightly altered version of Hawkesworth's 'Life'.[93] In 1765 Lyon also began to compile, apparently for Faulkner, extensive corrections and additions to Hawkesworth's 'Life'.[94] Faulkner's commercial and editorial flair seems to have been as eager as ever – his potential subscribers' enthusiasm perhaps less so.

The problem was taken up by Lord Chesterfield, the former Lord Lieutenant. In 1758 he asked after Faulkner's plan for a quarto edition ('Have you laid aside that design?'); and in 1760 he wrote to warn him explicitly against it:

> Let me advise you as a friend not to engage too deep in the expense of a new and pompous quarto edition of your friend Swift. I think you may chance to be what perhaps you would not choose to be, a considerable loser by it. Whosoever in the three kingdoms has any books at all, has Swift; and, unless you have some new pieces, and those too not trifling ones, to add, people will not throw away their present handy and portable octavos, for expensive and unwieldy quartos. How far indeed the name (you are so much superior to quibbles, that you can bear, and sometimes even smile at them) of *quartos* may help them off in Ireland, I cannot pretend to say.[95]

---

[93] Barry Slepian, 'Jonathan Swift and George Faulkner' (PhD dissertation, University of Pennsylvania, 1962), pp. 128–9; D. Woolley, 'The Textual History of *A Tale of a Tub*', p. 20; Mary Pollard, 'George Faulkner', *SStud*, 7 (1992), 79–96 (p. 85); *Dublin Journal*, 18 July, 5 August, 23 August 1759; TS 53, *ESTC* T73683.

[94] Elias, 'Swift's *Don Quixote*', pp. 30–1, 34–5.

[95] *The Letters of Philip Dormer Stanhope, 4th Earl of Chesterfield*, ed. Bonamy Dobrée, 5 vols. ([London: Eyre and Spottiswoode], 1932), vol. V, pp. 2297–8, 2361–2.

280   Part IV: Into the Future

One of the arguments against a Faulkner quarto was precisely that the octavos (not to mention the duodecimos) had been so successful. The modest format that had dominated lifetime Swift in print had in Chesterfield's view so effectively satisfied demand as to destroy the market for a Faulkner quarto (unless, Chesterfield sneers, Faulkner's Irish customers mistook it for something to drink). There may even be a hint that the notion of a large-format prestige edition had itself come to seem questionable: perhaps consumers (who had since 1735 been able to buy even Pope's *Works* in 'cheap, elegant, and readily available' annotated octavos) actually preferred a 'handy and portable' Swift to an 'expensive and unwieldy' one – just as Swift had in 1733 contrasted 'wealdable' Dublin octavo reprints of Pope's single poems with the 'monstrous' and expensive folios produced in London.[96]

The History of the Four Last Years of the Queen (1758)

Soon after Hawkesworth's edition reached the market in 1755 there emerged yet another threat to Faulkner. In 1758 the tally of major prose works that Swift had striven in vain to publish in his lifetime was finally completed by the London publication, in octavo, of *The History of the Four Last Years of the Queen*.[97] The title page gave Swift's name in full and asserted that it was 'Published from the / Last MANUSCRIPT COPY, Corrected and / Enlarged by the Author's OWN HAND'; but the bookseller named in the imprint was Andrew Millar (1705–1768), who had in 1752 published Orrery's far from complimentary *Remarks on the Life and Writings of Jonathan Swift* (as indeed had Faulkner, whose Dublin reprint turned out to be highly profitable, if questionable in its loyalty to his late author).[98] A member of a distinguished clerical family in the Church of Scotland, Millar had developed an impressive profile featuring Scottish writers such as James Thomson, David Mallet, Allan Ramsay and David Hume, as well as classics of the Whig tradition like Milton, Locke, Bayle and Burnet. He had also distinguished himself as promoter of new developments in the novel, counting Samuel Richardson, Henry and Sarah

---

[96] *Corr.*, vol. III, p. 615. See also Bronson, *Printing as an Index of Taste*, pp. 11–14; McLaverty, *Pope, Print and Meaning*, p. 209.

[97] *The History of the Four Last Years of the Queen. By the late Jonathan Swift, D. D. D. S. P. D. Published from the last manuscript copy, corrected and enlarged by the author's own hand* (London, 1758; TS 809, *ESTC* T143996). For the complex manuscript transmission, see H. Williams's Introduction to *PW*, vol. VII; *JSA*, Introduction; Karian, *Print and Manuscript*, pp. 92–8.

[98] Faulkner wrote to Orrery on 30 November 1751: 'I am likely to be hanged, drawn and quartered for printing and publishing this Libel against my best Friend and Benefactor, and am charged on this Account with the utmost Ingratitude to the Dean' (Ward, *Prince of Dublin Printers*, pp. 38–41 (p. 39)).

Ending and Going On (1736–1765) 281

Fielding, Charlotte Lennox and Tobias Smollett among his authors. Yet he continued to recognise the interest of Tory authors of the last generation: by the time he took on *The Four Last Years* he had already published John Sheffield, Duke of Buckingham, Bolingbroke and Pope (and also a play by Thomas Sheridan the younger). *The Four Last Years* was not therefore without precedent in his output (and in 1729 he had published, on the same topic but from an opposite point of view, *Memoirs of Queen Anne . . . wherein the transactions of the four last years are fully related*); but it may still seem ironic that Swift's political testament should in the end, after being repeatedly blocked in his lifetime by those most nearly concerned, appear under Presbyterian auspices.[99] Yet such irony was not without precedent, for Swift in print had first begun, long ago in 1691–2, with the publication of *An Ode. To the King* by John Brent and *Ode to the Athenian Society* by John Dunton. The difference was that Millar would now sponsor the framing of this vehemently Tory work with an explicit repudiation of its politics.

Like other booksellers in the years after Swift's death, Millar looked to an editor who had actually known him – but this time one implacably opposed to his politics. The long, unsigned Advertisement began in excitable and accusatory mode: '*THUS, the long wished for* HISTORY *of the* FOUR LAST YEARS *of the* QUEEN'*s Reign is at length brought to light, in spight of all attempts to suppress it!*'[100] It went on to tell the story of '*a gentleman, now in* Ireland, *of the greatest probity and worth, with whom the* DEAN *long lived in perfect intimacy*', to whom '*the* DEAN *intrusted a copy of his History, desiring him to peruse and give his judgment of it, with the last corrections and amendments the author had given it, in his own hand*'.[101] This person had only released it for publication when '*he and the world had full assurance, that the* DEAN'*s executors, or those into whose hands the original copy fell, were so far from intending to publish it, that it was actually suppressed, perhaps destroyed*'. Such accusations of literary skulduggery set the scene for an account that combined admiration for Swift's powers as historian with a careful rejection of his political opinions. Swift was depicted as a writer '*with strong passions, but with stronger prepossessions and prejudices in favour of a party*' from which the editor was keen to dissociate himself:

> *The editor considers this work in another light: he long knew the author, and was no stranger to his politics, connexions, tendencies, passions, and the whole*

---

[99] *ESTC* T90442.   [100] *The History of the Four Last Years of the Queen*, p. iii.
[101] *Ibid.*, pp. iii–iv.

Part IV: Into the Future

> *economy of his life. He has long been hardly singular in condemning this great man's conduct, amidst the admiring multitude; nor ever could have thought of making an interest in a man, whose principles and manners he could, by no rule of reason and honour, approve, however he might have admired his parts and wit.*[102]

He also singled out for condemnation some of Swift's more detailed judgements (with particular indignation at his calling the former James II *'the* abducated King').[103] Finally, he turned to editorial matters, making a distinction between the presumption of correcting Swift's *'seeming inaccuracies in stile or expression'* (which he left instead to *'the amending hand of every sensible and polite reader'*) and *'errors which are to be ascribed either to transcribers or the press'.*[104] From this diffuse and sometimes confusing Advertisement two things at least were clear: Swift deserved respect as a writer, but his party politics were indefensible. Editorial deference could no longer be taken for granted.

Controversy about the rights to the work, which Faulkner believed to be his, soon broke out in print, as the Dublin booksellers George and Alexander Ewing (active from 1718, *d.* 1764; active from 1744, *d.* 1765) added to the dispute by publishing a 1758 text of their own, which Carpenter has shown not to have been derived from Millar's, but probably from a manuscript belonging to William Rufus Chetwood (*d.* 1766), whose London apprenticeship to Curll and subsequent career as bookseller had early in life 'placed him in the right circles to have Swift material in manuscript', before a move to Ireland and into theatrical work and authorship in his own right left him 'living in straitened circumstances in Dublin'.[105] (The Ewings also in 1758 integrated the piece into volume IX of a cheaper, dubiously authorised Dublin *Works*, largely derived from Scottish reprints but also collecting for the first time, and in a revised text that would apparently later serve as copy for Faulkner and others, *A Short Character of His Ex. T. E. of W. L. L. of I—*.[106] This *Works*, though disfigured by editorial bombast and indiscriminately agglomerated paratext, was still, as Carpenter argues, in some ways

---

[102] *Ibid.*, pp. v–vi. [103] *Ibid.*, p. xiii. [104] *Ibid.*, p. xv.

[105] For the Ewings' edition, see TS 812–13, *ESTC* T154477, T139457; for their probable use of a manuscript source (rather than Millar's text), and for its possible transmission via Chetwood, see Carpenter, 'Reading Swift's Works', pp. 123–5.

[106] See textual account of *A Short Character* in *CWJS English Political Writings, 1701–1711* (forthcoming); and, for additional textual novelties in the Ewings' edition, Carpenter, 'Reading Swift's Works', pp. 123–4, and 'ST. PATRICK's Address to the People of IRELAND when he resigned his Patronage', in *CWJS Poems* III (forthcoming). The contents of each volume of the Ewings' *Works* (*ESTC* T52742) are listed in TS 98.

Ending and Going On (1736–1765)

preferable to Faulkner's, not least in adopting a more rational ordering.[107]) For his part, Faulkner issued *An Appeal to the Public* in March 1758 to protest against the Ewings' publication of the *History of the Four Last Years*, and in the same year incorporated his own edition into his *Works* under a different title: *The History of the Last Session of Parliament, and of the Peace of Utrecht. Written at Windsor in the year, 1713. By the Rev. Dr. J. Swift, D. S. P. D.*[108]

Twenty years later, in 1779, a possible identification of Millar's 'editor' would be published in the *Gentleman's Magazine*: Orrery, who disapproved of the publication, was cited to the effect that 'Lucas is most probably the person who has undertaken the invidious task of vilifying and abusing by Dr. Swift's pen.'[109] (The reviewer also cited a sneering suggestion that 'both the language and logic [of the Advertisement prefixed] prove him an Irishman who wrote it'.) Charles Lucas (1713–1771) had been a Dublin apothecary and radical controversialist (dubbed by Connolly 'the most prolific Irish political thinker of the mid-eighteenth century') who had moved to London to avoid imprisonment by the Irish Commons.[110] But although the identification added plausibility to the first editor's claim that he '*long knew the author*', it did not resolve doubts about the authenticity of the work itself. (Johnson, for instance, not only repeated Lucas's name in *Lives of the Poets*, but also spoke doubtfully of the attribution of the work to Swift.[111]) Millar's *History*, unlike Faulkner's *Directions*, had contained no invitation to inspect the evidence of 'the Author's OWN HAND'.

Deane Swift's Additions to Hawkesworth's Edition (1765)

In November 1763, readers were informed of a substantial effort to add further to Swift's published works, and this time Deane Swift was explicitly named as the source of the new material: 'Several Tracts Political and Historical', 'Two Political Sermons', 'several Pieces of Wit and Humour', 'About Seventy or Eighty genuine Letters' and 'Near Forty Copies of

---

[107] For detailed comparison between Faulkner's *Works* and the Ewings', see Carpenter, 'Reading Swift's Works'.

[108] *An Appeal to the Public* ([Dublin, 1758]; TS 1353, *ESTC* N3432); for *The History of the Last Session*, see TS 45A–46, TS 51A(8).

[109] *Gentleman's Magazine*, 49 (1779), p. 255 (reviewing John Nichols, *A Supplement to Dr. Swift's Works* (London, 1776–9). See also Mahony, *Jonathan Swift* (pp. 13–16); *CWJS Irish Political Writings after 1725* (pp. lxxxviii–lxxxix).

[110] Connolly, *Divided Kingdom*, pp. 241–4 (p. 242).

[111] Lonsdale, *Lives*, vol. III, pp. 199–200, 444.

284 Part IV: Into the Future

Verses'. But two significantly different proposals were circulating at the same time. One was the separately published four-page *Proposals for Printing by Subscription, several curious pieces, written by Doctor Swift, never before published*, dated 12 November 1763, which offered subscribers, for a standard price of 10s., their choice of one volume in quarto, two in large octavo, or three in small octavo, 'in order to accommodate those Gentlemen who are already possessed of the Doctor's other Works in any of the above Sizes'.[112] This appeared to be a London project: 'SUBSCRIPTIONS are taken in by / J. and R. TONSON in the *Strand*; / W. JOHNSTON in *Ludgate Street*; / and also by the following booksellers ...', none of whom was dignified by large and small capitals, and all of whom were based outside London.[113] Meanwhile, another set of *Proposals*, also dated 12 November, and seconded by an advertisement in *Jackson's Oxford Journal* for 19 November, made a slightly different offer, which was to be printed at the Clarendon Press.[114] It did not mention the Tonsons or Johnston, did not offer a quarto, and listed Oxford booksellers first – the second of whom was Daniel Prince (apprenticed 1726, d. 1796), Warehouse Keeper at the Press.

The situation is to an extent clarified by Deane Swift's letters to Sanderson Miller, to whom he also sent a draft proposal. This named no booksellers, envisaged publication in octavo only, left Deane Swift himself to administer subscriptions, and declared: 'These Volumes if the Vice Chancellor will please to grant his Imprimatur, to be printed at the Theatre in Oxford.'[115] Reminiscent of Faulkner's unfulfilled 1759 advertisement for a quarto Works to be printed at the Trinity College Printing Office in Dublin, Deane Swift's aspiration was also consistent with his passionate attachment to the University, for like his friend Miller he had taken his BA at St Mary Hall, Oxford, and in March 1763 his son Theophilus also matriculated there.[116] This was the college of Swift's late-career intermediary William King, now in his late seventies: both of Deane Swift's published proposals testify that King had confirmed the handwriting as Swift's. In November 1763 Deane Swift told Miller that he was in Oxford 'preparing all things requisite for printing those works which

---

[112] *ESTC* T231511.   [113] *Proposals for Printing by Subscription*, p. 4.

[114] *ESTC* N62130; Matthew Kilburn, 'The Learned Press: History, Languages, Literature, and Music', in Ian Gadd (ed.), *The History of Oxford University Press*, vol. I: *Beginnings to 1780* (Oxford University Press, 2013), pp. 419–59 (pp. 453–4), reproducing *Jackson's Oxford Journal*; Cook, 'Publishing Posthumous Swift', p. 217.

[115] Dickins and Stanton, *An Eighteenth-Century Correspondence*, pp. 70–2. University printing had formerly been based at the Sheldonian Theatre.

[116] *Ibid.*, pp. 66–7.

Ending and Going On (1736–1765) 285

I talked to you about', and he congratulated himself that 'All things promise well both at Oxford and Cambridge; and particularly at London all people who have seen my Proposals are delighted with them.'[117] Indeed, following King's death in 1763, Deane Swift spent the summer of 1764 in London, 'where I disposed of my Property in the Manuscripts, saving the Business of my Subscribers, to two of the prime Booksellers, Parson [Tonson?] and Johnson'. This was not necessarily incompatible with Oxford publication, since the Press produced far more 'authors' books' funded by authors, subscribers and others than it did 'Delegates' books' for the University.[118] But in the event the collection bore Johnston's London imprint and formed part of Hawkesworth's edition, a move facilitated by the inclusion of a quarto format in the London proposal.[119] The editors' preface mentioned 'circumstances, which at present, we rather chuse to pass over in silence'; but whatever had gone on behind the scenes, the London imprint underlined the incorporation of Deane Swift's materials into the canon of the London booksellers. Deane Swift wrote to Miller in November 1765 of his overwhelming contempt both for the Hawkesworth edition of which his collection was now part ('that whole injudicious wretched silly Edition printed in London') and for Faulkner's (though 'not half so bad as the English'); and he cited 'some of the Printers in London' to support his self-regarding claim 'that if I do not prepare an Edition for the use of Posterity, there will never be any one valuable Edition of the Dr.'s Works until the Day of Judgement'.[120] Experience of living in Ireland, familiarity with people and events known to Swift, and knowledge of 'many local Anecdotes' were, he insisted, indispensable qualifications; and he hoped (the tone is more febrile than persuasive) 'to finish it against the summer of the year 1768, if it please God that I should live so long'. Although he survived until 1783, no such edition appeared.

Thus Deane Swift's principal contribution to Swift in print remains his 1765 collection, which made substantial additions to Swift's published writing.[121] Some pieces supplemented already familiar works. *An Answer*

---

[117] *Ibid.*, p. 68.

[118] Martyn Ould, 'The Workplace: Places, Procedures, and Personnel 1668–1780', in Ian Gadd (ed.), *The History of Oxford University Press*, vol. I: *Beginnings to 1780* (Oxford University Press, 2013), pp. 193–240 (p. 194); Kilburn, 'The Learned Press', pp. 452–4. For the Clarendon Press imprints of books printed by Daniel Prince and sold by London booksellers, see *ESTC* in and around 1765.

[119] For the quarto, see TS 87, *ESTC* T52748; see also *CWJS Parodies*, pp. 627, 631–2; and, for Deane Swift's role in Hawkesworth's edition, TS headnote to 87–92, 'Third Stage', and table (pp. 81, 104).

[120] Dickins and Stanton, *An Eighteenth-Century Correspondence*, pp. 72–5.

[121] The following discussion is based on the quarto single volume; smaller formats comprised multiple volumes.

286 Part IV: Into the Future

to Bickerstaff presented a conclusion to the Bickerstaff hoax by a knowing 'Person of Quality' (very probably voiced by Swift himself), which had not been printed at the time.[122] *Laws for the Dean's Servants* contextualised *Directions to Servants* by revealing the rules by which Swift had governed his own household.[123] The *Preface to the History of the Four last Years of Queen Anne's Reign*, though written later than the *History* itself, is now routinely printed with it.[124] Other pieces amplified aspects of Swift's everyday creativity, such as the letters that filled most of Part II.[125] Alongside the letters, some of the discursive material was particularly revealing for Swift's biography. *Resolutions when I Come to be Old. Written in the Year MDCXIX* reflected on his early experience of life with the elderly Temple, and *On Barbarous Denominations in Ireland* told the story of his Uncle Godwin's misguided investment in the Swandlingbar iron foundry.[126] *On the Death of Mrs. Johnson*, meanwhile, offered personal testimony of Swift's relation to the woman whom some claimed had secretly been his wife. Some of the poems also focused on Swift's personal relationships, notably the sociable verses exchanged with Sheridan and Delany – which the volume put into context by printing their contributions as well as his own. Some new poems were printed here for the first time, but, as was standard across all the genres brought together in sets of Works, previously unpublished pieces were not routinely distinguished from published but previously uncollected pieces. Among Market Hill poems, for example, *Robin and Harry* really was appearing in print for the first time, but *The Dean's Reasons for not building at Drapier's Hill* had already been printed more than once.[127] But there was also a notable omission from the advertised list: the potentially inflammatory and as yet unpublished *A Discourse on Hereditary Right*, probably composed about 1710.[128] It would not be published at all until 1775, when its attribution to Swift was insinuated rather than directly stated; and *CWJS* will be the first Works to include it. Yet much of the new material that did achieve publication in 1765 is less than fully developed or echoes the themes of better-known works; and some fragments, notably *Hints on Good Manners*, recall the imagined defects of Motte's *Tale* by trailing off into asterisks.[129]

---

[122] *CWJS Parodies*, Appendix E, pp. 573–7.   [123] *Ibid.*, Associated Materials III, pp. 537–8.
[124] See *PW*, vol. VII.
[125] For the progressive addition of letters from the stock of Deane Swift and John Lyon to the Hawkesworth edition, see A. Williams, 'Epistolary Forms', p. 120.
[126] *CWJS Parodies*, pp. 244–53; Ehrenpreis, *Swift*, vol. I, pp. 63–4.
[127] *CWJS Poems* III (forthcoming).
[128] See Introduction and Textual Account in *CWJS English Political Writings, 1701–1711* (forthcoming).
[129] *CWJS Parodies*, pp. 193–7.

Ending and Going On (1736–1765)

In fact more than half of the posthumously published pieces in *CWJS Irish Political Writings after 1725*, devoted to the years when Swift became 'entirely alienated from Irish political life, very much the outside observer of a drama to whose essential plot-line he was indifferent', owe their first publication to Deane Swift's 1765 volume.[130] Yet there were also happier exhibits: *A Discourse to Prove the Antiquity of the English Tongue* furnishes a joyous example of discursive punning in Swift's best style of in-character satire.[131]

The quarto's two separately paginated parts, once bound together, made a substantial volume. Following the usual Hawkesworth design, the title page was set almost entirely in roman capitals, its only italics reserved for the Virgilian motto '*Hæ tibi erunt artes*' ('be these your arts'), taken from Anchises' prophecy to Aeneas of Rome's distinctively political contributions to human development.[132] At the top of the page 'WORKS' and the author's name were distinguished by rubrication and the largest and second-largest type; but considerable prominence was given beneath to 'DEANE SWIFT, ESQ; of GOODRICH, in HEREFORDSHIRE'. Eighteen pages of subscribers followed, with a final apology to other 'Persons of Rank and Distinction, both in Scotland and Ireland' whose names had not arrived in time.[133] From Oxford there were not only the two volumes subscribed for by 'Doctor William King, late Principal of St. Mary Hall, Oxford', but also many individual subscriptions and an impressive total of sixty-four sets for Oxford booksellers. (There were also twenty-four sets each for booksellers in Bath, Cambridge, Winchester and a 'Mr. R. Tovey', and twelve sets for Chester.) The list brought together nobility, gentry, clergy, universities and business across England, Ireland and Wales, with a scatter of copies going as far afield as Rotterdam and Philadelphia, and one to 'His Excellency Count Woronzow, Ambassador Extraordinary from Her Imperial Majesty of Russia'. Even at this late date, a few survivors of Swift's circle still made their appearance, notably 'The Honourable Lady Betty Germaine' and 'Mr. George Faulkner, of Dublin'; but newer institutional bases for literary consumption were also represented by 'The Book-Society of Grantham, in Lincolnshire' and 'The Sandwich Book-Society', as well as by two subscriptions from employees of 'the Sun Fire-Office, London'.[134]

---

[130] *CWJS Irish Political Writings after 1725*, p. cii.   [131] *CWJS Parodies*, pp. 230–42.
[132] 'Hae tibi erunt artes' (Virgil, *Aeneid*, VI. l. 852).   [133] Part I, p. xx.
[134] For the Grantham society, see the testimony of a clergyman who in 1775 told James Boswell that it 'has subsisted these thirty years', but 'that at first it consisted of clergymen only, and very respectable clergymen; but now they have apothecaries and others amongst them, and are not so respectable'. He added that they met 'once a month', that 'the expense of their books and pamphlets did not exceed a guinea a year each member', and that they ran a half-yearly account with a London

288 Part IV: Into the Future

A brief, one-page preface seemed at first sight to guarantee newness and authenticity, repeating the promise in the proposals that the manuscripts would be deposited 'in the British Museum, provided the Governors will please to receive them into their collection'.[135] Yet there were complications: the collection also included 'two or three Poems taken from the public prints', and manuscript material 'transcribed by his Amanuensis' or provided by 'our friends' – and the deposit seems not to have been carried through. Indeed, Deane Swift's 1778 correspondence with John Nichols (1745–1826) confirms that he shared the view, usual during Swift's lifetime, that manuscripts should be disposed of after printing ('not worth the skin of a turnip' being his memorable phrase).[136] Yet quite apart from their role in confirming attribution, such rare survivals as the manuscripts of *The Bubble*, or *A Modest Defence of Punning*, or the Rothschild manuscript of *Directions to Servants* also suggest how much of Swift's own material expression is lost when the only text that survives has been stripped of italics and capitalised nouns. The elegant plainness conferred on Deane Swift's new material was still varied with decorative endpieces, but new items were marked only by double rules at the head of the page, above titles set principally in roman capitals. In the texts themselves, one tiny but conclusive sign of the typographical distance that Swift in print had travelled was the decorous logic with which the new italic semicolons now matched preceding italic words. Annotation (supplemented to a degree by Hawkesworth's 'Life' in volume I) was slight and occasional, interfering little with the clean page. There were hardly any contextual headnotes, and footnotes focused for the most part on identifying people and places, or, at the end of the volume, adding a glossary to a game of 'Hard Latin' with Sheridan. Very occasionally readers were offered insights based on details of the manuscript text, as when Swift referred to '*personal civilities*' paid him by Harley: 'These words printed in Italicks are in the original erased, perhaps to avoid the imputation of vanity.'[137]

Going On

By offering so few notes, Deane Swift engaged far less obviously in contextualisation and advocacy than Faulkner, or than the *Essay* that he may

---

bookseller (*Boswell: The Ominous Years, 1774–1776*, ed. Charles Ryskamp and Frederick A. Pottle (London: Heinemann, 1963), pp. 83–4).

[135] Part I, p. xxiii.

[136] Nichols, *Illustrations*, vol. V, p. 376; Cook, 'Publishing Posthumous Swift', pp. 217–20.

[137] *Memoirs, relating to that Change which happened in the Queen's Ministry in the Year 1710* (Part I, p. 18).

Ending and Going On (1736–1765) 289

indeed have designed originally as a prefatory volume. But Faulkner, creating his printed role in the edition under the observation – if not always the direct instruction – of his author, had in the 1730s been laying the foundation for a rather different enterprise. As time went on, the resulting product looked increasingly old-fashioned; and, in the absence of his projected quarto edition, the prestige format for his reprinting of the London 1765 material was still the large octavo. In 1772, his expansion of the octavo edition to twenty volumes (with the *Tale* coming in as volume XX) represented not new ambition but the culmination of his long habit of reissuing stored sheets with new title pages.[138] Teerink notes: 'All these twenty volumes are earlier ones (Sm[all]. P[aper].), provided with new titles as above . . . ; but the renewal has not always been effected with proper care.'[139] The Dublin *Works* had fallen definitively behind.

In the mid-1730s Faulkner's modestly tempered ambition had been an advantage: it had enabled him to launch a major edition without over-reaching; to work with the discarded type of a superior printer; to cancel and replace parts of volume II after printing; to demote his elaborate volume I to volume IV; and to perform through all this the decorously passive role of an agent dependent on the textual mediation of '*Friends*' of '*the supposed Author*'. His strategy suited the Dublin market, the estab-lished association of Swift in print with unpretentious formats, and the author's insistence on both anonymity and authority: the result was a *Works* that put Faulkner at the head of the Dublin trade and kept him there for a lifetime. By giving monumental form to Ireland's most famous literary canon he had shown what could be achieved in the Dublin print trade by an entrepreneur alert to opportunity and effectively networked with the London trade. But in 1801, only a quarter of a century after his death in 1775, the system of legal reprinting in the other kingdom that had been fundamental to his business would be swept away, in the wake of the Act of Union, by the imposition of English copyright law.[140]

Even within twenty years of Swift's death in 1745 much had already changed. London copy-holders had seized the textual initiative, and it was Faulkner's turn to reprint from sheets supplied by Bowyer and his succes-sor. The printed canon had been substantially enlarged by two major prose works, a significant body of letters and many smaller pieces in prose and verse; and previously printed but obscure items had gained renewed currency in major collections. The Swift canon as we now receive it was

---

[138] TS 47, *ESTC* N31130, N31131; the new material formed vols. XII–XIII of the octavo edition.
[139] TS 48, and see final note, p. 46. [140] Pollard, *Dublin's Trade*, p. 31.

290 Part IV: Into the Future

already largely complete – although more still was to come (and probably to a lesser extent still is). A tradition of large sets of Works was well established; and in London, in contrast with the relatively modest formats of Swift's lifetime, the lavish large quarto was a familiar offering in editions that featured a preliminary biography as well as a sprinkling of contextual and critical notes. Presentation had meanwhile been adapted to new fashions, deploying typographical effects both more and less elaborate than Swift would have expected. In 1765 there were neatly rubricated title pages with roman full or large and small capitals for emphasis, and clean, carefully printed texts in which italic semicolons followed italic words in due sequence. But the text lacked typographical variety, and there was little opportunity for readerly negotiation between word and ornament. The 1765 quarto title, moreover, though confirming the transition over time from the double-framed 'Handbill' style to that of the unframed 'Inscriptional Tablet', still sat somewhat fussily on the large page – in striking contrast with the sculptural boldness enterprised in Birmingham in the previous decade in the Latin quartos of John Baskerville (1706–1775) – whose London agent, Dodsley, was now one of the London copy-holders.[141] Despite the new pomp of the Hawkesworth edition, Swift in print was by no means at the cutting edge.

Beyond 1765 there would be one more major eighteenth-century edition, the 1784 London *Works* commissioned from Thomas Sheridan the younger; and in 1801 a major revision and supplementation of that edition was carried through by Bowyer's apprentice and successor John Nichols.[142] After fifty years the field was still effectively dominated by the sons and successors of Swift's associates, a situation that would only come to an end with Scott's *Works* of 1814 and 1824 – although even then Scott was supplied with new material by Deane Swift's son Theophilus, who also showed him Mrs Whiteway's copy of the *Tale*.[143] By the early twentieth century, with the separation of Swift biography from the Works tradition and the establishment of Swift in university research and teaching, editions by Herbert Davis, Sir Harold Williams and others gave new emphasis to canonical completeness, historical contextualisation and textual transparency. Scholarly editions

[141] For the 1765 title, see above. For trends in title design, see Bronson, *Printing as an Index of Taste*, pp. 20, 24–5. For Baskerville and Dodsley, see *The Correspondence of Robert Dodsley, 1733–1764*, ed. James E. Tierney (Cambridge University Press, 1988), pp. 144–6, 169, 252–3, 264–5, 273.
[142] For an overview of these editions, see Cook, 'Publishing Posthumous Swift'.
[143] E.g. the sketches towards a preface to *Directions to Servants* placed by Scott in the notes to his *Memoirs* (Scott, *Works*, vol. I, pp. 429–33; *CWJS Parodies*, Associated Materials VI, pp. 549–50), and his report of the inscription in Mrs Whiteway's *Tale* (vol. IV, p. 378; *CWJS Tale*, p. 282).

Ending and Going On (1736–1765) 291

of Swift in this tradition offered, in stout, durable volumes, a succession of uniformly presented reading texts ordered predominantly by date of composition, supported by textual and contextual data and supplemented by tables, lists and indexes. Without the knowledge constituted by such editions, our current understandings of Swift would be inconceivable. But such texts also make everything look rather similar, muffling the effect of the diversely expressive printed papers, pamphlets and books that first constituted Swift in print. With their typographical, textual and paratextual oddities, their often strenuous but ill-resourced effort, their frequent achievement of decent print quality and their occasional touches of luxury, it was these texts, in their published sequence, that framed the meanings available to early readers. Now that these inky messengers from the analogue world are reaching more and more readers in digitally transfigured forms, it is a good time to think again about Swift in print.

Works Cited

Primary material, including lifetime publications by Swift, is not listed here.

All classical quotations and translations are taken from Loeb Classical Library (www.loebclassics.com).

Abbott, John Lawrence, *John Hawkesworth: Eighteenth-Century Man of Letters* (Madison, WI: University of Wisconsin Press, 1982)

An Impartial History of the Life . . . of Mr. John Barber (London, 1741)

Baines, Paul, and Pat Rogers, *Edmund Curll, Bookseller* (Oxford: Clarendon Press, 2007)

Baltes, Sabine, *The Pamphlet Controversy about Wood's Halfpence (1722–25) and the Tradition of Irish Constitutional Nationalism*, Bernfried Nugel and Hermann Josef Real (eds.), Münster Monographs on English Literature, vol. 27 (Frankfurt: Peter Lang, 2002)

Baltes-Ellermann, Sabine (ed.), *Swift's Allies: The Wood's Halfpence Controversy in Ireland, 1724–1725*, 2nd revised and augmented edition, Bernfried Nugel and Hermann Josef Real (eds.), Münster Monographs on English Literature, vol. 38 (Frankfurt: Peter Lang, 2017)

Barchas, Janine, *Graphic Design, Print Culture, and the Eighteenth-Century Novel* (Cambridge University Press, 2003)

Benson, Charles, 'The Irish Trade', in Michael F. Suarez and Michael L. Turner (eds.), *The Cambridge History of the Book in Britain*, vol. V: *1695–1830* (Cambridge University Press, 2009), pp. 366–82

Berry, Helen, *Gender, Society and Print Culture in Late-Stuart England: The Cultural World of the Athenian Mercury* (Aldershot: Ashgate, 2003)

Bibliotheca Annua, 1701–1703, English Bibliographical Sources, Series I, No. 4 (London: Gregg Press, 1964)

Boswell, James, *Boswell: The Ominous Years, 1774–1776*, ed. Charles Ryskamp and Frederick A. Pottle (London: Heinemann, 1963)

Bowers, Fredson, *Principles of Bibliographical Description* (Princeton University Press, 1949)

Boyle, John, 5th Earl of Cork and Orrery, *Remarks on the Life and Writings of Dr. Jonathan Swift*, ed. João Fróes (Newark, DE: University of Delaware Press; London: Associated University Presses, 2000)

Works Cited

British Book Trade Index (bbti.bodleian.ox.ac.uk)

Bronson, Bertrand H., *Printing as an Index of Taste in Eighteenth-Century England* (New York Public Library, 1963)

Bullard, Paddy, and James McLaverty (eds.), *Jonathan Swift and the Eighteenth-Century Book* (Cambridge University Press, 2013)

'Introduction', in *JS Book*, pp. 1–28

Carpenter, Andrew, 'A School for a Satirist: Swift's Exposure to the Wars of Words in Dublin in the 1680s', in *Münster* (2003), pp. 161–75

'Circulating Ideas: Coteries, Groups and the Circulation of Verse in English in Early Modern Ireland', in Martin Fanning and Raymond Gillespie (eds.), *Print Culture and Intellectual Life in Ireland, 1660–1941: Essays in Honour of Michael Adams* (Dublin: Woodfield Press, 2006), pp. 1–23

'Literature in Print, 1550–1800', in Raymond Gillespie and Andrew Hadfield (eds.), *The Oxford History of the Irish Book*, vol. III: *The Irish Book in English, 1550–1800* (Oxford University Press, 2006), pp. 301–18

'Reading Swift's *Works* in Dublin in the 1750s', in Kirsten Juhas, Patrick Müller and Mascha Hansen (eds.), *'The First Wit of the Age': Essays on Swift and his Contemporaries in Honour of Hermann J. Real* (Frankfurt am Main: Peter Lang, 2013), pp. 117–31

Carpenter, Andrew, and James Woolley, 'Faulkner's *Volume II. Containing the Author's Poetical Works*: A New Uncancelled Copy', in *Münster* (2019), pp. 47–58

Cibber, Theophilus, *The Lives of the Poets of Great Britain and Ireland*, 4 vols. (London, 1753)

Connolly, S. J., *Divided Kingdom: Ireland, 1630–1800* (Oxford University Press, 2008)

Cook, Daniel, 'Publishing Posthumous Swift: Deane Swift to Walter Scott', in *JS Book*, pp. 214–30

Cook, Daniel (ed.), *The Lives of Jonathan Swift*, 3 vols. (London and New York: Routledge, 2011)

Dickins, Lilian, and Mary Stanton (eds.), *An Eighteenth-Century Correspondence, being the letters of Deane Swift, Pitt, The Lytteltons and the Grenvilles, Lord Dacre, Robert Nugent, Charles Jenkinson, the Earls of Guilford, Coventry, & Hardwick, Sir Edward Turner, Mr. Talbot of Lacock, and others to Sanderson Miller, Esq., of Radway* (London: John Murray, 1910)

Dix, E. R. McClintock, 'The Crooke Family', *Bibliographical Society of Ireland* [papers], 2 (1921), 16–17

'The Ray Family', *Bibliographical Society of Ireland* [papers], 2 (1921), 84–5

'Cornelius Carter, Printer', *Irish Book Lover*, 17 (1929), 84–5

Dodsley, Robert, *The Correspondence of Robert Dodsley, 1733–1764*, ed. James E. Tierney (Cambridge University Press, 1988)

Donoghue, Denis, *Jonathan Swift: A Critical Introduction* (Cambridge University Press, 1971)

Dunton, John, *The Dublin Scuffle*, ed. Andrew Carpenter (Dublin: Four Courts Press, 2000)

294 *Works Cited*

Ehrenpreis, Irvin, *Swift: The Man, His Works, and the Age*, 3 vols. (London: Methuen, 1962–82)

Eighteenth Century Collections Online (www.gale.com/intl/primary-sources/eighteenth-century-collections-online)

Elias, A. C., Jr, *Swift at Moor Park: Problems in Biography and Criticism* (Philadelphia, PA: University of Pennsylvania Press, 1982)

'*Senatus Consultum*: Revising Verse in Swift's Dublin Circle, 1729–1735', in *Münster* (1998), pp. 249–67

'Swift's *Don Quixote*, Dunkin's *Virgil Travesty*, and Other New Intelligence: John Lyon's "Materials for a Life of Dr. Swift"', *SStud*, 13 (1998), 27–104

Elias, A. C., Jr, John Irwin Fischer and James Woolley, 'The Full Text of Swift's *On Poetry: A Rhapsody* (1733)', *SStud*, 9 (1994), 17–32

Elstob, Elizabeth, *An Apology for the Study of Northern Antiquities* [as prefixed to her *Rudiments of Grammar for the English-Saxon Tongue*, London, 1715], ed. Charles Peake, Augustan Reprint Society, 61 (Los Angeles, 1956)

English Short Title Catalogue (estc.bl.uk)

Ewald, William B., *The Masks of Jonathan Swift* (Oxford: Blackwell, 1954)

Fabricant, Carole, 'Swift the Irishman', in Christopher Fox (ed.), *The Cambridge Companion to Jonathan Swift* (Cambridge University Press, 2003), pp. 48–72

Faulkner, George, *Prince of Dublin Printers: The Letters of George Faulkner*, ed. Robert E. Ward (Lexington, KY: University Press of Kentucky, 1972)

Feather, John, 'The Stationers' Company and Copyright: Evidence in the Company Archives', in *Literary Print Culture* (www.literaryprintculture.amdigital.co.uk)

Ferguson, Oliver W., *Jonathan Swift and Ireland* (Urbana, IL: University of Illinois Press, 1962)

Fischer, John Irwin, 'The Government's Response to Swift's *An Epistle to a Lady*', *Philological Quarterly*, 65 (1986), 39–59

'Swift's *Miscellanies, in Prose and Verse, Volume the Fifth*: Some Facts and Puzzles', *SStud*, 15 (2000), 76–87

Flint, Christopher, *The Appearance of Print in Eighteenth-Century Fiction* (Cambridge University Press, 2011)

Foxon, David, *English Verse, 1701–1750: A Catalogue of Separately Printed Poems with Notes on Contemporary Collected Editions*, 2 vols. (Cambridge University Press, 1975)

Pope and the Early Eighteenth-Century Book Trade, revised and edited by James McLaverty (Oxford: Clarendon Press, 1991)

Frantz, R. W., 'Gulliver's "Cousin Sympson"', *HLQ*, 1.3 (1938), 329–34

Gadd, Ian, '"At Four Shillings per Year, Paying One Quarter in Hand": Reprinting Swift's *Examiner* in Dublin, 1710–11', in *Münster* (2013), pp. 75–94

'Leaving the Printer to his Liberty: Swift and the London Book Trade, 1701–1714', in *JS Book*, pp. 51–64

Gaskell, Philip, *A New Introduction to Bibliography* (Oxford: Clarendon Press, 1972)

Gentleman's Magazine, 49 (1779)

Gillespie, Raymond, *Reading Ireland: Print, Reading and Social Change in Early Modern Ireland* (Manchester University Press, 2005)

Griffin, Dustin, *Swift and Pope: Satirists in Dialogue* (Cambridge University Press, 2010)

Griffith, R. H., 'Swift's "Contests", 1701: Two Editions', *Notes & Queries*, 22 (1947), 114–17

Haley, K. H. D., *An English Diplomat in the Low Countries: Sir William Temple and John De Witt, 1665–1672* (Oxford: Clarendon Press, 1986)

Haslett, Moyra, '"With brisk merry lays": Songs on the Wood's Halfpence Affair', in *Münster* (2019), pp. 199–220

Higgins, Ian, 'A Preface to Swift's Test Act Tracts', in *Münster* (2013), pp. 226–43
'Censorship, Libel and Self-Censorship', in *JS Book*, pp. 179–98
'Swift's Whig Pamphlet: Its Reception and Afterlife', in *Münster* (2019), pp. 553–72

Highfill, Philip H., Jr, Kalman A. Burnim and Edward A. Langhans, *A Biographical Dictionary of Actors, Actresses, Musicians, Dancers, Managers and Other Stage Personnel in London, 1660–1800*, 16 vols. (Carbondale, IL: Southern Illinois University Press, 1973–93)

Hume, Robert D., 'The Economics of Culture in London, 1660–1740', *HLQ*, 69.4 (2006), 487–533

Jackson's Oxford Journal

Jarrell, Mackie Langham, '"Ode to the King": Some Contests, Dissensions, and Exchanges among Jonathan Swift, John Dunton, and Henry Jones', *Texas Studies in Literature and Language*, 7.2 (1965), 145–59

Johnson, Samuel, *The Lives of the Most Eminent English Poets*, ed. Roger Lonsdale, 4 vols. (Oxford: Clarendon Press, 2006)

Jonathan Swift Archive (ota-qa.bodleian.ox.ac.uk)

Karian, Stephen, 'Edmund Curll and the Circulation of Swift's Writings', in *Münster* (2008), pp. 99–129
Jonathan Swift in Print and Manuscript (Cambridge University Press, 2010)
'The Limitations and Possibilities of the *ESTC*', *The Age of Johnson: A Scholarly Annual*, 21 (2011), 283–97
'Swift as a Manuscript Poet', in *JS Book*, pp. 31–50

Kelly, Ann Cline, *Swift and the English Language* (Philadelphia, PA: University of Pennsylvania Press, 1988)
'The Semiotics of Swift's 1711 *Miscellanies*', *SStud*, 6 (1991), 59–68
Jonathan Swift and Popular Culture: Myth, Media, and the Man (Basingstoke: Palgrave, 2002)

Kelly, James, 'Political Publishing, 1700–1800', in Raymond Gillespie and Andrew Hadfield (eds.), *The Oxford History of the Irish Book*, vol. III: *The Irish Book in English, 1550–1800* (Oxford University Press, 2006), pp. 215–33

Kelly, Patrick, 'Swift on Money and Economics', in Christopher Fox (ed.), *The Cambridge Companion to Jonathan Swift* (Cambridge University Press, 2003), pp. 128–45

Kenner, Hugh, *Flaubert, Joyce and Beckett: The Stoic Comedians* (London: W. H. Allen, 1964)

Kilburn, Matthew, 'The Learned Press: History, Languages, Literature, and Music', in Ian Gadd (ed.), *The History of Oxford University Press*, vol. I: *Beginnings to 1780* (Oxford University Press, 2013), pp. 419–59

Lennon, Colm, 'The Print Trade, 1550–1700', in Raymond Gillespie and Andrew Hadfield (eds.), *The Oxford History of the Irish Book*, vol. III: *The Irish Book in English, 1550–1800* (Oxford University Press, 2006), pp. 61–73

Levine, Joseph M., *Dr. Woodward's Shield: History, Science, and Satire in Augustan England* (Berkeley, CA: University of California Press, 1977)

Lindsay, Alexander, 'Jonathan Swift, 1667–1745', in *Index of English Literary Manuscripts*, vol. III: *1700–1800*, Part 4 (London: Mansell, 1997), pp. 15–91

Literary Print Culture: The Stationers' Company Archive, 1554–2007, Adam Matthew Digital (www.literaryprintculture.amdigital.co.uk)

Locke, M., and J. V. Collins, 'Who was W. Goodall?', *The Linnean: Newsletter and Proceedings of The Linnean Society of London*, 17 (2001), 28–47

Loeb Classical Library (www.loebclassics.com)

Love, Harold, 'L'Estrange, Joyce and the Dictates of Typography', in Anne Dunan-Page and Beth Lynch (eds.), *Roger L'Estrange and the Making of Restoration Culture* (Abingdon: Routledge, 2016), pp. 167–79

Lowe, N. F., and W. J. McCormack, 'Swift as "Publisher" of Sir William Temple's *Letters* and *Miscellanea*', *SStud*, 8 (1993), 46–57

Luckombe, Philip, *A Concise History of the Origin and Progress of Printing* (London, 1770)

McBride, Ian, 'Renouncing England: Swift's *Proposal for the Universal Use of Irish Manufacture*', plenary lecture at Swift350 conference, Trinity College, Dublin, 9 June 2017

McEwen, Gilbert D., *The Oracle of the Coffee House: John Dunton's Athenian Mercury* (San Marino, CA: Huntington Library, 1972)

McKenzie, D. F., 'The London Book Trade in the Later Seventeenth Century' (Sandars Lectures, 1976; typescript held in Cambridge University Library)

McLaverty, James, 'The First Printing and Publication of Pope's Letters', *The Library*, 2 (1980), 264–80

    Pope, Print and Meaning (Oxford University Press, 2001)

    'The Failure of the Swift–Pope *Miscellanies* (1727–32) and *The Life and Genuine Character of Doctor Swift* (1733)', in *Münster* (2008), pp. 131–48

    'Swift and the Art of Political Publication: Hints and Title Pages, 1711–1714', in Claude Rawson (ed.), *Politics and Literature in the Age of Swift: English and Irish Perspectives* (Cambridge University Press, 2010), pp. 116–39

    'The Revision of the First Edition of *Gulliver's Travels*: Book-Trade Context, Interleaving, Two Cancels, and a Failure to Catch', *Papers of the Bibliographical Society of America*, 106.1 (2012), 5–35

    'George Faulkner and Swift's Collected Works', in *JS Book*, pp. 154–75

McTague, John, '"There Is No Such Man as Isaack Bickerstaff": Partridge, Pittis, and Jonathan Swift', *Eighteenth-Century Life*, 35.1 (2011), 83–101

Mack, Maynard, *Alexander Pope: A Life* (New Haven and London: Yale University Press, 1985)

Maggs Bros. Ltd, *Books and Readers in Early Modern Britain IV: A Selection of Books, Manuscripts and Bindings*, Catalogue 1393 (London: Maggs Bros. Ltd, 2006)

Mahony, Robert, *Jonathan Swift: The Irish Identity* (New Haven and London: Yale University Press, 1995)

Marshall, Ashley, 'Swift on "Swift": From *The Author upon Himself* to *The Life and Genuine Character*', *HLQ*, 75.3 (2012), 327–63

'The "1735" Faulkner Edition of Swift's *Works*', *The Library*, 14.2 (2013), 154–98

'Pope's Dedication of the "1736" *Dunciad* to Swift', in Kirsten Juhas, Patrick Müller and Mascha Hansen (eds.), *'The First Wit of the Age': Essays on Swift and his Contemporaries in Honour of Hermann J. Real* (Frankfurt am Main: Peter Lang, 2013), pp. 69–82

'Swift, Oldisworth, and the Politics of *The Examiner*, 1710–14', in *Münster* (2019), pp. 401–31

Maslen, Keith, *The Bowyer Ornament Stock* (Oxford Bibliographical Society, 1973)

'George Faulkner and William Bowyer: The London Connection', in *An Early London Printing House at Work: Studies in the Bowyer Ledgers* (New York: Bibliographical Society of America, 1993), pp. 223–33

Maslen, Keith, and John Lancaster (eds.), *The Bowyer Ledgers* (London: Bibliographical Society, revised online edition, 2017: www.bibsoc.org.uk; book and microform first published London: Bibliographical Society, and New York, Bibliographical Society of America, 1991)

May, James E., 'Re-Impressed Type in the First Four Octavo Editions of *A Tale of the [sic] Tub*, 1704–5', in Kirsten Juhas, Patrick Müller and Mascha Hansen (eds.), *'The First Wit of the Age': Essays on Swift and his Contemporaries in Honour of Hermann J. Real* (Frankfurt am Main: Peter Lang, 2013), pp. 85–108

'False and Incomplete Imprints in Swift's Dublin, 1710–35', in *Münster* (2019), pp. 59–99

Mayhew, George P., 'Swift's Bickerstaff Hoax as an April Fools' Joke', *Modern Philology*, 61.4 (1964), 270–80

The Monthly Catalogue, 1714–17, English Bibliographical Sources, Series I, No. 1 (London: Gregg Press, 1964)

Moxon, Joseph, *Mechanick Exercises on the Whole Art of Printing (1683–4)*, ed. Herbert Davis and Harry Carter, 2nd edition (London: Oxford University Press, 1962)

Munter, Robert, *The History of the Irish Newspaper, 1685–1760* (Cambridge University Press, 1967)

Nichols, John, *Literary Anecdotes of the Eighteenth Century; Comprizing Biographical Memoirs of William Bowyer, Printer, F.S.A. and many of his Learned Friends; an Incidental View of the Progress and Advancement of Literature in this Kingdom during the Last Century; and Biographical Anecdotes of a Considerable Number of Eminent Writers and Ingenious Artists; with a Very Copious Index*, 9 vols. (London, 1812–15)

Works Cited

Illustrations of the Literary History of the Eighteenth Century. Consisting of Authentic Memoirs and Original Letters of Eminent Persons; and Intended as a Sequel to The Literary Anecdotes, 8 vols. (London 1817–58)

O'Regan, Philip, *Archbishop William King of Dublin (1650–1729) and the Constitution in Church and State* (Dublin: Four Courts Press, 2000)

Ould, Martyn, 'The Workplace: Places, Procedures, and Personnel, 1668–1780', in Ian Gadd (ed.), *The History of Oxford University Press*, vol. I: *Beginnings to 1780* (Oxford University Press, 2013), pp. 193–240

The Oxford Dictionary of English Proverbs, 3rd edition, ed. F. P. Wilson (Oxford: Clarendon Press, 1970)

Oxford Dictionary of National Biography (www.oxforddnb.com)

Parkes, M. B., *Pause and Effect: An Introduction to the History of Punctuation in the West* (Aldershot: Scolar Press, 1992)

Parks, Stephen, *John Dunton and the English Book Trade: A Study of his Career with a Checklist of his Publications* (New York: Garland, 1976)

Pett, Craig Francis, '"I am no inconsiderable Shop-Keeper in this Town": Swift and his Dublin Printers of the 1720s: Edward Waters, John Harding and Sarah Harding' (PhD dissertation, Monash University, 2015)

Phiddian, Robert, *Swift's Parody* (Cambridge University Press, 1995)

Phillips, James W., *Printing and Bookselling in Dublin, 1670–1800* (Dublin: Irish Academic Press, 1998)

Phillips, Mabel (Mrs. William C. DeVane), 'Jonathan Swift's Relations to Science' (unpublished thesis, Yale University, 1925)

Philmus, Robert M., 'Dryden's "Cousin Swift" Re-Examined', *SStud*, 18 (2003), 99–103

Pilkington, Laetitia, *Memoirs of Laetitia Pilkington*, ed. A. C. Elias, Jr, 2 vols. (Athens, GA: University of Georgia Press, 1997)

Pollard, Mary, 'George Faulkner', *SStud*, 7 (1992), 79–96

Dublin's Trade in Books, 1550–1800, Lyell Lectures, 1986–7 (Oxford: Clarendon Press, 1989)

A Dictionary of Members of the Dublin Book Trade, 1550–1800 (London: Bibliographical Society, 2000)

Pope, Alexander, *Pope's Own Miscellany*, ed. Norman Ault (London: Nonesuch Press, 1935)

The Correspondence of Alexander Pope, ed. George Sherburn, 5 vols. (Oxford: Clarendon Press, 1956)

The Poems of Alexander Pope, vol. III: *The Dunciad (1728) and the Dunciad Variorum (1729)*, ed. Valerie Rumbold (Harlow: Longman, 2007)

Probyn, Clive T., '"Haranguing upon Texts": Swift and the Idea of the Book', in *Münster* (1985), pp. 187–97

'Swift and Typographic Man: Foul Papers, Modern Criticism, and Irish Dissenters', in *Münster* (1993), pp. 25–43

'Jonathan Swift at the Sign of the Drapier', in *Münster* (1998), pp. 225–37

Rawson, Claude, 'Savage Indignation Revisited: Swift, Yeats, and the "Cry" of Liberty', in Claude Rawson (ed.), *Politics and Literature in the Age of*

Swift: English and Irish Perspectives (Cambridge University Press, 2010), pp. 185–217

'The Typographical Ego-trip from "Dryden" to Prufrock', in Claude Rawson, *Swift and Others* (Cambridge University Press, 2015), pp. 11–47

Real, Hermann J., '"The Most Fateful Piece Swift ever Wrote": The Windsor Prophecy', *SStud*, 9 (1994), 76–99

Real, Hermann J., and others (eds.): *Proceedings of the First Münster Symposium on Jonathan Swift*, ed. Hermann J. Real and Heinz J. Vienken (Munich: Wilhelm Fink, 1985); *Reading Swift: Papers from the Second Münster Symposium on Jonathan Swift*, ed. Richard H. Rodino and Hermann J. Real (Munich: Wilhelm Fink, 1993); *Reading Swift: Papers from the Third Münster Symposium on Jonathan Swift*, ed. Hermann J. Real and Helgard Stöver-Leidig (Munich: Wilhelm Fink, 1998); *Reading Swift: Papers from the Fourth Münster Symposium on Jonathan Swift*, ed. Hermann J. Real and Helgard Stöver-Leidig (Munich: Wilhelm Fink, 2003); *Reading Swift: Papers from the Fifth Münster Symposium on Jonathan Swift*, ed. Hermann J. Real (Munich: Wilhelm Fink, 2008); *Reading Swift: Papers from the Sixth Münster Symposium on Jonathan Swift*, ed. K. Juhas, H. J. Real and S. Simon (Munich: Wilhelm Fink, 2013); *Reading Swift: Papers from the Seventh Münster Symposium on Jonathan Swift*, ed. Janika Bischof, Kirsten Juhas and Hermann J. Real (Munich: Wilhelm Fink, 2019)

Rivington, Charles A., *'Tyrant': The Story of John Barber, 1675 to 1741: Jacobite Lord Mayor of London and Printer and Friend to Dr. Swift* (York: William Sessions, 1989)

Rogers, Pat, 'The Uses of the Miscellany: Swift, Curll and Piracy', in *JS Book*, pp. 87–100

Rogers, Shef, 'Exploring the Bibliographical Limits of Gulliver's Travels', in *JS Book*, pp. 135–53

Rothschild, Nathaniel Mayer Victor, Baron, *The Rothschild Library: A Catalogue of the Collection of Eighteenth-Century Printed Books and Manuscripts formed by Lord Rothschild*, 2 vols. (Cambridge University Press, 1954)

Rounce, Adam, 'Swift's Texts between Dublin and London', in *JS Book*, pp. 199–213

Rumbold, Valerie, 'Locating Swift's Parody: The Title of "Polite Conversation"', in *Münster* (2008), pp. 255–72

'Burying the Fanatic Partridge: Swift's Holy Week Hoax', in Claude Rawson (ed.), *Politics and Literature in the Age of Swift: English and Irish Perspectives* (Cambridge University Press, 2010), pp. 81–115

'Merlinus Verax, T. N. Philomath, and the Merlin Tradition: Print Contexts for Swift's *A Famous Prediction of Merlin* (1709)', *The Library*, 12.4 (2011), 392–412

'Ignoring Swift in Dublin? Swift's Bickerstaff Hoax in the Dublin Print Trade', *Publishing History*, 57 (2017), 9–42

Scouten, Arthur H., 'Jonathan Swift's Progress from Prose to Poetry', in *The Poetry of Jonathan Swift: Papers Read at a Clark Library Seminar, 20 January 1979* (Los Angeles: William Clark Memorial Library, *c.* 1981)

Works Cited

Sheridan, Thomas, Jr, *The Life of the Rev. Dr. Jonathan Swift, Dean of St. Patrick's, Dublin. By Thomas Sheridan, A.M. Vol. I.* (London, 1784)

Simms, John Gerald, *Jacobite Ireland, 1685–91* (London: Routledge & Kegan Paul, 1969)

Slepian, Barry, 'Jonathan Swift and George Faulkner' (PhD dissertation, University of Pennsylvania, 1962)

'George Faulkner's "Dublin Journal" and Jonathan Swift', *Library Chronicle*, 31 (1965), 97–116

Smith, John, *The Printer's Grammar, 1755*, English Bibliographical Sources, Series 3, No. 2 (London: Gregg Press, 1965)

Stanhope, Philip Dormer, 4th Earl of Chesterfield, *The Letters of Philip Dormer Stanhope, 4th Earl of Chesterfield*, ed. Bonamy Dobrée, 5 vols. ([London: Eyre and Spottiswoode], 1932)

Suarez, Michael F., 'Toward a Bibliometric Analysis of the Surviving Record, 1701–1800', in Michael F. Suarez and Michael L. Turner (eds.), *The Cambridge History of the Book in Britain*, vol. V, *1695–1830* (Cambridge University Press, 2009), pp. 39–65

Swift, Jonathan, *The Works of Jonathan Swift*, ed. Walter Scott, 2nd edition, 19 vols. (Edinburgh, 1824)

The Drapier's Letters to the People of Ireland against Receiving Wood's Halfpence, ed. Herbert Davis (Oxford: Clarendon Press, 1935)

The Prose Writings of Jonathan Swift, ed. Herbert Davis and others, 16 vols. (Oxford: Basil Blackwell, 1939–74)

A Discourse of the Contests and Dissentions between the Nobles and the Commons in Athens and Rome, ed. Frank H. Ellis (Oxford: Clarendon Press, 1967)

Swift vs. Mainwaring: The Examiner and The Medley, ed. Frank H. Ellis (Oxford: Clarendon Press, 1985)

The Correspondence of Jonathan Swift, D.D., ed. David Woolley, with index by Hermann J. Real and Dirk F. Passmann, 5 vols. (Frankfurt am Main: Peter Lang, 1999–2014)

The Cambridge Edition of the Works of Jonathan Swift (Cambridge University Press, 2008–): vol. I, *A Tale of a Tub and Other Works*, ed. Marcus Walsh (2010); vol. II, *Parodies, Hoaxes, Mock Treatises: Polite Conversation, Directions to Servants and Other Works*, ed. Valerie Rumbold (2013); vols. III–VI, *Poems I–IV*, ed. James Woolley and Stephen Karian (forthcoming); vol. VII, *English Political Writings, 1701–1711: The Examiner and Other Works*, ed. Ian Gadd and Ian Higgins (forthcoming); vol. VIII, *English Political Writings, 1711–1714: The Conduct of the Allies and Other Works*, ed. Bertrand A. Goldgar and Ian Gadd (2008); vol. IX, *Journal to Stella: Letters to Esther Johnson and Rebecca Dingley, 1710–1713*, ed. Abigail Williams (2013); vol. XII, *Writings on Religion and the Church after 1714*, ed. Ian Higgins (forthcoming); vol. XIV, *Irish Political Writings after 1725: A Modest Proposal and Other Works*, ed. David Hayton and Adam Rounce (2018); vol. XV, *Gulliver's Travels*, ed. David Womersley (2012)

Works Cited

Swift, Jonathan, and Thomas Sheridan, *The Intelligencer*, ed. James Woolley (Oxford: Clarendon Press, 1992)

The Tatler, ed. Donald F. Bond, 3 vols. (Oxford: Clarendon Press, 1987)

Teerink, H., 'Swift's *Discourse . . . Contests . . . Athens and Rome*, 1701', *The Library*, 4 (1949), 201–5

    A Bibliography of the Writings of Jonathan Swift, 2nd edition revised and corrected by the author, ed. Arthur H. Scouten (Philadelphia, PA: University of Pennsylvania Press, 1963)

Treadwell, Michael, 'London Trade Publishers, 1675–1750', *The Library*, 4.2 (1982), 91–134

    'Swift's Relations with the London Book Trade to 1714', in Robin Myers and Michael Harris (eds.), *Author/Publisher Relations during the Eighteenth and Nineteenth Centuries*, Publishing Pathways (Oxford Polytechnic Press, 1983), pp. 1–36

    'Benjamin Motte, Andrew Tooke and *Gulliver's Travels*', in *Münster* (1985), pp. 287–304

    'Observations on the Printing of Motte's Octavo Editions of *Gulliver's Travels*', in *Münster* (1998), pp. 157–77

Walsh, Marcus, 'Swift's *Tale of a Tub* and the Mock Book' in *JS Book*, pp. 101–18

Walsh, Patrick, *The South Sea Bubble and Ireland: Money, Banking and Investment, 1690–1721* (Woodbridge: Boydell, 2014)

Watt, Ian, *The Rise of the Novel: Studies in Defoe, Richardson and Fielding* (London: Chatto & Windus, 1957)

Weedon, Margaret, 'An Uncancelled Copy of the First Collected Edition of Swift's Poems', *The Library*, 22.1 (1967), 44–56

    'Bickerstaff Bit, or, Merlinus Fallax', *SStud*, 2, (1987), 97–106

Wilkinson, Hazel, *Edmund Spenser and the Eighteenth-Century Book* (Cambridge University Press, 2017)

Williams, Abigail, *Poetry and the Creation of a Whig Literary Culture, 1681–1714* (Oxford University Press, 2005)

    'Epistolary Forms: Published Correspondence, Letter-journals and Books', in *JS Book*, pp. 119–34

Woolley, David, 'Swift's Copy of *Gulliver's Travels*: The Armagh Gulliver, Hyde's Edition, and Swift's Earliest Corrections', in Clive T. Probyn (ed.), *The Art of Jonathan Swift* (London: Vision Press, 1978), pp. 131–78

    'The Canon of Swift's Prose Pamphleteering, 1710–1714, and *The New Way of Selling Places at Court*', *SStud*, 3 (1988), 96–117

    'A Dialogue upon Dunkirk (1712), and Swift's "7 penny Papers"', in *Münster* (1993), pp. 215–23

    'The Textual History of *A Tale of a Tub*', *SStud*, 21 (2006), 7–26

Woolley, James, 'Sarah Harding as Swift's Printer', in Christopher Fox (ed.), *Walking Naboth's Vineyard: New Studies of Swift* (University of Notre Dame Press, 1995), pp. 164–77

'John Barrett, "The Whimsical Medley", and Swift's Poems', in Howard D. Weinbrot, Peter J. Schakel and Stephen E. Karian (eds.), *Eighteenth-Century Contexts: Historical Inquiries in Honor of Philip Harth* (Madison, WI: University of Wisconsin Press, 2001), pp. 147–70

'Swift's First Published Poem: *Ode. To the King*', in *Münster* (2003), pp. 265–83

'Poor John Harding and Mad Tom: "Harding's Resurrection" (1724)', in Charles Benson and Siobhán Fitzpatrick (eds.), *That Woman! Studies in Irish Bibliography: A Festschrift for Mary 'Paul' Pollard* (Dublin: Lilliput Press, 2005), pp. 102–21

'Swift and Lord Berkeley, 1699–1701: Berkeley Castle Swiftiana', in Kirsten Juhas, Patrick Müller and Mascha Hansen (eds.), *'The First Wit of the Age': Essays on Swift and his Contemporaries in Honour of Hermann J. Real* (Frankfurt am Main: Peter Lang, 2013), pp. 31–68

'Swift's Most Popular Poems', in *Münster* (2013), pp. 367–82

'The Circulation of Verse in Jonathan Swift's Dublin', *Eighteenth-Century Ireland: Iris an dá chultúr*, 32 (2017), 136–50.

Index

This index focuses on four areas: Swift's attitudes, actions and engagements with print and publication; his published writings and relevant collections; general topics relating to print; and individuals variously connected with Swift and his published work. For works attributable to individuals other than Swift, see references under their names; for Swift's correspondence, see addressee. For a more general overview of the book's contents, see chapter summaries in the Preface; and, for modern scholarship and editions, see the listing in Works Cited.

Acheson, Sir Arthur and Lady Anne, 205, 206–7, 215, 286
Addison, Joseph, 94, 107, 108, 132
Allen, Joshua, second Viscount Allen, 214
All Fools' Day, 69
almanacs and astrological writing, 4, 10, 28, 67–8, 72, 74, 78, 83–4, 159
Amy, Robert, 254
Anderson, Andrew, 92
Anne, Queen, 79, 89, 102, 114–15, 120, 123, 124, 129, 131, 195, 240–1
Answer to the Proposal for the Universal Use of Irish Manufactures, An, 151
Arbuthnot, John, 130–1, 185–6, 191, 195, 196, 255–6, 258
Armagh Robinson Library, 83, 193
Ashe, St George, 107
astrological writing, *see* almanacs and astrological writing
Atterbury, Francis, 108–9, 143, 146–7, 255

B., M., Drapier (fictitious author), 28, 29, 84, 87, 145, 146–7, 161–2, 173, 174, 176, 247, 260–1
Baldwin, Abigail, 30, 39, 71, 79, 80, 86, 104–5, 215
Baldwin, Richard, 18, 30, 39, 79, 215
Barber, John, 52, 103–4, 105, 108, 112, 115, 116, 117, 118–19, 120, 123, 130–1, 132, 133, 139, 143, 153, 216
Barber, Mary, 217–18, 262
Baskerville, John, 290
Bathurst, Allen, first Earl Bathurst, 17
Bathurst, Charles, 251, 255, 256, 262, 264, 269, 272

Baudrier, Sieur de, 121–2
Beckingham, Charles, 255
Bentley, Richard, 110, 130–1, 240
Berkeley, Charles, second Earl of Berkeley, 35, 41, 48, 91, 126–7
Berkeley, Elizabeth, Countess of Berkeley, 91, 95
Berkeley, Lady Elizabeth, *see* Lady Betty Germain
Best in Christendom, The, 198–9
Bettenham, James, 188
Bettesworth, Arthur, 254
Bible, 4, 165
Bickerstaff, Isaac (librettist), 72
Bickerstaff, Isaac (fictitious author), 28, 66, 67, 68, 71, 72–3, 74, 78, 81, 84, 93, 98, 105–6
Bickerstaff, John (actor), 72
Bickerstaff, John and Jane (of Dublin), 72
Bladen, William, 6, 7
Bolingbroke, Viscount, *see* Henry St John, Viscount Bolingbroke
Book of Common Prayer, 4, 7
book trades, 4
  Cork, 204
  Dublin, 5–12, 26–30, 144–5, 176, 211
    blackguard boys, 169, 173–4
    English copyright legislation not applicable in, 9, 289
    Guild of St Luke, 10–11
    King's Printer in Ireland, patent monopoly of, 4, 6–12, 27–8, 154
    London publications, Dublin reprinting of, 9, 19, 29, 65, 67–84, 91–2, 93n.82, 103, 133–9, 153, 154, 167, 178, 193–4, 203, 214–15, 216–17, 218–19, 259, 280
    verse, rarity of in Dublin print, 5–6, 15

304   *Index*

book trades (cont.)
  Edinburgh, 92, 133, 214
  London, 4–5, 33, 176, 178
    copyright in, 4–5, 9, 100, 212, 216, 248, 289
    Dublin publications, London reprinting of,
      134, 153, 154, 174, 207, 208, 209–10, 213,
      214, 217–19, 248, 268
    English Stock, 4, 43
    exchange of copies, 187
    Licensing Act (1662), 49
    London publications, unauthorised
      London reprinting of, 80–2, 95–6
    stamp duty, 111–12
    Stationers' Company, 4
    Stationers' Company Entry Books of
      Copies (i.e. 'Stationers' Register'), 45,
      50, 100, 108, 110–11, 116, 120, 130–1, 186,
      194n.67
    subsidy by authors, 6
    trade publishers, 18, 49–50, 120
    — *and see* Abigail and Richard Baldwin;
      John Morphew; John Nutt; James
      Roberts
Bowyer, William (the elder) and William (the
  younger), 124, 125, 146, 174, 203,
  209–10, 213, 214–15, 216, 219, 221, 227,
  228, 230, 247, 251, 255, 262, 268, 269,
  275, 278, 289, 290
Boyer, Abel, 44, 86
Boyle, Charles, fourth Earl of Orrery, 240
Boyle, John, fifth Earl of Orrery, 262, 264, 272–3,
  280, 283
Brent, Ann, *see* Ann Ridgeway
Brent, Jane, 16–17, 143–4
Brent, John, 12–17, 26–7, 29
British Library, 75–8
British Museum, 288
Brocas, John, 26–7, 29, 148
Brodrick, Alan, 1st Viscount Midleton, 88, 90, 92,
  130, 159, 173, 175, 235–6
Brodrick, Thomas, 90, 92, 130, 235–6
Brothers' Club, 115
Browne, John, 29
Bunyan, John, 191
Burnet, Gilbert, 53, 122, 135, 215
Burnet, Thomas, 147–8
Butler, Theophilus, Lord Newtown Butler, 30

Calves' Head Club, 112
Cambridge University, *see* University of
  Cambridge
Carter, Cornelius, 28–9, 65, 83, 135–7, 139, 146,
  148, 157, 277
Carteret, John, second Earl Granville, 174, 204,
  241–2

Caroline, successively Princess of Wales and
  Queen Consort of George II, 182, 212,
  213–14, 217–18, 256, 257
Cato, 40
Cervantes Saavedra, Miguel de, 189
Charles I, 39, 112
Chesterfield, *see* Philip Dormer Stanhope, 4th
  Earl of Chesterfield
Chetwood, William Rufus, 282
Churchill, Awnsham and John, 40
Churchill, John, 1st Duke of Marlborough, 116
Cibber, Colley, 263, 274
Cicero, 155
Claudian, 230
Clements, Henry, 125
Congreve, William, 200–1, 258
Cooper, Anthony Ashley, 3rd Earl of
  Shaftesbury, 97, 274
Coryton, William (bookseller), 119, 136
Coryton, Sir William (MP), 119
Crooke, John and Mary, 6–8, 264
Crooke, Andrew, 7, 9, 11, 27, 29, 204
Crooke, Bankes, 43
Curll, Edmund, 95, 97, 126, 128, 182, 198–9,
  200–1, 251, 257–9, 282
Cutts, John, 127–8

Daniell, Combra, 204
Davenant, Charles, 51–2, 122
Davis, Charles, 199, 210, 247, 248, 269
Davis, Herbert, 290
Declaratory Act, 145, 147
Defence of English Commodities, A, 198–9
*Defence of the Conduct of the People of Ireland,
  A*, 174
Delany, Patrick, 135n.139, 173, 210, 214, 215,
  252–3, 286
Derry and Raphoe, Diocese of, 12
Dickson, Francis, 82
Dingley, Rebecca, 252
— *and see* Esther Johnson and Rebecca Dingley
  as joint correspondents
Dobson, Eliphal, 9
Dodd, Ann, 109, 213, 254
Dodsley, Robert, 264–5, 268, 269, 290
Downes, Thomas, 41
'Dring', *see* Daniel Tompson
Dryden, John, 14, 56, 58, 93, 94
Duck, Stephen, 263
Dunton, John, 18–21, 23–30, 139

*Elegy upon the Death of the Famous Dr. John
  Partridgd* [sic], *An*, 78
*Elegy on the Much-Lamented Death of John
  Harding Printer*, 171

Index

305

Elliston, Ebenezor, 158–9, 242
Elstob, Elizabeth, 133n.128
Erskine, John, styled 22nd or 6th Earl of Mar, 120
Eusden, Laurence, 94
Ewing, George and Alexander, 282–3

Fairbrother, Samuel, 29, 203, 209, 247–8
Faulkner, George, 5, 146, 173, 174–6, 178, 209–10,
    212–13, 214–48, 251, 252, 253, 254,
    256–7, 259, 260–1, 262–8, 269, 272–3,
    275, 278–80, 282–3, 287, 289
— *and see* George Faulkner and James Hoey,
    partnership of; Jonathan Swift (*Fraud
    Detected*; *Works of J. S, D. D,
    D. S. P. D.*)
Faulkner, George, and James Hoey, partnership
    of, 210, 213–14
Finch, Anne, Countess of Winchilsea, 94
Finch, Daniel, 2nd Earl of Nottingham, 112–14
FitzRoy, Charles, 2nd Duke of Grafton, 150–1
Ford, Charles, 122, 147, 151–2, 154, 173, 184–5, 187,
    192, 203, 246
*Form of Prayer with Thanksgiving for the Safe
    Delivery of the Queen, and Happy Birth
    of the Young Prince, A*, 8
Fountaine, Sir Andrew, 80
*Funeral Elegy on the much lamented Death of Robert
    Lord Viscount Molesworth, A*, 203–4

Gadbury, John, 67–8, 79–80, 129
Gay, John, 183–4, 185, 191, 192, 195, 199, 215,
    230–1, 255–6, 258
Gellibrand, Edward, 37–8
Gellibrand, Samuel, 36, 37
George I, 150, 204, 232
George II, 212, 213–14, 217–19, 263
Germain, Lady Betty, 126–7, 287
Giffard, Martha, Lady, 38, 41, 84–7
Gildon, Charles, 24–5
Gilliver, Lawton, 202, 217–19
Godolphin, Sidney, 1st Earl of Godolphin, 110
Goodall, William, 198–9
Goodwin, Timothy, 44, 46
Grafton, *see* Charles FitzRoy, 2nd Duke of
    Grafton
Grantham, Book Society of, 287
Granville, George, Baron Lansdowne, 258
Grattan, John, 170, 173
Guiscard, Antoine de, 108
Gulliver, Lemuel, 73, 84, 87, 227, 234,
    242, 246
Gunne, Matthew, 148

Halifax, *see* Charles Montagu, 1st Earl of Halifax
Hall, John, 15

Hanmer, Sir Thomas, 150–1
Harding, John, 146–7, 155–61, 162–5, 166–70,
    171–2, 173, 175, 234, 241–2
Harding, John Draper, 171–2
Harding, Sarah, 146–7, 158, 168, 169, 171–2, 178,
    203–9
Harley, Edward, 2nd Earl of Oxford and
    Mortimer, 236
Harley, Lady Henrietta Cavendish
    Holles, 255
Harley, Robert, 1st Earl of Oxford and Mortimer,
    53–4, 102, 103, 105, 108–9, 111, 115, 116, 118,
    119, 122, 123, 124, 128, 131–2, 133, 134, 241
Harris, Frances, 126–7
Harrison, William, 30, 96, 105–6, 206
Haukyns, John, 80
Hawkesworth, John, 252, 271–3, 274–6, 279
— *and see* Jonathan Swift (*The Works of Jonathan
    Swift, D. D. Dean of St. Patrick's,
    Dublin*)
Hayman, Francis, 278
Helsham, Richard, 135n.139, 201n.94
Henly, John, 134–5, 137, 145–6
Herbert, Henry, 8th Earl of Pembroke and 5th
    Earl of Montgomery, 85
Hills, Henry, 82, 92, 95–6
Hoey, James, 214–15
— *and see* George Faulkner and James Hoey,
    partnership of
Holcroft, Francis, 75
Horace, 47, 89–90, 110, 112–14, 130–1, 134,
    226, 227
Hort, Josiah, 254, 260
Hopkins, John, 220
Huggonson, John, 218–19
Hussey, Nicholas, 207
Hyde, John, 29, 138–9, 146–7, 148, 154–5, 193–4,
    209, 215, 234
Hyde, Sarah, 29, 146–7, 154, 209, 215–16, 218–19

Intelligencer, see Jonathan Swift and Thomas
    Sheridan
Ireland, Lords Justices and Council, *see Whereas
    in expectation of Conformity*
Irenaeus, 61

James II, 8–9, 11, 73, 282
Johnson, Esther, 286
— *and see* Esther Johnson and Rebecca Dingley
    as joint correspondents
Johnson, Esther, and Rebecca Dingley as joint
    correspondents (including *Journal to
    Stella*), 17, 35, 104, 108–9, 110, 111–12,
    114, 115–16, 119, 121–3, 127, 128, 131,
    132, 134

Johnson, Samuel, 274, 283
Johnson, William, *see* William Johnston
Johnston, William, 284, 285
Jones, David, 39, 44
Jones, Edward, 17
Juvenal, 118

Kendall, Thomas, 143–4
King, William (Archbishop of Dublin), 43, 90, 91, 159, 173
King, William (of Christ Church, Oxford), 125–6
King, William (of St Mary Hall, Oxford), 125–6, 255–7, 284, 285, 287
Knapton, James, 52

Lansdowne, *see* George Granville, Baron Lansdowne
Last Farewell of Ebenezor Elliston to this Transitory World, The, 158–9
Last Speech and Dying Words of Captain Collins, The, 159
Last Speech of Wisdom's Defeat, The, 204
L'Estrange, Sir Roger, 20
Leach, Dryden, the elder, 30, 71, 80, 86
Lely, Peter, 40
Letter from some Electors, A, 51
Letters, Poems and Tales: Amorous, Satyrical, and Gallant (compilation by Curll), 198–9
Lewis, Erasmus, 192
Lily, William, 4
Lindsay, Thomas, 235–6
Lintot, Bernard, 125
Longshaw, R., 68
Lucan, 40, 118
Lucas, Charles, 252, 281–2, 283
Luckombe, Philip, 64n.93
Lucretius, 50, 61
Lyon, John, 252, 279

Maggs Bros., 82
Mainwaring, Arthur, 108–10, 133n.128
Malone, James and Richard, 9, 148
Manley, Delariviere, 104
Mar, John Erskine, Earl of, *see* John Erskine, styled 22nd or 6th Earl of Mar
Marlborough, *see* John Churchill, 1st Duke of Marlborough
Marsh, Narcissus, 45
Marshall, William, 75
Masham, Abigail, Baroness Masham, 115
Masham, Samuel, Baron Masham, 116

Memoirs of Queen Anne . . . wherein the transactions of the four last years are fully related, 281
Methuen, Sir Paul, 240
Midleton, *see* Alan Brodrick, 1st Viscount Midleton
Millar, Andrew, 17, 280–1, 282, 283
Miller, Sanderson, 284–5
Misosarum, Gregory, 122
Mist's Weekly Journal, 204
Molesworth, Robert, 1st Viscount Molesworth, 125, 134–5, 150–1, 165, 166, 169, 173, 203–4
Montagu, Charles, 1st Earl of Halifax, 53, 85
Moor[e], A. (fictitious bookseller), 210, 213, 215
Mordaunt, Charles, 3rd Earl of Peterborough, 103, 111, 257–8
Moreton, Henry, 43
Morice, Mary, 255
Morphew, John, 71, 82, 89, 100, 104–5, 106, 108, 109, 116, 119–20, 124, 125–6, 130–1
Motte, Benjamin (the elder), 54–5, 71, 97, 98, 99–100, 110–11, 124, 125, 179, 263, 264
Motte, Benjamin (the younger), 29, 148, 177, 178, 179, 182–5, 186–9, 191–3, 195, 197, 199–200, 202, 212, 216–19, 234, 243, 248, 251, 255, 256, 262–3, 264
Moxon, Joseph, xiv, 19n.72, 20n.75, 117n.66, 128n.112
Mr. P—dg's [*sic*] *Elegy on the Death of Mr. John Gadbury, the Famous Astrologer*, 67–8

N., T., Philomath, 71, 79–80, 215
Nichols, John, 117, 288, 290
Nutt, John, 46, 49–50, 57, 71, 100, 105, 124

Oldmixon, John, 44, 132, 133n.128
On Wisdom's Defeat in a Learned Debate, 204
Ovid, 118
Oxford University, *see* University of Oxford

Parker's Penny Post, 191
'Parson', *see* Jacob and Richard Tonson
Partridge, John, 28, 44, 67, 68, 69, 72, 73–4, 75, 78, 79–80, 81, 82, 83
Patrick (Swift's servant), 110
Pembroke, *see* Henry Herbert, 8th Earl of Pembroke and 5th Earl of Montgomery
Penny London Post, The, 189–91
Peterborough, *see* Charles Mordaunt, 3rd Earl of Peterborough
Philips, Ambrose, 93, 94, 125
Pilkington, Laetitia, 252–3
Pilkington, Matthew, 203, 216–19

Index

307

Pindarick Ode on His Majesties Return from the Campaign, 1691, A, 13n.44
Pittis, William, 68
Pliny the younger, 85
Poem to the Whole People of Ireland, A, 171
Pope, Alexander, xv, 5, 13, 94, 100, 177, 180, 182, 183–4, 186, 187, 188, 194–5, 207, 209–10, 216–17, 239, 242–3, 251, 255–6, 257–9, 264, 268, 269, 274, 280, 281
Powell, Stephen, 26–7, 29, 213
Present Miserable State of Ireland, The, 158
Prince, Daniel, 284
print design, production and marketing
  advertising
    in books, pamphlets and single sheets, 9, 58–60, 93–4, 107, 110, 171, 176, 278–9
    in periodicals, 18, 86, 106, 107, 108, 110, 112, 114, 135, 136, 157, 166, 167, 175, 178, 217, 222, 262, 265, 269n.68, 279, 284
  annotation, 53, 63, 78, 96–7, 99–100, 123, 134, 136, 152, 162, 215, 220, 233, 239–42, 256–7, 269, 271, 273, 274–6, 278, 288, 290
  asterisks, 55, 62, 214–15, 256, 257, 286–7
  black letter, 7, 8, 8n.18, 19, 37, 39, 40, 52, 61, 73, 114, 117, 118, 129, 132, 134, 138, 155, 162, 209, 238, 277
  bulk purchase for free distribution, 92, 119, 161
  casting off (and reduction in type size to accommodate problems arising), 10, 18–19, 57–8, 136, 137, 164, 208
  dedication, 15, 41, 91, 101, 201–2
  editors of Works, status, qualifications and expectations of, 251–2, 274–6, 285, 290
  epigraph, 40, 50, 61, 85, 89–90, 117, 118, 155, 165
  errata list, 36, 42, 137, 195
  format, xi–xii, 187
    broadside, 71, 74, 129
    duodecimo, 107, 109, 184–5, 189, 192, 193, 203, 248, 280
    folio, 5, 13, 20, 23, 107, 123, 162n.74, 217–18, 255, 269, 280
    half sheet, 7, 18, 20, 23, 24, 71, 79, 80, 81, 82, 103, 105–16, 118, 277
    octavo, 33–4, 39, 40, 51–2, 54, 55, 56, 63, 65, 66, 71, 73, 78, 81, 85, 89, 92, 93, 94, 101, 103, 105, 107, 116, 117, 123–5, 129, 130, 132, 136, 162, 164, 178, 189, 192, 194, 195, 205, 207–8, 213, 220, 221, 222–3, 256, 260–1, 263–4, 269, 271, 273, 277, 279–80, 284, 289
    octodecimo, 273, 279
    quarto, 12–13, 36, 50, 51, 71, 74, 82, 89, 92, 116–17, 134, 162n.74, 214, 253, 269–71, 273, 278, 279–80, 284, 285, 287, 290

glossary, 288
hawkers, 81, 110, 214
illustrations, 40, 60, 94, 96–7, 99, 123, 139–40, 180, 183, 192, 222, 226–7, 269, 273
  maps, 60, 180, 183, 187, 193–4
  Swift depicted in, 139–40, 180, 186, 187, 193–4, 226–7, 243–4
imprint, 6
  absent, defective, misleading or fictitious, 71–2, 83, 92, 102, 110, 114, 116, 137, 144, 149, 167–70, 176, 211, 212, 213–18, 219, 277
  — *and see names of individual printers and booksellers*
letters, layout of, 20–1, 40–1, 124, 131–2, 164, 166
multi-volume sets, problems in sequencing of, 196–9, 225–7
ornaments, 78, 148, 150, 164, 166, 174, 180, 187, 193–4, 195–6, 205, 210, 213–14, 215–16, 223, 227–32, 288, 290
  angler, 228, 231
  cockerel, 255
  eagle, 152, 153
  fleurons, 150, 165–6, 180, 203, 227
  flowers and foliage, 124, 164, 228
  fox and goose, 231
  Gadbury as Merlin, 79, 82, 129, 215
  lamb and flag, 231
  lion, 194, 230–2, 227–8n.59
  London perspective, City Arms and postboy, 189
  monogram, 195, 199, 223, 243, 258–9
  mourning compartment and imagery, 74, 75–8, 79, 129
  national imagery
    English and Scottish, 7, 11, 209, 228, 231, 232
    Irish, 7, 11, 228–32
  peacock, 152, 175–6
  phoenix, 230, 231, 232, 260
  putto, 139–40, 150, 153, 228, 255, 258–9
  royal arms and imagery, 7, 8, 209
  sunrise over cityscape, 180
  Swift depicted in, 158n.56, 228, 260–1
pagination, 57, 58, 61, 62, 101
pamphlets, political, 12–13, 48, 49, 50, 89, 103, 116–23, 143, 144
paper, 10, 13, 16, 23, 71, 73, 80, 82, 92, 137, 138–9, 162, 164, 193, 208, 216–17, 221, 222–3
preliminaries, 24, 33, 36–8, 46–7, 56–8, 84–6, 96–8, 100, 123, 183, 195, 197, 199, 243–7, 265–7, 274, 275, 288

308 · *Index*

print design, production and marketing (cont.)
  pricing, 10, 45–6, 63, 81, 92, 96, 106, 110, 112,
    116, 117–18, 119, 139, 166, 168, 169, 178,
    187, 189–91, 206, 221, 222, 256, 260,
    262, 269–71, 278–9, 284
  — *and see* Jonathan Swift (copy, sale of)
  print genres, material allusion to, 11–12, 63, 69,
    71, 72, 74–8, 79–80, 105, 110–16, 117,
    118, 129, 162, 179, 263, 277
  print, poor quality, 17–25, 28–9, 78, 82, 83, 116,
    134–5, 136–7, 138, 155–7, 162, 169–70,
    176, 189, 191, 193–4, 205, 207–8,
    216–17, 238, 260, 262
  'printers' normal', xiv, 33, 34, 42–3, 55–65, 74,
    98, 101, 133, 179, 188–9
  provocative material blanked by rules, asterisks
    or gaps, 92, 112, 256–7
  punctuation, italic, 63, 253, 288, 290
  rubrication, 10, 73, 273, 275, 290
  rules, composite, 13, 65n.93, 136, 136n.142,
    137, 138
  serialisation, 189–91
  signatures, 20, 33, 56, 57, 58, 62, 101, 137, 176,
    239–40
  styling of text, 52–3, 63–5, 93, 117, 133, 134, 150,
    152, 178–9, 188, 193, 195, 238, 253, 262,
    263, 271, 277–8
  subscription and mock-subscription projects
    and proposals, 107, 109–10, 125, 135–6,
    174–5, 211, 215–16, 220–2, 257, 269–71,
    278–9, 283–9
  title page, design of, 13, 24, 36, 39–40, 41, 45, 52,
    58–61, 72, 73, 77, 80–2, 83, 85, 89, 93–4,
    99, 117, 118, 124, 128–9, 132, 134, 139–40,
    150, 176, 179, 195, 203, 205, 208–10,
    223–5, 273, 275–6, 280, 287, 290
  type, 7–8, 10, 13–14, 14n.48, 81, 83, 138, 138n.152,
    148, 160, 162, 208, 222, 223, 262, 278
    mis-sorted, 14, 18, 19, 83, 135, 136, 137
    standing, 118, 162
  typography, 'noisy' expressivity of, 20–1, 23,
    155, 162, 164, 208, 277–8
  white space, 57, 125, 178–9, 195, 196,
    223, 273
Prior, Matthew, 108–9, 111, 121–2, 144, 154, 255
Pue, Richard ('Dick'), 26, 28, 29, 157
Purser, John, 213

Ray, John, 27–8, 29, 154
Ray, Sarah, *see* Sarah Hyde
Rhames, Aaron, 138, 194, 215
Ridgeway, Ann, 16, 30
*Right of Precedence between Phisicians and
    Civilians Enquir'd Into, The*, 198–9,
    200–1

Roberts, James, 198–9, 201, 213, 214–15,
    216–17, 219
Roper, Abel, 108, 114
Roscommon, Wentworth Dillon, 4th Earl of
    Roscommon, 95, 96
Rothschild Library, *see* University of Cambridge
    (Trinity College, Wren Library)
Rowe, Nicholas, 93, 94, 240
Royal Irish Academy, 137
Rymer, Thomas, 108

Sadleir, Elizabeth, 158, 171
St John, Henry, Viscount Bolingbroke, 102, 116,
    119, 123, 130, 153, 154, 258, 281
St Patrick's Cathedral, Dublin, 35, 45, 104, 123,
    134, 162, 175, 184, 226, 243
Sandwich Book-Society, The, 287
Sandys, Ann, 93n.82
Sault, Richard, 18
Scott, Sir Walter, 272–3, 290
*Second Collection of Miscellanies, Written by
    Jonathan Swift, D. D., A*, 198–9
Seneca, 255
Seymour, Elizabeth, Duchess of Somerset, 114–15
Shaftesbury, *see* Anthony Ashley Cooper, 3rd Earl
    of Shaftesbury
Sheridan, Thomas (the elder), 17, 158, 173, 198–9,
    202, 205–6, 207, 209, 228, 247, 254,
    264–5, 286, 288
Sheridan, Thomas (the younger), 264–5, 281, 290
Simpson, Richard, 38, 40, 64n.93, 183
Smith, John, 8n.18, 14n.48, 19n.72, 55n.82,
    117n.66, 128n.112, 271n.73,
    277n.91
Society for the Reformation of Manners,
    43, 89
*Some Considerations upon the late Attempt to
    Repeal the Test Act*, 147n.16
*Some Reasons shewing the Necessity the People of
    Ireland are under, for continuing to
    refuse Mr. Wood's Coinage*, 175
Somers, John, 1st Baron Somers, 40, 43, 49, 53,
    57, 85
Somerset, *see* Elizabeth Seymour, Duchess of
    Somerset
South, Robert, 108
Southerne, Thomas, 43
Southwell, Sir Robert, 15
Spectator, The, 239–40
Spencer, Robert, 2nd Earl of Sunderland, 48–9,
    53, 85
'Squire Bickerstaff Detected, 68, 240
Stanhope, George, 60n.88
Stanhope, Philip Dormer, 4th Earl of
    Chesterfield, 279–80

Index

309

Stationers' Company, *see* book trades (London)
Steele, Sir Richard, 68, 73, 78, 90, 93, 105–8, 116–17, 121, 126, 134, 239–40
Sunderland, *see* Robert Spencer, 2nd Earl of Sunderland
Sun Fire-Office, 287
Swearers-Bank, The, 198–9
Swift, Abigail, 16
Swift, Deane, 252–3, 271–3, 279, 283–9, 290
Swift, Godwin, 272, 286
Swift, Jonathan
  as author
    anonymous, xiii–xiv, 12, 15, 40, 45, 49–50, 54, 57, 84, 92, 93, 95–6, 97–8, 102, 108–9, 119–20, 122–3, 124–5, 126, 130, 139–40, 144, 151, 155, 189, 241, 242–3, 244, 277
    'author of the Tale of a Tub, the', 95–6, 97–8, 125
    confirmed (or alleged) by printing Swift's name, 12, 21, 39–40, 41, 84–5, 102–3, 124, 128, 131–2, 154, 195, 200, 251, 255, 260–1, 277, 280
    implied by partially blanked name, initials, imprint, association with other texts, etc., 50, 95–6, 102, 126–7, 128, 139, 187, 214–15, 228, 235, 243, 256
    mediated by George Faulkner as 'the publisher', 243–7, 251, 256, 265–7, 278–9
    performed by authorial voices, 21, 25, 41–2, 45, 55–6, 57, 66, 71, 74, 79, 81, 84–92, 93, 98, 102, 107, 109, 121, 145, 161–2, 183–5, 215, 216–17, 244, 267–8, 277, 285–6, 287
    referred to in the third person by authorial voice, 90, 97–8, 125–6, 127
    — *and see* Isaac Bickerstaff; Lemuel Gulliver; T. N. Philomath; Richard Sympson; Simon Wagstaff
  biography of, prefatory to Works, 252, 269, 272, 274, 275–6, 278, 279, 290
  books owned by, posthumously auctioned, 265
  book-trade professionals, sociability with, 11, 16, 43–4, 66, 81, 103–4, 108, 123, 143–4
  conservative linguistic preferences applied to published texts of, 133, 238–9, 271
  copy for works by
    delivery to press of, 152–3, 169, 173–4, 180–2, 186
    disposal or retention of after printing, 56, 152, 153, 192, 265, 266, 267, 283, 288
    doubtful or unknown authority of, 128, 137, 138

    gift of to Mary Barber, 262
    preparation of, 21, 56, 151–2, 155, 162, 194
    sale of, 35, 44–5, 46, 84, 179, 184–5, 186, 191, 202, 252, 285
    Swift annoyed by editing of provocative content of, 180, 187–8, 191–2, 193–4
    transcribed by third party, 114, 122–3, 153, 168, 169, 173, 247, 288
  copyright, views on, 212, 216, 248, 269
  early modern formation of, xv, 21–3, 242–3
  editorial beliefs and practice of, 38, 46–7, 85, 86–7, 98–9, 108
  — *and see* Jonathan Swift (revision by Swift and others after first printing/ publication)
  Grub Street and, 63, 65, 67, 68–9, 71, 74–5, 110–16
  London publication, attraction of, 11, 25, 35, 151–2, 177–8, 189, 194, 216, 219
  manuscript circulation of works by, 15–16, 21–3, 92–3, 189, 216–17, 233, 252, 253, 254–5, 256–7
  miscellanies and Works traditions in canon formation of, 55, 123–4, 199, 200, 225, 290
  modest material form typical of publications of, 16, 179, 211, 222–5, 277, 290
  posthumous editors, qualifications and expectations of, 251–2, 271–3, 278
  Presbyterianism, dissent, deism and atheism (and perceived Whig support for), opposition to, 11, 16–17, 18, 25, 27, 39, 67, 75, 83, 87, 90, 91, 102, 114, 121, 128, 129, 212–13, 216–17, 231, 235–6, 241, 281
  presentation copies of works by (typically featuring large paper and/or special bindings), 40, 45, 53, 85, 192, 214
  proofreading personally undertaken by, 38, 109, 118, 133, 220
  relation to publication process
    distancing from, 42–3, 143, 149–50, 152–3, 170, 177, 180–2, 183, 206, 211, 219–20, 242–3, 275
    involvement with, 69, 104, 117, 118, 175, 220, 225, 232, 244–5, 246, 275
  revision by Swift and others after first printing/ publication, 83, 94, 105, 118–19, 130, 136–7, 153, 162, 192, 193–4, 199, 203, 214, 217–19, 220, 221–2, 233–4, 236–7, 246, 275–6, 282
  stages and events in life of, 3–4, 9, 17–18, 26, 35, 38, 46, 66, 87, 91, 102, 103, 104, 105, 108, 123, 131, 133, 134, 143, 182, 202–3, 243, 251, 255–6, 258, 259, 264, 265, 286

310 *Index*

Swift, Jonathan (cont.)

surveillance, investigation, prosecution and imprisonment (actual, apprehended, or circumvented) in relation to Swift and his associates, 91, 104, 116, 119–20, 137, 146–7, 148–50, 153–4, 166–9, 171, 182, 183–4, 187–8, 204, 212–14, 217–19, 241–2, 253, 254–5, 257, 260

— *and see* Sir William Temple, *and names of individual booksellers and printers*

Works and collections by or edited by (major title variants in square brackets)

Accomplishment of the First of Mr Bickerstaff's Predictions, The, 29

— *and see* Bickerstaff papers

Advantages Proposed by Repealing the Sacramental Test, The, 213

Answer to a Paper, called A Memorial of the Poor Inhabitants, Tradesmen and Labourers of the Kingdom of Ireland, A, 154, 204–5

Answer to Bickerstaff, An, 285–6

— *and see* Bickerstaff papers

Answer to Dr Delany's Fable of the Pheasant and the Lark, An, 215

Answer to the Ballyspellan Ballad, An, 209

Apology for the Tale of a Tub. With explanatory notes by W. W-tt-n, B. D. And others, An, 100–1

Argument to Prove that the Abolishing of Christianity in England, may . . . be attended with some Inconveniences, An, 128, 129, 231

Battle of the Books, The, 55, 61, 62

— and *see A Tale of a Tub*

Baucis and Philemon, 93, 93n.82, 94–6, 127

Bavcis and Philemon: A Poem on the Ever-lamented Loss of the two Yew-Trees, in the Parish of Chilthorne, near the Count-Town [sic] of Somerset. Together with Mrs. Harris's Earnest Petition: and an Admirable Recipe. By the Author of the Tale of a Tub. As also an Ode upot [sic] Solitude: by the Earl of Roscommon (compilation by Hills), 95–6

Beautiful Young Nymph Going to Bed, A, 219

Bickerstaff papers, 66, 67, 107, 126, 127, 129, 145, 238, 239–40, 285–6

Bubble, The, 151–3, 175–6, 288

Cadenus and Vanessa, 196

Cassinus and Peter, 219

Character of the Legion Club, A, 253–5

City Shower, A, 93, 93n.82

Collection of Poems, &c. Omitted in the Fifth Volume of Miscellanies in Prose and Verse, A, 247

Conduct of the Allies, The, 117–19, 122, 134, 137, 138–9, 154

Considerations upon Two Bills (and the related 'Some Queries humbly offered'), 212–13

Contests and Dissensions, 35, 47–54, 126, 127, 129–30, 147–8, 230–1, 240

Dean's Reasons for not Building at Drapier's Hill, The, 286

Decree for Concluding the Treaty between Dr Swift & Mrs Long, A (possibly by Swift), 198–9

Description of a Salamander, A, 127–8

Description of the Morning, A, 93

Dialogue between Mad Mullinix and Timothy, A, 237

Directions to Servants, 251, 252, 264, 265–8, 286, 288

Discourse concerning the Mechanical Operation of the Spirit, A, 55, 61–2, 101, 187–8

— *and see A Tale of a Tub*

Discourse on Hereditary Right, A, 286

Discourse to Prove the Antiquity of the English Tongue, A, 287

Drapier's Letters, 34, 155–7, 161–76, 203–4, 211, 226, 234, 238, 241–2, 277

— *and see separate titles*

Elegy on Mr. Patrige, the Almanack-maker, An, 126, 129, 159, 160

— *and see* Bickerstaff papers

Elegy on the much lamented death of Mr. Demar, An (by Swift and others), 149

Epilogue . . . In the Behalf of the Distrest Weavers, An, 157–9

Epistle to a Lady, who Desired the Author to Make Verses on Her, in the Heroick Stile, An, 217–18, 237

Examiner, The, 29n.102, 105, 108–10, 112, 114, 135–6, 206

Excellent New Song, Being the Intended Speech of a Famous Orator against Peace, A, 114

Fable of Midas, The, 115–16

Faggot, The, 240–1

Famous Prediction of Merlin, A, 30, 110–11, 114, 129, 215, 238

— *and see* Bickerstaff papers

Fraud Detected [*The Hibernian Patriot*], 174–6, 209–10, 221, 225, 226, 241–2

Index

311

Full and True Account of the Solemn Procession to the Gallows, at the Execution of William Wood, A, 159

Grand Question Debated, The, 215

Gulliver's Travels, see Travels into Several Remote Nations of the World

Harding's Resurrection (sometimes attributed to Swift), 159–61

Harrison's Tatler, 30, 105–8, 206, 239–40

Hibernia's Passive Obedience (compilation including extracts from *Contests and Dissensions, The Sentiments of a Church of England-Man*, and *A Letter ... concerning the Sacramental Test*), 147–8

Hints on Good Manners, 286–7

History of Poetry, A, 247–8

History of the Four Last Years of the Queen [*History of the Last Session of Parliament, and of the Peace of Utrecht*], *The*, 252, 264, 280–3, 286

Hue and Cry after Dismal, A, 111, 114

Humble Address of the Right Honourable the House of Lords, The, 123

Humble Address to Both Houses of Parliament, An (Drapier's letters, additional letter, no. 7 of the expanded series), 226, 233, 234–5

Humble Petition of Frances Harris, The, 95, 126–7

Importance of the Guardian Considered, The, 121

Journal of a Dublin [Modern] Lady, The, 206–7

Journal to Stella, see Esther Johnson and Rebecca Dingley

Lady B—B— finding ... some Verses Unfinished, 126–7

Lady's Dressing Room, The, 214–15

Last Speech and Dying Words of Ebenezor Ellison, The, 158–9, 242

Last Speech and Dying Words of the Bank of Ireland (sometimes attributed to Swift), 158

Laws for the Dean's Servants, 286

Letter from a Member of the House of Commons in Ireland to a Member of the House of Commons in England, concerning the Sacramental Test, A, 87–9, 90, 91–2, 127, 128, 130, 147–8, 159, 235–6

Letter from Dr. Swift to Mr. Pope, A, 151

Letter from a Lay-Patron to a Gentleman, designing for Holy Orders [*A Letter to a Young Gentleman, lately enter'd into Holy Orders. By a person of quality.*], *A*, 153, 231

Letter from the Pretender, A, 111, 116

*Letter of Thanks from My Lord W***** to the Lord Bp of S. Asaph, A*, 121

Letter to Mr. Harding the Printer, A (Drapier's letters, no. 2), *see* Drapier's letters

Letter to the Lord Chancellor Middleton, A (Drapier's letters, additional letter, no. 6 of the expanded series), 175, 226, 233, 234–5, 244

Letter to the Right Honourable the Lord Viscount Molesworth, A (Drapier's Letters, no. 5), 234

— *and see* Drapier's letters

Letter to the Shop-keepers, A (Drapier's letters, no. 1), 228

— *and see* Drapier's Letters

Letter to the Whole People of Ireland, A (Drapier's letters, no. 4), 172, 241–2

— *and see* Drapier's letters

Letters to the King (by Sir William Temple), 46–7, 49

Letters written by Sir W. Temple ... in Two Volumes, 39–42, 183

Libel on D—— D—— and a Certain Great Lord, A, 202, 210, 213–14

Life and Genuine Character of the Rev. Dr. S—t, D. S. P. D. Written by Himself, The, 216–17, 256

Meditation upon a Broom-stick, A, 95, 128

Meditation upon a Broomstick, and somewhat beside; of the same Author's, A, (compilation by Curll), 95

Memoirs of Capt. John Creichton. Written by Himself, 215–16

Memoirs. Part III (by Sir William Temple), 84–7

Miscellanea. The Third Part (by Sir William Temple), 44–6, 129–30

Miscellanies in Prose and Verse (by Swift; 1711), 50, 74, 98, 99, 100, 101, 104, 123–30, 240, 245

Miscellanies in Prose and Verse (by Swift; second edition, 1713), 139–40

Miscellanies in Prose and Verse. Volume the Fifth (London collection from advance sheets of Faulkner's Dublin edition), 199, 219, 247

Index

Swift, Jonathan (cont.)

Miscellanies in Prose and Verse (1727–32, edited by Pope, containing work by Swift, Pope and others), 29, 177, 194–203, 205–6, 211, 216–17, 218–19, 221, 225, 245, 251, 264

– and, for Dublin reprints, *see* Samuel Fairbrother

Modest Defence of a Late Poem by an Unknown Author, Call'd the Lady's Dressing Room, A, 214–15

Modest Defence of Punning, A, 288

Modest Proposal, A, 171, 177, 178, 202, 207–9, 211, 230–1

Mr. C—n's Discourse of Free-thinking, 121

Mr. Pope's Literary Correspondence ... Volume the Fifth (including letters by Swift), 257–9

New Journey to Paris, A, 121–2

New Letters of Mr. Alexander Pope (partial reprint of *Mr. Pope's Literary Correspondence ... Volume the Fifth*), 258

New Way of Selling Places at Court, The, 120, 121, 130–1, 136–7

Ode to the Athenian Society, 3, 17–25, 26, 79, 128, 131, 132, 244, 275

Ode. To the King, An, 3, 12–17, 23, 26, 128, 247–8

On Barbarous Denominations in Ireland, 286

On the Death of Mrs. Johnson, 286

On the Irish Bishops, 231

On Mrs. Biddy Floyd, 93, 94–5, 127

On Poetry: A Rapsody, 29, 218–19, 241

On the Words – Brother Protestants, and Fellow Christians, 241

Panegyric on the D—n, A, 237

Paraphrase on the Seven Penitential Psalms, A, 204–5

Peace and Dunkirk; Being an Excellent New Song upon the Surrender of Dunkirk, 111, 114

Poem, Occasion'd by Reading Dr. Young's Satires, A, 217–18

Poetical Miscellanies: The Sixth Part (additional volume of Tonson's miscellany, edited by Nicholas Rowe, including *Baucis and Philemon* and *On Mrs. Biddy Floyd*), 93–4, 127, 139–40

Predictions for the Year 1708, 67, 263

— *and see* Bickerstaff papers

Preface to the B—p of S—r—m's Introduction, 122, 134–5

Preface to the History of the Four Last Years of Queen Anne's Reign, A, 286

Presbyterian's Plea of Merit ... Impartially Examined, The, 213

Project for the Advancement of Religion, and the Reformation of Manners. By a Person of Quality, A, 87, 89–90, 91, 92, 126, 129, 132, 187

Proposal for Correcting, Improving and Ascertaining the English Tongue, A, 102–3, 124, 130–3, 187, 238–9, 241, 244

Proposal for Giving Badges to the Beggars, A, 260–1

Proposal for the Universal Use of Irish Manufacture, A, 138, 147–51, 153–4, 228, 230, 236

Publick Spirit of the Whigs, The, 120, 122, 134, 137, 262, 263–4

Reasons why we should not Lower the Coins now Current in this Kingdom (including a speech by Swift), 260

Resolutions when I Come to be Old, 286

Robin and Harry, 286

Run upon the Bankers, The, 153

Seasonable Advice, 157, 167–70

Sentiments of a Church of England-Man, The, 128, 147–8, 231

Seventh Epistle of the first Book of Horace Imitated, The, 134

Short Character of his Ex. T. E. of W. L. L. of I—, A, 119, 136, 282

Short View of the State of Ireland, A, 204

Some Advice Humbly Offer'd to the Members of the October Club, 121, 122–3, 137, 152–3

Some Arguments against Enlarging the Power of Bishops, 154, 155, 230–1

Some Free Thoughts upon the Present State of Affairs, 152–3

Some Observations upon a Paper... relating to Wood's Half-pence (Drapier's letters, no. 3), *see* Drapier's letters

'Some Queries humbly offered', *see Considerations upon Two Bills*

Some Reasons to Prove, that no Person is Obliged by his Principles as a Whig, to Oppose her Majesty or her Present Ministry, 121, 137

Some Remarks on the Barrier Treaty, 117–18, 120, 122, 137–8, 139

Some Remarks upon a Pamphlet, Entitled, A Letter to the Seven Lords of the Committee, 138n.152

S—t contra omnes, 254

Index

313

Strephon and Chloe, 219

Tale of a Tub, A, 4, 24, 29, 30, 34, 35, 44, 49, 54–65, 68, 96–101, 104, 105, 110–11, 117, 123, 124–5, 128, 179, 184–5, 216–17, 237–9, 247, 251, 261, 263, 264, 269, 272, 273, 277, 278, 279, 286–7, 290

Tatler, no., 62–3, 131, 230, 238–40

Three Sermons, 264–5

To Dr Delany, on the Libels Writ against him, 214

T—l—nd's Invitation to Dismal, 111, 112–14

Traulus, 214, 237

Travels into Several Remote Nations of the World, 29, 139, 177, 178–94, 203, 211, 221–2, 231–2, 233–4, 242, 246, 251, 277

Treatise on Polite Conversation, A [A Complete Collection of Genteel and Ingenious Conversation], 42, 128, 261–4

Tritical Essay upon the Faculties of the Mind, A, 128

Verses on the Death of Dr. Swift, 216–17, 253, 255–7

A Vindication of His Excellency the Lord C—T, A, 210

Vindication of Isaac Bickerstaff, A, see Bickerstaff papers

Virtues of Sid Hamet the Magician's Rod, The, 110–11, 127

Whitshed's Motto on his Coach, 241

W—ds-r Prophecy, The, 114–15

Wonderful Wonder of Wonders, The, 238

Wood, an Insect, 241

Works of Jonathan Swift, D. D. Dean of St. Patrick's, Dublin, The (London copy-holders' edition edited by Hawkesworth), 13, 252–3, 269–78, 283–9

Works of J. S, D. D, D. S. P. D, The (Faulkner's Dublin edition), 5, 34, 72, 139–40, 147, 175, 194, 199, 211, 217–48, 251, 262–4, 265, 269, 285, 289

– and see individual titles for non-Swiftian works and works of contested attribution

Swift, Jonathan, and Thomas Sheridan the elder, *The Intelligencer*, 177, 202, 205–7, 230–1

Swift, Theophilus, 284, 290

Swift, Thomas, 23, 24, 97, 98

Sympson, Richard (fictitious correspondent), 183–5, 186, 188, 192, 234, 242, 246

Sympson, William, 183

Tatler, The, 68, 72, 73, 78, 90, 93, 105–6, 205, 206, 239–40

Temple, Sir John (father of Swift's patron), 36

Temple, Sir William (grandfather of Swift's patron), 36

Temple, Sir William (Swift's patron), 3, 4, 14, 15, 17–18, 21, 23, 24, 25, 34–43, 44–7, 84–7, 97, 98–9, 108, 117, 129–30, 183, 286

— *and see* Jonathan Swift (*Letters to the King*; *Letters written by Sir W. Temple . . . in Two Volumes*; *Memoirs. Part III*; *Miscellanea. The Third Part*)

Theobald, Lewis, 263

Tickell, Thomas, 94

Toland, John, 112, 114

Tompson, Daniel, 134–5, 145–6

Tom Punsibi's Dream (pseudonym used by Thomas Sheridan the elder), 228

Tonson, Jacob (the elder), 40, 93, 97, 100

— *and see* Jonathan Swift (*Poetical Miscellanies: The Sixth Part*)

Tonson, Jacob (the younger), 185

Tonson, Jacob and Richard (sons of Jacob Tonson the younger), 284, 285

Tooke, Andrew, 183, 185, 187–8, 234, 246

Tooke, Benjamin (the elder), 6–8, 10, 29, 35, 43, 264

Tooke, Benjamin (the younger), 11, 29, 35, 43–65, 66, 71, 81, 84, 85, 86, 87, 89, 97, 98, 99–100, 101, 103–4, 105, 117, 123–5, 126, 127, 130–1, 132, 133, 139, 143, 153, 182, 264

— *and see* Jonathan Swift (*Tatler* no. 230)

Trapp, Joseph, 94

Trinity College, Dublin, 3, 8, 11, 12, 15, 30, 91, 154, 279

University of Cambridge

Cambridge University Library, 116, 198–9, 256–7

Trinity College, Wren Library, 194n.67, 197–8

University of Oxford

Bodleian Library, 176

St Mary Hall, 284

Oxford University Press, 284–5

Vanessa, *see* Esther Vanhomrigh

Vanhomrigh, Esther, 143–4, 196

Vertue, George, 222, 226–7, 243–4

Vindication of the Protestant Dissenters, from the Aspersions Cast upon Them, A, 213

Virgil, 165, 287

Index

W., E., *A Poem to his Most Sacred Majesty King William upon his Return from Flanders*, 13n.44

Wagstaff, Humphrey (fictitious author), 93

Wagstaff, Simon (fictitious author), 42, 84, 93, 261, 263

Walpole, Sir Robert, 17, 158n.56, 182, 212, 213–14, 217–19, 242, 263

Walsh, Peter, 7

Warner, T., 214

Waters, Edward, 137–8, 139, 146–51, 153–4, 157, 166, 216–17, 230, 260

Waters, Sarah, 148

Watts, John, 71

Wesley, Samuel, the elder, 18

Wesley, Samuel, the younger, 255

Whalley, John, 10, 28, 67, 72, 83, 84, 134–5, 157, 159

Wharton, Thomas, 1st Marquess of Wharton, 119, 121, 136, 150–51

'Whimsical Medley, The', 30, 247–8

Whereas in expectation of Conformity to the Laws of the Land (Dublin, 1662), 7n.17

White, Robert, 36

Whiteway, Martha, 252–3, 256, 268, 272, 290

Whitshed, William, 150, 151, 165, 171, 241–2

Wilford, John, 217–19

William III, 14–15, 17, 28, 35, 41, 53, 67, 75

Williams, Sir Harold, 116, 198–9, 290

Wise, T., 81–2

Wonder of all the Wonders, that ever the World Wondered at, The, 238

Wood, William, 145, 159, 160, 165, 166, 167, 203–4, 231–2, 241

Woodward, John, 114–15

Woodward, Thomas, 210

Woronzow, Count, 287

Worrall, John, 170–71, 173, 209

Wotton, William, 99

Wright, John, 202